D1602579

CARSON CITY LIBRARY
900 North Roop Street
Carson City, NV 89701
775-887-2244   MAY 0 4 2016

The NFRW Literacy Committee

"Only the educated are free"
~Epictetus~

This book is presented by

Carson City
Republican Women

Club Name

Nevada

State Federation

In Memory of
Mae and Jim Thorpe

Under the sponsorship of the
National Federation of Republican Women
124 N. Alfred Street
Alexandria, VA 22314-3011

WHY COOLIDGE MATTERS

The Daily Grind in Washington

Coolidge holding Congress's nose
to the grindstone of the economy,
January 15, 1925.

COURTESY OF THE JAY N. "DING" DARLING
WILDLIFE SOCIETY

WHY COOLIDGE MATTERS

MATTERS

Leadership Lessons from

America's Most Underrated President

CHARLES C. JOHNSON

Encounter Books

NEW YORK · LONDON

© 2013 by Charles C. Johnson

All rights reserved. No part of this publication may be reproduced,
stored in a retrieval system, or transmitted, in any form or by
any means, electronic, mechanical, photocopying, recording,
or otherwise, without the prior written permission of
Encounter Books, 900 Broadway, Suite 601,
New York, New York, 10003.

First American edition published in 2013 by Encounter Books,
an activity of Encounter for Culture and Education, Inc.,
a nonprofit, tax exempt corporation.
Encounter Books website address: www.encounterbooks.com

Manufactured in the United States and printed on
acid-free paper. The paper used in this publication meets
the minimum requirements of ANSI/NISO Z39.48–1992
(R 1997) (*Permanence of Paper*).

FIRST AMERICAN EDITION

LIBRARY OF CONGRESS CATALOGING-IN-PUBLICATION DATA

Johnson, Charles C., 1988-
Why Coolidge matters : leadership lessons from America's
most underrated president / Charles C. Johnson.
pages   cm
Includes bibliographical references.
ISBN-13: 978-1-59403-669-9 (hardcover : alk. paper)
ISBN-10: 1-59403-669-1 (hardcover : alk. paper)
ISBN-13: 978-1-59403-670-5 (eBook)
1. Coolidge, Calvin, 1872–1933. 2. Political leadership—United States—
Case studies. 3. United States—Politics and government—1923–1929.
I. Title.
E792.J65   2013
973.91'5092—dc23
2012043096

10 9 8 7 6 5 4 3 2 1

CONTENTS

For the Corcos family,
with thanks for everything

ACKNOWLEDGMENTS

I owe many debts that I, unlike President Coolidge and his Secretary of the Treasury Andrew Mellon, am hard pressed to repay. Here I shall list my necessary debts, ever thankful that I incurred them and hopeful that they are sufficient.

The list begins with Professors Kesler and Rossum, who kept me out of (most) trouble at college. What Charles Garman was to Coolidge, Rossum and Kesler are to me. They have opened their minds, their libraries, and even their homes to me. "The great distinguishing mark of all of [my professors] was that they were men of character," Coolidge noted about his time at Amherst. So, too, I can say of my favorite professors at Claremont. In particular, special thanks go to Professor Kesler. It was said that Garman alone in the wilderness would be a university; the same is true of Professor Kesler, who gave his attention – and more important, his encouragement – to this project.

Ryan Williams, Linnea Powell, Bryce Gerard, John Kienker, Sam Corcos, and, as always, Bernadette, listened to me recount my love of the '20s. Coolidge once said that it takes a "great man to be a good listener." I am surrounded, then, by great men and women, who tolerated me even when I was intolerable, which, I am ashamed to say, was often.

An especially patient man is David Frisk. He is a good friend and a magnificent editor, and he poured his attention into this project with all the enthusiasm that the perennial student of history and government can muster.

The family Corcos, to whom this work is dedicated, are the greatest friends I have ever had. When I had not a lot, they took me in for Christmas, not once, not twice, but thrice, and gave me the greatest Christmases ever.

This is fitting because in some key respects, it is always Christmas with them. When I read Coolidge's reminder that those who have "the real spirit of Christmas" are those who "cherish peace and good will" and are "plenteous in mercy," I picture the Corcos family. How lucky I am to count them among my friends; how different these years would have been without them.

My parents inspire from afar, in the land that so desperately needs another Coolidge. They are truly public servants, serving the public schools where they teach, not for their pay, but for the love of, and respect for, the children in their charges. I, of course, was their first pupil – and for that I am always grateful.

I am grateful as well for the opportunity to study Calvin Coolidge. He was not silent but *silenced*, and here I hope to have him speak for himself. As we shall see, he has much to say – if only we care to listen.

Nothing in the world can take the place of persistence. Talent will not; nothing is more common than unsuccessful men with talent. Genius will not; unrewarded genius is almost a proverb. Education will not; the world is full of educated derelicts. Persistence and determination alone are omnipotent. The slogan "press on" has solved and always will solve the problems of the human race.

CALVIN COOLIDGE
quotation from a 1933 Coolidge memorial program

FOREWORD

YOU WOULD NOT want Charles Johnson to look into your background, not if you had anything to hide. He is an indefatigable investigator, who, at the campus conservative magazine, the *Claremont Independent* – and at his own rollicking blog – for four years kept Claremont McKenna College buzzing with revelations about affirmative action, politically tendentious speakers, and abuses in student government. He held college administrators' feet to the fire, and they got singed.

It was easier to condemn than to refute him, and his critics soon gave up on the latter. Outside CMC, more disinterested judges quickly discovered the boldness of his reporting and commentary. Soon he had been awarded virtually every prize a young journalist of conservative disposition could receive: the Robert L. Bartley Fellowship at the *Wall Street Journal*, the Eric Breindel Award, the Robert Novak Award from the Phillips Foundation, and a Publius Fellowship at the Claremont Institute. Hitting the trifecta is hard, but what Charles achieved is so remarkable as to be nameless: hitting – what, the quadrifecta?

While leading his very public life as a student journalist, Charles pursued, more quietly but just as intrepidly, the study of politics. His senior thesis, a precocious work of political biography, became the starting point for the book (his first) you are now reading. *Why Coolidge Matters* marks the appearance of a major new conservative talent – and the reappearance of a major old one.

We are on the verge of Calvin Coolidge revival, and it is long overdue. It has kindled for a while, at least since the publication in 1982 of Thomas B. Silver's brilliant *Coolidge and the Historians*. This was not long after President Ronald Reagan had rearranged the presidential portraits in the Cabinet Room: Thomas Jefferson's went out, and Coolidge's in, to the consternation of liberal society. Reagan, born in 1911, remembered the Coolidge years in blessed contrast to the times surrounding them. In Silver's words: "The hallmarks of the years proceeding Coolidge were war and depression; the hallmarks of the years following were depression and war. The hallmarks of the Coolidge era were prosperity and peace."

Doubtless, Harry V. Jaffa, Silver's teacher who had set him on the path of studying Coolidge, was right to complain that "Calvin Coolidge would have been more honored if his portrait had been side by side with that of the author of the Declaration of Independence." After all, Coolidge was the only president to have been born on the Fourth of July. Perhaps Reagan, who had made his own study of Coolidge, counted him not as a replacement for Jefferson but as a representative of genuine twentieth-century Jeffersonianism, as opposed to the spurious kind circulated by, say, Franklin D. Roosevelt.

Before a Coolidge revival can proceed very far, it has to confront the damaging myths about him. These originated in the political charges hurled against him by his partisan opponents, which, with anger and bias aplenty, were then transcribed into the history books by the court historians of the New Deal. Read the accounts by Allan Nevins, Henry Steele Commager, and above all Arthur Schlesinger Jr., and you will see this mythology, part of the official narrative of modern liberalism, passed down to later historians who credulously repeat the same stories. Schlesinger's indictment of Coolidge in *The Crisis of the Old Order*, the first volume (published in 1957) of his admiring *Age of Roosevelt*, is classic:

> [Coolidge's] speeches offered his social philosophy in dry pellets of aphorism. 'The chief business of the American people,' he said, 'is business.' But, for Coolidge, business was more than business; it was a religion; and to it he committed all the passion of his arid nature. . . . As he worshipped business, so he detested government. . . . The federal government justified itself only as

it served business. . . . And the chief way by which the federal government could serve business was to diminish itself.

It is easy to imagine President Barack Obama denouncing Mitt Romney in substantially the same terms half a century later – because he did.

Although Silver's book demolished Schlesinger's suave assertions and misrepresentations, it got little notice. Drawing on its young author's prodigious research skills, *Why Coolidge Matters* adds impressive evidence and argument to the case and should command fresh attention. Consider, for example, some of the passages and arguments from Coolidge that never make it into the books of liberal historians. In the same paragraph in which he remarked that "the chief business of the American people is business," Coolidge proceeded to say: "Of course, the accumulation of wealth cannot be justified as the chief end of existence. But we are compelled to recognize it as a means to well nigh every desirable achievement. So long as wealth is made the means and not the end, we need not greatly fear it." What are those desirable achievements, those ends of existence? "In all experience," he explained, "the accumulation of wealth means the multiplication of schools, the increase of knowledge, the dissemination of intelligence, the encouragement of science, the broadening of outlook, the expansion of liberties, the widening of culture."

He dilated on that point in another speech that escaped Schlesinger's notice. Coolidge lamented the decline of liberal education in America:

> Great captains of industry who have aroused the wonder of the world by their financial success would not have been captains at all had it not been for the generations of liberal culture in the past and the existence all about them of a society permeated, inspired, and led by the liberal culture of the present. If it were possible to strike out that factor from present existence, he would find all the value of his great possessions

diminish to the vanishing point, and he himself would be but a barbarian among barbarians.

Dry pellets of aphorism? Business as a religion? The real Coolidge was one of the most cultured, thoughtful, and eloquent of modern presidents. He was hardly "Silent Cal," although thanks to the prevailing historians he has been, as Charles Johnson well expresses it, effectively *silenced*.

Did Coolidge, like Scrooge, detest government as a distraction from moneymaking? Hardly, and in certain respects he was, in Jaffa's formulation, "the most notable interpreter of the Declaration since Abraham Lincoln." As proof, here is one last passage, one of the loveliest in his writings, from "The Inspiration of the Declaration," his address on the sesquicentennial of the Declaration of Independence:

> We live in an age of science and of abounding accumulation of material things. These did not create our Declaration. Our Declaration created them. The things of the spirit come first. Unless we cling to that, all our material prosperity, overwhelming though it may appear, will turn to a barren scepter in our grasp. If we are to maintain the great heritage which has been bequeathed to us, we must be like-minded as the fathers who created it. We must not sink into a pagan materialism. We must cultivate the reverence they had for the things that are holy.

On at least three counts the present book makes striking contributions to our knowledge of this neglected president. Johnson fills in the picture of the young Coolidge as a moderate Progressive of the Republican ilk. Most Progressives in the early twentieth century were Republicans, to be sure, and in some states most Republicans were Progressives. But which was typically the adjective and which the noun (Progressive Republican or Republican Progressive?) remained unclear; it had to be puzzled out case by case. In retrospect, and maybe even to contemporaries, President Coolidge was important as one of those statesmen who attempted to subordinate Progressivism to timeless republican principles reaching back to Lincoln's statesmanship, Hamiltonian constitutionalism, and the Declaration's doctrine of natural rights.

Second, the book helps to render explicit what Coolidge usually left implicit, namely, the distance between his conservatism (not a word he favored) and Woodrow Wilson's and Theodore Roosevelt's Progressivism, their far-reaching impatience with the Constitution and its premises. It is fair to say the book may raise as many questions as it answers on this front, but it is a service to explore the issue, so rife with implications for the definition and conduct of twenty-first-century American conservatism.

Finally, and above all, the reader should welcome such a winning portrait of such an underrated human being and president. After finishing Charles Johnson's bracing book, no one should doubt why Coolidge matters.

CHARLES R. KESLER

WHY COOLIDGE MATTERS

Calvin Coolidge is the only President on record who did not seem to care what was written about him.[1]

It will be said of [Coolidge] as of Sir Harry Vane – leader of the Puritans on both sides of the water, Governor of Massachusetts in 1636 – "He made men think that there was somewhat in him of extraordinary; and his whole life made good that imagination."[2]

IMAGINE A COUNTRY in which strikes by public-sector unions occupied the public square; where, after nearly a decade of military adventurism, foreign policy wandered aimlessly as America disentangled itself from wars abroad and a potential civil war on its southern border; where racial and ethnic groups jostled for political influence; where a war on illicit substances led to violence in its cities; where technology was dramatically changing how mankind communicated and moved about – and where the educated harbored increasing contempt for the philosophic underpinnings of our Republic.

You might say that such a world looks a lot like our own – except that it doesn't. The 1920s were a period of "general prosperity that was historically unique in its experience or that of any other society," in the words of historian Paul Johnson.[3] They were, as their popular name would suggest, "roaring," with unemployment at the lowest – and economic growth at the highest – ever recorded in the twentieth century. Cars and radios rolled off the assembly lines as industrial titans made unheard-of fortunes. We know their names still: Edison, Ford, Firestone, and Disney. More and more people of modest means could afford the conveniences of modern life as real per capita income rose from $522 to $716 during the Coolidge years.[4] This prosperity, as we know in hindsight, did not last, but what prosperity does? It was real enough for those who experienced it.

President Calvin Coolidge knew this well, telling reporters at one of his many press conferences: "If you can base the economic conditions of the people on their appearance, the way they are dressed, the general appearance of prosperity, I should say it was very good. . . . I noticed most of the ladies had on silk dresses and I thought I saw a rather general display of silk stockings."[5] Prosperity, in other words, wasn't something to turn away from, but to embrace – so long as it was on a sure foundation and designed to truly benefit the people. For, as Coolidge also warned, there "is no surer road to destruction than prosperity without character."[6]

It was far more important, Coolidge knew, to recognize where prosperity comes from than to set about chasing it for its own sake. "Prosperity is only an instrument to be used," he is reported to have said, "not a deity to be worshipped." Whether or not he uttered these exact words, they reflect his deep beliefs. As often happens, great men have great words spoken for them by an admiring public. Having learned such lessons, Coolidge had much to teach, and he did so frequently. In Fredericksburg, Virginia, he told those assembled:

> It is sometimes assumed that Americans care only for material things, that they are bent only on that kind of success which can be cashed into dollars and cents. That is a very narrow and unintelligent opinion. We have been successful beyond others in great commercial and industrial enterprises because we have been a people of vision. Our prosperity has resulted not only by disregarding but by maintaining high ideals. *Material resources do not, and cannot, stand alone; they are the product of spiritual resources.* It is because America, as a nation, has held fast to the higher things of life, because it has had a faith in mankind which it has dared to put to the test of self-government,

because it has believed greatly in honor and righteousness, that a great material prosperity has been added unto it.[7]

This is not the Coolidge of popular memory, who, if the persisting legend is true, was too friendly with business and couldn't see economic questions objectively. The cartoonish portrayal remains lodged in the popular imagination in part because "Silent Cal" wasn't so much silent as he was *silenced*. Other scholars have wrestled with why he was silenced without delving deeply into what he had to say, only compounding the problem of his obscurity. I am much more interested in exploring what he has to say for his time – and perhaps for our time and all time – than in pursuing detailed arguments with his generations of detractors. Coolidge did, after all, publish three collections of speeches, an autobiography, hundreds of letters, and a syndicated post-presidential column, all of which he wrote himself. He also took great pride in his speeches, showing them off in the library that had helped produce them.

To introduce the reader to this overlooked statesman, I have chosen six aspects of his life and thought: Coolidge's strong sense of public service as a calling, particularly evinced in his approach to the labor movement; his education; his relation to the founding and Lincoln; his general approach to the presidency; his view of racial issues; and his foreign policy. In the Afterword, I examine the advice he offered in his very popular post-presidential column, "Calvin Coolidge Says." His economic and agricultural policies receive due mention, but I have mostly left them for another time. In studying Calvin Coolidge's theory of progressive yet constitutional self-government, I hope to restore to public familiarity a great, well-read American thinker – and none too soon.

Coolidge – the last president to pay down the national debt – has important lessons for politics in our day, too. Government's scope has expanded beyond Coolidge's worst nightmare. The federalist impulse that undergirded his approach, which would urge leaving much power

to the states, is often ignored today. But a new resistance to government's growth has emerged from the very sorts of people who raised
Coolidge in his rustic Vermont town. The people have awoken in the
form of the Tea Party, whose adherents wish to restore America's
Constitution. These patriots draw a link from the founding generation
to our day in hopes that constitutional governance has not faded
from this earth. Often literally cloaked in the garb of that founding
era, they muster all their passion and petition their government to do
as each of us must in our own life: live within our means.

But passion, though important, is not sufficient. However buoyant,
it needs the ballast of discipline and wisdom. Tea Party activists
ignore important constitutional thinkers at their peril: Now is the
time for less talk radio and fewer blogs, and more books with better
arguments, for quietude in our loquacious, anxious age. For too long,
we have neglected our history. But delving into the details of the past
can help us better connect the dots between the politics of today and
the essential ideals of yesteryear. Seeing more clearly what we have
lost may help us return to America's founding principles. A few among
us remember the Coolidge presidency and – notwithstanding the
long assault on its record – look to it for inspiration.

If the Tea Party and other limited-government conservatives study
Coolidge, they will find much to love; the farmer from Vermont may
serve as a guide even in our postindustrial age. In calling for an
"industrial democracy" with constitutional underpinnings, Coolidge
argued that capitalism's excesses were, rather than a harbinger of the
proletarian revolution, a challenge to return to the principles that
animated our nation's earliest days. Coolidge appreciated the unique
moment of America's founding, and, unlike his predecessor Woodrow Wilson, he saw little to correct and much to admire in the Founders. On Forefathers' Day in 1920, he remarked: "On their abiding
faith has been reared a nation, magnificent beyond the dreams of
Paradise. No like body has ever cast so great an influence on human
history."[8] We feel that influence even today. If the founding doesn't
have anything important to teach, why do we continue to make our

arguments and appeals in constitutional language? Why do so many make what Coolidge called pilgrimages to the monuments that celebrate our Republic's achievements?

Like Alexander Hamilton, who was one of his greatest heroes, Coolidge believed that the people really were capable of governing themselves based on reflection and choice. He followed Washington, Jefferson, and Madison, too, in his insistence that governments are instituted not for the rulers, but for the people. Further, he believed that this principle, though it had its fullest practical application in America, would one day govern the world. All free people, Coolidge expected, would someday be governed under his beloved Declaration of Independence's formulation that governments derive their just authority from the consent of the governed. For Coolidge, this bond between the people and their freely chosen representatives was nothing short of sacred.

In this view of freedom sweeping over all the peoples of the earth, Coolidge may have been one of the first "national greatness" conservatives. He made no apologies for believing that the goal of American foreign policy ought to be protecting America, including American businesses and property. Coolidge also believed that America's allies deserved protection, and he repeatedly used the military to safeguard their freedom, too, contrary to current notions that America in the 1920s was isolationist. In those days, it was common to believe that America's foreign policy ought to be narrowly defined, but Coolidge would have agreed with John Quincy Adams: America is the friend of liberty everywhere, but custodian only of her own.

That pro-liberty maxim, perhaps still inspiring in his day, is neglected in our own, when a ruling class based in the seemingly imperial capital of Washington, D.C., regulates and taxes its fellow citizens without limit, supposedly for the public interest. Such overreach and profligacy are anathema to the American way, and the American people have taken notice and become engaged once more. Now that they are finding their voice, so-called Silent Cal has much to offer them. Indeed, Coolidge's thinking – close as it is to the sorts of slogans that sprout up wherever Tea Party demonstrations take place – seems tailor-made for today's conservative activists: "Patriotism is easy to understand in America. It means looking out for yourself by looking out for your country. In no other nation on earth does this principle have such complete application"[9]; "There is no dignity quite so impressive, no one independence quite so important, as living within your means"[10]; "To live under the American Constitution is the greatest political privilege that was ever accorded to the human race"[11]; "The Constitution is the sole source and guaranty of national freedom."[12]

And yet too few are heeding Coolidge's words. Pro–New Deal historians promulgated a myth that continues today of Coolidge as taciturn and passive. Coolidge's recent defenders seem to be swinging to the opposite end of the spectrum, attempting to replace the myth with a Coolidge cult of their own.[13] Led by, among others, talk-show host Glenn Beck; Amity Shlaes of the George W. Bush Foundation; Gene Healy, a fellow at the Cato Institute; and Larry Kudlow, a Reaganite turned CNBC host, well-meaning fans of Coolidge claim him as the "last liberal president"[14] and thus as the antidote to the near-imperial presidency that we suffer today.[15] Steven Hayward gives Coolidge an A+ in his book, *The Politically Incorrect Guide to the Presidents*. These Coolidge enthusiasts miss the mark somewhat, but they represent a welcome departure from the scurrilous attacks against Silent Cal that characterized the New Deal historians.

Some politicians buck this trend of unserious worship of Coolidge-the-libertarian-hero, notably Governor Mike Pence of Indiana, who seems to understand Coolidge especially well, as evident in his comments on the presidency at Hillsdale College, on September 20, 2010:

> There is no finer, more moving, or more profound understanding of the nature of the presidency and the command of humility placed upon it than that expressed by President Coolidge. He, like Lincoln, lost a child while he was president, a son of sixteen.
>
> Young Calvin contracted blood poisoning from an incident

on the South Lawn of the White House. Coolidge wrote, "What might have happened to him under other circumstances we do not know, but if I had not been president . . . " And then he continued, "In his suffering, he was asking me to make him well. I could not. When he went, the power and glory of the Presidency went with him."

A sensibility such as this, and not power, is the source of presidential dignity, and must be restored. It depends entirely upon character, self-discipline, and an understanding of the fundamental principles that underlie not only the republic, but life itself. It communicates that the president feels the gravity of his office and is willing to sacrifice himself; that his eye is not upon his own prospects but on the storm of history, through which he must navigate with the specific powers accorded to him and the limitations placed on those powers both by man and by God.[16]

In any event, while the net effect of some of his policies may well have been economically liberal,[17] Coolidge's political philosophy could best be characterized as that of a "constitutional progressive." Nowhere is his constitutionalism more on display than in his thinking on the presidency. Here we find that he had all the qualities of what Hamilton, in *Federalist* 70, considered necessary for a successful executive: unity, energy, secrecy, and dispatch.

Attempts on both the right and the left to portray Coolidge as a feeble executive are more political than historical. To many on the right, his do-nothing side is admirable – as if a president really should do nothing. To the left, it is lamentable – a president should do everything! In rendering these judgments, both the left and right ignore his times, as if the greatest economic expansion in American history happened by accident and as if the budget in his day balanced itself by magic (a magic unavailable to today's Republican House) – in spite, or perhaps because of, Silent Cal's weakness as an executive. Such critics are wrong. Coolidge achieved a great deal – few presidents have been more committed to presidential control of the executive branch. And in his time, people held a more accurate view of him as a decisive executive.

Progressive historians tend to see his administration as a failure, and they are invested in that misconception because Coolidge's thought traces a route back to the Founders' understanding of the Constitution. It also refutes the political philosophy of his predecessor, Woodrow Wilson, which has done so much to shape modern American government, often with detrimental results. But we can rediscover the past's way of looking at our Republic. Coolidge points the way.

CHAPTER ONE

"IN THE EYE OF THE NATION"
The Political Service and Practice
of Calvin Coolidge

The Police Strike did not make Coolidge, it revealed him. . . . The Police Strike provided a theatrical situation. Governor Coolidge plucked from it and gave the American people a vital truth, the obviousness of which had been forgotten.[1]

Local issues are sometimes civilization-wide. Those, pledged by heart to the interests of civilization, instinctively look to the man of quality to help bear the burdens of civilization, and to tug at its problem. . . . In the day of our world-anguish, unrest, and conflicting voices, we will trust much to the man of that sort. "He that would be greatest among you, let him be the servant of all." Calvin Coolidge is showing the largeness of persistent servanthood.[2]

We are in the eye of the nation. Other cities are looking on. If the Soviet theory succeeds here, it will spread to other battle grounds and become nation wide.[3]

THE BOSTON POLICE STRIKE of 1919 and then-governor Coolidge's response to the lawlessness of the police department have been the subject of movies and books.[4] His simple declaration – "There is no right to strike against the public safety by anybody, anywhere, any time" – launched the national political career of a once-obscure politician from Massachusetts and rural Vermont. That frank statement, and the show of resolve behind it, curtailed the excesses of public-sector unionism at a time of national recession brought on by profligate federal spending, overly friendly labor poli-cies, and the dangerous aftermath of World War I.

The repercussions of Coolidge's controversial yet necessary deci-sion to call in the State Guard extend to our day.[5] When resolving the 1981 strike of the air-traffic controllers, President Ronald Reagan reportedly drew inspiration from Coolidge's proclamation and his telegrammed response to Samuel Gompers of the American Federa-tion of Labor[6] – and in doing so, Reagan may have hastened the end of the Cold War by impressing America's Soviet antagonists.[7] Rea-gan wrote to a Coolidge enthusiast that he was "an admirer of Silent Cal," whom he believed had been "badly treated by history." He added: "I've done considerable reading and researching of his presi-dency. He served his country well and accomplished much."[8]

Indeed, although Reagan often invoked other presidents in speeches, Coolidge was the only one he claimed to have studied. He also invited Coolidge historian Tom Silver to the White House for a lecture and discussion. And he saved Coolidge quotations from the editing pens of his speechwriters. Reagan insisted on Coolidge's suc-cesses in an interview with *Newsweek* at the beginning of his presidency:

> I don't know if the country has ever had a higher level of pros-perity than it did under Coolidge. And he actually reduced the national debt, he cut taxes several times across the board. And maybe the criticism was in both cases that they weren't activist enough. Well, maybe there's a lesson in that. Maybe we've had instances of government being too active, interven-ing, interfering. You have here a couple of cases of men who were abiding by the rule that says if it ain't broke don't fix it.[9]

Reagan had honored Coolidge already by integrating him into his writings as early as 1975. He now had the former president's por-trait hung in the Oval Office.[10] He read a biography of Coolidge while recovering from surgery in 1985.[11]

Reagan's critics were quick to pounce on his fondness for Coolidge. To one commentator, Coolidge was the embodiment of "repressed sentimentality chained in a prison of smooth, flinty New England exterior." Another called him a "throwback to earlier times – a museum piece of old fashioned New England values." Senator Edward Kennedy of Massachusetts castigated Reagan for "saddl[ing] us with the tattered old philosophy of Calvin Coolidge that will work no better in the 1980s than in the 1920s."[12] Mark Shields, the Democratic speechwriter turned columnist, responded angrily to Reagan's choice of Coolidge over Thomas Jefferson for one of his Oval Office portraits, calling it "almost a national sacrilege."[13] Reagan, who after all came of age during the Coolidge presidency, rightly rejected these assessments in a July 1981 interview with Haynes Johnson of the *Washington Post*:

> Now you hear a lot of jokes about Silent Cal Coolidge, but I think the joke is on the people that make jokes because if you look at his record, he cut the taxes four times. We had probably the greatest growth and prosperity that we've ever known. And I have taken heed of that because if he did nothing, maybe that's the answer [for] the federal government."[14]

That the Great Communicator found Silent Cal so worthy of study and public praise should make us wary of lists that routinely rank Coolidge as one of the worst presidents of the twentieth century.[15] It should make us even more wary of scholars who downgrade the strike-breaking actions in Boston that ultimately led him to the presidency. His popularity – he was the only president to ever be featured on a coin in his lifetime[16] – cannot be explained away. As William Allen White, a prominent Republican journalist and leader of the Progressive movement, wrote in 1925 in an early Coolidge biography: "When a man has gone into twenty elections and has won nineteen, he had something in him which compels confidence and which represents the popular will."[17] Thomas Edison, the man who personified American genius and the inventiveness of the 1920s, thought Americans ought to re-nominate and reelect Coolidge in 1928, in part because Coolidge had fostered an economic prosperity that helped spread the benefits of technology throughout society.[18] "The United States is lucky to have Calvin Coolidge," Edison noted after a visit to the Coolidge homestead in Vermont.[19]

It is my contention that Coolidge is ignored (in some cases even hated) not because he was ineffective as an executive, but because he was *spectacularly* effective at helping the common man while defeating attempts to socialize America. Coolidge steered the country through what Jay Lovestone, a Communist union leader, called the "eve of giant class conflicts." Coolidge's earlier strong support of the war effort had already earned him the ire of Socialists, who saw him as little more than a shill for the war industry.

But Lovestone's real indictment of Coolidge in the 1920s was that he did not support labor unions as much as people like himself would have liked. Within weeks after the new president took office, Lovestone said as much in his pamphlet "What's What – About Coolidge?" in which he explained the former governor's rise to prominence:

> The rise of Coolidge, who has ridden into national infamy thru outright strikebreaking activities, portrays with painful clarity the unbridled domination of the employing class over the working masses. Nothing can clinch this truth as forcefully as an examination of the President's record.[20]

In fact, examining that very successful record undermines such critics and enemies. (Lovelace himself later turned against Communism and became a government informant and labor critic.) Coolidge was not in the service of capital any more than he was in thrall to labor. Historian Robert H. Ferrell, while far from sympathetic to Coolidge, notes that the reason so many workers did not join unions was that they were doing very well under Harding and Coolidge. Union membership declined from 5.1 million in 1920 to 3.5 million in 1923. From 1920 to 1929, "real wages rose, the workweek declined, and unemployment was low" – so low that it was a mere 3.7 percent in this period, compared with 6.1 percent for the period of 1911–1917.[21] Coolidge was not opposed to the efforts of union leaders and their political allies to help workers. That's not why labor leaders opposed him. They were roused against him because he had rendered them increasingly irrelevant. By effectively distinguishing police officers who serve the public in the most essential sense from laborers who toil for their earnings as private employees, Coolidge dealt a deathblow to the Socialists' dream of creating a nationwide, revolutionary labor union. The Industrial Workers of the World (IWW) and other left-wing extremists hoped that such a union would bring the country to its knees and peacefully establish Bolshevism in America. As his speeches after the strike make clear, Coolidge knew that the issue at stake wasn't the pay of the police officers, which he had long favored increasing, but the faithful maintenance of public order, of the people's law. Or, as he put it at the Middlesex Club in Boston on October 27, 1919:

> [The police officers who went on strike] determined to substitute their will and their welfare for the will and welfare of all the people. Unless those in authority would permit this, they were to be forced to permit it by turning over Boston to terrorism. Force was to be substituted for law.

The triumph of force is the first stage of revolution – or anarchy. The question for Coolidge, as an officer of the Commonwealth charged by his oath to maintain its constitution and its order, was how best to put force back on the side of the people.

* * *

Coolidge's reactions during the strike were the logical results of studied thought, character, and prior practice, dating back long before the events of September 1919. Without proper context, it's impossible to understand the importance of the strike.

It is undoubtedly true that Coolidge was more reluctant than other politicians of his time to use government's power, but that reluctance does not mean he dithered. On the contrary, he rationed himself with political purposes in mind – a tactic long recognized as prudence in other statesmen.[22] Tom Silver of the Clement Institute has shown in *Coolidge and the Historians* that Coolidge worked all along with Mayor Andrew Peters and Commissioner Edwin U. Curtis: He "played the lion and the fox," while honoring the separation of powers in Massachusetts law.[23] He did not take command of the State Guard immediately to subdue the looting because he believed this problem – absent concerns for the public's safety in the wake of rather minor property damage – lay outside his jurisdiction. He thought local matters should be taken care of by local officials. Out of principle and experience – he once quipped that his hobby was "holding office"[24] – Coolidge believed that local government was the best "informed of local needs" and the most "responsive to local conditions."[25]

It helps to understand the history immediately preceding Coolidge's involvement in the strike. The Boston situation reflected serious national problems, not least of which was the high cost of living that central planning imposed. As governor of a populous and industrialized state, Coolidge had to confront the economic upheaval of the end of the First World War, which brought with it some of the greatest labor strikes in American history. Some four million servicemen had returned to work, only to find little employment or housing. War industries, which had employed nearly a quarter of the labor force, were shutting down. Rampant inflation (prices doubled in this period, while earnings increased by only 6 percent) eroded what little savings families had. Allegations of profiteering by landlords were widespread. Lawmakers wondered what they could do to alleviate "the high cost of living," what we now call inflation.

As lieutenant governor, Coolidge had already confronted the problems that a wartime economy imposed. His administration appropriated money for a commission to investigate allegations of wartime profiteering, but he urged caution before he laid blame. He did not want to provoke anti-capitalist behavior. In a speech about the high cost of living, Coolidge cautioned, "Let us refrain from suspicion; let us refrain from indiscriminate blame; but let us present at once to the proper authorities all facts and all evidence of unfair practices."[26] Government claimed for itself the "right and duty" to investigate profiteering, to be sure. But it must rely upon the court of public opinion to try those responsible, for ultimately the American system was one of "public opinion," of shame. "And above all, we claim the right of publicity," he told the audience at Faneuil Hall. "That is a remedy with an arm longer and stronger than that of the law." He would write later that while "public opinion is of slow development and slow to act . . . once set in motion, it proceeds with a completeness which is overpowering."[27]

Publicity could help shape public opinion. And public opinion, Coolidge reasoned (probably from having read James Bryce's masterful *The American Commonwealth*[28]), was playing an increasingly important role in all the world's republics. In recently defeated Germany, public opinion had held that the country's "only protection lay in . . . a military despotism." Men, be they Germans or anyone else, would submit to a government of force, Coolidge believed (echoing Hobbes), only so long as "they believe it is necessary for their security, necessary to protect them from the imposition of force from without." Americans submitted to the force of the Wilson war administration because it protected them from the threat of German submarine warfare, not because they approved the restrictions on their liberty. But in safer times, "when the mind is free, it turns not to force, but to reason for the source of authority."[29] Reason is accessible to all men at all times; Coolidge agreed with Wilson that the Great War might be the war to end all wars, once reason prevailed and the public fully understood war's senselessness.

In analyzing the wartime economy, Coolidge carefully distinguished the "patriot" in business from the "profiteer." He saw businessmen generally as loyal citizens who helped finance the war effort and who shared in the national sacrifice.

The man who seeks to stimulate and increase the production of materials necessary for the conduct of the war by raising the price he pays [for them] is a patriot. The man who refuses to sell at a fine price whatever he may have that is necessary for the conduct of the war is a profiteer. One man seeks to help his country at his own expense, the other seeks to help himself at his country's expense. One is willing to suffer himself that his country may prosper, the other is willing his country should suffer that he may prosper.[30]

Unlike other politicians of his day, Coolidge did not criticize profit per se or join the radical agitators' calls for the abolition of property in the nation's name. Instead, he argued, "We are coming to see that we are dependent upon commercial and industrial prosperity . . . for the solving of the great problem of the distribution of wealth." Wealth's problems could be solved only by more wealth. Only then could society complete its great endeavor, which was "to extend equal blessings to all." In other words, only business could ameliorate inequality. As Coolidge explained to a meeting of industrialists in Boston, the distribution of wealth could be made just only by justly rewarding those who had contributed to an enterprise. The problem of maldistribution could not be solved "by law, it cannot be done by public ownership, it cannot be done by socialism," for "when you deny the right to a profit you deny the right of a reward to thrift and industry." Referring to a recent wartime recession, he asked: "Have we not seen what happens to industry, to transportation, to all commercial activity which we call business when profit fails? Have we not seen the suffering and misery which it entails upon the people?"[31]

Instead of socialism, Coolidge called for a free-market "industrial democracy," in which republican ideals would be extended into commerce in the sense that "each individual would become an owner, an operator and a manager, a master and a servant, a ruler and a subject."[32] Developments fostering this kind of democracy were essential and indeed already under way, Coolidge believed. He took the maxim of American revolutionary James Otis – kings were made for the good of the people, not the people for good of the kings – and applied the concept to industry. There, the corporate executive or owner, who once ruled as "absolute lord," was giving way to owners of stock, which meant ownership by members of the general public although not by government. Where Marx called for a Communist system guided by the principle "from each according to his ability, to each according to his need,"[33] Coolidge argued that in an industrial democracy, the proper maxim was "unto each who contributes in accordance with his ability, there is due equal consideration and equal honor."[34] The best industries would be those that ennobled men through work and that served shareholders.

"Industry" in the sense of work – and its by-products, profit and property – must be protected, though, from government interference. And attempts to demonize businessmen, he warned, were misguided and counterproductive. Some of the effort to increase business regulation "has proceeded on the theory that if those who enjoy material prosperity used it for wrong purposes, such prosperity should be limited or abolished," he said. "That is as sound as it would be to abolish writing to prevent forgery." He favored anti-trust laws but hoped there would be no need to enforce them. Businessmen, being gentlemen who understood their essential role in society, should, like all good Americans, police themselves first. Every man should stand ready to serve his fellow, for the good of the whole: "It must always be remembered that the obligation to serve the State is forever binding upon all, although office is the gift of the people."[35] Coolidge understood this as a moral edict, not a legal one, but believed it was binding on men of good character all the same. He appealed to their honor.

Business and property owners, then, did not have free rein to prey upon the people – and even less liberty to do so in time of war. When he was lieutenant governor and later as governor, Coolidge used the bully pulpit to curtail aggressive rent hikes at industrial war centers (really manufacturing plants), but he did little to redistribute property, as the federal government had done. In September 1918, Coolidge noted that he retained power under state law to set the terms and conditions of property ownership during wartime for the defense of the Commonwealth. "Up to the present time," he added, "it has not been necessary to take property."[36] He credited the patriotism of Massachusetts citizens for the fact that he had never needed to use this power. It was vintage Coolidge: using the force of reason and patriotism, rather than the direct force of law, to achieve his ends.

Self-policing by business was necessary because, as Coolidge had known at least since 1914, legislation very often could not deliver on its promises. Legislative acts could not take the place of character, industry, or economy. Writing later in his autobiography, Coolidge recalled that he was vindicated when a spate of Progressive candidates went down for defeat nationally and in Massachusetts in the midterm election of 1914. "It appeared to me in January 1914 that a spirit of radicalism prevailed which unless checked was likely to prove very destructive," he wrote. "It consisted of the claim in general that in some way the government was to be blamed because everybody was not prosperous."[37]

In the very different atmosphere of postwar economic malaise, however, the spirit of radicalism succeeded in setting off anarchy in Seattle, in January 1919, when a general strike, one of only a handful in American history, shut down the city. Some twenty-five thousand shipyard workers took to the streets in the weeks after Mayor Ole Hanson took office. They were soon joined by forty thousand other workers, paralyzing the city. Hanson had at one time been a Progressive, but the Russian Revolution in 1917, together with developments in Seattle, caused him to change his views, and he took a stand against the city's organized labor movement in the mayoral election. Labor forces, sensing weakness, retaliated with what became a general strike. According to one historian, everything was disrupted: "Public schools closed; newspapers ceased publication; the city's transportation system grounded to a halt; restaurants were shuttered; and soup kitchens had to be organized."[38] The strikers set up a "virtual counter-government for the city," which suggested something akin to a revolution. Hanson perceived it as such, later writing emphatically:

The so-called sympathetic Seattle strike was an attempted revolution. That there was no violence does not alter the fact. . . .
The intent, openly and covertly announced, was for the overthrow of the industrial system; here first, then everywhere. . . .
True, there were no flashing guns, no bombs, no killings. Revolution, I repeat, doesn't need violence. The general strike, as
practiced in Seattle, is of itself the weapon of revolution, all
the more dangerous because quiet. To succeed, it must sus-
pend everything; stop the entire life stream of a community. . . .
That is to say, it puts the government out of operation. And
that is all there is to revolt – no matter how achieved.[39]

The situation was so dire that Hanson told reporters, "Any man
who attempts to take over the control of the municipal government
functions will be shot." He was adamant that "the seat of government is the city hall," not the "communes" establishing themselves
throughout Seattle. President Woodrow Wilson offered federal military aid to Mayor Hanson, but by that time, the strike was ebbing.[40]
It ended after just five days, but only after horrifying the nation. Soon
thereafter, in April 1919, there was a failed bombing attempt on
Hanson's life.[41]

In August, the mayor resigned and went on a speaking tour across
the country, warning about the threat of publicly managed utilities in
particular and of socialism generally. Discussing "domestic Bolshevism," he was popular on the lecture circuit, making nearly five times
the amount he had when he was mayor.[42] He was even touted as a
possible vice-presidential choice.[43] (On his tour of America and thanks
to the IWW strikes that were paralyzing America, Mayor Hanson
came to the attention of a then-conservative young man named
Whittaker Chambers.[44] Chambers liked Hanson's response to the postwar unrest and complimented "the long-forgotten mayor of Seattle"
– but he loved Coolidge, writing to "every Republican newspaper editor in the country" in support of him for vice president.) Hanson,
during his tour, went so far as to visit the New England Association

of Gas Engineers' convention, where his views were met with rapt attention.[45] The mayor turned author wrote eloquently in his book *Americanism versus Bolshevism* about the threat the IWW posed to the nation: "No effort whatever . . . was made by the authorities to punish the open teaching of sedition. Sabotage, too, came into general use as was consistent with safety, and the preaching thereof became as free and untrammeled as the preaching of the Gospel."[46] Lawlessness was being preached from the streets, while Bolshevism, broadcast from Russia and finding a home around the world,[47] was being heralded, Hanson charged, from Woodrow Wilson's Oval Office.

Wilson had long flirted with socialism. "[In] fundamental theory socialism and democracy are almost if not quite one and the same," he had argued as a young man. "They both rest at bottom upon the absolute right of the community to determine its own destiny and that of its members. Men as communities are supreme over men as individuals."[48] These early views were not ones he later recanted. During the presidential election of 1912, Wilson, a devout Presbyterian, argued: "When you do socialism justice, it is hardly different from the heart of Christianity."[49]

Coolidge disagreed with Wilson about the value of socialism, as about so much else, and his awareness of the radical implications of the police strike earned him a reputation as "the man who defied Bolshevism and more."[50] He flatly opposed the "Bolshevik state" in Russia that, along with the IWW in America, threatened to "pervert and enslave the people." He felt for the "misgoverned, misguided people of Russia" who languished under their new dictatorship, and he cautioned against "aid[ing] Russia by becoming like her."[51] The Russian Revolution was not a true revolution at all, in Coolidge's eyes, but a rejection of democracy and civilization. Indeed, Russia was a civilization that had committed suicide.[52] In the revolution's wake were nothing but "starving victims."[53] Throughout his time in government and afterward, Coolidge denounced the Soviet regime and refused to give it diplomatic recognition.[54] In an unusually passionate speech at a reformatory in Concord, Coolidge placed the blame for the persistent nationwide disorder on American and foreign Communists, who must be checked. He did not think they would bring down America and believed they could be defeated by educating Americans and changing public opinion:

> Every government always has enemies. Our government at this moment is no exception. We have more just now than is usual, and if they are in the pay of the revolutionary authorities in Russia, as I believe to be the case, the danger is somewhat greater than in normal times simply because these enemies to-day are better financed than usual. Even so, I do not regard the menace as genuinely serious. . . . It is right to punish overt acts, but the only way to deal with beliefs is to meet them, to expose their fallacy, to present the facts which prove them wrong. This is the American way.[55]

Wilson, on the other hand, had a disturbingly ambiguous attitude toward the Bolshevists, whom he dismissed as the "dreamers of Russia." He told the Executive Committee of the American Federation of Labor, "My heart is with them, but my mind has a contempt for them."[56] Nevertheless, according to Socialist turned anti-Communist Max Eastman, Wilson wished "good luck to the 'republic of labor unions' in Russia" and hoped the Allied Powers of World War I would treat the Soviet Union with "good will . . . intelligence and unselfish sympathy."[57] Revolutionary leader Leon Trotsky told an interviewer on March 5, 1918, that Wilson was a "fellow traveler." "Historians must never forget," Jennings C. Wise wrote in 1938, "that Woodrow Wilson, despite the efforts of the British police, made it possible for Leon Trotsky to enter Russia with an American passport."[58] To those watching the scene from 1918 to 1920, it was a real possibility that the nation might be veering off into a socialist state.[59] "Men have dared to fly the red flag in the face of the law," as one contemporary noted in December 1919.[60]

Hewing to the more American red-white-and-blue, Coolidge

asserted proudly on Flag Day of that year that the Stars and Stripes spoke with a "voice" proclaiming the "sanctity of revelation." The citizen "who lives under it and is loyal to it is loyal to truth and justice everywhere, " he added. "But he who lives under it and is disloyal to it is a traitor to the human race everywhere."[61]

*   *   *

In the election of 1912, Theodore Roosevelt failed to win the Republican nomination and the party re-nominated William Howard Taft; Roosevelt then created the Progressive Party and ran for president as its leader. This Taft–Roosevelt split caused the reliably Republican Massachusetts to tip to the Democrats' nominee, Woodrow Wilson. Coolidge told his father he was pleased that Roosevelt had gone down to defeat. "I am sorry that Taft could not win but am glad TR made so poor a showing," he wrote.[62] Coolidge's support for Taft may have been more personal than political, as Coolidge was always a loyal party man.[63] Nonetheless, his dislike of Roosevelt in 1912 marks perhaps the first time that he began to openly question Progressivism, although it was quite some time before he voted against it as a state legislator. Massachusetts had long been a center of Progressivism. It had passed child-labor legislation as early as 1836, for instance, long before the nation debated a constitutional amendment against child labor in the 1920s. The Commonwealth had laws requiring factory inspection by the state for safety, and a limited workday for women and children, as well as food- and drug-safety regulations, and laws to allow the recall of judges. Curiously, Massachusetts Progressives did not believe a Progressive government needed to be a larger government. Governor Curtis Guild Jr., for instance, favored Progressive causes, yet reduced the state's debt by 12 percent in 1906.[64]

The discord between the traditional wing (the "standpats") of the Taft supporters and the Progressive wing of Roosevelt fans found its way into Massachusetts politics, where Senators Winthrop M. Crane and Henry Cabot Lodge vied for influence. This divide was both ideological and geographical, with Crane representing the western part of the state and Lodge the eastern. There were educational and class overtones in the dispute, too: Crane graduated from high school and began a career in small business, while Lodge received Harvard's first Ph.D. in political science in 1876, one of the first Ph.D. politicians.[65]

Coolidge, though he was always independent of the party "organization,"[66] agreed with the eastern, anti-Progressive, "standpat" wing of the party. He was somewhat in the political orbit of Senator Crane, because of his western Massachusetts roots, but he also courted the support of Senator Lodge, with whom he would later have a complicated relationship. Lodge, for his part, congratulated the young Coolidge on his "Have Faith in Massachusetts" speech and for his courage, writing in 1914:

> I am more struck with it on the second reading even than I was with it on the first. It is not only able but you have put the propositions with epigrammatic force and often in a very original way. That is saying much, for you are stating what you and I believe to be fundamental truths. . . . What I like best of all is the courage with which you state those fundamental truths which it is the fashion just now to put aside and hide. For some years past political leaders, great and small, have been talking to the people as though these truths did not exist. For example, directly and indirectly it has been continually declared that everybody would be happy and successful by [means of] legislation, a most pernicious doctrine. . . . As a citizen of Massachusetts I congratulate myself that we have a president of the senate who not only is able but who is ready to make such a speech.[67]

Lodge, in a letter to former president Roosevelt, later backed Coolidge for governor. Coolidge was "ardently for the war from the beginning," he wrote. "And in his campaign he has not been talking for himself at all but just making war speeches."[68] Roosevelt did back

Coolidge for the governorship, writing in his endorsement that he was "a man who has the forward look and who is anxious to secure genuine social and industrial justice in the only way it can be effectively secured, that is, by basing a jealous insistence upon the rights of all, on the foundation of legislation that will guarantee the welfare of all."[69]

Coolidge and Roosevelt profoundly differed, however, about that "foundation." Coolidge agreed with Lodge that the notion that legislation might uplift all was a pernicious doctrine. Unsurprisingly, then, as governor and later as president, Coolidge favored no legislative agenda in any broad sense, because he generally did not believe in legislation. His skepticism about new laws was rooted in his conviction that the purpose of politics was not to achieve certain ends, but to defend rights and protect the public safety. His second inaugural address as governor on January 9, 1920, made this clear: "In general, it is time to conserve, to retrench rather than to reform, a time to stabilize the administration of the present laws rather than to seek new legislation."

This speech was the logical extension of one in his campaign for lieutenant governor in 1916, in which he had said: "We do not need more legislation. Repeal is even unnecessary. What Massachusetts needs – what the nation needs – is wise administration of the law. Look not to the legislature for relief; look to the executive."[70] Coolidge was clear on what kind of governor he would be. Legislation wasn't meant to uplift, but merely to maintain the conditions sufficient to continued prosperity. More often than not, his advice on legislation was: "Do nothing. It is more important that the law be permanently fixed than that experiments in new legislation should be tried."[71] He deplored the increasing tendency "to run to government for relief from the consequences of conditions which no act of government causes, and which no device of government can correct." On the subject of unemployment bills, he declared to the *Boston Journal* on March 29, 1921, that "anyone who is not capable of supporting himself is not fit for self-government." "If people can't support themselves," he warned, "we'll have to give up self-government."

Part of this disdain for legislative uplift stemmed from a lesson Coolidge had learned early: that progressivism often has unintended consequences. He entered the state legislature, the Massachusetts General Court, in 1907 as something of a Progressive, but he served only one two-year term. After that, he ran for, and served as, Northampton mayor instead. Biographer William Allen White detailed Coolidge's successes as a young legislator, a record he considered that of a "mild Progressive." Indeed, Coolidge was described as "uncomfortably Progressive for some of his constituents" by a legislative colleague. His record shows a strong Progressive streak. He supported bills providing for one day's rest per week in industry, for reduced working hours for women and children, for lower railroad fares for workmen, for honest weighing in coal yards, for pensions for firemen's widows, and for municipal playgrounds.[72] As governor, he established a commission to look into the feasibility of providing pensions to state employees.[73] He even wrote a section of the 1914 state Republican platform that was Progressive to the core in advocating support for a long list of boons:

Every means of compulsory and public education, vocational and technical; merited retirement pensions, aid to dependent mothers, helpful housing and fire protection, reasonable hours and conditions of labor, and amplest protection to the public health, workingmen's compensation and its extension to interstate railroads, official investigation of the price of necessities, pure food and honest weight and measure, homestead commission, city planning, the highest care and efficiency in the administration of all hospital and penal institutions, probation and parole, care and protection of children and the mentally defective, rural development, urban sanitation, state and national conservation and reclamation, and every other public means for social welfare consistent with the sturdy character and resolute spirit of an independent, self-supporting, self-governing, and free people.[74]

Coolidge soon became disillusioned, though, with the politics of Progressive improvement. It seemed as if the General Court was legislating faster than it could ever hope to administer. Coolidge explained his political evolution – which had been spurred perhaps more by pragmatism than philosophy – to Frank W. Stearns, Amherst man, business tycoon, Coolidge confidant, and first political backer:[75]

> When I first went to the Legislature I was a very young man. I suppose those who voted for me considered me a Radical or a Liberal. I had only been a member of the Legislature a few months when I made up my mind that Massachusetts at any rate was legislating faster than it could administer and that the sane thing was to call a halt for the time being.[76]

Writing to his business associate Robert Maynard on August 16, 1916, Stearns made much of this transformation:

> [Coolidge] told me once that when he first went into the legislature he supposes he was considered a radical, especially along the lines of legislation in favor of social betterment. There came a time around the middle of his legislative experience when he came to the conviction *not* that his previous ideas were wrong but that Massachusetts, at any rate, was going too fast. As he put it, legislation was outstripping the ability to administer. He felt that unless we were willing to get into serious trouble that would take years to rectify, a halt must be called; and he faced about and was probably then considered a conservative.[77]

Experience, not ideology, started Coolidge down the path to fiscal conservatism. He wanted to move slowly and prudently. As if to justify Coolidge's reluctance to legislate quickly, January 17, 1915, produced a record number of bills, with some 1,700 reported out of committee. By this time and after his stint as mayor, Coolidge had returned to the state legislature, where he served as Senate president,

and he worried that the proliferation of proposed legislation made it
impossible to give proper deliberation to the issues affecting the state.
A letter from his office dated March 30, 1914, was titled "ALARM"
and noted that the committees in the legislature were not keeping up
with the deluge. Such volume meant bills would not receive proper
consideration and would fail the test of narrow tailoring that he had
recommended in a letter to his father, shortly after his father became
a Vermont state senator, in 1910:

> You need not hesitate to give the other members your views on
> any subject that arises. It is much more important to kill bad
> bills than to pass good ones. . . . See that the bills you recom-
> mend from your committee are so worded that they will do
> just what they intend and not a great deal more that is unde-
> sirable. Most bills can't stand that test.

Coolidge's belief in limiting the amount of legislation also owed
something to his long-standing emphasis on efficiency and brevity.
After he was unanimously chosen president of the Massachusetts
Senate, he delivered a notably simple inaugural message of just forty-
four words. Its essence was clear: "Above all things, be brief." A belief
in brevity lent itself naturally to a belief in limited legislation and,
ultimately, limited government. Coolidge's position was especially
important because the ever-increasing administrative bloat in Massachusetts threatened to drown self-government in a morass of regulation and bureaucracy. In his autobiography, he would recall his
wish to curtail "the great complication of laws and restrictive regulations, from a multiplicity of Boards and Commissions, which had
reached about one hundred, and from a large increase in the number
of people on the public pay rolls."

By reorganizing the departments and making them smaller,
Governor Coolidge delivered a rebuke to the Progressives' ideal of a
disinterested bureaucracy. Some 118 separate departments had arisen
since 1900, demanding more space in the already crowded State

House. By means of a ballot measure he had supported, Coolidge won the authority to reorganize the state government's departments into no more than twenty.[78] But in picking a fight he might have shirked, he exposed himself to real political fallout. At a time of national recession, he was eliminating well-paying government jobs. As Claude M. Fuess, Coolidge's best biographer, notes: "Every public official who lost his comfortable job was likely to become an enemy, and the number of friends made in the process would inevitably be much smaller than the foes.[79] Coolidge himself noted to a friend: "They say the Police Strike required executive courage; reorganizing one hundred and eighteen departments into eighteen required a good deal more. Every time a man makes an appointment he creates one ingrate and a thousand enemies."[80]

Under the new constitution that passed after the Massachusetts Constitutional Convention of 1917, Coolidge could easily have left to his successor the related, and also technically difficult, challenge of reducing the state's boards and commissions, because the constitution did not require any change be made until January 1, 1921. But he undertook the task himself, attacking at much political risk the sluggish but growing and politically formidable administrative state in Massachusetts. He did so because he recognized that an excess of bureaucracy and legislation led to a decline in self-government.

Coolidge was ever the guardian of self-government. This was the highest calling of the public servant. He insisted that the purpose of public service was to serve, not to get rich. The members of the General Court should "look on [public service] only as an avocation," not an occupation. If legislators became dependent on their public salaries, Coolidge knew, charges of self-dealing would ensue, imperiling the government by reducing the public's respect for it. "No system of government can stand that lacks confidence," he wrote in his undated essay "On the Nature of Politics." "Public administration is [supposed to be] honest and sound and public business is transacted on a higher plane than private business."

It was only natural, then, that Coolidge should recoil so strongly

from legislators' attempts to fatten their wallets out of the public's treasury. When legislators asked him to join them at a party before the
legislature adjourned for the summer in 1919, he said nothing at first,
waiting for them to leave. As they did, he said, "I trust you won't forget
to vote yourselves some compensation." It was a cool rhetorical pay-
back – perhaps an ineffectual one, given that the legislators had already
pushed through an annual pay increase for themselves, from $1,000 to
$1,500, overriding Coolidge's veto of what the press dubbed the "Sal-
ary Grab Bill." As Fuess notes, Coolidge had laid out all his arguments:
that the measure was extravagant at a time of recession, that no man
in the legislature was so poor that he could not serve for a session of
about five months, and that there was more to being a legislator than
mere compensation. "When membership is sought as a means of
livelihood, legislation will pass from a public function to a private
enterprise," Coolidge warned, also reminding the legislators that
"men do not serve here for pay" but rather sought something else –
"their honor."

Nothing less than the honor and reputation of the General Court
was at stake, he believed.[81] That honor would "never depend on [a
legislator's] salary, but on the ability and integrity with which he does
his duty; not on what he receives, but on what he gives; and only out
of the bountifulness of his own giving will his constituents raise him to
power." It was the legislators' "solemn duty" to "think last of themselves." Otherwise their decisions would "lack authority." Coolidge
wished to protect the legislature from itself and to guarantee that a
republican spirit would continue in the state's government.

* * *

Although he had stood fast against attempts to raise the salaries of
legislators, Coolidge favored increasing them for schoolteachers,
believing that bad teachers would imperil republican government by
failing to teach the convictions essential for republican life. He also
exalted good teachers throughout his career. As vice president, he said:

The standards which teachers are required to maintain are continually rising. Their work takes on a new dignity. It is rising above a calling, above a profession, into the realm of art. It must be dignified by technical training, ennobled by character, and sanctified by faith.[82]

Coolidge feared wrong teaching in addition to inadequate teaching. Those who promoted false convictions, he told students at a Harvard commencement on June 19, 1919, were rejecting the truth upon which the American Revolution was founded and sowing the seeds of "anarchy or despotism."[83] Proper civic instruction, in contrast, exemplified by the great educators John Adams and James Bowdoin, "recognizes with the clear conviction of men not thinking of themselves that the cause of America is the cause of education, of education with a soul, a trained intellect but guided by an enlightened conscience." The Republic needed men who "recognize . . . that when these fail, America has failed." Men such as Ephraim Williams (who founded Williams College, where Coolidge gave a speech in October 1919) understood that "enlightening the soul of his fellow man . . . made his mark which all eternity cannot erase." They recognized that their fellow citizens "find their true satisfaction in something higher, finer, nobler" than a "greatly increased material prosperity."[84]

With so much at stake, it is not surprising that Coolidge wrote a letter to the mayor of Boston expressing support for increasing teachers' pay:

It is perfectly clear that more money must be provided for these purposes, which surpass in their importance all our other public activities, both by government and by private charity. . . . Unless a change is made, the cause of education will break down."[85]

Ultimately, inadequate education would cause the Republic to fall, in Coolidge's opinion; in the past, the sovereign had tutors, but now the people were sovereign both politically and culturally, and "what they think determines every question of civilization." Teachers had the great duty of transmitting thought down through the generations, but they were not treated as if they did, suffering neglect in a time when society overly indulged its "pursuit of prosperity," Coolidge told graduating Harvard students in 1919. Failing to pay them salaries commensurate with their value to civilization and to "the foundations of our liberties" might make them "listen too willingly to revolutionary doctrines." Republican principles required that they be generously paid because our government of "public opinion" needed to be well cultivated. "The compensation of many teachers ... is far less than the pay of unskilled labor," Coolidge noted. "We compensate liberally the manufacturer and the merchant; but we fail to appreciate those who guard the minds of our youth."[86]

CHAPTER TWO

LABOR, BLOWS TO BOLSHEVISM, AND TAKING UP "MANLY BURDENS"

Let everybody keep at work. Profitable employment is the deathblow to Bolshevism, and abundant production is disaster to the profiteer. Our salvation lies in putting forth greater effort, in manfully assuming our own burdens, rather than in entertaining the pleasing delusion that they can be shifted to some other shoulders. Those who attempt to lead people on in this expectation only add to their burdens and their dangers.[1]

COOLIDGE CANNOT BE dismissed as anti-government. For the simple reason that he stood opposed to "desertion of duty,"[2] he would very likely have opposed strikes by teachers' unions that place the self-interest of teachers above that of their charges. For that kind of desertion, Coolidge had nothing but scorn, which he expressed in his long tussles with the near-anarchist labor movement that hoped to seize upon the bedlam of the recession and other postwar troubles. He rightly saw the transition to peacetime as fraught with danger. How would the country win the peace and find work for the soldiers returning home? In his inaugural address as governor on January 2, 1919, Coolidge asked: "How shall we emerge from the autocratic methods of war to the democratic methods of peace, raising ourselves again to the source of all our strength and all our glory – sound self-government?" Self-government had frayed, it must be restored, and idleness, unemployment, and rioting endangered it.

A successful transition required a thoughtful leader who was willing to stand firm for the principle of law and order while being sensitive to the underlying concerns that led to the unrest. Coolidge had experience with law and negotiation, and he saw both as necessary to preserve the Commonwealth. He had successfully resolved a dispute between workers and the textile industry in 1912, on terms favorable to labor, as a state senator on the legislative affairs and agriculture committee. In the postwar era, similar disputes were proving harder and harder to resolve peacefully, but Coolidge still tried. In January 1919, the American Woolen Company in Lawrence asked Coolidge to send in the state militia to break up a textile strike; Coolidge instead dispatched F. F. Fuller, an even-handed member of the *Boston American* editorial staff, to the town to investigate conditions and report his findings. After he listened to Fuller's report, Coolidge decided he would not send in the militia.

Another strike took place soon thereafter as eight thousand telephone operators held up business for several days in April 1919. Coolidge wired a request for federal permission to seize the telephone system in the interest of the public welfare. He was betting on the support of Postmaster General Albert S. Burleson, who, as Coolidge knew, favored anti-labor policies and government control of communications. In short order, the parties reconciled, but Coolidge remained wary, writing in a statement after the strike concluded that he didn't think it "should ever have been permitted." Those who served the public – owners and workers alike – had a duty to resolve their differences, he explained:

> There is another principle involved which has received very little attention, and that is the obligation that exists on those who enter public service to continue to furnish such service even at some personal inconvenience. This obligation reaches from the highest officer or government official to the humblest employee. The public has rights which cannot be disregarded.[3]

Union sympathies spread nationwide as the IWW sought to establish "one big union" to advance its socialist aims; and, in 1919 alone, some 3,630 strikes occurred involving more than four million workers.[4] By March 1919, workers in the wool, silk, tobacco, marine, and building trades had all gone on strike. The railroads in California, Arizona, and Nevada had all been shut down by striking railroad workers.[5]

A strike was, at base, a violation of a contract. Violating contracts threatened to upend public safety and threaten the rule of law. Coolidge resolved to uphold law and order, at least in his own Commonwealth of Massachusetts. President Wilson, acting under the Federal Possession and Control Act and on the grounds of easing the war effort, had nationalized most of the nation's railways, and they remained nationalized after the war ended. Coolidge ably kept the railroads of his state from falling prey to union demands. Michael E. Hennessy, in *Four Decades of Massachusetts Politics: 1890–1935*, described how Coolidge dealt with the conflict between streetcar companies and the Salem jitneys, small buses that were underbidding streetcars and taking some of their passengers. The streetcars contended that the jitneys were operating illegally, in violation of an order from the Salem municipal government; the jitneys had been encouraging urchins to disrupt streetcar traffic. Coolidge agreed with the streetcars because the jitneys were operating in defiance of municipal code, which he was bound to uphold.

He encouraged the railroad trustees to put their streetcars back into operation and pledged the support of the state police if necessary. For his efforts, he was threatened with political defeat: "The labor people will go into every town in the state and crucify you politically." Coolidge's response was that they were welcome to try: "Don't let me deter you. Go right ahead."[6]

Coolidge knew he had established a reputation for fairness and therefore believed the people would side with him. He rode the streetcar to work, just as his constituents did.[7] "It was widely known – and widely applauded – that the new governor traveled in Boston by streetcar," notes Garland S. Tucker III in his recent book, *The High Tide of American Conservatism*.[8] Coolidge knew that a strike by streetcar unions would probably expand beyond Salem and inspire other streetcar operators throughout the state to go on strike. Fortunately, he was well prepared to preempt any statewide strike before one occurred. Months earlier, he had argued *in favor* of employees of the Boston Elevated Street Railway, helping to win the workers a sizeable pay increase.[9] Meanwhile, Coolidge sought to resolve the streetcar issue by eliminating the jitneys. In July 1919, at the end of a special session of the legislature, he urged the creation of a commission on streetcars, which would report to the legislature in November (so as not to affect the coming election). Coolidge had previously argued, in January, that

> street railway service in some form is a public necessity . . .
> [but as] every one knows, the difficulty is where to get more
> money. There are only two sources – increased fares and the
> public treasury, directly by grant or indirectly by remission of
> taxes or other payments. Public ownership is no answer . . . as
> it would increase no revenue. *The question is one of our needs and of*
> *our duty, and it must be squarely met.* . . . So long as a street railway
> can be operated with fair service, paid for by its patrons, it is on
> a sound and enduring basis. That ought to be standard. The
> moment that it is abandoned there is no standard to measure
> the soundness of the principle applied.[10]

This application of political philosophy to a mundane issue such as transportation was typical of Coolidge. Similarly, the touchstones of public "needs" and governmental "duty" would also be essential to his handling of the police strike.

With these political victories in hand, Coolidge was adequately prepared for the police-strike crisis. Contrary to Fuess, who argues that he never mentioned the police strike by name, Coolidge suggested to the people of Massachusetts the nature of his law-and-order response by giving two speeches in early September of that year on the topic of duty, work, and sacrifice in a constitutional republic. In them, we have a fine answer to the question he posed: How could self-government be restored after the horror of world war? While the country had remained largely unscathed physically – American casualties were barely above 115,000 – its institutions were imperiled by strikes and unrest. Americans' rights had been violated by their government; some citizens had been jailed for criticizing Woodrow Wilson, and war-related bigotry was high. Republican self-restraint and virtue, not socialism, were the correct way forward for the newly emergent world power.[11]

The war had ended mere days after Coolidge won the governor-ship, and Americans now grappled with what kind of government they would have in peacetime. Many now favored a socialized system, believing it would temper the excesses of capitalism – which they saw as the root cause of the war. Coolidge rejected this "criticism of commercialism" that "advocate[d] the destruction of all enterprise and the abolition of all property,"[12] and he did so at a time when it was not yet clear that his side (the side of "law and order," as his collection of speeches from this era is titled)[13] would triumph. If anything, his side seemed hopelessly outnumbered. Coolidge knew, though, that the most useful approach was to fight for public opinion, which, as governor, he could shape through his statements and actions. In those days newspapers reprinted government speeches on the front page, and Coolidge, who in his post-presidency would write for a newspaper as a columnist, knew how to write speeches that would please an editor. They were short and to the point. His speeches in September, which eloquently reflect his belief that the first duty of a statesman is to teach, accordingly have a timeless quality appropriate to any age. In them, Coolidge earned his rise to statesmanship.

* * *

In the first of these speeches, delivered in Plymouth on Labor Day, Coolidge cast the issue through the prism of American history and labor's own progress, which had been achieved not through socialism, but through hard work and service to one's fellow man: "Not only have the hours and conditions of labor been greatly improved, but wages have increased about one hundred per cent," he noted. Most important, Coolidge reminded his audience that it was the law that had made this progress possible, and indeed that had instituted Labor Day itself, established by law as a national holiday. Labor, aligned with law, would continue to make rapid gains.

Coolidge recognized that labor would always be important to a republic. In true Calvinist fashion, he believed that man set himself apart in America through his labor and its fruits. A republic that was "founded on a recognition of the sovereignty of the citizen" must necessarily be "led to a realization of the dignity of his occupation." America's creed of hard work rejected "the age-old European conception that work is the badge of the menial and the inferior." Coolidge considered that European notion responsible for World War I because it had allowed one class – the Kaiser and his court – to rule over others, without even the pretense of serving the people. Americans would not stand for rule by a Kaiser, as Coolidge made clear in a speech at Boston's Tremont Temple:

> The great pretender to the throne of earth thought the time had come to assert that we were his subjects. Two million of our men are already in France, and each day ten thousand more are hastening to pay their respects to him at his court in Berlin in person. He has our answer.[14]

Coolidge often remarked that the assassination of royalty in 1914 was the "newest shot heard 'round the world." The implication was clear: America was not a place for royalty, but she would extend her ideal of the natural equality of all men all the way to the European battlefields. Work was "the crowning glory of men free and equal." Its fruits through the war effort and industrial production demonstrated the "loyalty, devotion, and sacrifice of American labor." The war was a continuation of "that principle, which is known as the Monroe Doctrine, that European despotism shall make no further progress" in the world.[15]

The hour had come, Coolidge thought, to extend that principle at home. It had already come far. The socialist assumption that the worker did not own the means of production was "growing more and more contrary to the facts," because the increasing ownership of stock meant that "the wealth of the Nation is owned by the people of the Nation." Coolidge listed the industries – railroad, commerce, shipping, and banking – in which hundreds of thousands of everyday workers owned stock. It was now dubious to assume that "we can take from one class to give to another," he argued, because the propertied and employed classes were increasingly one and the same.

This progress would continue – so long as Americans recognized that socialism was inimical to progress because it retarded the incentive to "build up our industries and make them strong."

> When they fail, all fails. When they prosper, all prosper. Workmen's compensation, hours, and conditions of labor are cold consolations, if there be no employment. And employment can be had only if some one finds it profitable. . . . Industry must expand or fail.[16]

Taxing industry too heavily would make it fail because taking any more than is just would lead naturally to injustice, waste, and failure. It would lead the country closer to socialism, in which the choice, as Coolidge put it in a later speech, would be between "Russia past and present: anarchy and despotism."[17]

The country was emerging from an autocratic war footing, which, though not ideal, had been necessary. But efforts to take away profit in order to prevent profiteering had entailed great sacrifices that were now unnecessary. Coolidge rebuked the socializing practices of the war years: The railroads had been so restricted through government control of fuel, he said, that they were "unable to do good" – and the nationalization of the railroads came at a price. New England, for instance, had even given up its supplies of coal during the winter in order to power the trains.

Those days were in the past, however, and the new question for America was not sacrifice, but surviving the excesses of prosperity.

> The day of adversity has passed. The American people met and overcame it. The day of prosperity has come. The great question now is whether they can endure their prosperity.[18]

Coolidge believed they could, because Americans of all classes and occupations had answered "the call of duty" during the war. The workingman had rejected the "sodden selfishness" of people who just wanted to "make money" and who preferred "peace at any price."

Coolidge wondered if America, having emerged from World War I as the world's strongest economy, would turn toward socialism, abandoning the path that had brought so much success throughout its history. He astutely invoked the country's most prominent labor leader as he issued this warning:

> The counsel that Samuel Gompers gave is still sound, when he said in effect, "America may not be perfect. It has the imperfections of all things human. But it is the best country on earth, and the man who will not work for it, who will not fight for it, and if need be die for it, is unworthy to live in it."[19]

Quoting Gompers was especially clever because Gompers, as Coolidge probably knew, could not quickly reply – he had gone to Europe for the peace conference at the behest of Woodrow Wilson, with the hope of extending the labor movement's influence in Europe. The labor chieftain's words underscored Coolidge's own notion of America as a collective undertaking that would stretch as far into the future as the country might exist. "The day when it is duty of all Americans to work will remain forever." America would live forever if everyone worked. The cause of America was the cause of labor, called upon to do its best, and labor's best efforts had helped America outpace her European adversaries in wartime production:

Such a course saved us in war; only such a course can preserve us in peace. The power to preserve America, with all that it now means to the world, all the great hope that it holds for humanity, lies in the hands of the people.[20]

"Talents and opportunity exist," Coolidge said, so long as Americans continue to "work for America." He reiterated his point often and emphatically before, during, after the police strike. The striking police were out for themselves, he suggested, and had deserted the ideal of hard work for the common good – an ideal that had contributed to America's past, wartime, and future successes. The strikers were, in effect, un-American because they lacked a sense of duty.

*   *   *

While his first speech of September 1919 employed recent history to denounce organized labor's efforts to take over the police union, the second speech Coolidge gave that month, delivered two days later in Westfield, referred to the American founding and especially to the establishment of the Constitution. Here the governor was at his best, carefully using America's revolutionary history to illuminate the unchanging "principles of government and of citizenship," which would "never be untimely or unworthy of reiteration," in defense of his actions against the strike. He deftly showed himself to be, as his political backer Frank Stearns had put it years before, Lincoln's "heir."[21]

Coolidge's first purpose in the Westfield speech, delivered at the town's 250th-anniversary celebration, was to honor General William Shepard, an "illustrious son of Westfield" who had put down the insurrection of Shays' Rebellion in 1787. General Shepard, already much beloved by some of his fellow citizens for defending Massachusetts "at all hazards" in the Revolutionary War, had feared that Shays's 1,400 men would use the weapons in the local arsenal to destroy the countryside. Coolidge pointed out that Shepard knew he had to act quickly and decisively, because once armed, the rebels would be difficult to stop. Shays's men had encircled the arsenal and stood ready to attack, preparing a siege of Shepard's poorly equipped force. Shepard was expecting General Lincoln from the Continental Army but knew he could not afford to wait any longer. He ordered his men to fire at "waistband height." They killed two rebels instantly with cannon fire and wounded more than twenty others with grape-shot, successfully defending the Springfield Armory. The insurgents quickly abandoned their assault on the armory and fled.

In the context of the Boston strike, Coolidge's decision to speak at an event honoring Shepard – and his direct invocation of Shepard's defense of the arsenal – can only be seen through a political prism. General Shepard, present at both Lexington and Concord and Valley Forge, had long been a patriot, Coolidge pointed out. To protect law and order against the assault of the Shays rebels, he had disobeyed an order from Secretary of War Henry Knox, who had denied him permission to use the weaponry at the Springfield Armory because Congress was not in session and could not authorize its use. Shepard, reaching the armory before Shays, took the arms anyway and restored order with a local unpaid militia of some nine hundred men who lacked food and adequate arms. Shepard acted at great personal cost, which he described a few years later in a letter to Secretary Knox:

> [My actions] . . . excited against me the keenest Resentments of the disappointed Insurgents, manifested in the most pointed Injurys, such as burning my Fences, injuring my Woodlands, by Fire, beyond a Recovery for many Years – wantonly & cru-elly butchering two valuable Horses, whose ears were cut off and Eyes bored out before they were killed – insulting me per-sonally with the vile Epithet of the Murderer of my Brethren, and, through anonimous Letters, repeated by threatening me with the Destruction of my House and Family by Fire. – which kind of Injuries I occasionally experience even to this day.

Shepard died much reduced, having to pay to restore his property after he had furnished his own troops with supplies to stave off the rebellion. For Coolidge, Shepard's political significance was clear: Here was a patriot who had freely given of himself so that his community could have an "establishment of liberty, under an ordered form of government." The true patriot gives of himself to his fellows and they, in turn, return the duty. "When we turn to the life of her patriot son," Coolidge told the Westfield crowd, "we see that [Shepard] no less grandly illustrated the principle, that to such government, so established, the people owe an allegiance which has the binding power of the most solemn obligation." Just as Shepard opposed the Shays mob, so too would Coolidge oppose the mob-like actions of an attempted general strike, because it was the governor's "solemn obligation" to uphold the law of the Commonwealth. "All usurpation is tyranny," Coolidge observed, and America's founding patriots "hated the usurper whether king, or Parliament, or mob, but they bowed before the duly constituted authority of the people."

Coolidge went on to explain that Shays' Rebellion, led by eighteen rebellious military men[22] "hostile . . . to the execution of all law," had resulted in the Constitutional Convention, where witnesses to the rebellion, such as Jonathan Smith, a farmer from nearby Lanesboro and delegate to the Massachusetts ratifying convention, defended the new Constitution against its anti-Federalist enemies. Similarly, other patriots from around the country, motivated by the need to prevent future rebellions, now sought to build stronger foundations for civic order. Smith earned Coolidge's high praise: There was "no better example of a man of the people desiring the common good," he said, and he "spoke the common sense of the common man of the Commonwealth." The common sense Coolidge praised consisted of Smith's rebuke to Amos Singletary, an anti-Federalist farmer at the Constitutional Convention who worried that the moneyed elite would become the real "managers of the Constitution." Smith, relying on common sense, defended of the Constitution on the grounds that all Americans were "embarked in the same cause" and "must all sink or swim together." In Coolidge's summation of Smith's arguments for the Constitution, one can hear him referring to the police strike:

> Shall we throw the Constitution overboard because it does not please us all alike? Suppose two or three of you had been at the pains to break up a piece of rough land and sow it with wheat: would you let it lie waste because you could not agree what sort of a fence to make? Would it not be better to put up a fence that did not please every one's fancy, rather than keep disputing about it until the wild beasts devoured the crop? Some gentlemen say, Don't be in a hurry; take time to consider. I say, There is a time to sow and a time to reap. We sowed our seed when we sent men to the Federal Convention, and now it is time to reap the fruit of our labour; and if we do not do it now, I'm afraid we shall never have another opportunity.

In this invocation of the biblical command to sow and reap, Coolidge reflected on the challenge of self-government, and thus of republican government, in his own time. He wanted to resolve the conflict with the police officers as peacefully as possible. The police who had shirked their duty, he stated in a later proclamation, had acted in a "voluntary" manner, "against the advice of their well wishers," and had "long discussed" and "premeditated" their strike.

The strikers had given Coolidge no choice. He recognized that supporting them and their aims – or even failing to act against the strikes – would ultimately undo the "duly constituted authority of the people" who, in making the law, had given Police Commissioner Curtis the authority to govern the police department and exercise his own judgment to that end. Though the strikers wanted Coolidge to remove Curtis, Coolidge informed Samuel Gompers by telegram that he would do no such thing because he had no power to do it: "[The Commissioner] can assume no position ... except what the people by the authority of their law vested in him." Coolidge also let Gompers know that he stood "determined to defend the sovereignty of Massachusetts" and to maintain the laws of her people. The success of the strike, Coolidge wrote to Gompers, would have "meant anarchy" and "letting in the enemy," who would undo the principle of the nobility of work. "No man," Coolidge proclaimed on September 24, "has a right to place his own ease or convenience or the opportunity of making money above his duty to the State." Coolidge was calling for an ancient republican government, not a libertarian utopia, as both his immoderate classical-liberal admirers and his liberal detractors maintain. Rights were never far from duties in Coolidge's understanding.

But what went for the strikers went for the wartime manufacturers, too. World War I, like the Revolutionary War, had brought hardship in its wake. That was the nature of war. Now, as then, there would be no "season of easy prosperity," however longed for or expected. But Coolidge also knew that the people could rebound, especially if they accepted that the "great promise of the future lies in the loyalty and devotion of the people to their own Government."

Liberty – by which he meant the virtue that enables self-government – could be increased if men increased their determination to support and defend their government of the people, as other patriots had in Massachusetts a century and a half before and at the Second Battle of the Marne. Again and again in speeches, Coolidge stressed that the soldiers of World War I were the spiritual inheritors of the American fight for independence, and of the struggle against slavery and for the Union in the Civil War. Those WWI soldiers fought what he called "European despotism," as their ancestors had fought earlier despotisms.

* * *

The Commonwealth[23] was well prepared, then, when Coolidge called forth the State Guard to restore order to Boston after police officers walked off their jobs to protest a ban on their recent affiliation with the American Federation of Labor. The situation could no longer be resolved through arbitration, and Coolidge was called back from Greenville where he was to give a speech on September 8. (Ironically, Coolidge was scheduled to give a speech before the state convention of American Federation of Labor, the very group that encouraged the strike.[24]) The night roll call at the police stations revealed that 1,117 of the 1,544 police officers had not reported to their posts.[25] Bedlam befell the city on the evening of September 9, 1919. The *Boston Herald* reported:

> Lawlessness, disorder, looting, such as were never known in this city, ran riot last night in South Boston, the North and West ends, and the downtown sections of the municipality, following the departure of the striking policemen from their station houses.

With more rioting likely and a sympathetic strike planned by the Boston Fire Department and the telephone operators,[26] Coolidge called in the State Guard. By September 11, peace was restored. President Wilson declared that Boston had been "at the mercy of an army of thugs" and called the strike a "crime against civilization."[27] Governor Frank Lowden of Illinois, who would be touted as a potential presidential candidate or a vice-presidential running mate with Coolidge,[28] supported his reelection in 1919, arguing that Coolidge's defeat would be a "repudiation of his stand in the Boston riots."[29] The press largely supported Governor Coolidge as well. The *New York Times*, for example, wrote that the police strike "sharpened the nation's conception of the strike problem and defined for everyone the line upon which the public must make its fight for self-preservation."[30]

Coolidge had supported World War I when he ran for governor in 1918, depicting it as a struggle for self-government and against tyranny. Now, he maintained, tyranny's animating principle had come to American shores: the desire that men have masters to direct their fates. Released weeks after the strike was broken, Coolidge's political proclamation on September 24, 1919, explained the philosophical problem posed when public servants acted against the interest of the public:

There is an obligation, inescapable, no less solemn, to resist all those who do not support the government. The authority of the commonwealth cannot be intimidated or coerced. It cannot be compromised. To place the maintenance of the public security in the hands of a body of men who have attempted to destroy it would be to flout the sovereignty of the laws the people have made. It is my duty to resist any such proposal. Those who would counsel it join hands with those whose acts have threatened to destroy the government. There is no middle ground. Every attempt to prevent the formation of a new police force is a blow at the government. That way treason lies. No man has a right to place his own ease or convenience or the opportunity to make money above his duty to the state.[31]

In this proclamation, Coolidge was encouraging the public servants to execute their duties. In doing so, though it might seem that he was attacking what we would call public-sector workers, he was appealing to their higher natures. He was far from anti-labor, whether in regard to public or private-sector workers. He had long favored "a properly compensated police force" and had spoken out against deplorable conditions in the stationhouses, lest "danger ... arise." In "The Wardens of Civilization," a 1921 review of a book on police forces, he granted that officers' work was increasingly difficult and that "their importance has not been sufficiently appreciated and their functions have been too little understood."[32] But policemen, like legislators, worked for far more than their pay: They worked for the public good. Without a proper consideration of that good, anarchy would ensue, and with it an end to Americans' cherished liberties.

The problem of crime, the very reason we have police officers, stemmed from the vitality of America. We have crime because we are a "new civilization which attracts to itself the restless and adventurous spirits and the dissatisfied from the older countries," Coolidge, then the vice president elect, wrote in the same book review.[33] This restlessness was a good thing because it led to great feats of industry, but it was also a dangerous one because it threatened to undo order. It was necessary, then, to form police departments because the "first and foremost duty of any government is the preservation of order," and yet the actual administration of the police was fraught with danger, especially for a republic. That was all the more reason that its guardians ought to be treated well and compensated fairly:

> There is nothing so destructive of our liberties as a misuse of police power. No people will submit to it for long, least of all Americans. The worst thing that could happen would be to have the conviction abroad that police, courts, and the government were more concerned with the protection of property than with the protection of the personal rights of the individual. Under a wise and judicious leadership, a well-trained and properly compensated police force, this danger would not arise. Under a police force which is the sport of political conditions [or favoritism] it is likely to arise at any time.[34]

In other words, a political system could not allow its guardians to decide when or whether they would serve it. The police force must be separate from politics, and not susceptible to the venal bribery that was widespread in the union boss–controlled cities.[35]

Coolidge believed this separation had become "almost impossible," in part because of the American disdain for bureaucracy. Americans, he noted approvingly, were a nation of "amateurs" who looked with annoyance, if not contempt, on the professionalization of political machines that would administer the police departments. Americans needed to understand that crime prevention was a science "no less than the profession of law or medicine."[36] Police officers constituted a "peace army," which "must be under the direction and command of trained administrators" in order to be effective. Citing "political and scientific consideration," Coolidge favored using a commissioner appointed by the governor, rather mayors and city councils, to keep corruption in check: "It is an axiom of political science that if a representative is desired he should be chosen by popular vote; if professional skill is wanted, it can best be secured by appointment." Coolidge also made clear that duty could not be shirked, whatever the arrangement. If police could strike against the public, conflict and "the destruction of all order" would result:

> Members of the force should have no private interests and should serve no selfish ends. . . . They cannot . . . be permitted to join any outside organization that would in any way interfere with their complete allegiance to the execution of the law or create in the public mind the feeling that they were no longer impartial in the performance of their duties.[37]

*　*　*

But with a duty comes the solemn need to enforce it. Only a spiritual imperative could emancipate man from his selfish temptations to harm the state. Journalists were coming to think of Coolidge as the leader to deliver it. Bruce Barton[38] was one of the first journalists to notice him as a statesman of national caliber. In "The Silent Man on Beacon Hill," which appeared in the March 1920 issue of *Women's Home Companion,* Barton praised Coolidge's quiet, religious poise:

> The greatest leaders we have had have been spiritual leaders. In Washington, in Lincoln and Roosevelt, in every man who has stirred America, there has been always an appeal that reached down beneath the material to something large, and unselfish, and eternal in man. And Calvin Coolidge also is a leader of that sort.[39]

For what spiritual cause would Coolidge speak? The war provided a ready answer. His principles, as articulated during the strike and earlier in his career, would now come through most clearly. Coolidge had run for governor in 1917 on a platform of support for the war.

His aides found it puzzling that he seldom mentioned himself on the campaign trail; he stressed instead the threat posed by the Kaiser's way of thinking.[40] He passionately sounded the alarm against German militarism and even suggested, as Lincoln did in response to the *Dred Scott* decision, that there was a conspiracy afoot to enslave mankind and bring down man's best hope.

> The past four years had shown the existence of a conspiracy against mankind of a vastness and a wickedness that could only be believed when seen in operation and confessed by its participants. This conspiracy was promoted by the German military despotism. It probably was encouraged by the results of three wars – one against Denmark which robbed her of territory, one against Austria which robbed her of territory, and one against France which robbed her of territory and a cash indemnity of a billion dollars. These seemingly easy successes encouraged their perpetrators to plan for the pillage and enslavement of the earth.[41]

And as with Lincoln, Coolidge foretold a new birth of freedom after the defeat of that danger, calling it, before Election Day in 1919, a "new glory":

> America has been performing a great service for humanity. In that service we have arisen to a new glory. The people of the nation without distinction have been performing a great service for America. In it they have realized a new citizenship. . . . Education is to teach men not what to think but how to think. Government will take on new activities, but it is not more to control the people, the people are to control the government.[42]

Critics dismissed these speeches as blather, designed to avoid specificity. After all, Richard Long, Coolidge's Democratic challenger, also supported the war and even promised veterans a bonus of $360, in effect waging a populist campaign against a popular governor. Long also pledged to abolish the poll tax and soak the rich with higher taxes – two very popular proposals.[43] While Coolidge refused to mention his opponents by name, Long felt no such compulsion, even with all the chaos surrounding the strike. "Governor Coolidge," he claimed, "has shown himself to be the weakest, most helpless and incompetent governor that our state has ever had."[44]

It is true that Coolidge spoke in generalities when he campaigned. But in doing so, he avoided his predecessor's ambitious Progressivism, which, among other specific things, called for state-provided health insurance. Coolidge placed himself above ordinary politics. In addition to not discussing his opponents by name, he wrapped himself in the flag. He campaigned in this manner because he rightly perceived that something greater than his own election was at stake – he remarked at Amherst College, his alma mater, that the "German War was won by the influence of classical ideals." A failure to win that war would have been a loss for the principles that had made America a world power. The classical ideal of duty, of "doing the day's work," had been preserved by the blood of America's men in Europe.

In 1919, Coolidge knew well that the failure to adequately address the dangers implicit in a public-employees' union was potentially – given the extent of Socialist and anarchist forces and ambitions at the time – as great a constitutional challenge as that which Lincoln had faced. The Boston police strike, he believed, subverted the natural equality of the Declaration of Independence by threatening to create two classes of men: the subjects, who toiled for the state, and the bureaucrats and public employees, who were their masters. That was why Coolidge cited Lincoln in his acceptance speech upon his nomination for the vice presidency a year later. He argued that Americans, as a people governed by law, must begin "restoring the Lincoln principles" of a "government of the people, for the people, and by the people." The postwar strikes around the country threatened to undo that government, he believed, and required a response. "The chief task which lies before us is to repossess the people of their government and their property. . . . Unless the government and property of the nation are in the hands of the people, and there to stay as their permanent abiding place, self-government ends and the hope of America goes down in ruins."[45] If America's guardians would not uphold the law, they were acquiescing in mob rule and "accepting the sword of force."[46]

Would America continue to be a government of laws? That depended on how she responded to the threat of organizations that undermined the law and order that had made the nation's great progress possible. Public servants, too, had helped make that progress possible, and they were so charged with the public trust that they could not abandon it. Coolidge put the situation in such terms when he spoke on Roosevelt Night at the Middlesex Club in Boston on October 27, 1919:

> A policeman is a public officer. He is the outward symbol of
> the law. He represents the authority of the people. It is a high
> crime to interfere with him in any way in the discharge of his
> duties. On him depends the peace and order of the state. He
> is a judicial officer. Well might he remember the words of
> Grover Cleveland that "a public office is a public trust." They
> are not employees. They are not holders of a job.

Coolidge knew well his duty, telling the audience, "so long as I am in authority it is my solemn duty to resist those who resist the Government." The supremacy of the government, in the sense of upholding and enforcing the law, was so important that no other question of public policy could rise to its level. He warned:

> We cannot arbitrate the duty of all persons to be obedient to
> the law. When that is done, government ceases to exist. The
> will of all the people ends and the arbitrary will of some class,

some dictator, begins. That is revolution. That is disorder. That is anarchy. That is destruction.[47]

Coolidge, then, had rechristened the Declaration's central premise – that men institute government to protect their rights against both tyranny and mob rule – to illuminate the politics of his day, much as Lincoln had understood the Declaration as a Rosetta stone to his own. In Coolidge's proclamation announcing that he was calling out the entire State Guard of Massachusetts, he gave the date in terms of Christendom – "in the year of our Lord" – and by referring to the years since the announcement of "the Independence of the United States of America."[48]

Coolidge's invocation of the Declaration of Independence is telling. Like Lincoln, he seems never to have had a guiding idea that did not come from the Declaration. Coolidge, in the words of his first biographer, had been "revealed" to his fellow men and had revealed the truth – that no man might live solely at the expense of another – upon which a republic stands. Or, in the words of the Rev. John Wise, a pre-Revolutionary-era patriot Coolidge often quoted: "Democracy is Christ's government in church and state." That simple phrase, Coolidge thought, illuminated the origins of "the doctrine of equality, popular sovereignty, and the substance of the theory of inalienable rights."[49] Such a doctrine meant service to one's fellow man, not enslavement to him. It also meant a different sort of nobility, nobility suited to a democracy. Coolidge explained to a convention of the American Legion:

> Titles to nobility cannot be granted or seized. They can only be achieved. They come through service, as yours came, or they do not come at all. If men in civil life, in these days of peace, would put their thought and effort into the success of the people of the whole country, as in military life you put your thought and effort, in time of war, into the success of the whole army, the victories of peace would follow as surely as did the victories of war.[50]

The "title of American" came from sacrifice and service, and for Coolidge it was the only title worth having. Self-government meant self-sacrifice. "Nothing is ever felt to be of value," he said, "which is not won as a result of sacrifice."[51]

CHAPTER THREE

EARLY EDUCATION
"Do the Day's Work"

The Declaration of Independence is a great spiritual document. It is a declaration not of material but of spiritual conceptions. Equality, liberty, popular sovereignty, the rights of man are not elements which we can see and touch. They are ideals. They have their source and their roots in the religious convictions. They belong to the unseen world. Unless the faith of the American people in these religious convictions is to endure, the principles of our Declaration will perish. We can not continue to enjoy the result if we neglect and abandon the cause.[1]

In the fullest sense of the term, [Coolidge's] conservatism is remarkably progressive. It grapples with the facts: it uses the past to make the future; it welcomes changes for the better; it rejoices in the blessings we now enjoy; it enters militantly into the struggle for sound progress.[2]

CALVIN COOLIDGE thought himself a Progressive, at least initially, and yet he is among the finest modern interpreters of the American founding, the Constitution,[3] the Declaration of Independence, and Abraham Lincoln. For the Progressives of Coolidge's era, the insights from earlier statesmen presented something of a paradox.[4] He celebrated progress, and his strong belief in limiting taxation stemmed partly from a belief in progress, but he remained thoroughly wedded to American political thought, and especially to the Declaration of Independence, as giving that progress its animating principles. Implicit in the paradox is a question: How is it that a "puritan in Babylon" presided over the largest economic expansion in American history? This man who disdained material things, who lived in a two-family home and seemingly cared nothing for wealth or riches, forged the Roaring Twenties from the wreckage of America's greatest economic depression to date. How he did this has been the great Coolidge mystery. But to Coolidge, the source of his success was no mystery at all. It came from his classical education, which, as he would often put it, had taught him the nature of the things that are unseen.

Educating the Young Coolidge

Coolidge's education and his religious piety sprang from his natural inclination to preserve what would, like New England granite, stand the test of time. His teachers at Black River Academy had sharpened his mind, but his parents had prepared him for that sharpening. In fact, his whole village had. He learned about the hardship of unnecessary taxes as he followed his father on his tax-collecting routes, and he learned of civic life while living a Tocquevillian existence. Tocqueville's description of rural America easily applies to Coolidge's Plymouth Notch, Vermont:

> The Americans never use the word "peasant," because they have no idea of the class which that term denotes; the ignorance of more remote ages, the simplicity of rural life, and the rusticity of the villager have not been preserved among them; and they are alike unacquainted with the virtues, the vices, the coarse habits, and the simple graces of an early stage of civilization.[5]

Tocqueville's description of "local freedom," which "perpetually brings men together, and forces them to help one another, in spite of the propensities which sever [ties]," is an apt description for Plymouth Notch. Tocqueville continues:

> In the United States, the more opulent citizens take great care not to stand aloof from the people. On the contrary, they

47

constantly keep on easy terms with the lower classes: they listen to them, they speak to them every day.

So it was with Coolidge. Young Coolidge worked alongside his fellows and pitched the hay with everyone else. Unlike current leaders, who tend to bemoan the fact that they worked as children or to boast about it for political gain with middle-class voters, Coolidge expressed genuine fondness for early days, especially his work in a smithy. The blacksmith "always pitched the hay on the ox cart and I raked after," Coolidge recalled. "If I was getting behind he slowed up a little. He was a big-hearted man. I wish I could see that blacksmith again." Coolidge didn't seek to distance himself from his youth.

In a post-presidential column for *Hearst's International-Cosmopolitan* (June 1929), he recalled his upbringing in stark yet beautiful prose, in an extract titled, "Scenes of My Childhood." These extracts, later collected in his autobiography, recall the residents of Plymouth Notch and an egalitarian way of life:

> The break of day saw them stirring. Their industry continued until twilight. They kept up no church organization, and as there was little regular preaching the outward manifestation of religion through public profession had little opportunity, but they were without exception a people of faith and charity and good works. They cherished the teachings of the Bible and sought to live in accordance with its precepts.

Coolidge may have had modest origins, but he was no country bumpkin. His home had books, most of them great books. Biographer Claude Fuess once listed the books that Coolidge mentioned in an article, "Books of My Boyhood." They included the *Orations of Cicero*, Harriet Beecher Stowe's *Men of Our Times*, *From Canal Boy to President* (a biography of James Garfield), *Livingstone Lost and Found*, Hilliard's *Sixth Reader*, *Choice Poems and Lyrics*, *Captain John Brown*, *History of the Indian Wars*, *The Young People's Bible History*, the New Testament, and *The Life, Public Service and State Papers of Abraham Lincoln,* edited by Henry J. Raymond.[6]

Ever curious, Coolidge read avidly and deeply, especially in American and ancient history. Coolidge's two favorite teachers from his high school years were George Sherman and Belle Challis – he thanked both of both of them in his autobiography, and both teachers lived to see him in the White House. Coolidge thanked them for teaching him ancient history:

> Under their guidance I beheld the marvel of old Babylon, I marched with the Ten Thousand of Xenophon, I witnessed the conflict around beleaguered Troy which doomed that proud city to pillage and flames. I heard the tramp of the invincible legions of Rome, I saw the victorious galley of the Eternal City carrying destruction to the Carthaginian shore, and I listened to the lofty eloquence of Cicero and the matchless imagery of Homer. They gave me a vision of the world when it was young and it is almost impossible for those who have not traveled that road to reach a very clear conception of what the world now means.[7]

Most of all, Coolidge learned that ancient thought shaped present realities and therefore politics.

Coolidge read romantic literature, too. Even when he was sent home from Amherst with a temporary illness, he assiduously read the poems of Sir Walter Scott. Fuess notes the role his mother played in cultivating an appreciation for poetry by teaching him "to enjoy Tennyson and Scott, from whom he could recite long passages."[8] The insight in Scott's "Marmion" might have pleased him well: "Oh! What a tangled web we weave/ When first we practice to deceive!"[9] And the moral themes of Tennyson's work – the conflict between science and religion, the necessity of perseverance, the importance of tradition and history to literature – would not have been lost on Coolidge.

His love of literature dominated his evening studies as a country lawyer as well. By day, he read Chancellor James Kent's *Commentaries on American Law*, the great early-nineteenth-century treatise, which begins by emphasizing that the "faithful observance" of the law is "essential to national character, and to the happiness of mankind." By night, he studied the speeches of statesmen such as Thomas Erskine, 1st Baron Erskine;[10] Daniel Webster;[11] and Rufus Choate.[12] He read many of the British historian Lord Macaulay's essays and found the writings of Thomas Carlyle and John Fiske "very stimulating."[13] He even translated Cicero's defense of the poet Archias, "because in it," Coolidge later explained, Cicero "dwelt on the value and consolation of good literature."[14] He kept abreast of modern English writers as well, reading "much in Milton and Shakespeare" and finding "delight in the shorter poems of Kipling, Eugene Field, and James Whitcomb Riley."[15] It is easy to imagine a young Coolidge delighting in Kipling, especially the poems "If," "The Gods of the Copybook Headings," and "Recessional."

As with his frequent recitations of the Bible, literature would come to play a role in his political thought. Contrary to what one biographer contends,[16] Coolidge indeed drew upon his study of literature in many of his speeches, but he cited works always without attribution and never ostentatiously. He trusted his audience to recognize the allusions – in that era, many did.

* * *

At Black River Academy, which Coolidge entered at age thirteen, he grew interested in government and the American founding. In his autobiography, he wrote with affection of that time:

> This was my first introduction to the Constitution of the United States ... the subject interested me exceedingly. The study of it which I then began has never ceased, and the more I study it the more I have come to admire it, realizing that no

other documented devised by the hand of man ever brought so much progress and happiness to humanity. The good it has wrought can never be measured.[17]

The Constitution, he learned, had been possible only because the American Revolution had laid down its founding principles. And if the Revolution meant anything, "it meant the determination to live under a reign of law," Coolidge observed. "It meant the assertion of the right of the people to adopt their own constitutions, and when so adopted, the duty of all the people to abide by them."[18] Its meaning was clear even to the teenaged Coolidge: "It was conservative," he wrote at the time, and it sought "the preservation of the ancient rights of English freemen, which were not new even when they were set out in the Great Charter of the day of King John." The Constitution, he saw, "represented an extension of the right of the people to govern themselves."[19] Coolidge had considered, also while a teenager, the even more fundamental question of how man could live in a community, in his readings in the Latin and Greek classics. There he "discovered that our ideas of democracy came from the agora of Greece, and our ideas of liberty came from the forum of Rome."[20]

Religion, classical education, and a love of country all strengthened Coolidge's resolve against the excesses of Progressivism, which, Coolidge feared, would become predatory if it were not checked.[21] The Progressives' intention to minister to souls all too often resulted, he saw, in a byzantine, indifferent bureaucracy that mastered the people it aimed to serve.

A student of history throughout his life, Coolidge read H. G. Wells's *The Outline of History* (1919) shortly after he went off to Washington in 1921, in which Wells argues that Roman freedom declined because there was "no wide organization of education to base the ordinary citizen's mind upon the idea of service and obligation to the republic."[22] Wells attacked the history textbooks of the day, and Coolidge, though he did not share Wells's leftism or his sexual libertinism, likely agreed with his diagnosis of the problem facing America in its opulent age. Rome, as Coolidge understood it, fell because it abandoned its own ideals and became "a prey, first to itself and then to the barbarians." The same fate could befall America if it neglected its own ideals. Coolidge therefore sought to shore up education to save the American republic from the Roman republic's fate.

For direction, he drew on spiritual principles. Character and strong religious faith, Coolidge believed, would prevent the people from needing excessive administration and bureaucracy. "Faith," he told the Boy Scouts in July 1924, "is the great motive power, and no man realizes his full possibilities unless he has the deep conviction that life is eternally important, and that his work, well done, is a part of an unending plan."[23] But that plan was revealed to man through revelation and reason, not through a bureaucrats' discretion or presidential rhetoric.

Coolidge delivered his first recorded public address, "Oratory in History," when he was seventeen, on May 23, 1890, before his alma mater, Black River Academy. It borrows heavily, almost to the point of plagiarism, from William Matthews's 1879 work, *Oratory and Orators*. The speech's rousing rhetoric, à la Matthews, is not characteristic of the famously taciturn Coolidge, and it does not match the tone of the career that would follow, but the speech's themes would become familiar. In the address, we see that Coolidge believed "the triumphs of the tongue have rivaled, if not surpassed, those of the sword." Taking inspiration from great men of history,[25] he understood full well the power of oratory, but also its danger. Coolidge quotes Matthews:

> When eloquence . . . is armed with the thunderbolt of powerful thought and winged with lofty feeling . . . when it divests men of their peculiar qualities and affections, and turns a vast multitude into one man, giving to them but one heart, one pulse, and one voice . . . then, indeed, it becomes not only a delight, but a power, and a power greater than kings or military chieftains can command.

To him who masters the art of oratory, Coolidge continues, all power is his:

> As there is no effort of the human mind which demands a rarer combination of faculties than does oratory in its loftiest flights, so there is no human effort which is rewarded with more immediate or more dazzling triumphs. To stand before a vast assembly of men composed of the most various callings . . . and mold them at will – this, perhaps, is the greatest triumph of which the human mind is capable, and that in which its divinity is most signally revealed.

Even in pagan times, Coolidge said, divinity had a way of coming to the fore and guiding, through oratory, the fate of nations: "Oratory, as every schoolboy knows, was the master spirit of both great nations of antiquity, Greece and Rome, and plays an important part in modern nations." Classical thought had deeply influenced Coolidge, and it showed in the influence of Cicero and Demosthenes on this speech, in the notion that oratory could shape thought and thus master men and their actions.

The emphasis on oratory's role was deliberate on Coolidge's part. As a young man thirsting for distinction, he aspired to the kind of rhetorical success Cicero and Demosthenes had attained, perhaps because these seemed so elusive to him. Coolidge was never a demagogue or even much of a speech giver. After delivering his first inaugural address in 1924, he continued the Jeffersonian practice of submitting written messages to Congress each year rather than speaking to it directly.[25] (That was the standard practice up until President Wilson.)

In later life, Coolidge wrote that he had studied the orations of Cicero with "much interest." They held "my attention to such a degree," he wrote, "that I translated some of them in later life."[26] Though Coolidge acquired Greek with some difficulty, he still managed to understand enough of it to reap what he called the "rewards" of the "moving poetry of Homer" and "the marvelous orations of

Demosthenes."[27] As an Amherst student, he wrote to his father upon reading Demosthenes's "On the Crown" with Professor William S. Tyler, "Eloquence does not seem to grow very fast if after 2,000 years we can produce nothing to rival this speech."[28]

In his speech before the Black River Academy, Coolidge celebrated such oratorical prowess, pointing to Philip of Macedonia's remark that had he heard Demosthenes's oratory, he would have been persuaded to take up arms against himself.[29] Despots, Coolidge argued, must silence such oratory if they are to maintain their tyrannical rule:

> We are told that such was the force of Cicero's oratory, that it not only confounded the audacious Cataline, and silenced the eloquent Hortensius – not only deprived Curio of all power of recollection, when he rose to oppose that great master of enchanting rhetoric – but made even Cæsar tremble, and changing his determined purpose, acquit the man he had resolved to condemn. It was not till the two champions of ancient liberty, Demosthenes and Cicero, were silenced, that the triumph of Despotism in Greece and Rome was complete.

The powers of oratory, Coolidge believed, did not entirely dissipate after the classical era; they were in full flower in modern times, in the era of the American Revolution, when orators argued the rightness of parliamentary supremacy and of the American desire for independence. British thinkers and statesmen of that day – William Pitt the Elder, William Pit the Younger, Edmund Burke, and Adam Smith, among others – deployed the power of persuasion so that America might have her English liberties restored.

Coolidge also cited Daniel Webster (whom he would quote again and again in his speeches) approvingly on this point. "When the Federal Constitution, the product of so much sacrifice and toil, was menaced by the Nullifiers of South Carolina, it was the great orator of Massachusetts that sprang to its rescue." Burning with an "ignited logic," Webster demanded "Liberty *and* Union, now and forever, one and inseparable," and because of him, the "whole North was ready to fight." Coolidge also commented favorably on the "master spirit" oratory of the French Revolution, the prudent speech of British parliament, and the sagacious rhetoric of the American Revolution. He marveled at the "sacred oratory" of John the Baptist, Saints Paul and Peter, and churchmen George Whitefield, Thomas Chalmers, Thomas Knox, Jonathan Edwards, Henry Ward Beecher, and Charles Timothy Brooks.[30] Men of "silvery and impetuous speech," as he put it in his Black River Academy speech, had always been able to exert mastery over the public. Such skill could serve a good purpose in crises such as the American Revolution, but he rejected this approach in his own career. He would become not the public's master, even in a rhetorical sense, but its servant, armed with simple words that were well polished. A more modest and reasoned rhetoric befitted a more modest, republican statesmen, who, avoiding the temptation to demagoguery, deferred to public deliberation.

Sound deliberation required firm education, Coolidge argued throughout his speeches. A contemporary believed that his collections of speeches would "take a permanent place in our literature of political science, not for the originality of their ideas, but for the way in which those ideas are set before the minds of the people, for their teaching power."[31] Another argued that if Coolidge were an author, a "builder of books, his books would win their way to every empire of earth," adding:

> His style, his grip on the truth, and his conveyance of it are among the most thrilling delights to any who yield to the charm of style. . . . The student of literature will soon list Calvin Coolidge among those who command for the faultless style, and for stalwart utterance. This man of learning and letters, who loves law and lives it, has lit a new light in literature, which will glow after all of us are long dead.[32]

Like great works of literature, Coolidge's speeches communicate on different levels and are especially rewarding to readers who understand, or listeners who understood, their classical references. He sought to cultivate the best in his listeners, as Cicero had done, and he didn't talk down to his audience. "There is no moral standard so high that the people cannot be raised up to it," he told an audience gathered to celebrate Lincoln's birthday. [33] He often thought of his role as a teacher – the first duty as a statesman was to educate, he believed – and he seems to have loved every minute of teaching. He was "thrilled at the thought of his audience," he told one audience of Boy Scouts.[34] "I never address boys without thinking, among them may be a boy who will sit in this White House."[35]

The College Commencement Speeches and the Threat to the Liberal-Arts Order

Coolidge's second speech, delivered two years after his Black River Academy speech, was to the people of his hometown, Plymouth Notch. As his town's only college student, he delivered the Independence Day oration on July 4, 1892.[36] Stirring his audience with mentions of the great heroes of the Republic – Washington, Jefferson, and the citizen-soldiers at Lexington and Concord all got due attention – he ended with a tribute to America's greatness: "Roll on, America! Roll on, bearing rich blessings with o'erflowing hand through the endless ages of all eternity, until freedoms' golden course has traversed all the earth and tyranny and oppression are no more."[37]

The problem for the American Republic, as Coolidge came to see it in the years after college, was that freedom's golden course was increasingly misdirected by the very institutions that should be guiding the way: America's liberal colleges. Coolidge's advocacy of liberal-arts education was based on its importance in his own life. The faculty at Amherst had never had "any superior," he said, and the students there were motivated by a "serious purpose. He concluded nonetheless that America was not rolling on as she should, because her academy was not fulfilling its purpose, which was to cultivate the arts that make men free. In a series of speeches delivered during the summer and fall of 1919, Coolidge addressed these deficiencies and provided a theory of education that merits consideration.

Recalling his education at Amherst, in a commencement address there, Coolidge quoted Walter Scott's "The Vision of Don Roderick": "So passed that pageant. Ere another came. . . . " Suggesting the cyclical nature of life, this line suggested that one generation would go to school, another would replace it, and so forth.[38] Coolidge turned his attention to the next pageant – the next generation. Now, Coolidge lamented, more and more institutions were walking the path from liberal-arts college to research university, a course whose wisdom he doubted because it overstressed the immediately practical at the expense of the classics and their indispensable wisdom. Amherst, he noted, had chosen to stress what was really "the most practical of all – the culture and classics of all time."[39] There was no need to depart from what worked. On the contrary, the classical education Coolidge had received at Amherst was needed *more*, not less, in the postwar days. All the promise of technology had not uplifted man, but mechanized his destruction on Flanders fields.

The World War, as it was called in Coolidge's time, was construed as a product of science because it was the technical advances in weaponry that had enabled the mass killing. Coolidge, however, argued in the commencement speech that such a view was "too narrow." It was the lack of culture, the narrowness of life, that had made war possible. He called for "a more liberal culture" that would "reveal the importance and nobility of the work of the world, whether in war or peace." In this, he followed the thinking of his professor, Charles Garman. To reduce or eliminate the dangers of industrialization and modern warfare, Garman taught, capitalism would need to evolve. "The 'sweating system' makes impossible the decencies of life simply because [it presumes that] money is worth more than manhood," he warned.[40] "It is far from enough to teach our citizens a vocation," Coolidge added. "Our industrial system will break down unless it is humanized." Humanization, including treating workers better, required expanding classical ideals through the "whole body of our citizenship." Liberal-arts colleges – and the liberal arts alone – were capable of disseminating such teaching. Indeed, if they were successful, Coolidge's prophesied, "the day when a college education will be the portion of all may not be so far distant as it seems." He looked upon the prospect with anticipation and happiness.

Scientific and technical colleges were "important and necessary" but were "not enough," because modern science was a byproduct of classical ideals, not their equal.[41] "In fact," Coolidge noted in another speech, "the natural sciences are so much the product of . . . the classics that, without such training, their very terminology cannot be fully understood."[42] (Coolidge was no doubt referring to the need of doctors and scientists to know Latin and Greek.) When classical ideals have first priority, war might more easily be avoided. When they are ignored, men can become machine-like in their capacity for killing. In so arguing, Coolidge broke with the Progressives, who held that progress in modern science inevitably meant progress in political science and thus in overall quality of life. This argument of the Progressives undergirded their belief that man was perfectible, a notion that Coolidge rejected out of hand in a commencement address at Holy Cross College: "We have no right to expect as our portion something substantially different from human experience in the past. The constitution of the universe does not change. Human nature remains constant."[43] It follows from this assertion that the study of the classics, which speak to that human nature and have existed down throughout the ages, teach important lessons to mankind. For Coolidge, men come to the study of the classics because they "realize that the only road to freedom lies through a knowledge of the truth."[44] The classics were a repository of truth.

Mankind have always had classics. They always will. That is only another way of saying they have always set up ideals and always will. Always the question has been, always the question will be, what are those ideals to be, what are to be the classics?[45]

Coolidge continued this praise for classics when he gave the commencement address at Harvard University, a day after his speech at Amherst. He noted that the teachings of Harvard, so important to America's government because of Harvard's always-large influence, had found their way into the Massachusetts constitution. The president of the state's constitutional convention in 1779 was fellow Harvard graduate James Bowdoin II. The framers of the Massachusetts constitution, Coolidge argued, had intertwined religion, morality, and self-governance. They had understood their alma mater to be a "defender of righteous convictions, of reverence for truth and for the heralds of truth." Because these Massachusetts founders were religious people who hoped to enshrine truth and virtue in the government, Coolidge noted, they preserved "teaching," which after all amounted to "leading," and had given it the "same safeguards and guaranties as freedom and equality." The state's constitution had insisted, he pointed out, that "wisdom and knowledge, as well as virtue, diffused generally among the body of the people, are necessary for the preservation of their rights and liberties."[46] In those "days of reverence and of applied reverence," the alumni of Harvard – John Adams and Bowdoin chief among them – "knew that freedom was the fruit of knowledge" and drew their conclusions from the truth of the Bible, itself a classical text.

Then, as now, those principles had "the same binding force . . . when they were recognized and proclaimed." The problem, as Coolidge apprehended, was that too many Americans no longer proclaimed these principles; they were jettisoning them in favor of new, hollow principles. He bemoaned the state of a society that paid its clergy and teachers, "the pillars of liberty and equality," less than their full worth: "We have lost our reverence for the profession of teaching and bestowed it upon the profession of acquiring." In the pursuit of that prosperity, the citizens of Massachusetts had "forgotten and neglected its foundations" – the classics. The only "remedy" for this defect was a "public opinion" that would restore these "noble professions" to the "place of reverence" they held in the days of the Revolution. If they were ignored, if Massachusetts's older and more scholarly leadership was "exchanged" for an inferior one "bred of the marketplace," then the proper scope of statesmanship would vanish:

> We must turn our eyes from what is to what ought to be. The men of the day of John Adams and James Bowdoin had a vision that looked into the heart of things. They led a revolution that swept on to a successful conclusion.

And they did this because they cared more for spiritual things than material ones.

The Commonwealth needed more men who understood that the "cause of America is the cause of education," he told his Harvard audience. Only leaders with a "trained intellect . . . guided ever by an enlightened conscience" would share this vision, prevalent at the American founding, and thereby ensure America would endure "until its flag is the ancient among the banners of the earth."

Coolidge continued this line of argument in his Holy Cross commencement speech, delivered on June 25, 1919. He began by complimenting the Roman Catholic institution, which like all colleges – and, he added, unlike political environments – was a place where "ideals are cherished for their own sake" by the "servants of the truth." Both students and alumni, Coolidge said, were obligated to apply this truth in their lives, and thus to serve their country and mankind: "If college-bred men are to exercise the influence over the progress of the world which ought to be their portion, they must exhibit in their lives a knowledge and a learning which is marked with candor, humility, and the honest mind." They should be guided, he urged, by what Patrick Henry called "the lamp of experience." One of its lessons was that "mankind is finite," and that contrary to the Progressives' promises of perfection on earth, "processes of government are subject to the same limitations."

Coolidge believed that the Progressives and other critics of American civilization fell into a habit of the "unlearned," by "forever proposing something which is old, and, because it has recently come to their own attention, supposing it to be new." These criticisms of American life – aimed especially at immigrants and their children, including his Holy Cross audience – "sometimes take the form of a claim that our institutions were founded long ago; that changed conditions require that they now be changed." At times, these critics even suggested that immigrants, if not of the race of the Founders, had no claim to American institutions and "therefore . . . owe it no support."[47]

They were wrong, Coolidge argued. The nation wasn't in need of anything new, but rather must rededicate itself to the old. "The forms and processes of government are not new," after all. "They have been known, discussed, and tried in all their varieties through the past ages." America had drawn from their experience in drafting her Constitution, which more than any other yet devised gave "promise of being the most substantial and enduring." America's Constitution survived because it preferred changing itself "not by the total overthrow of institutions," but by "preserving that which was good": not revolution but "evolution." Coolidge reasoned that the American Constitution, like all other institutions and governing documents before it, was imperfect, but he saw this as something to expect and correct. Even the "most beneficient [*sic*] of our institutions" began "in forms which would be particularly odious to us now," he noted. "Civilization began with war and slavery; government began in absolute despotism; and religion itself grew out of superstition which was oftentimes marked with human sacrifices." America was but a part of this process, and thus, "out of our present imperfections we shall develop that which is more perfect."

In this thinking, Coolidge was following a philosophically pure conservatism, imploring "the candid mind of the scholar" to "remedy all wrongs with the same zeal with which it defends all rights." And America, like all nations, has flaws, even if she is slow to acknowledge them. "The long and toilsome processes which have marked the progress of the past cannot be shunned. . . . That service and sacrifice which have been the price of past progress are the price of progress now." Lest America worry, as Scipio Aemilianus did when he wept at the destruction of Carthage,[48] Coolidge reassured listeners that his evolutionary vision of the nation was one "of hope and high expectation." The teaching of "all of history" was: "That which is necessary for the welfare and progress of the human race has never been destroyed." Therefore America would have a kind of immortality, because "whatever America holds that may be of value to posterity will not pass away." It was to make sure America had traditions worthy of passing on that colleges such as Holy Cross had been founded. Their purpose was to teach and show "the way, the truth, and the light." Education meant soul-craft and soldiering for justice. At Holy Cross, which Coolidge called a "defender of righteousness," the school halls had become "the armories from which are furnished forth the knights in armor to defend and support our liberty."

Coolidge and Academia

As we have seen, Coolidge took academia seriously. There was some speculation, upon his leaving the presidency, that he would be the president of Amherst College, but Coolidge, with characteristic wit, declined any such role. "Easier to control Congress than a college faculty," he famously joked. Quarrelsome though college faculty might be, Coolidge's own college experience was a happy one. It is no exaggeration to say that he got his political start on the Amherst campus, where a diffident boy came out of his shell to deliver the Grove Oration (in which, to his later chagrin, he poked a little too much fun at his 1895 graduating class). As a speaker and thinker, he began to come into his own at Amherst. He would later write fondly of those years in his autobiography:

> In the development of every boy who is going to amount to anything there comes a time when he emerges from his immature ways and by the greater precision of his thought and action realizes that he has begun to find himself.[49]

For Coolidge, that time was his junior year at Amherst. He defeated the skilled debater – who was also the captain of the football team – in a debate, by vote of the public-speaking students, and won the J. Wesley Ladd Prize for an oration on the Spanish epic of El Cid.[50] Before his junior year, Coolidge was by his own admission a lackluster student, although a hard worker. His grades were mediocre at first[51] – Cal earned a C in Logic, a C in public speaking, and a C in rhetoric – but he worked hard and later graduated cum laude. He learned firsthand what it was like to exert real intellectual effort, and the habit stayed with him in later years.[52] His post-college plans were "undecided," according to an Amherst registration form completed his senior year.[53] There are no anecdotes to suggest that the undergraduate Coolidge was a budding genius. Nor does he seem to have impressed his classmates socially or politically. Dwight Morrow, whom President Coolidge would appoint as ambassador to Mexico, was handily voted most likely to succeed. Cal received only one vote for that honor – although it was from Morrow, college lore has it.[54]

Among Coolidge's most important experiences at Amherst were his studies under two professors who altered how he viewed the world and whose influence stayed with him during his long political life. Biographer Fuess rightly concluded that his "political philosophy . . . was formed" under Anson D. Morse and Charles E. Garman, and that "the doctrines of which he was to become the symbol may be traced back to his teachers."[55] Coolidge's old math professor, George Olds, later noted the rich debt he owed to Garman.

> Consciously or unconsciously . . . this teacher seems to be with
> him at all times. One need only instance certain salient points
> in Garman's teachings to make this clear to those [who] are
> familiar with "Have Faith in Massachusetts" and other public
> utterances of the President.[56]

Coolidge's wife, the vivacious and aptly named Grace Goodhue Coolidge, noted that during his presidency, her husband kept three books at their nightstand: *Paradise Lost*, the Bible, and a collection of Garman's writings. Never philosophically (or, perhaps, physically) far from his professor's lectures, he never forgot or opposed their political teachings. In the classroom of what one biographer called "this almost worshiped teacher," Coolidge learned:

> "Philosophy is simply intelligence at its best." "The scripture name for service is love." "Property is coined service." "Service given and received is business." "Constructive public service with a supreme emphasis on character." . . . "The Amherst system demands self-reliance, self-government; the students must choose for themselves." "Great artists have often used few tools and simple materials." "To make the right supreme choice is to be born again."[57]

With government, Coolidge was certainly "born again." Like Garman, he believed that choosing the right thing would refresh the soul, sharpen the mind, and bring its just reward from Providence. Coolidge considered Garman "one of the most remarkable men" with whom he had ever come into contact. "He drew men out," Coolidge wrote, perhaps referring to himself.

While Professor Garman taught Coolidge how to think, Professor Anson Morse inculcated a respect for history. As recounted in Coolidge's autobiography, Morse taught him European history from Charlemagne to Napoleon; he showed the young Coolidge the influence of Pope Gregory VII and Pope Innocent III. In class, students considered the works of great theologians and religious thinkers – Abélard, Erasmus, Luther, and Calvin. Coolidge took to ancient, English, and American history. He understood American history as a culmination of the Whig tradition, writing in his autobiography:

> The significance of the long struggle with the Crown before the Parliament finally reached a position of independence was disclosed, and the slow growth of a system of liberty under the law, until at last it was firmly established, was carefully explained. We

saw the British empire rise until it ruled the seas. The brilliance of the statesmanship of the different periods, the rugged character of the patriotic leaders, of Anselm and Simon de Montfort, of Cromwell and the [English] Puritans, who dared to oppose the tyranny of the kings, the growth of learning, the development of commerce, the administration of justice – all these and more were presented for our consideration. Whatever was essential to a general comprehension of European history we had.[58]

Coolidge keenly understood that the struggle for self-government continued even in his day, and he believed he had a role in this battle. As the newly elected governor of Massachusetts, he saluted the General Court and celebrated its role in his inaugural address on January 2, 1919. Addressing the legislators, he said:

You are beholding the fulfillment [sic] of the age-old promise, man coming into his own. You are to have the opportunity and responsibility of reflecting this new spirit in the laws of the most enlightened of Commonwealths. *We must steadily advance.* Each individual must have the rewards and opportunities worthy of the character of our citizenship, a broader recognition of his worth and a larger liberty, protected by order – *and always under the law.*[59]

Coolidge was not, however, a progressive in the sense of following the Progressive movement of his era, for he warned that the steady "advance" he advocated was subject to a higher law, not the result of elite manipulation, bureaucratic planning, charismatic leadership, or even a plebiscite.[60] He also made clear to the legislature that he looked to the past for guidance:

In the promotion of human welfare Massachusetts happily may not need much reconstruction, but like, all living organizations, forever needs continuing construction. What are the

65

lessons of the past? How shall they be applied to these days of readjustment? How shall we emerge from the autocratic methods of war to the democratic methods of peace, raising ourselves again to the source of all our strength and all our ground – sound self-government?[61]

Sound-self government required an understanding of its history. For that, Coolidge turned to the American founding as Professor Morse had taught it to him.

Washington was treated with the greatest reverence, and a high estimate was placed on the statesmanlike qualities and financial capacity of Hamilton, but Jefferson was not neglected. In spite of his many vagaries it was shown that in saving the nation from the danger of falling under the domination of an oligarchy, and in establishing a firm rule of the people which was forever to remain, he vindicated the soundness of our political institutions. The whole course was a thesis on good citizenship and good government. Those who took it came to a clearer comprehension not only of their rights and liberties but of their duties and responsibilities."[62]

In turn, this exploration of history led Coolidge to new questions. What were those duties, and where did they come from? For answers, he turned to Charles Garman, one of the faculty's leading professors – "Amherst's mystic" and its crown jewel. When the great philosopher William James visited Garman, he remarked afterward, "That man is the greatest teacher in the United States today." When asked if he meant the greatest teacher of philosophy, James replied, "No, no. The greatest teacher."[63] Though Garman published little, his students loved him and built a memorial tablet in his memory when he died in 1907. The memorial read, "He Chose to Write on Living Men's Hearts."[64] It was said that "no education force in [Garman's] generation was more widely felt and less known to fame."[65] Garman's students saw in him qualities that they wished to develop in themselves: "intellectual curiosity, tolerance and idealism."[66] Some students did develop them in abundance, and Coolidge drew upon those men to form his government in times of crisis: Dwight Morrow '95 (Ambassador to Mexico during a bellicose time), William F. Whiting '96 (Secretary of Commerce who undid much of Hoover's handiwork), and Harlan F. Stone '94 (Attorney General and later Supreme Court Chief Justice).[67]

Nowhere did Garman make his presence more felt than with the young Calvin Coolidge, who devoted some six and half pages of his slim autobiography to his former professor. "It always seemed to me that all our other studies were in the nature of a preparation for the [Garman] course in philosophy," Coolidge wrote. His favorite professor's deeply held and infectious beliefs seemed to prove the existence of divinity through the working out of philosophical problems posed to his students. "We looked upon Garman as a man who walked with God," Coolidge recalled.

> His course was a demonstration of the existence of a personal God, of our power to know Him, of the Divine immanence, and of the complete dependence of all the universe on Him as the Creator and Father "in whom we live and move and have our being." Every reaction in the universe is a manifestation of His presence. Man was revealed as His son, and nature as the hem of His garment, while through a common Fatherhood we are all embraced in a common brotherhood. . . . *The conclusions which followed from this position were logical and inescapable.* It sets man off in a separate kingdom from all the other creatures in the universe, and makes him a true son of God and a partaker of the Divine nature. This is the warrant for his freedom and the demonstration of his equality. It does not assume all are equal in degree but [that] all are equal in kind. On that precept rests a foundation for democracy that cannot be shaken."[68]

This passage underscores Coolidge's appreciation of the role a great teacher might play in a man's philosophical life. By revealing God's role in the political thought of America, Garman made it seem as if you had no choice but to follow the professor's reasoned conclusions.[69] Professor Garman spoke to Coolidge's initial progressive instincts and his Christian, classical education when he argued that the role of a college needs to change with the times, but that change must be based in righteousness and truth. American government, Coolidge knew, was driven by public opinion, but public opinion must be shaped through great works, which were themselves the product of great thought. He inherited this idea of shaping public opinion from Garman – and to a lesser extent Lord Bryce, who once "compared public opinion to a cake of ice which yields to slow pressure but cracks under a sharp blow." In other words, decisive statesmen could provide the catalyst for necessary changes.[70]

Garman sought to teach students how to be philosophical while remaining practical. He believed that every student must at some point make a "choice between a spiritual and a material world."

Men must act, he would have said; whatever they do implies basic, though often inarticulate, premises. Those premises they must choose, and from that choice, the fundamental discrimination between the material and the ideal, they could not escape. From that choice all other choices stemmed.[71]

His class pamphlets, which he required every student return at the end of the class, covered subjects that would prove thematic in Coolidge's later career: "Pleasure and Righteousness, Will and Sentiment, plus Expediency as a Working Principle to the Twentieth Century."[72] These pamphlets – which Garman wrote, printed on his home printing press, and even bound himself – were designed to be "succinct statements of long philosophical treatises."[73] The problems were short yet complex; the solutions were left up to the students.

The twentieth century – what Garman surmised would be a century of profound problems, particularly related to the economy and labor – promised to be vastly different than any that had come before it, he told his students. It would require that men of character become "men of power" – men who, as Coolidge later said he learned from Garman, had "the courage and industry to hold to the main stream without being washed ashore by the immaterial cross currents."[74] The new age required closer attention to public service among those who practiced it, Garman argued, because

> business is asking for men of ability and integrity to take posi-
> tions of greater responsibility, and the same is true of munici-
> pal affairs and of politics. In short, citizenship is the great
> need of the present time.[75]

Only a citizen could appeal to his fellow men as men first. The businessman would, Garman worried, see them only as tools. Garman saw to it to teach morality to the future businessmen at Amherst. It was his duty as a teacher, he believed, to develop his students' "desire to service society."[76] As one of his students put it, the esteemed professor "filled us with a consuming desire to serve and dedicate our lives and our talents to the making of a better world."[77] Another claimed: "Garman in a wilderness would be a university."[78] The core of his teaching was about helping students discover God and the rules He had made. Garman, Coolidge wrote, "was given a power which took his class up into a high mountain of spiritual life and left them alone with God." There on the mountain with Him, the student discovered the bare truth that Garman believed animated politics in a republic: "Man was revealed as His Son, and nature as the hem of His garment, while through a common Fatherhood we are all embraced in a common brotherhood."[79] This natural equality came with duties: "The doctrine of stewardship, or service, was the climax of Garman's course and the heart of his philosophy."[80]

Like Lincoln, Garman believed that the natural equality among men resulted in clear political obligations, and he wondered what public servants might do to help man survive industrialization. Garman died in 1907, long before Coolidge or any of his other students made their mark, but he had made his mark on Coolidge. Garman's teachings about work and the importance of good relations between manager and laborer helped prepare Coolidge for the role he would assume in dealing with the labor strikes that occurred during his political career.

Years before, while discussing the Railroad War of 1877 – the first national strike that ended only after ten governors called out the National Guard – and the Pullman Strike of 1894,[81] which had occurred while Coolidge was a junior, Garman had instilled in his students a distrust of strikes as well as of those who organized and led them. To Garman, strikes were psychological as much as economic in nature, resulting from "anxious forebodings when times become hard and there is great suffering among the lower classes."[82] The desire to strike might be understandable, but workers would be wise to refrain. Disrupting the normal operation of industry and society reflected one of man's baser motives and selfishly undermined the stability of the community. Instead, he reminded his students, whom he saw as society's future leaders, they should appeal to the spiritual nature in each man – workers and leaders alike – and "which never can be quite obliterated even in the blackest criminal."[83] In short, workers had a duty to stay on the job. Garman taught that man's spiritual nature, if recognized and respected, could be developed,

> not merely in the palace and the counting-room, but in the workshop and among the rank and file of the industrial army, and it is quite possible that the mission of America in the history of the world is to accomplish just this task.[84]

This insight later helped Coolidge deal humanely but dispassionately with workers who went on strike. Striking endangered the health of the Republic, he was sure, but the strikers, however selfish, misguided, or even criminal, were still men and needed to be treated that way. Garman continued: "The true reformer . . . will discover in men the image of God, and He will establish institutions that will stand the test of divine standards."[85] In other words, institutions, well designed, have divine inspiration and will be protected by Providence.

Speaking before the Brockton Chamber of Commerce in 1916, Coolidge again reflected Garman's teachings when he told an audience of bankers that commerce was "the foundation of human progress and prosperity" but that "material rewards," while necessary, were "only incidental." "Men must work for more than wages," he said. "Factories must turn out more than merchandise, or there is naught but black despair ahead."[86] (Coolidge was probably referring to the omnipresent strikes.) There was, fortunately, a solution, but it required men to "forever realize that material rewards are limited . . . but the development of character is unlimited and is the only essential."[87] When men acknowledged this teaching, commerce could fulfill its ultimate end: "to minister to the highest needs of man and to fulfill the hope of a fairer day."[88] Coolidge understood his role in government as helping commerce, primarily by not interfering with it; by not interfering, the government could help commerce fulfill its highest purpose. Men needed, in Garman's formulation, to stop loving commercialism – "a sort of moral cocaine"[89] – and start loving their fellows.

Practical Politics from Garman's Lessons

Garman's influence on Coolidge as a politician is especially clear in Coolidge's handling of two major strikes – not only the famous Boston police strike of 1919 during his governorship, but a lesser-known one in 1923, when strikes threatened to derail him. The latter strike, the most politically dangerous of the two, occurred during his first months in office, shortly after Harding's death, when a Harding-initiated labor peace agreement in the Pennsylvania coalfields broke down. The resulting miners' strike periodically made fuel less available in the Northeast, causing fears of "another winter of hardships and unhappiness." Seemingly every winter, the strikers held the nation's heat-deprived homes hostage to their demands.

Republican leaders insisted that Coolidge intervene. Senator Walter E. Edge of New Jersey advised the president that although the strike did not, strictly speaking, fall under his constitutional authority, Coolidge would face little political backlash if he became involved. "When an Executive . . . somewhat exceeds his authority in order to provide the public with necessities of life," the senator pointed out, he invariably gets public opinion on his side.[90] A New York businessman, fearing a spike in the price of coal, urged the president to "declare martial law. . . . Seize the mines, draft men to work. . . . Give them Hell."[91] The *New-York Tribune* declared on August 8 that Coolidge, with his party's nomination the following year far from assured, had no choice but to break the strike with bold, dramatic action.

Pennsylvania's governor, Gifford Pinchot, was a leading Progressive Republican, formerly Theodore Roosevelt's head of the U.S. Forest Service and instrumental in driving the split between the Progressive and conservative wings of the party in 1912.[92] He was easily elected governor in 1922 after defeating the establishment-Republican candidate in the primary. Many political commentators thought the politically ambitious governor could defeat Coolidge in the upcoming presidential-nomination battle if he responded effectively to the impending strike.[93] Coal strikes caused price spikes and political turmoil in 1900, 1902, and 1919 and were very much on Pinchot's mind, and he saw the one now looming as an opportunity to attain the presidency.[94] Coolidge, according to biographer Ferrell, "knew that something had to be done and that whoever did it would attract the dissatisfaction of both parties. Pinchot wanted to step in, and Coolidge let him."[95]

Coolidge did not plan to get involved himself, although he did suggest that the power industry use substitutes for Pennsylvania's anthracite coal.[96] He authorized Francis R. Wadleigh, who served as federal fuel distributor, to assemble officials from eleven states to prepare emergency plans for getting alternative coal and coke to the areas affected by a strike. Pinchot, meanwhile, approached Coolidge at President Harding's funeral on August 23 and offered his assistance.

No doubt sensing that Coolidge was dithering, Pinchot telephoned the president's secretary and threatened – or more accurately blustered – that it was his duty as governor to intervene and so he would.

When told of the call, Coolidge said nothing, but he acted within hours, inviting Pinchot and John Hays Hammond, a famous mining engineer who was chairman of the U.S. Coal Commission, to the White House for lunch the next day. Both Coolidge and Hammond suspected that Pinchot would have a plan of his own,[97] and rather than wait for it, they sought to neutralize him by using a three-thousand-page report from the Coal Commission, which Hammond had helped craft.[98] Coolidge and Hammond both probably surmised that because Pinchot had been instrumental in the formation of the federal commission, he would have no choice but to follow its decisions, so the two men planned how they would outmaneuver him the next day. Lunch was a social affair, complete with Coolidge's customary afternoon cigar, but when they adjourned to talk, it was another situation altogether. Hammond later recalled the scene in his autobiography:

> The moment we reached the President's study after lunch, I pulled from my pocket the report Coolidge had already read, and handed it to him, saying: "Mr. President, the commission has studied the conditions in the coal industry with great care, and considers this report covers the situation. After you've examined it, I'm sure Governor Pinchot will wish to read it also."
>
> I had seen Pinchot's hand go towards the pocket where I assumed his own plan reposed. I had beaten him to the draw.
>
> For form's sake, Coolidge glanced briefly over the report and then handed it to Pinchot. As soon as I saw Pinchot had finished, I said, "Don't you agree that this covers the situation?"
>
> The governor had to admit he approved the report, with the result that the coal crisis was met by the Coolidge, and not the Pinchot, plan.
>
> President Coolidge many times referred to this as our "coup."[99]

By the time the meeting ended, Coolidge named Pinchot as "Special Coal Strike Mediator" – and told him to carry out the plan in the commission's report.[100] Pinchot hoped for some autonomy, no doubt to implement his own plan, but Coolidge did not grant it. According to the White House press release, Pinchot was to act with the "cooperation" of federal authorities,[101] a forced cooperation that later angered Pinchot, who wrote to a friend: "The talk of my being the President's agent in this matter is pure nonsense."[102] Still fuming fourteen years later, Pinchot wrote to Progressive Republican editor William Allen White that the idea that he was the president's agent was "a lie out of the whole cloth" that "left him with no respect for [President Coolidge] whatsoever."[103] That Pinchot was still upset long after Coolidge had died indicates that Pinchot critics were probably right to explain his actions entirely through the prism of politics.[104]

Pinchot began the process of negotiating an agreement between strikers and mine owners, which he promised would occur "with conciliation if can be, with fire and sword if need be."[105] The *New York Times* suggested that Coolidge had "made a tactical error" by turning over the details to Pinchot, who quickly settled the strike by getting the owners to agree to full recognition of collective bargaining rights, an eight-hour work day, a 10 percent wage increase, and a compromise on the question of automatic dues collection by the union, the United Mine Workers, headed by the aggressive and outspoken John L. Lewis.[106]

Progressives rejoiced, thinking Pinchot was almost certain to replace Coolidge as the Republican candidate for president. Similarly, the *Baltimore Sun* wrote that the Progressive governor would "be in the minds of the people and the politicians when the nomination is made."[107] "It is one of those things that happened to work out just exactly right," Pinchot wrote. "Of course I am perfectly delighted."[108] But despite such expectations, Pinchot's victory was pyrrhic. Many of the forty million anthracite users quickly blamed him for their steeper fuel bills.[109] The press reversed its initial praise – the Rochester, New York, *Herald* remarked, for instance: "The dear old public has graciously been allowed the privilege of keeping warm this winter at

[the] expense of paying" higher and higher coal prices.[110] Despite his campaign to expose "profiteering," Pinchot was left out in the cold politically. Much to Pinchot's irritation, Coolidge sent his "heartiest congratulations," writing that it was a "very difficult situation . . . in which I invited your cooperation."[111]

Coolidge's refusal to involve himself heavily thus paid political dividends and isolated Pinchot. The press, which once condemned him for doing nothing, now saw him as a shrewd tactician.[112] As they soon saw it, Coolidge had nipped a competitive bid from Governor Pinchot in 1924 when he recommended that the governor agree to a costly increase in the price of anthracite coal. The governor did agree to the price increase because he was beholden to the unions and, in doing so, slit his own throat, politically. Time and again, Coolidge's deft management of strikes worked to his political advantage. He did not move quickly, but deliberately. By temperament and also due to the influence of Garman's teaching, Coolidge eschewed political expediency as often illusory and dangerous.[113] "Expediency as a working principle is bound to fail," Coolidge wrote in his autobiography.[114] "While I am not disposed to minimize the amount of evil in the world, I am convinced that the good predominates and that it is constantly all about us."[115] The statesman has to go out and find it.

Coolidge had patiently waited for Pinchot to spoil his own chances at the presidency. Despite all of Pinchot's scheming, the press noted that "the President will get the credit for the ensuing general tranquility" while Pinchot would receive all the political risk.[116] Coolidge had learned to use political timing to powerful effect and had done so by following Professor Garman's principles. The irony is that, in all likelihood, Pinchot settled the strike in much the same manner Coolidge would have.[117] Coolidge received acclaim from those who liked the settlement, and Pinchot received criticism from those who didn't. Secretary of the Treasury Andrew Mellon, whose coal company was involved in the strike, was said to have seen to it that even the Pennsylvania delegates lacked enthusiasm for a Pinchot candidacy.[118]

Pinchot had fallen victim to the politics of expediency, and before long, the consequences were clear. The labor peace he negotiated quickly in 1923 came unraveled only two years later, in September 1925, in a strike that lasted more than six months. But Pinchot appears to have learned his lessons from negotiating the 1923 strikes too hastily. "This time," according to biographer McGreary, "the Governor was not in as much of a hurry."

> As the end of November approached ... [Pinchot] informed President Coolidge by letter that he had invited the miners and operators to meet with him in Harrisburg on the very next day. Representatives of the miners arrived in Pinchot's office at the appointed time for the conference; the operators, now distrustful of the Governor, stayed away.[119]

Even so, he had not learned the lesson that he needed to be fair to both sides in a labor dispute, a lesson Coolidge had mastered as governor in Massachusetts. Pinchot always sided with labor. Miners "have given me confidence in their integrity and public spirit," he said in 1927. Pinchot, in his final message to the Pennsylvania legislature, attacked the coal operators, who had confirmed his opinion of them as "hard-boiled monopolists, whose sole interest in the people is what can be got of them."[120] Pinchot made enemies of the coal operators and approached the 1925 strike with a markedly pro-union bias, a decision that wound up severely harming his political career. He lost his bid for a Senate seat in 1926.

The politics of expediency also ended the 1920 presidential campaign of the governor of Illinois, Frank Lowden. Lowden had proposed conferences to cartelize wheat production during a period of disastrously low prices but couldn't get a workable deal, and before long, his window of opportunity closed.[121] Coolidge was surely unsurprised by Lowden's failure to elevate the price of wheat. In 1923, he had told Congress that any plan to ameliorate the lot of farmers had to begin with tax reduction, not subsidies. "No complicated scheme of relief, no plan for Government fixing of prices, no resort to the public Treasury will be of any permanent value in establishing agriculture," he maintained, with a hint of tragedy,[122] because the plight of those who worked the earth was a constant in human life. "Farmers have never made money," he told agriculture expert R. A. Cooper. "I don't believe we can do much about it."[123] Such proposals were also wrong because they were based on the false premise that work was undesirable and that men should therefore be compensated by earning more, independently of their products' value. As Coolidge noted in 1926, echoing Garman once again in his emphasis on spiritual matters over material ones:

> We can not expect to be relieved from toil, but we do expect to divest it of degrading conditions. Work is honorable; it is entitled to an honorable recompense. We must strive mightily, but having striven there is a defect in our political and social system if we are not in general rewarded with success. To relieve the land of the burdens that came from the war, to release to the individual more of the fruits of his own industry, to increase his earning capacity and decrease his hours of labor, to enlarge the circle of his vision through good roads and better transportation, to place before him the opportunity for education both in science and in art, to leave him free to receive the inspiration of religion, all these are ideals which deliver him from the servitude of the body and exalt him to the service of the soul. Through this emancipation from the things that are material, we broaden our dominion over the things that are spiritual.[124]

Coolidge's dedication to Garman's philosophy was so complete that his campaign advertisements for reelection even featured Garman prominently. A pamphlet titled "Do the Day's Work" described what the president had learned from Garman in his years at Amherst:

At Amherst College he learned well the lesson of service from the great philosopher Garman, and the influence of this teacher imbued him, as an undergraduate, with the firm conviction which has never been shaken, that character is the real foundation on which our institutions stand.[125]

This early education in the centrality of character to America's founding institutions helps to explain why Coolidge took such pains to restore America's heritage of freedom while in Washington.[126]

CHAPTER FOUR

Born on the Fourth of July
Coolidge's American Forefathers

No greater company ever assembled to interpret the voice of the people or direct the destinies of a nation.[1]

COOLIDGE'S RELIGIOUS GROUNDING prevented him from making Progressivism's gravest mistake: rejecting the exceptional statesmanship of the American founding. As he saw it, the Great Awakening's religious teaching ennobled – and indeed enabled – America's founding. He believed in America's moral force and saw it at work in the world. He encouraged Massachusetts, as her men fought in Europe in 1918, to recall America's cardinal virtues:

> Have faith in the moral power of America. It gave independence under Washington and freedom under Lincoln. Here, right never lost. Here, wrong never won.... Courage and confidence are our heritage.[2]

En route to Europe, men in the maritime industries from Massachusetts and other Americans disdained the "infamous servitude" that the Edict of Potsdam – broadly interpreted in international law as the right to travel to and from nations in the interest of commerce – had imposed upon American ships in a false declaration of neutrality. Americans preferred instead to plant "seeds of the same righteousness ... which later flourished with such abundance at Saratoga, at Gettysburg."[3] Massachusetts would not sail under the Edict of Potsdam, but "under the ancient Declaration of Independence, choosing what course she will, maintaining security by the guns of ships of the line, flying at the mast the Stars and Stripes, forever the emblem of a militant liberty."[4] If America was militant, it was only because she had something to be militant about, and her truths could not be limited to her shores. Coolidge's militancy in World War I had an evangelical flair. He believed that Americans were not only a religious but perhaps even a messianic people, who judged progress by "two great standards": "creation" and "redemption," twin forces that sent two million of America's men across the sea so "that the cause of a Christian civilization might still remain supreme."[5] Germany's belief that others were to be ruled by superior nations was, in Coolidge's analysis, a profoundly un-Christian – and un-Jeffersonian[6] – thought.

Coolidge had celebrated Jefferson's Declaration early in his career, telling an audience assembled at the home of Daniel Webster on July 4, 1916, of the importance of the Declaration in world events.

> The events of history may have added to it, but subtracted nothing. Wisdom and experience have increased the admiration of it. Time and criticism have not shaken it. . . . But, however worthy of our reverence and admiration, however preeminent, it was only one incident of a great forward movement of the human race, of which the American Revolution was itself only a larger incident. It was not so much a struggle of the Colonies against the tyranny of bad government, as against wrong principles of government, and for self-government. It was man realizing himself.

That realization persisted through time and touched all men's souls, as it moved from Concord or Yorktown, marching "on to Paris, to London, to Moscow, to Pekin." "Men of every clime" respected the Declaration, for "it marked the entry of new forces and new ideals into human affairs." The "realization of the true glory and worth of man," encouraged by the noble document, had "wrought vast changes that have marked all history since its day."[7]

Man's triumphal progress through time owed much to consider-

ations of "natural rights." But, unfortunately, these were "not sufficient to live by," Coolidge reminded the audience in Webster's home.
Their preservation required citizens to honor their duty and pledge
to one another and the body politic.

> The signers knew that well; more important still, the people
> whom they represented knew it. So they did not stop there.
> After asserting that man was to stand out in the universe with
> a new and supreme importance, and that governments were
> instituted to insure life, liberty, and the pursuit of happiness,
> they did not shrink from the logical conclusion of this doctrine.

The Declaration and those who clung to its teachings understood
that "the rights of citizens are to be protected with every power and
resource of the State, and a government that does any less is false to
the teachings of that great document, of the name American." These
teachings made up the heart of American civic life, Coolidge believed,
and he urged that we live by them:

> Here lies the path to national preservation, and there is no
> other. Education, the progress of science, commercial pros-
> perity, yes, and peace, all these and their accompanying bless-
> ings are worthy and commendable objects of attainment. But
> these are not the end, whether these come or no; the end lies
> in action – action in accord with the eternal principles of the
> Declaration of Independence.

To act upon the eternal principles of the American founding, then,
was to act righteously, even if "doctrinaires and visionaries shudder"
at the notion. Men with "privilege of birth may jeer" and "the practical politician may scoff" at it, but other Americans, Coolidge stressed,
"respond to" the Declaration. After all, "the assertion of human
rights is naught but a call to human sacrifice," he said.[8]
Coolidge's strong faith in the document's principles and his under-

standing of its centrality in the American republic relieved him of some of the worry about reelection and saved him from practicing a politics of expediency, because he understood that a people is always bound to its foundational charter or faith – at least as long as it clings to man's spiritual nature. As Coolidge would later write in his autobiography:

> In time of crisis my belief that people can know the truth, that when it is presented to them they must accept it, has saved me from many of the counsels of expediency. The spiritual nature of men has a power of its own that is manifest in every great emergency from Runnymede [birthplace of Magna Carta] to Marston Moor [a key battle in the English Civil War], from the Declaration of Independence to the abolition of slavery."[9]

The American people's spiritual response to the Declaration, he believed, compelled them to fight for it – which they did. Jefferson may receive "the immortal honor of having drafted the Declaration" that "proclaimed the great truths of our national life,"[10] and Washington's army in the field may have given America its independence, but Coolidge kept the flame alight.

Coolidge's Declaration of Independence

For Coolidge, the cultivation of our form of government and the maintenance of its policies depended on first principles and their reinforcement by religion and liberal education, not modern-day political science. In this light, he is best defined as a "Declaration of Independence progressive," a "conservative progressive," or a "constitutionalist progressive." He believed in human progress but saw it emanating from divine inspiration – in America's case, that of the Declaration of Independence – rather than from any new knowledge. The Declaration, and indeed all valid American political thought, was "the product of centuries of an earlier culture, a culture which was [no less] real because it supposed the earth was flat . . . which was pre-eminent in the development of the moral and spiritual forces of life."[11]

Without these religious and civic truths, no progress in politics was possible. With them, man would realize untold success. Coolidge believed, like Aristotle, that the arts and sciences are capable of infinite progress, and he celebrated those who broke new ground.[12] But he knew that advancement owes a great deal to the underlying principles that animate it.

One day after the Declaration's sesquicentennial anniversary in Philadelphia, he reminded an audience of America's first principles:

> We live in an age of science and of abounding accumulation of material things. These did not create our Declaration. Our Declaration created them. The things of the spirit come first. Unless we cling to that, all our material prosperity, overwhelming though it may appear, will turn to a barren sceptre in our grasp. If we are to maintain the great heritage which has been bequeathed to us, we must be like-minded as the fathers who created it. We must not sink into a pagan materialism. We must cultivate the reverence which they had for the things that are holy. We must follow the spiritual and moral leadership which they showed.[13]

Coolidge believed in progress, but he eschewed the label "progressive" as too vague, telling a press conference in 1924:

> I don't think I can give any definition of the word "reactionary" and "progressive" that would be helpful. . . . Sometimes the person is not well thought of and he is labeled as a reactionary. Sometimes he is well thought of and he is called a progressive. As a matter of fact all the political parties are progressive. I can't conceive of a party existing for any length of time that wasn't progressive, or of leadership being effective that wasn't progressive.[14]

Ever the loyal party man,[15] Coolidge judged that the most progressive party of all time was his own Republican Party, which under its first president both freed the slaves and saved the Union. The GOP, in his view, still had much to give. In Massachusetts, it had "lit the fire of progress," and he himself, Coolidge added with pride, had tended that fire "faithfully" with a whole body of now-settled legislation.

> [The GOP] has provided here conditions of employment, and safeguards for health, that are surpassed nowhere on earth. There will be no backward step. The reuniting [after 1912] of the Republican Party means no reaction in the protection of women and children in our industrial life. These laws are settled. These principles are established.[16]

Coolidge as president argued in favor of a constitutional amendment[17] to "protect the child life of the Nation from the unwarranted imposition of toil," as part of the same "advance toward the realization of the vision of Washington and Lincoln"[18] – a steady but sure "fulfillment of an age-old promise, man coming into his own."[19] But such progress was lasting, healthy, and possible only when it rested on a secure theoretical foundation. As he wrote in "On the Nature of Politics," "No system of government can stand that lacks public confidence and no progress can be made on the assumption of a false premise."[20] Examination of classic thought and history helped the prudent statesman distinguish true premise from false dogma. Coolidge knew that premises must be arrived at through argument, understood as true rather than expedient, and then disseminated in the body politic through education. America's very existence owed much to history's repository of such premises, argued and then conveyed down through the ages – and embodied in the immortal Declaration of Independence. Founded on self-evident truths and grounded in reverence for "nature and nature's God," Coolidge's political philosophy owes much to the Declaration and its contributions to political theory.

Other scholars – most notably the late Tom Silver of the Claremont Institute, Harry V. Jaffa of Claremont McKenna College, and Burt Folsom Jr. of Hillsdale College – have noted Coolidge's connection to the Declaration. In his recent essay "An Enabler of Prosperity," Folsom explores Coolidge's careful study of the document, which, as he argues, distinguishes Coolidge from the other progressives in both parties.

> During these years, the "progressive spirit" led many politicians to argue that a stronger central government was needed to solve the economic problems of the day. Coolidge resisted this trend and argued that adherence to the Constitution and the principles of the Declaration of Independence well served the nation before the 1900s, and would continue to do so afterward.[21]

Folsom is correct: The homage to the Declaration runs throughout Coolidge's writings. His first speech, his prize essay, and his finest speech[22] all mention it, as do many others.

Coolidge was perhaps especially appreciative of the Declaration's dual character as a product of both religion and education, both revelation and reason – in his view the two greatest supports of civilization.[23] These had to function together, and in a self-governing society such as America must be taught to all. "The question for consideration is not what shall be taught to a *few* individuals ... [but] what does the public welfare require for the purpose of education?" he asked fellow Amherst alumni shortly after the 1920 election. "What are the fundamental things that young Americans should be taught? What is necessary for society to come to a larger comprehension for life?"[24] Far from being a decade of cultural sloth and self-indulgence, as portrayed by later progressives, the 1920s saw a renewed appreciation for learning.

> Between 1910 and 1930 ... total education spending in America rose fourfold, from $425.25 million to $2.3 billion a year.

Spending on higher education rose fourfold, too, to nearly a billion a year. Illiteracy fell from 7.7 percent to 4.3 percent. The 1920s was the age of the Book of the Month Club and the Literary Guild, of booming publishing houses and book-shops, and especially a popular devotion to the classics. Throughout the 1920s, *David Copperfield* was rated "America's favorite novel," and those voted by Americans as "the ten greatest men in history" included Shakespeare, Longfellow, Dickens, and Tennyson.[25]

Coolidge looked upon these developments with pleasure but warned his fellow Americans not to ignore spiritual or moral themes in their education. It is significant that he began his second collection of speeches, *The Price of Freedom*[26] – the first speeches he delivered while in federal office – by stressing the importance of character education. For Coolidge, the very "process of civilization" consisted in men's "discovery . . . of the laws of the universe and of living in harmony with those laws," and this discovery required "education, the method whereby man is revealed to himself."[27] Such revelation had special importance as the starting point of self-government, which began with the individual and extended outward to his community and nation.

"Education which is not based on religion and character," Vice President Coolidge asserted, "is not education."[28] True education was enormously consequential, for it was "the process by which each individual recreates his own universe and determines its dimensions."[29] It therefore had crucial importance in a republic based on public opinion. If students limited their moral universe to what was material, they would not grow into full Americans. If they broadened their universe to include first spiritual – and only then material – considerations, they would be worthy citizens in a republic. Sound public opinion required an educated citizenry, without which it would lack direction.

Education fails which does not help in furnishing this with some solution. It ought to confer the ability to see in an unfolding history the broadening out of the base of civilization, the continued growth of the power and the dignity of the individual, the enlarging solidarity and stability of society, and the increasing reign of righteousness.[30]

Coolidge returned to this theme often. At Amherst, he had noted the central role of knowledge – and its chief advocate, the college – in improving society:

Civilization depends not only upon the knowledge of the people, but upon the use they make of it. If knowledge be wrongfully used, civilization commits suicide. Broadly speaking, the college is not to educate the individual, but to educate society. The individual may be ignorant and vicious. If society have learning and virtue, that will sustain him. If society lacks learning and virtue, it perishes. *Education must give not only power but direction*. It must minister to the whole man or it fails.[31]

The insistence on "direction" raises the question of whether Coolidge found the education of his day lacking. For Coolidge, education and the proper use of knowledge were to be the "handmaid of citizenship."[32] An increasingly educated citizenry portended well for the American republic, and without it, America would have nothing to unite it and would fall apart. "We must have every American citizen well grounded in the classical ideals," he told an audience at his alma mater.[33] Universal teaching of America's founding ideals would help shape what Lord Bryce called its government of public opinion, which had "drawn its inspiration from the classics."[34]

Americans not only gained wisdom and found inspiring examples by studying the classics; they also got a clearer sense of God's commands. And the greatest repository of truth in Coolidge's view – "the classic of all classics"[35] – was the Bible. As he wrote to an Episcopal Sunday-school teacher in 1927, "the foundations of our society and Government rest so much on the teachings of the Bible that it would be difficult to support them if faith in these teachings should cease to be practically universal in our country." It was because religious teachings were concerned with how man should live, individually and in community, that people should universally accept them. Like Garman, Coolidge believed men could deduce their natural equality from both reason and revelation and go about the project of instituting a government where men serve one another. On this point, he often quoted the Rev. John Wise's formulation that "democracy is Christ's government in church and state."[36] Wise was one of many eighteenth-century ministers of the Great Awakening who influenced the founding. Coolidge noted that his works, reprinted in 1772, had been "declared . . . nothing less than a textbook of liberty for our Revolutionary fathers."[37] Through teachings like Wise's, the Founders learned that democracy, as Coolidge said at the July 4 commemoration at Daniel Webster's home, is "the alpha and omega of man's relation to man, the beginning and the end."[38]

Democracy, the people's government, was instituted in America because it was the best means of preserving rights and the people's natural liberty. But its ultimate justification was the word of God: The Founders, according to Coolidge, believed that "the ultimate sanction of law rests on the righteous authority of the Almighty."[39] Democracy secures law, and it would eventually triumph because "its foundation lays hold upon eternity."[40] The Declaration, which secured that democracy, became a covenant among the American people, thus becoming "immortal." Like the Founders, Coolidge believed that self-government required religion and education; only through tradition (which he saw as a codification of human wisdom, derived from long experience) and education could a people learn republican principles.

Coolidge believed that the great thinker (and first American professor of sociology) William Graham Sumner missed the mark by claiming that economic principles came long before democracy. On the contrary, he wrote to Dwight Morrow (the future ambassador to Mexico who had introduced him to Sumner's writings), it was philosophy and religion that made possible good economics and democracy. In Coolidge's view, Sumner's overemphasis on economics made him unable to appreciate the animating principle of service that made the American experiment possible. Sumner "nowhere enunciates the principle of service," he told Morrow.[41] Coolidge would certainly have rejected Sumner's denial of natural rights, his contention that in "the tribunal of nature a man has no more right to life than a rattlesnake; he has no more right to liberty than any wild beast; his right to pursuit of happiness is nothing but a license to maintain the struggle for existence."[42]

Religion and education were also the bulwarks that protected Coolidge, in his thinking, from Progressivism's excesses. "Education," he told a convention of the National Education Association in 1924, is the "cornerstone of self-government,"[43] while religion[44] kept America safe from tyranny because "Christ spent no time in the antechamber of Cæsar."[45] This was because Christ had no desire for an earthly kingdom, preferring to come down to earth and live only as a servant. Christ wanted, in Coolidge's interpretation, to use religion's power to cultivate an appreciation for ideals – spiritual principles – in men. As ideals undergird American government, so religion undergirds American self-government.

Despite his great respect for religion and tradition, Coolidge elaborated on his understanding of the American founding by noting how much it owed to religious dissidents in particular, people who reasoned anew about religion and government. The effort to create something new, building on the best reasoning from older times, attracted pilgrims the world over who were dedicated to the American experiment. For such pilgrims, journeying to their own would-be Garden of Eden, politics was in a sense religious (and religion was in a sense political). "Our nation cannot live without morality," he warned, "and morality cannot live without religion."[46] Morality, like truth, was accessible to all peoples – a lesson America came to learn from its long experiment in separation of church from state.

By becoming part of American culture, new peoples would belong fully American society. "Common spiritual inspiration" was a "potent [force] to bring and mold and weld together into a national unity," he told Washington's Jewish residents at the laying of the cornerstone of their community center on May 3, 1925. At the Founding,

> there were well-nigh as many divergencies of religious faith as there were of origin, politics and geography. Yet, in the end, these religious differences proved rather unimportant. While the early dangers in some colonies made a unity in belief and all else a necessity to existence, at the bottom of the colonial character lay a stratum of religious liberalism which had animated most of the early comers. From its beginnings, the new continent had seemed destined to be the home of religious tolerance. Those who claimed the right of individual choice for themselves finally had to grant it to others. *Beyond that – and this was one of the factors which I think weighed heaviest on the side of unity – the Bible was the one work of literature that was common to all of them. The scriptures were read and studied everywhere. There were many testimonies that their teachings became the most important intellectual and spiritual force for unification.*[47]

Coolidge celebrated the new community center as a testament to that American history and the Jews' place in it, telling those assembled that he agreed with historian William Edward Hartpole Lecky's contention that "Hebraic mortar cemented the foundations of American democracy." America had a common history with Jews because they worshiped the same Bible and both had turned to it as the font of their government, as the "chief source of illumination for their arguments in support of the patriot cause."

> [The Founders] knew the Book. They were profoundly familiar with it, and eminently capable in the exposition of all its justifications for rebellion. To them, the record of the exodus from Egypt was indeed an inspired precedent. They knew what arguments from holy writ would most powerfully influ-

ence their people. It required no great stretch of logical processes to demonstrate that the children of Israel, making
bricks without straw in Egypt, had their modern counterpart
in the people of the colonies, enduring the imposition of taxation without representation!

"The Jewish faith," Coolidge reasoned, is "predominantly the
faith of liberty." Coolidge welcomed the contribution of Jewish mer-
chants who had cast their lot with America and, in the run-up to the
American Revolution, "unhesitatingly signed the non-importation
resolution of 1765: Isaac Moses, Benjamin Levy, Samson Levy,
David Franks, Joseph Jacobs, Hayman Levy Jr., Matthias Bush,
Michael Gratz, Bernard Gratz, Isaac Franks, Moses Mordecai, Benjamin Jacobs, Samuel Lyon and Manuel Mordecai Noah." America
would repay the debt by welcoming the sons of Abraham to her
shores. Coolidge also expressed his "sympathy with the deep and
intense longing which finds such fine expression in the Jewish
National Homeland in Palestine." Proclaiming that "from earliest
colonial times, America has been a new land of promise to this long
persecuted race," Coolidge promised his audience that any bigotry
against Jews would be overcome:

> Factional, sectional, social and political lines of conflict yet
> persist. Despite all experience, society continues to engender
> the hatreds and jealousies whereof are born domestic strife
> and international conflicts. But education and enlightenment
> are breaking their force. Reason is emerging.[48]

Reason would lead all of America's faiths to a better understanding, in which they could use the lessons of their shared Bible to build
a community. Moral life was inseparable from political and religious
questions, yet it was attainable through reason. Democracy – "the
spirit of the people themselves" – needed to become "conscious of its
authority." In accord with Christ's teaching in Psalm 103:8, it should

be "slow to anger, plenteous in mercy."[49] People with political disagreements ought to follow suit, trusting to their institutions, which they administer, to deliver earthly justice.

Similarly, Coolidge told the National Council of the Boy Scouts, "Our Government rests upon religion . . . the source from which we derive our reverence for truth and justice, for equality and liberty, and for the rights of mankind."[50] Even among peoples who had hitherto been seen as savages, the influence of Christianity had "always and everywhere . . . been a force for illumination and advancement."[51] In Coolidge's view, religion breaks down all barriers of race or culture and replaces them with concern for universal truth. "New arrivals" could be Americanized if they "[kept] up their devotion to religion."[52]

"Religion is the essential," Coolidge insisted. If the country were to grow less religious, he feared, much of its civilization would be lost, destroying in its wake Americans' ability to remain largely independent of government in their lives. "The community without the church goes to pieces," he warned. "I have seen it again and again in New England," he noted, referring, no doubt, to the turn away from religion in some of the region's mill towns. This could not be allowed to happen because "our Nation was founded by men who came over for the sake of religion."[53] On the other hand, Americans should not depend on government "to do the work of religion" because "there is no way by which we can substitute the authority of law for the virtue of man."[54] Trying to get government to save men's souls or meet their material needs, rather than merely protect their rights, led inexorably to tyranny because it denigrated the spiritual side of man.

Those most in danger from such a prospect were the poor new immigrants, susceptible as they were to Tammany Hall–style promises from the machines. "One of the greatest dangers" that affect new immigrants and "especially those of the younger generation," Coolidge warned, "is that they will fall away from the religion of their fathers, and never become attached to any other faith."[55] This must not be allowed to happen, because the country "owes its beginnings to the determination of our hardy ancestors to maintain complete freedom in religion."[56] New arrivals, whether from Sweden or Japan, as well as "Negroes" long settled here, could ultimately participate in self-government if they found their own complete freedom in religion.

Coolidge's understanding of the civic role of education and religion show him to be at least arguably a progressive, but he was a progressive of a kind rarely seen before or since. Our need for Coolidge-type progressivism is great; it is perhaps the only variety of progressivism that can counter the movement's typical excesses, because it offers a clear understanding of what true progress is and how it might realistically flourish in a government operating within limits, administered by men who know theirs.

* * *

Of course, some apparent "progress" *is* founded on false premises. Progressivism's excesses were due especially to one of its great enunciators, Woodrow Wilson, who, long before he was president, denied that the Declaration taught self-evident truths applicable to all men at all times. Instead, he saw the Declaration as a product of now-outgrown times and therefore unworthy of study as a philosophic work. It was a mere document of history, one whose signers did not see it as an "attempt to dictate the aims and objects of any generation but their own."[57] Wilson also argued that the Declaration "did not afford a general theory of government to formulate policies upon." He asked skeptically whether we still hold to the Declaration, whether its doctrine "still lives in our principles of action, in the things we do, in the purposes we applaud, in the measures we approve." In our day and age, Wilson maintained, "we are not bound to adhere to the doctrines held by the signers of the Declaration of Independence" and "are as free as they were to make and unmake governments," seemingly with little concern for whether such governments are founded upon eternal principles. All that was really necessary in a free society, in Wilson's view, was consent.

Wilson continued his broadside on the Declaration by dismissing the ultimate importance of its author, the problematic genius Thomas Jefferson:

> It is fashionable, it is easy, to talk about Jeffersonian principles of government. Men of all kinds and of the most opposite doctrines call themselves by Mr. Jefferson's name; and it must be admitted that it is easy to turn many of Mr. Jefferson's opinions this way or that. But no man's name settles any principle, and Mr. Jefferson was originating no novel doctrine, announcing no discoveries in politics, when he wrote the Declaration of Independence. What it contains is in fact the common-place of political history. There can be no liberty if the individual is not free; there is no such thing as corporate liberty. There is no other possible formula for a free government than this: *that the laws must deal with individuals, allowing them to choose their own lives under a definite personal responsibility to a common government set over them*; and that government must regulate, not as a superintendent does, but as a judge does; it must safeguard, it must not direct.[58]

A government that existed "over them," led by even a divine "judge," could never be a government of the people, by the people, and for the people. At its worst, in Wilson's conception of free government, men could choose to have an enlightened dictator, who – though elected – would know what the people wanted better than they knew it themselves. At its best, if "each generation must form its own conception of what liberty is," men would descend into moral relativism and government would decay. With no recourse to the higher principles of the Declaration, our governing bodies would devolve into anarchy, for the freest state is no government at all. In such a world, people would bicker constantly over just what government may – or even can – be, and over its legitimate ends. In the wake of Wilson's philosophical revolution and its cultural consequences, we appear to live in such a world today.

*   *   *

Coolidge opposed Wilson's views of the Declaration because he believed rights came from God, not government – and certainly not from history or evolution.[59] For Coolidge, "history is revelation," led by an Almighty God – through great men who are "ambassadors of Providence sent to reveal to their fellow men their unknown selves."[60] These ambassadors acted upon, but crucially also *with*, a great people who produced "stupendous results" by "working with an everlasting purpose."[61]

The people could find greatness from among their ranks, and they had done so with Lincoln. In a speech commemorating Lincoln's birthday, Coolidge remarked that Lincoln "made the same appeal to his countrymen which all great men have made . . . it came not from his belief in their weakness but in their strength."[62] Coolidge praised the Lincolnian vision, which "saw . . . more clearly . . . the moral relationship of things" and believed his "great achievement consisted in bringing the different elements of his country into a more truly moral relationship."[63] The efforts of Lincoln, the great student of the Declaration, made him a Christ-like figure in the people's estimation, sacrificed on Good Friday, Coolidge suggested, so that the people might live.

> There is in the people themselves the power to put forth great men. . . . There is no problem so great but that somewhere a man is being raised up to meet it. There is no moral standard so high that the people cannot be raised up to it. God rules, and from the Bethlehems and the Springfields He sends them forth, His own, to do His work. In them we catch a larger gleam of the Infinite.[64]

That Infinite was God, whose presence was felt through great men who produced great works that would endure, even in some cases throughout the world.[65] God, Coolidge believed, would not only give rights but also allow men to perfect, through labor, what he had already given – hence his commandment to work. "True great-ness," according to Coolidge, "enlarges man's dominion." It comes from "obedience to that admonition given on creation morn to sub-due the earth."[66] Following that commandment ennobled the soul and enabled men to do great things while working out the divine plan. Only great men follow God. Greatness would come in the form of "men of larger vision and higher inspiration," who come "with a power to impart a larger vision and a higher inspiration to the people, to make history."[67] But only a people who worshiped shared things could become great itself. Coolidge more or less believed that a peo-ple that prays together stays together:

> It is only when men begin to worship that they begin to grow. A wholesome regard for the memory of the great men of long ago is the best assurance to a people of a continuation of great men to come, who shall still be able to instruct, to lead, and to inspire. A people who worship at the shrine of true greatness will themselves be truly great.[68]

Following Scripture, Coolidge reminded his audience that while searching for such men to lead them, the people ought to consider "men of low estate" rather than looking first to the elite.[69] After all, he said, "the greatest epoch in all human history began in a manger," and Lincoln was the "great American" who "came out of a frontier clearing and spent his early manhood in a village of a few hundred souls."[70] Those few hundred souls were able to understand his great-ness because he lived among and like them, and because, according to Coolidge, they worshiped a God intimately involved in their lives. Their shared worship enabled them to do amazing things, eventually winning a war of seemingly biblical proportions. "A great people responded to a great man," Coolidge remarked of the outpouring of support for the low-born Civil War general, later President Grant.

But there were limits to the potential for greatness. Great men cannot be atheists because "without the sustaining influence of faith in a divine power we could have little faith in ourselves," he told the Boy Scouts later in his presidency. "Doubters do not achieve; skeptics do not contribute; cynics do not create. Faith is the great motive power, and no man realizes his full possibilities unless he has the deep conviction that life is eternally important, and that his work, well done, is a part of an unending plan."[71] Trust in God, Coolidge might have said, and he shall provide for us to provide for ourselves. In a sense, faith in America was faith in God and vice versa.

Coolidge's strong religious rhetoric was grounded in real faith. He had, as biographer Gamaliel Bradford would note, an "unshaken belief in an anthropomorphic God, who guides the destinies of nations and also the petty affairs of individuals, and to whom it is of real importance what you or I or Calvin Coolidge may or may not do."[72] He believed, too, that God had formed a pact with a chosen people: He had chosen America, and America would continue to prosper so long as she continued to worship God. "Behind such a deity," writes Bradford of Coolidge's theology, is an afterlife, "a future, perhaps unending, existence, in which all the inequalities of this world, riches and poverty, brains and dullness, will be amply adjusted and compensated, and in which again, you, and I, and Calvin Coolidge will richly receive the reward of all of our labor and endurance here."[73]

Perhaps Coolidge's embrace of the afterlife was what kept him going. Death was always a constant companion, felling those close to him. Early in his presidency, Coolidge had to face one of Scripture's darker teachings: What the Lord giveth, he also taketh way. Calvin Coolidge Jr. died when a blister he got while playing tennis produced a fatal infection. After his death, the president told a delegate to the Republican National Convention, "When I look out the window, I always see my boy playing tennis on that court out there." In his autobiography, he wondered why a just God would take his son from him.[74] "I do not know why such a price was exacted for occupying the White House," the ex-president wrote. When his son died, "the power and glory of the Presidency went with him," Coolidge said. It vexed him that he was powerless to help his sick child. "In his suffering, he was asking me to make him well. I could not." Yet his faith in a personal and benevolent God seems to have remained unshaken. The president later told his father, who would pass away shortly thereafter: "I suppose I am the most powerful man in the world but great power does not mean much but great limitations. I am only in the clutch of forces that are greater than I am." In this, Coolidge echoes Lincoln, who wrote to a friend in 1864, "I claim not to have controlled events, but confess plainly that events have controlled me." These were the same forces – the same unpredictable events – Coolidge had in mind when, noting the sudden death of President Harding the previous year, he said in a piece of campaign literature in 1924, "I have faith that God will direct the destinies of our nation."[75]

* * *

In his first inaugural address as President in his own right, in 1925, Coolidge affirmed America's missionary and implicitly Christian character:

> Here stands our country, an example of tranquility at home, a patron of tranquility abroad. Here stands its Government, aware of its might but obedient to its conscience. Here it will continue to stand, seeking peace and prosperity, solicitous for the welfare of the wage earner, promoting enterprise, developing waterways and natural resources, attentive to the intuitive counsel of womanhood, encouraging education, desiring the advancement of religion, supporting the cause of justice and honor among the nations. America seeks no earthly empire built on blood and force. No ambition, no temptation, lures her to thought of foreign dominions. *The legions which she sends forth are armed, not with the sword, but with the cross. The higher state to which she seeks the allegiance of all mankind is not of human, but of divine origin. She cherishes no purpose save to merit the favor of Almighty God.*[76]

All just regimes seek the favor of a God or gods and believe themselves to act in accordance with them. But Coolidge, one of America's most religious presidents, saw a divine plan at work in America, and indeed in all of human history.

In this assessment, he followed the Whig analysis of history, as laid out in the work of Thomas Macaulay and elsewhere. "What is the teaching of all history?" Coolidge asked in his 1919 commencement address at Holy Cross. He answers:

> That which is necessary for the welfare and progress of the human race has never been destroyed. The discoverers of truth, the teachers of science, the makers of inventions, have passed to their rewards, but their works have survived. The Phoenician galleys and the civilization which was born of their commerce have perished, but the alphabet which that people perfected remains. The shepherd kings of Israel, the temple and empire of Solomon, have gone the way of all the earth, but the Old Testament has been preserved for the inspiration of mankind. The ark of the covenant and the seven-pronged candlestick have passed from human view; the inhabitants of Judea have been dispersed to the ends of the earth, but the New Testament has survived and increased in its influence among men. The glory of Athens and Sparta, the grandeur of the Imperial City, are a long-lost memory, but the poetry of Homer and Virgil, the oratory of Demosthenes and Cicero, the philosophy of Plato and Aristotle, abide with us forevermore. Whatever America holds that may be of value to posterity will not pass away.[77]

History, then, has a way of conserving what is best, even as its creators vanish. The idea that what is necessary for human welfare shall not disappear suggests an involved God who chooses both the best among mankind's leaders and the best among civilizational achievements to live down through the ages.

"About the Declaration," Coolidge observed on its 150th anniversary, "there is a finality that is exceedingly restful." It was his strong belief in this finality that most clearly shows the vast differences between Coolidge's understanding of good politics and Wilson's. Coolidge believed that progress depended on the truths eloquently identified in the Declaration:

> It is often asserted that the world has made a great deal of progress since 1776, that we have had new thoughts and new experiences which have given us a great advance over the people of that day, and that we may therefore very well discard their conclusions for something more modern. But that reasoning can not be applied to this great charter. If all men are created equal, that is final. If they are endowed with inalienable rights, that is final. If governments derive their just powers from the consent of the governed, that is final. No advance, no progress can be made beyond these propositions. If anyone wishes to deny their truth or their soundness, the only direction in which he can proceed historically is not forward, but backward toward the time when there was no equality, no rights of the individual, no rule of the people. Those who wish to proceed in that direction can not lay claim to progress. They are reactionary. Their ideas are not more modern, but more ancient, than those of the Revolutionary fathers.

Coolidge, owing to his belief in divine intervention, used highly religious language when discussing the Declaration of Independence. In his eyes, the document was a "miracle," inspiring a "reverence" that helped bring pilgrims of every nation to American shores. People "at home and abroad" alike, Coolidge said, considered Independence Hall a "hallowed ground" and revered the Liberty Bell as a "sacred relic." These symbols represented a "spiritual event," and America had become a "Holy Land."

The Declaration of Independence has come to be "regarded as

one of the great charters that not only was to liberate America but was everywhere to ennoble humanity." This was because the Founders "proposed to establish a nation on new principles" and did so. An inquiry into those new principles finds that they were religious. And it was those religious teachings that had made the formation of a new polity possible – and that religious teaching, although it found new ground in America, had come from the Continent. Indeed, Coolidge also celebrated the fact that other peoples had also been reasoning their way toward the just principles embodied in the Declaration – which owed much to "what the Dutch had done in 1581 and what the English were preparing to do" in the English Civil War.[78] The Dutch, Coolidge knew, declared in their own Declaration of Independence that "God did not create the people slaves to their prince, to obey his commands, whether right or wrong, but rather the prince for the sake of the subjects," while the English fought their King over the supremacy of parliament.

All of these principles had long been taught to the fledgling American people, who were learning as early as 1638, Coolidge noted, from thinkers such as the Rev. Thomas Hooker of Connecticut. In a sermon quoted by Coolidge, Hooker told the colony's General Court: "The foundation of authority is laid in the free consent of the people. . . . The choice of public magistrates belongs unto the people by God's own allowance." Before America could be founded, her citizens had first to be saved – and her clergy played a key role. Coolidge also often cited the aforementioned Rev. John Wise, who spent time in the royal governor's prison in Massachusetts for having promoted rebellious ideas in his treatise "The Church's Quarrel Espoused" in 1710. In it, Wise explained how Christianity taught the principles of civil government. He was, Coolidge noted, just one of a long list of eighteenth-century preachers who informed his congregation of the "principles of human relationship which went into the Declaration of Independence." These principles "are found in the text, the sermons, and the writings of the early colonial clergy who were earnestly undertaking to instruct their congregations in the great mystery of how to live."

The question of how man should live was inseparable from that of who should rule. Because the clergy "believed in the divine origin of mankind," they knew man's "dignity and glory," and "through a common father" they "perceived a common brotherhood." A common brotherhood meant a common politics, grounded in natural equality.

> From this conception there resulted the recognition that free- dom was a birthright. It was the natural and inalienable con- dition of beings who were created "a little lower than the angels." With it went the principle of equality, not an equality of possessions, not an equality of degree, but an equality in the attributes of humanity, an equality of kind. Each is pos- sessed of the divine power to know the truth. It is in accor- dance with these standards that the American people adopted their Constitution and set up their government.[79]

To Coolidge, that divine fraternity is understood by all men and constitutes the heart of the American system. A common spiritual life lent itself to a common political one. For that reason, those who touched the spiritual nature of the American public were greatly rewarded; in the same way, the Declaration, at base a spiritual docu- ment, had long met with great favor among Americans. In the speech commemorating the Declaration's sesquicentennial, Coolidge notes that the document draws inspiration from divine sources, which are explicitly mentioned three times in the Declaration. "Coming from these sources," he says, "it is no wonder that Samuel Adams could say 'The people seem to recognize this resolution as though it were a decree promulgated from heaven.' "

But our political life would quickly descend into a Hobbesian hell, he adds, if Americans ignored certain "conclusions" and "courses of action which have been a great blessing to the world." To keep their Republic, Americans "must go back and review the course" the Founders followed and "think the thoughts which they thought."

While there were always among them men of deep learning, and later those who had comparatively large possessions, the mind of the people was not so much engrossed in how much they knew, or how much they had, as in how they were going to live. While scantily provided with other literature, there was a wide acquaintance with the Scriptures. Over a period as great as that which measures the existence of our independence they were subject to this discipline not only in their religious life and educational training, but also in their political thought. They were a people who came under the influence of a great spiritual development and acquired a great moral power.

America's moral mission in the world, Coolidge thought, would never be divorced from the font of her spiritual power, the Declaration. When this religious origin is seriously considered, it is only "natural that the first paragraph of the Declaration of Independence should open with a reference to Nature's God and should close in the final paragraphs with an appeal to the Supreme Judge of the world and an assertion of a firm reliance on Divine Providence." It is only natural because man is, at base, a spiritual creature who wants to live in harmony with God's laws. That spiritual impulse is never eradicated:

Something in all human beings makes them want to do the right thing. Not that this desire always prevails; oftentimes it is overcome and they turn toward evil. But some power is constantly calling them back. Ever there comes a resistance to wrongdoing. When bad conditions [begin] to accumulate, when the forces of darkness become prevalent, always they are ultimately doomed to fail, as the better angels of human nature are roused to resistance.[80]

The people need "reverence," however, for it is "the beginning of a proper conception of ourselves, of our relationship to each other, and our relationship to our Creator. Human nature cannot develop very far without it." There was no progress without God and no government without his hand, Coolidge insisted, and even a cursory examination of American government revealed that

> [the Founders] did not deny the existence of authority. They recognized it and undertook to abide by it, and through obedience to it secure their freedom. They made their appeal and rested their cause not merely upon earthly authority, but in the very first paragraph of the Declaration of Independence asserted that they proposed "to assume, among the powers of the earth, the separate and equal station to which the laws of nature and of nature's God entitle them."

But leadership required loyalty to His self-evident truths and a willingness to affirm that loyalty. Coolidge knew this well:

> When finally our Constitution was adopted, it contained specific provision that the President and members of the Congress and of state legislatures, and all executive and judicial officials, should be qualified for the discharge of their office by oath or affirmation. By the statute law of the United States, and I doubt not by all States, such oaths are administered by a solemn appeal to God for help in the keeping of their covenants.[81]

In contrast to Coolidge, Wilson had once written: "If you want to understand the real Declaration of Independence, do not read the preface," meaning the opening paragraph with its affirmations that all men are created equal. "The Declaration expressly leaves to each generation of men the determination of what they will do with their lives," wrote the political scientist turned politician. "In brief, political liberty is the right of those who are governed to adjust the government to their own needs and interests."[82] In Wilson's view, each generation could make and unmake governments as it saw fit.

Coolidge did not believe that the new social-science framework promoted by Wilson represented new principles capable of shaping a worthy politics; nor did he want a new politics. The first speech Coolidge placed in *Foundations of the Republic* was a proclamation issued after Wilson's death on February 3, 1924. In it, he gently responded to the Wilsonian brand of new politics. Wilson had admittedly "left his impress upon the intellectual thought of the country," but it was not altogether clear that his views would or should remain influential, Coolidge said. Coolidge's entire collection of speeches in the *Foundations* volume, especially because it begins with Wilson's death and ends with the sesquicentennial address on the Declaration, may be seen as a thinly veiled rebuttal to the theory and politics of Progressivism. The question perhaps implicit in the collection is this: Now that Wilson has passed from the scene, what ought to replace him?

Coolidge did not doubt that Wilson "was moved by an earnest desire to promote the best interests of the country as he conceived them." His "acts were prompted by high motives and his sincerity of purpose can not be questioned." Coolidge did not point out, though, that the Harding-Coolidge ticket had questioned Wilson's motives a few years before, in 1920, by promising a "return to normalcy," suggesting that Wilson's governance was anything but normal. We can also see a course correction to a major aspect of Wilson's presidency, its violations of civil liberties, in Coolidge's decision to issue pardons to all thirty-one "political prisoners" (as the press frankly called them) found guilty of violating Wilson's Sedition Act.[83]

Coolidge challenged Wilson's legacy most directly by rejecting his views on the presidency as both unconstitutional and ill advised. Wilson had set forth a concept of the president as a man who would rise above his fellow men to become a "spokesman for the real sentiment and purpose of the country." He thought Americans needed a president who would "seem to the country in some sort of an embodiment of the character and purpose it wishes its government to have – a man who understood his own day and the needs of his country."[84] Coolidge, out of reverence for the Constitution, veered away from this view of the president as a superior being. He saw to it that Wilson's experiments, which were grounded on a "false premise," would get needed correction. As Coolidge told the Associated Industries Dinner in Boston on December 15, 1916, all of this questioning of how we ought to live had been not only tedious, but also destructive of the nation's purpose:

> During the past few years we have questioned the soundness of many principles that had for a long time been taken for granted. . . . We have debated again the theories of the men who wrote the Declaration of Independence, the Constitution of the Nation, and laid down the fundamental law of our own Commonwealth. Along with this examination of our form of government has gone an examination of our social, industrial, and economic system. What is to come out of it all?[85]

Nothing good, it seemed, and indeed something downright sinister if people followed Wilson's line of thought to completion. Wilson went well beyond the Founders' belief in government by intelligent and honorable representatives and presidents. He believed that one man, the president, should direct the national conversation that led to legislation – in essence, that the president should tell people what to think.

This was not Coolidge's belief, nor was it in any sense his way. He was a president who maintained a profound sense of humility, a republican in both temperament and philosophy. Regarding the "consent of the governed," he writes:

> It is from that source [that] our Government derives its just powers and promulgates its righteous laws. They are the will of the people, the settled conviction derived from orderly deliberation, that take on the sanctity ascribed to the people's voice.[86]

If followed, the people's voice, codified into law and expressed through representatives, contributes mightily to human civilization and flourishing. As he said in his speech in Daniel Webster's home in

1916, the Declaration "was, indeed, a great document," ranking among mankind's best. It had, he noted, been "drawn up by Thomas Jefferson when he was at his best."

> It was a product of men who seemed inspired. No greater company ever assembled to interpret the voice of the people or direct the destinies of a nation. The events of history may have added to it, but subtracted nothing. . . . It stands with ordinance and law, charter and constitution, prophecy and revelation, whether we read them in the history of Babylon, the results of Runnymede, the Ten Commandments, or the Sermon on the Mount.[87]

As in the Old Testament, however, the people of the Covenant must keep their end of the bargain or lose God's protection. Coolidge noted:

> It seems to me perfectly plain that the authority of law, the right to equality, liberty and property, under American institutions, have for their foundation reverence for God. If we could imagine that to be swept away, these institutions of our American government could not long survive.[88]

Whereas Woodrow Wilson sought to read Nature's God out of the Declaration – and hence out of political life – entirely, Coolidge sought to put him back in. America was the fulfillment of God's promise. The Declaration was a promissory note and a covenant with the American people. So long as they clung to its truth, the system would endure. The Declaration and the self-evident truths behind it bind all Americans together in a common race.

Lincoln had also known this to be true, which was why in his pre–Civil War speech in Chicago, he appealed to the Declaration. Those who cannot trace their heritage back to the Revolutionary era could appeal to America's founding document:

They have a right to claim it as though they were blood of the blood, and flesh of the flesh, of the men who wrote that Declaration – and so they are. That is the electric cord in that Declaration that links the hearts of patriotic and liberty-loving men together, that will link those patriotic hearts as long as the love of freedom exists in the minds of men throughout the world.

Coolidge used the Declaration as Lincoln had – to remind Americans of their shared spiritual principles and to make a political appeal to the nation. This emphasis on the Declaration is what makes Coolidge unique among American progressives: He wanted his progressivism to have at its core a natural equality, grounded in reason and consecrated with the blood of American patriots such as Lincoln and the patriots of the Revolutionary generation. He was like Lincoln also in that he "never had a feeling politically that did not spring from the sentiments embodied in the Declaration."[89] Coolidge, it seems, never had a political thought that veered far from Lincoln – the statesman who, he said, "wrought out" an "all-embracing freedom."[90]

Lincoln and Coolidge

Coolidge celebrated those who put their faith in God's plan as they accomplished great things. Eagerly and often, he singled out Civil War veterans and thanked them for preserving the Union. At a ceremony in Pennsylvania honoring Major General George Meade, of Gettysburg fame, Coolidge approvingly cited his deep religious convictions:

When [Meade] entered the service he said, "I go into the field . . . trusting to God to dispose of my life and actions in accordance with my daily prayer that His will, not mine, shall be done." Throughout his entire military career he constantly acted in harmony with that sentiment. Time and again, in his letters and statements, he acknowledged his dependence upon Divine Providence.[91]

Coolidge noted that Lincoln, long an agnostic, eventually called on God to preserve the nation by pointing Americans toward a common understanding of their mutual duties. At a Lincoln birthday event in Springfield, Illinois, on February 12, 1922, Coolidge quoted a letter from Lincoln to a friend, in which he wrote: "Can we, as a nation, continue permanently – forever – half slave and half free? The problem is too mighty for me – may God in His mercy superintend the solution." "It was Lincoln who pointed out that both sides prayed to the same God," Coolidge reminded an audience at the dedication for the Confederate Memorial at Arlington National Cemetery.[92] Since they worshipped the same God, it was "only a matter of time" when the two sides would "seek a common end." That end had been revealed: "It is the maintenance of our American form of government, of our American institutions, of our American ideals, beneath a common flag, under the blessings of Almighty God."[93] Lincoln, too, revered the founding, "pondered over the dangers which were incurred by the men who . . . framed and adopted that Declaration of Independence," and believed that the Founders still had wisdom to teach.

Lincoln appears often in Coolidge's political thought, and a number of contemporary commentators saw Coolidge as the political successor to the first Republican President. He is not a second Lincoln, though some in his day praised him as one. Frank W. Stearns appears to have made the comparison earlier than most. In a letter on January 10, 1916, he told a friend that Coolidge was the "political heir of American Lincoln."[94] Stearns later considered that Coolidge belonged in the same company as Washington and Lincoln, though he confessed that he was "not sane on the subject."[95] That some recognized Lincoln, an Illinois backwoodsman who aspired to greatness, in Coolidge, a Vermont backwoodsman who aspired to greatness, should come as no surprise. After all, candidates often claim (as do their supporters) that they are the second coming of the last venerated candidate who came before them.

Still, the Coolidge-Dawes campaign of 1924 explicitly invoked the Lincolnesque qualities of Coolidge and incorporated memories of Lincoln and the Civil War in its message. The five-thousand-mile "Coolidge-Dawes Lincoln Tour" left from Coolidge's hometown of Plymouth Notch and set out on "the great Lincoln Highway" with the express purpose of "acquainting the voters of the country with the Calvin Coolidge" whom his supporters knew and admired. Before they left, President Coolidge presented his campaigners with a book of names of Civil War veterans from Plymouth Notch that he had collected as a boy. He requested that the caravan, wherever it stopped, write down the names of veterans who had voted for Lincoln so that he might register them. Before the group reached Indiana, so many such voters had enrolled that another volume was added. Coolidge was reminding the veterans that he was the political heir to Lincoln, as the newspapers understood, running headlines such as: "Coolidge Appeals for Support of Principles of Lincoln," "Classmates Liken Coolidge to Lincoln," "Will Address Lincoln Birthday Dinner," and "Coolidge Declared of Same Caliber as Lincoln."[96]

Although Coolidge never did become a second Lincoln (Stearns, the newspapermen, and the Coolidge-Dawes campaign notwithstanding), he was perhaps the finest interpreter of Lincoln of his generation. A preface he wrote to a short book on Lincoln shows that he found something admirably democratic in the sixteenth president's humble origins:

> When Americans cease to admire Abraham Lincoln the Union which he perpetuated will be no more. The strongest proof of the continued power of Lincoln's legacy is the ceaseless publication of books about him. His greatness increases with each exploration. It has not been bounded. The authority of his words grows with time. He spoke and lived the truth.
>
> The practice of canonization is inherent in the human mind. Men of the past grow into giants, history takes the form of the good old days, all deeds become heroic. This has advantage, it is inspiring; but it is not human experience, and it is not true. There is too much written of what men think of Lincoln

in proportion to that which tells [us instead] what he was. He does not need to be glorified. That but degrades. To idealize him destroys him. The greatest inspiration his life can give is in the whole truth about him. Leave him as he is. He came from the soil, he was born of the people, he lived their life. To make it all heroic, like giving him drawing-room airs, destroys the mighty strength of his example.[97]

Coolidge well understood the great success of Lincoln and the timeless quality of his sacrifice: "In him is revealed our ideal, the hope of our country fulfilled."[98] In his Lincoln Day Proclamation of 1920, Coolidge spoke of Lincoln as one might speak of Christ:

Divine Providence . . . sent into the world a new life, destined to save a nation. No star, no sign, foretold his coming. About his cradle all was poor and mean save only the source of all great men, the love of a wonderful woman. . . . There can be no proper observance of a birthday which forgets the mother.

Coolidge, too, had lost a mother at a young age. He knew that the illness or death of a mother changes a young man, even if it might also help make him great.

In wisdom great, but humility greater, in justice strong, but in compassion stronger, he became a leader of men by being a follower of truth. He overcame evil with good. His presence filled the Nation. He broke the might of oppression. He restored a race to its birthright.[99]

But most of all, Lincoln kept his faith in America, God, and the nation's true "political religion." He urged his fellow citizens in the Cooper Union address of 1860: "Let us have faith that right makes might, and in that faith, let us, to the end, dare to do our duty as we understand it." That was, of course, the best he could do. Right and might will never be one and the same – the best that we can do is work to make it so and pray that luck ("faith") is on our side. And so Lincoln appealed to the "better angels of our nature" – to our American political religion – against both mob rule and dictatorship.

America's civil religion saved her from the seduction of glory or bloodlust. Americans, Coolidge reminded an audience at Arlington, have "not sought military glory." The only wars they fought were for "the purpose of securing conditions under which peace would be more permanent, liberty would be more secure, and justice would be more certain."[100] But America's civic religion needed to be taught, and it was increasingly clear to Coolidge that America's colleges, founded on religious truths, had started to go awry. Progressivism, with its ceaseless indictment and diminution of fundamental principles, had been a phenomenon of the universities and was starting to have a corrosive effect on the nation's civic life because few sought to check its false premises. Coolidge was among a small number of prominent Americans who did.

CHAPTER FIVE

"I Thought I Could Swing It"

Energy in the Executive Office

It is difficult for men in high office to avoid the malady of self-delusion. They are surrounded by worshippers. . . . They live in an artificial atmosphere of adulation and exaltation, which sooner or later impairs their judgment. They are in grave danger of becoming arrogant or careless.[1]

He who gives license to his tongue only discloses the content of his own mind. By the excess of words he proclaims his lack of discipline. By his very violence he shows his weakness.[2]

The words of the President have an enormous weight and ought not to be used indiscriminately.[3]

Those who believe in reincarnation may well see that in the thin and ascetic body of Calvin Coolidge is the austere and silent soul of George Washington. With him there is no compromise, no weakness. When one speaks to him of rights he answers duty. When one speaks to him of pleasure he answers work. Public life is for him a sacred ceremony and the statesman is priest. He knows only one law, that of the public good.[4]

P RESIDENT COOLIDGE's capacious understanding of the powers of the presidency saved him from being a mere time-server when, on August 3, 1923, he ascended to the office upon the death of President Harding. Portrait painter Charles Hopkinson had asked Coolidge what his first thought was when he learned that Harding had died. "I thought I could swing it," he replied.[5] The Republican Party was then reeling from the bribery scandal of Teapot Dome and from the largest midterm defeat of any political party in the twentieth century. The party was badly depleted in Washington, having lost seventy-seven seats in the House and seven in the Senate in the elections of 1922. In such a political environment, it seemed as if the presidency itself was well within the Democrats' grasp. One Democratic senator suggested that it was "not so much whether the Republican Party will be defeated as to whether it will survive."[6] The *New York Times* noted that the Republican majority had "practically disappeared," with control of the Senate "in the balance."[7] Though Republicans still held control of both chambers, their caucus was deeply divided between its Progressive and traditional wings – and neither side cared much for Coolidge.

Progressive Republicans especially thought little of him, enamored as they were of Senators Hiram Johnson of California and Robert La Follette of Wisconsin, and Governor Gifford Pinchot of Pennsylvania. Even before Harding's illness and death, there had been a movement among them in April 1923 to replace Coolidge as presidential nominee the following year.[8] The strain on Coolidge began on his first day as president. The day Coolidge took office, the *Times* warned: "Alignments within the Republican Party have become all awry. The national convention, which will assemble in September of 1924, will not be a ratification meeting . . . it will be the scene of a stupendous battle in which every element of the party will take part."[9] Senator Peter Norbeck of South Dakota said flatly that Coolidge could "no more run this big machine at Washington than could a paralytic."[10] In September, Secretary of Commerce Herbert Hoover – perhaps suggesting himself, a can-do businessman, in his place – dismissed Coolidge as "not a man to start a corporation."[11] Still, William Howard Taft, the former president, disagreed. Taft wrote to his brother on February 16, 1924, praising Coolidge for the "quickness with which he acts, the hardheadedness that he displays and the confidence he is stirring in the people."[12] In short order, Coolidge became "one of the most popular presidents in history,"[13] making, as a critic put it, something of a "fetish of honesty and propriety."[14]

At root, these criticisms resulted from what has proved to be a lasting misunderstanding of what the president must be – a view that still predominates in Americans' conception of the office. We are often told that we need a president who will "run America like a business," or that we need outsiders who can "shake up Washington" or overturn the "system." These slogans dangerously misrepresent the president's proper role, which is not to treat citizens as shareholders or customers or subjects, but as members of a republic, partners in self-government. The CEO is beholden to shareholders; the president is first among equals. This insight requires that the president direct Americans' attention toward a common good and a public morality. It means that the first duty of the president or any statesman is to teach his fellow citizens. Coolidge, as noted previously, could be an effective teacher despite his reserved manner and humility, because he was a perennial student of the Constitution, *The Federalist*, and executive power. His political philosophy, as he showed in his conduct while president and also in his speeches and writings, was a conscious rediscovery of Publius's political science in the *Federalist Papers* and a rejection of Woodrow Wilson's.[15]

Part of what allows a president to become an effective teacher is the ability to shape public opinion indirectly, often through the "power of initiation," – a president can initiate either action or public understanding by communicating with voters (and with the government) through the media. In this task, Coolidge – contrary to his later reputation – was a master. He held, for example, a then-record number of press conferences, 7.8 per month on average. He also used radio, then a brand-new technology, to present his ideas to the public, which loved his radio addresses. According to Senator James E. Watson, who recounted it in his memoirs, Coolidge told him on the *Mayflower* that the advent of radio had been a godsend: "I am very fortunate that I came in with radio. I can't make an engaging, rousing, or oratorical speech to a crowd . . . and so all I can do is stand up and talk to them in a matter-of-fact way about the issues of my campaign; but I have a good radio voice, and now I can get my messages across to them without acquainting them with my lack of oratorical ability or without making any rhetorical display in their presence."[16] Technology increased Coolidge's ability to reach the people. He was the first president to deliver a speech by radio, the first to make use of loud speakers, and the first to appear on a film with sound.

He also knew when to keep silent, a practice that was a tactic as well as a habit. He clung to his old maxim: "They can't hang you for what you don't say."[17] Although not even U.S. senators could usually get a comment out of Coolidge, one prominent journalist tried his luck. When he insisted that Coolidge grant him an exclusive interview, the president finally relented, but he responded to each question with "no comment." When the journalist finished, Coolidge bid him adieu, telling him, "By the way, don't quote me."[18] That dry wit when dealing with the press served him well and even endeared him to some of them. As early as his first official press conference, he earned the "hearty applause" of the "boys," as he called the press. In his 1924 campaign, he joked about what had become his trademark silence: "I don't recall any candidate for President that ever injured himself very much by not talking."[19] Though often compared to a "sphinx," Coolidge, in his silence, communicated exactly what he intended.[20] "He was logical in his theory of the value of silence," wrote John Hammond, the mining engineer and Coolidge confidant, recalling Coolidge's "brilliant flashes of silence."[21]

Upon Harding's death, Coolidge refused repeated requests to make a speech about his own policies until the late president was interred, much to the disappointment of newspapermen who wanted to get him on record. In fact, he would outline no legislative agenda at all (and did not) until he spoke before Congress in December. He explicitly instructed the postmaster general to "continue right along in the same old way"[22] and implicitly gave much the same advice to other members of the cabinet. In avoiding the limelight, Coolidge assured that there would be ample press coverage when he did present his agenda eventually. The *New York Times* editorialized that the policy address, when it came, promised to put Coolidge on the political map – "See the Message as Party Platform" was the *Times*'s headline.[23]

In limiting his words to create a positive effect, Coolidge showed he understood the importance of public opinion. Indeed, he shared the view of Lord Bryce, one of his favorite thinkers, that American was governed by public opinion.[24] Coolidge was a careful reader of Bryce's *American Commonwealth*, and Bryce's belief that "great men" could not be president may have made a strong impression on Coolidge. He later wrote in his autobiography, in a passage that has since become famous, that he did not consider himself a "great man."

> When the events of August, 1923, bestowed upon me the Presidential office, I felt at once that power had been given to me to administer it. This was not any feeling of exclusiveness. When I felt qualified to serve, I was well aware that there were many others who were better qualified. It would be my providence to get the benefit of their opinion and advice. It is a great advantage to a President, and a major source of safety to the country, for him to know that he not is a great man. When a man begins to feel that he is the only one who can lead in his republic, he is guilty of treason to the spirit of our institutions.

Coolidge was paying his old history Professor, Anson D. Morse, a compliment as well. The Whiggish Morse believed that a good leader could help the people grow, that he could become the means by which "the crude first thoughts and blind first feelings of the people" are "transformed into rational thinking and feeling," and thus "public opinion."[25] Coolidge believed the chief executive should influence the public, and in this he was like Wilson, but he rejected Wilson's ideal of a president who led the nation, through public opinion, into radical new policies.

Of course, Coolidge's studied silence and self-effacement were also careful rhetoric and good politics: Great or high-profile men often have great adversaries – and great adversaries tend to distract from accomplishing a presidential agenda, especially if that agenda is, as it was with Coolidge, a modest one. As a governor, he had learned "adequate brevity."[26] As president, he mastered it.[27]

In his first message to the American people, he mourned Harding's death, asked the help of the country and God, and promised to continue the Harding policies wherever possible.[28] "Whatever his [Harding's] policies were are my policies," he reassured at the first of his many press conferences. He asked Hoover, Mellon, and Hughes to stay on as secretary of commerce, secretary of the treasury, and secretary of state, but he set about putting his own mark on the presidency. He moved quickly, and in the short space of a week the veteran correspondent Clinton Gilbert noted, "The only things there were in common [between] Mr. Coolidge, the vice president, and Mr. Coolidge, the president, was his name."[29] As vice president, he listened; as president, he led.

President Coolidge avoided the usual agenda-driven style of Washington politics. Owing to his "general disdain for programmatic initiatives,"[30] he preferred letting Congress go its own way when it wanted, although he was quick to get it in line when he thought necessary, ably using the bully pulpit and the press.[31] He gave 520 press conferences during his five and half years in office and used the press expertly: "Sometimes I made an appeal direct to the country by stating my position at the newspaper conferences. I adopted that course in relation to the Mississippi Flood Control Bill. . . . The press began a vigorous discussion of the subject, which caused the House greatly to modify the [Senate] bill, and in conference a measure that was entirely fair and moderate was adopted."[32]

With no real legislative program of his own, Coolidge told the truth when he later said he "never felt it was my duty to attempt to coerce Senators or Representatives, or to make reprisals" – and yet he got much of what he wanted passed by taking a long view. Most of the policies he advocated in his first annual message "have become law," he said in 1929, although "it took several years to get action on some of them." Perhaps these successes owed to his understanding of the virtues of a deliberative body, which he elaborated upon in his

autobiography: "About a dozen able, courageous, reliable and experienced men in the House and the Senate can reduce the problem of
legislation almost to a vanishing point."[33]

Coolidge preferred using his veto pen – or the threat of it – to direct
policy. In this, he harked back to an earlier notion of the president, a
view that the president should not diminish the office by wheeling and
dealing, as the bloviating Harding or the hectoring Wilson had done.
Besides, Coolidge had gotten elected governor of Massachusetts while
avoiding a specific, well-defined agenda and presumably saw no reason
to break with that successful pattern.[34] He thought a legislature's role
was to legislate, while his job as chief executive was to execute – and
this became his sole agenda. As he told Congress in his first annual
message on December 6, 1923, he viewed enforcing the law as a spiritual matter:

> The law represents the voice of the people. Behind it, and sup-
> porting it, is a divine sanction. Enforcement of law and obedi-
> ence to law, by the very nature of our institutions, are not
> matters of choice in this republic, but the expression of a
> moral requirement of living in accordance with truth. They
> are clothed with a spiritual significance, in which is revealed
> the life or death of the American ideal of self-government.[35]

Executing his office proved difficult, however, because congressional power seemed ascendant. To truly become president in his
own right, Coolidge had to defend the presidency from its congressional foes and from opportunistic opponents within the party. Some
of these foes were ideologically opposed to Coolidge's agenda; others
believed strongly in legislative supremacy. Forces were at work that
sought to redefine the presidency itself. Republican senator Albert B.
Cummins of Iowa, president pro tempore of the Senate and twice a
presidential contender, favored a constitutional amendment limiting
the president to one term only. He couched his proposal in terms
of concern for the executive's health, but it was a clear threat to

presidential prerogative. The senator effectively wanted to gut the presidency[36] – even before the Teapot Dome scandal became a household name.

*   *   *

Coolidge defended the presidency in this initially difficult environment through a series of decisions that underscored his robust understanding of its rightful powers. In the wake of Teapot Dome, he knew he needed to defend the office against congressional assaults. His full-throated belief in what constitutional scholars call the "unitary executive" guaranteed that his administration had one of the key virtues of successful executives as cited by Publius in the *Federalist Papers*: energy.

Coolidge's administration, for example, was energetic in jealously guarding presidential power against the growing administrative state. It zealously sought presidential control of the bureaucracy, repeatedly pursuing its case on this question all the way to the Supreme Court. On behalf of his administration, Coolidge used seemingly every power at his disposal – pardons,[37] vetoes,[38] executive orders,[39] and removal – in order to assert his control of the executive branch and guarantee its unity, another essential quality of successful administrations. Relying on his shrewdness and his understanding of the Constitution, Coolidge became one of the greatest wielders and interpreters of executive power.

This is all the more remarkable given that he was not initially elected president, he carried out his predecessor's policies to a great extent, and he inherited and retained Harding's main officials. In his autobiography, he readily conceded that he may not have been the best person for the presidency, but he felt that God was acting through him and that the institution of the presidency directed him.[40] In 1924, not much more than a year into his presidency, he was rewarded with the largest popular vote for a Republican up to that time.[41] This political success owes much to the fact that he applied constitutional guidelines to the workings of the Oval Office: It worked politically, not just on the merits. As an accidental president, he came to office with the disadvantage of having no popular mandate; in such a seemingly weak position, he used the powers of the presidency to keep Congress from running roughshod over him.

Coolidge's successes owe much to Chief Justice William Howard Taft, who expanded or favorably clarified the powers of the president in a series of important Supreme Court decisions. Taft, the only president who became a Supreme Court justice, probably empathized with the new president and wished to guard him from his congressional foes. Though Taft wore robes, he never lost his presidential spectacles. The affinity went two ways, because Coolidge was described as "almost as judicial as Bill Taft" in his temperament. Some speculated that Coolidge belonged on the Supreme Court, not in the Oval Office.[42]

* * *

In becoming a strong executive, Coolidge also benefited from Harding's decision to give him more rein than previous vice presidents had enjoyed. On the campaign trail, Harding had promised that Coolidge would be the first vice president to sit in on cabinet meetings, an experience that proved invaluable to Coolidge.[43] As vice president, he also had the opportunity to "think his way through some of the great principles of the American government and American civilization," in the words of biographer Robert Woods.[44] He was widely respected in Washington. The *New-York Tribune*, for instance, recommended that "the way to end for all time the naming of a Vice-President of mediocre ability is precisely by giving Mr. Coolidge room for his ability"[45] Perhaps Harding hoped Coolidge might be a co-president. Harding had, after all, admitted that he wasn't up to the task of being president, remarking to Nicholas Murray Butler, president of Columbia University, "I am not fit for this office and should never have been here."[46]

Coolidge, in contrast, seemed born to fill that role. Although he later expressed grave doubts as to whether he was "qualified to fill the exalted office of President," he said when Harding died that he "felt at once that power had been given" to him by God.[47] The *New York Times* noted the transformation: "The growth of Mr. Coolidge from a colorless Vice-President into the fame which is already attached to his name in the presidency, is one of the human and political marvels of our time."[48] Secretary of State Hughes would also remark upon the change from Harding to Coolidge. In his autobiography, Hughes wrote:

> President Harding's keen desire to please and his accessibility to all sorts of visitors made his days especially arduous. Visiting the Executive Office, I usually found his Secretary's room filled with persons seeking an audience, and when I was slipped in, so that I should not be kept waiting, he would often put his arms across my shoulders and exclaim, "Hughes, this is the damnedest job!"
>
> There was a marked change when Mr. Coolidge became President. As he was taciturn and non-committal, visitors got little advantage from a personal interview and were generally content with a word with his Secretary. Such appointments as he had he could dispose of in the morning. So that when in the afternoon I would take my telegrams or proposals over to the Executive Office, I would find the President alone, smoking a cigar and reading his papers in an atmosphere of quiet and relaxation.[49]

After two and a half years of sitting in on cabinet meetings, Coolidge knew which cabinet officers were trustworthy – and which were not. Coolidge later commented on that education in his autobiography:

> If the Vice-President is a man of discretion and character, so that he can be relied upon to act as a subordinate in such position, he should be invited to sit with the Cabinet, although some of the Senators, wishing to be only the advisers of the President, do not look on that proposal with favor. He may not

help much in its deliberations, and only on rare occasions would he be a useful contact with the Congress, although his advice on the sentiment of the Senate is of much value, but he should be in the Cabinet because he might become President and ought to be informed on the policies of the administration. He will not learn of all of them. Much went on in the departments under President Harding, as it did under me, of which the Cabinet had no knowledge. But he will hear much and learn how to find out more if it ever becomes necessary. My experience in the Cabinet was of supreme value to me when I became President.[50]

While the experience was "of supreme value," Coolidge never had any doubt that the president retained control and that the vice president, despite his knowledge of the Senate, was there by invitation only. Seated in the cabinet meetings, Coolidge learned of the policies of the administration and defended them in his stump speeches as vice president (which he later collected for his second volume of addresses, *The Price of Freedom*). Having made the case for those policies on his own, Coolidge could more willingly retain them and more easily maintain political continuity after Harding's death. He issued a proclamation promising "no sweeping displacement of the men then in office and . . . no violent changes in the administration of affairs."[51] Coolidge disdained change for its own sake. So long as Harding's officers agreed with his policies, he kept them in place.[52]

He also disdained an activist approach to the presidency. "Perhaps one of the most important accomplishments of my administration has been the minding of my own business," he told a gathering of the press after he had left office.[53] But while libertarians and others have seized upon that quotation as indicative of Coolidge's laissez-faire approach, in truth, by "business" Coolidge probably meant executive affairs. The chief business of America was business, but the business of the executive was, in Coolidge's view, to execute the laws. And contrary to what today's libertarians or politicos sometimes claim about him, he was a quick and decisive executive who seemed minimalist mainly because he knew how to ration his actions. "In order to function at all," he warned future presidents, the president "has to be surrounded by many safeguards." If these were to be "removed for only a short time," the President "would be overwhelmed by the people who would surge in upon him."[54] Even so, Coolidge remained keenly aware of a president's limits, knowing that a president must understand that he was "only in the clutch of forces that are greater" than himself, as he wrote his father on New Year's Day, 1926.

Scholars Steven G. Calabresi and Christopher Yoo focus on Coolidge's defense of the president's prerogatives in their 2008 book on the unitary executive. "The degree of influence [Coolidge] exerted over the independent agencies indicates that he envisioned them as being subject to his will," they contend. He believed that the Federal Trade Commission and other commissions "'should subordinate their judgment to the opinions of the Executive' and that 'they properly were mere agencies to register the policies of the administration.'" Perhaps showing his contempt for excessive bureaucratic power, Coolidge appointed to the commission an attorney who had once described the FTC as "an instrument of oppression" against the lumber industry.[55]

In open hostility to the prevailing Progressive notion that bureaucratic administration of the law must be disinterested, Coolidge aligned the bureaucracy with his administration's interests. He sought outright control of the independent agencies by, for example, altering the policies of the Federal Reserve and the U.S. Shipping Board. The Shipping Board dutifully trimmed itself into irrelevancy, selling off 104 vessels to private operators for one-tenth of their cost.[56] On the Tariff Commission, Coolidge removed one commissioner, appointed another to an ambassadorship, and drove a third to resign, all to create his protectionist majority. To guarantee compliance with his administration, he required that all commissioners submit signed and undated letters of resignation before appointment.

This last bit was cleverly practical. Coolidge understood that the president embodies popular opinion and that every care must be taken to insulate him from scandal. If, as the saying goes today, "mistakes were made," Coolidge would see to it that heads rolled.

> The president can't resign. If a member of the cabinet makes a mistake and destroys his standing with the country, he can get out, or the president can ask him to get out. But if he has involved the president in the mistake, the president has to stay there to the end of his term, and to that extent that the people's faith in their government has been diminished. So I constantly said to my cabinet: "There are many things you gentlemen must not tell me. If you blunder, you can leave, or I can invite you to leave. But if you draw me into all your department decisions and something goes wrong, I must stay here. And by involving me you have lowered the faith of the people in their government.[57]

Here Coolidge was surely rebuking his predecessor's cozy relations with administrators and lobbyists. As the nation learned after the Teapot Dome scandal, President Harding's personal failings had political consequences.

Faith in government was what Coolidge tried to restore – and with alacrity – after Teapot Dome. He gave the Congress the illusion of control by appointing two theoretically independent special prosecutors, one a Republican and one a Democrat, to investigate the mishandling of the scandal. It was a political gesture, not a constitutional one, and Coolidge's post-midnight statement, quoted in the *New York Times* on January 27, 1924, underlined this critical point by making clear that he was appointing the counsels to carry out one specific task: investigate malfeasance. This would not be a special-counsel show trial such as we've come to know in recent years.

Coolidge's special counsels were the first – and to date only – special counsels appointed by the Senate, which confirms that he accomplished what he wanted: a faithful enforcement of the law, without hands-on involvement by the presidency. Coolidge, unlike other presidents facing special counsels, had little to lose with two special counsels traipsing about, because there was no way any part of the investigation would reflect poorly on him. Coolidge, after all, had no connection at all with Teapot Dome. In fact, the investigation would serve as a perfect way of discerning which Harding cabinet members to retain. His statement to the *Times* does not read as if it were written by a president willing to diminish himself. Coolidge was seeking, rather, to execute the law and avoid the appearance of impropriety that would come from acting as both judge and jury.

It is not for the President to determine criminal guilt or render judgment in civil causes. . . . Acting under my direction the Department of Justice has been observing the course of the evidence which has been revealed at the hearings conducted by the senatorial committee investigating certain oil leases made on naval reserves, which I believe warrants action for the purpose of enforcing the law and protecting the rights of the public. This is confirmed by reports made to me from the committee. If there has been any crime, it must be prosecuted. If there has been any property of the United States illegally transferred or leased, it must be recovered.

I feel the public is entitled to know that in the conduct of such action, no one is shielded for any party, political or other reason. As I understand, men are involved who belong to both political parties, and having been advised by the Department of Justice that it is in accord with the former precedents, I propose to employ special counsel of high rank drawn from both political parties to bring such action for the enforcement of the law. Counsel will be instructed to prosecute these cases in the courts so that if there is any guilt it will be punished; if there is civil liability it will be enforced; if there is any fraud it will be revealed; and if there are any contracts which are illegal they will be canceled. Every law will be enforced. And every right of the people and the Government will be protected.

Coolidge's deft use of the "I" pronoun in this statement reveals his determination to seize the reins. The *New York Times* celebrated his take-charge stance, headlining an article on his response: "President Takes Hold." In response to Coolidge's request that Congress appoint special counsels from each party, the Senate selected former Democratic senator Atlee Pomerene of Ohio and Republican (and later Supreme Court justice) Owen Roberts of Pennsylvania, who set about investigating and prosecuting.

Chief among those they snared was Secretary of the Interior Albert Fall, who had persuaded Harding to issue an executive order that transferred three oil reserves from the Navy to the Interior Department on June 1, 1921. Under existing law, this decision gave the secretary the power to award lucrative leases to the reserves in Elk Hills, California, and Teapot Dome, Wyoming. Fall was then entrusted with the authority to use oil from those leases to provide for the Navy's needs. In an atmosphere of "secrecy," as his critics put it, Fall awarded the California and Wyoming leases respectively to E. L. Doheny, an oil tycoon and his close friend, and Harry F. Sinclair, the noted oil industrialist.

Today we think of Teapot Dome as synonymous with a great scandal, but at the time, Secretary Fall's move elicited little criticism.[58] Indeed, it received accolades from the *New York Times*, which complimented him for protecting the oil reserves against the severe drainage and disrepair that befell them during the Wilson years.[59] By putting the oil reserves under the control of the Interior Department, Fall, a former senator from New Mexico, insured they would be properly developed. What made for good policy, alas, did not make for good politics. Fall inadvertently started a political fight that he could not have foreseen, but in which he alone would be the unwitting victim.[60] (Found guilty of bribery in 1929, Fall was fined and sentenced to a year in prison. He became the first presidential cabinet member to be incarcerated for actions performed in office.)

Progressive politicians who supported the Wilson administration's policies on the oil lands were up in arms about Fall's proposals to reverse them. Among them were Governor Pinchot of Pennsylvania and Senator Robert La Follette of Wisconsin, the nation's most prominent Progressive spokesman after the death of Theodore Roosevelt. La Follette and Pinchot considered themselves true conservationists, and both of them disliked the Harding administration's general policy of rapid development of Western resources, which Fall also supported.[61] Fall's Interior Department had tussled with Pinchot before, and as a result Pinchot deeply distrusted him, noting: "On the record, it would have been possible to pick a worse man for Secretary of the Interior, but not altogether easy."[62] In comments reminiscent of today's debate over opening more of Alaska's northern slope to oil extraction, Pinchot expressed dismay at Interior Department plans to encourage private exploitation of the territory's natural resources.[63]

Both La Follette[64] and Pinchot[65] would be touted as possible Progressive Republican standard-bearers in 1924 over Vice President Coolidge, who was still almost unknown. Pinchot's close friend and former secretary, Harry Slattery, was something of a Progressive muckraking journalist who became counsel to the National Conservation Association (NCA), an organization that Governor Pinchot had founded. Slattery persuaded Senator La Follette to investigate Fall and the Teapot Dome deal and began a publicity campaign against the Interior Department, publishing a series of articles in the *Christian Science Monitor* in 1921.[66] Believing Harding was a weak president and hoping to bully him, the Senate unanimously adopted La Follete's resolution to begin a congressional investigation on April 29, 1922.

Curiously, hearings did not begin until October 22, 1923, several months after President Harding had died. For the Progressives, who loathed Coolidge, this was no accident. The hearings were timed to begin after the new president's honeymoon period and were intended to provoke an intra-Republican contest in 1924. To defeat the president, who had pledged to continue Harding's conservative policies, the Progressive Republicans had to defeat those policies where they had the most ability to do so: in the Senate, where they held the balance of power.[67]

Democrats, also sensing an opportunity in 1924,[68] began to get involved. The young Thomas J. Walsh, a Democrat from Montana, was appointed head of the Senate's own inquiry. But for Democrats, too, the scandal soon proved embarrassing as several prominent figures in the party were ensnared. The oil tycoon Doheny had apparently kept several prominent Democrats on his payroll, including Wilson's Secretary of the Interior, Franklin K. Lane, and William G. McAdoo, Wilson's son-in-law and Secretary of the Treasury. (The revelations abruptly ended McAdoo's rumored bid for the presidency, allowing John W. Davis to become the nominee.)

The press and the hostile Senate quickly pursued Albert Fall, despite scientific evidence in favor of his privatization plan.[69] He was judged unethical for his receipt of some $40,000 in loans[70] from Doheny and Sinclair, despite his insistence that the loans were unrelated to his official duties.[71] His biographer, David Stratton, notes that if Fall were really angling for bribes, he sold out quite cheaply, in view of the fact that the value of the oil-well contract at Teapot Dome alone was worth well over $2 million in 1921 dollars.[72] As another scholar suggests, Fall was guilty of ethical insensitivity more than corruption: "[Fall] displayed extraordinarily bad judgment in embroiling himself with Sinclair and Doheny. . . . Teapot Dome therefore involved a brazen and inexcusable conflict of interest rather than bribery, pure and simple. . . . [P]roblems of public policy were subordinated to political expediency."[73]

Coolidge moved quickly to insulate himself from Fall's faux pas, shifting oil policy from exploitation to conservation. Along the way, he appointed Curtis D. Wilbur as Secretary of the Navy in Edwin Denby's stead. Wilbur, in turn, appointed Commander Nathan W. Wright, a known conservationist, to oversee oil projects. Tactically, this shift made both political and military sense. The urgent need to exploit America's federal oil wells had passed with the end of the war, while a glut of oil, following new discoveries in California and the Gulf of Mexico, made exploitation of federal lands too costly. Indeed, the quickening pace of private oil exploitation on private lands to meet the new automotive demand made the staff of United States Geological Survey worry that the oil supply might be depleted within a decade. So it was only natural that Coolidge, who suspected that the next war would be fought with oil-guzzling aircraft,[74] began to favor conservation. In December 1924, he created the Federal Oil Conservation Board to help guide the nation's oil policy. Meanwhile, the issue had retreated from the public view.

*   *   *

The Senate mistook Coolidge's decision to appoint special Teapot Dome counsels for weakness rather than political cunning. Sensing blood in the water with the imminent downfall of Secretary Fall, the Senate proceeded apace with its own inquiry, led by the Senate Committee on Lands and Public Surveys and targeting Secretary of the Navy Denby and Attorney General Daugherty. Democratic senator Joseph Robinson of Arkansas quickly authored a resolution demanding Denby's resignation. Robinson's resolution passed the Senate on February 11, 1924, and was joined by ten Republicans, making the tally 47 to 34, but Coolidge refused to be cowed. "I do not propose to sacrifice any innocent man for my own welfare, nor do I propose to retain in office any unfit man for my own welfare," he fired back in a statement on February 13, indicating that he would not heed the resolution.[75] He also had Senator Henry Cabot Lodge of Massachusetts enter his objections into the Congressional Record.

Coolidge's statement masterfully defended the president's removal power. He made clear that removal was "exclusively an Executive function," and that he regarded this as "a vital principle of our Government." He then invoked Madison's understanding of the separation of powers, writing:

> In discussing this principle Mr. Madison has well said: "It is laid down in most of the constitutions or bills of rights in the Republics of America; it is to be found in the political writings

of the most celebrated civilians, and is everywhere held as essential to the preservation of liberty that the three great departments of government be kept separate and distinct."[76]

It is important to underscore that Coolidge was quoting from Madison's June 17, 1789, speech on the president's removal powers, delivered during the state debates on the ratification of the federal Constitution. Here again, we see that Coolidge knew his history well.

Next, Coolidge invoked the Democratic president Grover Cleveland, who had himself tussled with those seeking to limit the removal power. Coolidge quoted him warmly:

President Cleveland likewise stated the correct principle in discussing requests and demands made by the Senate upon him and upon different departments of the Government, in which he said: "They assume the right of the Senate to sit in judgment upon the exercise of my exclusive discretion and Executive function, for which I am solely responsible to the people from whom I have so lately received the sacred trust of office. My oath to support and defend the Constitution, my duty to the people who have chosen me to execute the powers of their great office and not to relinquish them, and my duty to the Chief Magistracy, which I must preserve unimpaired in all its dignity and vigor, compel me to refuse compliance with these demands."

Here Coolidge understood that the presidency would be hobbled by senatorial hindsight. By invoking Cleveland, he lent his position bipartisan support.

The President is responsible to the people for his conduct relative to the retention or dismissal of public officials. I assume that responsibility, and the people may be assured that as soon as I can be advised so that I may act with entire justice to all parties concerned and fully protect the public interests I shall act. . . . I shall try to maintain the functions of the Government unimpaired, to act upon the evidence and the law as I find it, and to deal thoroughly and summarily with every kind of wrongdoing.[77]

Congress could advise him, but Coolidge made it clear that it was legitimately his power and his alone to dismiss Secretary Denby, and that he stood ready to defend that power from usurpation. Ultimately, the issue was moot. Although Denby promised to fight it out and went so far as to demand a recorded vote so he could know which senators were "willing to besmirch"[78] his good name, he resigned a week after Coolidge issued his statement,[79] to keep "embarrassments" from mounting against the president.[80] In accepting Denby's letter of resignation, the president was quick to defend his reputation, telling him: "You will go now with the knowledge that your honesty and integrity have not been impugned."[81]

Despite Coolidge's defense of Denby, the Senate was further emboldened. When Fall's physicians declared he was too ill to testify, the inquiry – now looking like a witch hunt – turned to Attorney General Daugherty, a Harding confidant and, as it turned out, the owner of a small amount of Sinclair Oil stock.[82] On January 29, Democratic senator Burton K. Wheeler of Montana introduced a resolution that demanded Daugherty be fired for incompetence in prosecuting the corruption related to Teapot Dome. The resolution had the effect of reigniting the whole scandal once more and threatened to split the party.

Despite earlier advice from prominent Republicans, particularly Senator William Borah of Idaho, advising him to jettison Daugherty, Coolidge had thus far refused. As he wrote to Raymond Robbins, the organized-labor activist:

I will not so remove the attorney general, for two reasons. First, it is a sound rule that when the president dies in office, it is the duty of his successor for the remainder of that term to maintain the counselors and policies of the deceased president. Second, I ask you if there is any man in the cabinet for whom – were he still living – President Harding would more surely demand his day in court, would more surely *not* dismiss because of the popular clamor than the man who was his closest personal and political friend? I am satisfied that you are right, the people would be pleased, the party would be helped, my campaign would be advanced, by the summary removal of Mr. Daugherty. We shall have to bear that burden. Regarding my being afraid to dismiss Mr. Daugherty, I can assure you that if the attorney does any act I regard as wrong while I am president, he will be removed.[83]

Coolidge refused to back down from defending his attorney general publicly, but privately it was another matter entirely. He summoned Senator Borah to explain why he thought the Attorney General ought to be fired. After Borah made his case, Coolidge brought in Daugherty, and the two men, in a contentious hour-long debate, fought it out while Coolidge observed them both in silence, weighing the arguments.[84] Daugherty eventually couldn't take it and stormed from the room, prompting Coolidge to say to Borah, "Senator, I reckon you are right."[85] Firing Daugherty, though, proved politically problematic: He was well-defended by Ohio's Republican senators, who promised that the Buckeye State's substantial electoral vote would go to Coolidge's challenger in 1924 in the general election if Coolidge got rid of him.[86]

Chief Justice Taft, with whom Coolidge often consulted,[87] began to see the whole matter as something akin to the Pinchot–Ballinger affair of his own presidency. (Indeed, he probably suspected that Pinchot, whom he viewed as a Progressive rabble-rouser, was behind this plot as well, as he was behind the Couzens–Mellon controversy, which I shall turn to in a moment.) Taft held that the response to the scandal among Coolidge critics was nothing but a plot to dishonor men of good will – which Daugherty, in Taft's eyes, certainly was. As Harding's confidant, Daugherty had after all helped Taft get appointed to the Supreme Court. Coolidge, meanwhile, described the Republican senators who thought the Teapot Dome investigations had gone too far as "a lot of damned cowards,"[88] as he told Taft. Taft's protestations to the contrary, the tumult soon grew too loud, and Coolidge was forced to respond. Before long, Senator George W. Pepper of Pennsylvania and his fellow Republican colleague Henry Cabot Lodge joined Borah in calling for Daugherty to resign, while Coolidge's cabinet maneuvered to force him out. Fearing the worst, the attorney general offered to resign, telling Coolidge: "If the time comes that you wish my resignation, just put it in writing and give me your reasons."[89]

Senate Democrats sensed that the scandal would keep growing and issued yet another resolution. Introduced by Kenneth McKellar of Tennessee, the resolution asked the administration to provide the Public Lands Committee with all income tax returns of Fall, Doheny, Sinclair, and their attendant companies.[90] Coolidge refused to comply, calling it a violation of the Revenue Act of 1921 and of the proper executive-legislative relationship:

> Whatever may be necessary for the information of the Senate or any of its Committees in order better to enable them to perform their legislative or other constitutional functions ought to always be furnished willingly and expeditiously by any Department [but] the attack which is being made on the Treasury Department goes beyond any of these legitimate requirements [and would damage the] comity between the Executive departments and the Senate."[91]

Coolidge recognized it as "the duty of the Executive to resist such intrusion and to bring to the attention of the Senate its serious consequences."

The Senate committee never secured concrete evidence against Daugherty, who was acquitted twice (although in the second trial, he survived by only a single vote).[92] Democrats perceived the entire administration as corrupt, thanks to the alleged scandal, but Daugherty suffered the most because his patron, Harding, was dead. Among his political enemies, Daugherty was a most sought-after target because he had impressively outmaneuvered Progressive forces to help get Harding the nomination in 1920.[93] But Daugherty wasn't corrupt, at least in a legal sense. Nor was he, as one Democratic senator claimed, a "third-rate Justice of the Peace lawyer."[94] Indeed, he was the sole reason that Coolidge wanted special counsels to investigate Tea Pot Dome in the first place. It was Daugherty's idea. In fact, Coolidge favored him for the job, but Daugherty turned it down.

But the Senate committee did unearth quite a lot about Daugherty – but the shady goings-on reflected personal failings, rather than criminal acts. In the words of one Coolidge biographer, "A fantastic record of questionable transactions, deals, and actions by the Attorney General and his friends was revealed."[95] By the time the Senate was done with him, Daugherty's reputation stood in tatters. He could no longer defend himself against accusations and be a loyal adviser to the president. He had to go, and he couldn't continue claiming executive privilege for all Justice Department files. Coolidge wrote to him on March 27, 1924:

You will see at once that the Committee is investigating your personal conduct, and hence you have become an interested party, and the Committee wants these papers because of a claim that they disclose your personal conduct of the Department. Assuming that the request of the Committee is appropriately limited to the designated files, still the question will always be the same. *In view of the fact that the inquiry relates to your personal conduct, you are not in a position to give to me or the Committee what would be disinterested advice as to the public interest. . . .*

I am not questioning your fairness or integrity. I am merely reciting the fact that you are placed in two positions, one your personal interest, the other your office of Attorney-General, which may be in conflict. How can I satisfy a request for action in matters of this nature on the ground that you, as Attorney-

General, advise against it, when you as the individual against whom the inquiry is directed necessarily have a personal interest in it? I do not see how you can be acting for yourself in your own defense in this matter, and at the same time and on the same question acting as my adviser as Attorney-General.[96]

Daugherty pugnaciously replied:

Your suggestion that an attack upon a cabinet officer disqualifies him from further official service is a dangerous doctrine. Mr. President, all the pretended charges against me are false. But, whether true or false, if a member of the cabinet is to be incapacitated or disqualified by the preferment of charges against him, no matter how malicious and groundless, and he is compelled to give up his responsible position and sacrifice his honor for the time being because of such attacks, no man in any official position is safe, and the most honorable, upright, and efficient public servant could be swept from office and stable government by clamor.[97]

Nevertheless, having made his reservations clear, the attorney general resigned the following day.[98] He returned to Columbus to resume his law practice, but even so, the Senate voted to censure him by a vote of 70 to 2. With the mounting pressure, Daugherty cracked, saying that the files he refused to disclose showed "abundant proof of the plans, purposes, and hellish designs of the Communist International."[99] In any event, the political import was clear: The president believed he must retain control over who served in his administration in order to protect the office, but he also knew that the Senate could, nevertheless, extract its pound of flesh.

It seemed that the Senate inquiries resulting from Teapot Dome would implicate American foreign policy as well. After it came to light that then-Secretary Fall had favored a planned oil treaty with

Colombia, Senator Clarence Dill of Washington introduced two resolutions that hinted at a worldwide oil conspiracy. Senate Resolution
149 requested all correspondence between the U.S. government and
its foreign counterparts related to oil concessions, while Resolution
150 asked Secretary of State Hughes to turn over correspondence in
connection with the ratification of the Colombian agreement and
the securing of American oil interests there. Coolidge rebuffed these
attempts.

Despite his strong belief in the presidency's constitutional prerogatives, Coolidge advocated prudence when it came to separation
of powers. He refused to take sides in any debate over the limits of
the vesting clause, preferring to read it in whatever manner the
immediate situation required, as was the president's right.

> The Constitution specifically vests [the president] with execu-
> tive power. Some Presidents have seemed to interpret that as
> an authorization to take any action which the Constitution, or
> perhaps the law, does not specifically prohibit. Others have
> considered that their powers extended only to such acts as
> were specifically authorized by the Constitution and the stat-
> utes. This has always seemed to me to be a hypothetical ques-
> tion, which it would be idle to determine in advance. It would
> appear to be better practice to wait to decide each question on
> its merits as it arises. . . . For all ordinary occasions, the specific
> powers assigned to the President will be found sufficient to
> provide for the welfare of the country. That is all he needs.[100]

In wielding those powers, Coolidge proved adept.

* * *

Deliberative bodies have a habit of being too deliberative and of
spending too much time on things not needing much attention. It

was when Congress proved unyielding that Coolidge wielded his veto pen most effectively. Coolidge also instituted novel ways of managing Congress. A good example, famous at the time, was his practice of having White House breakfasts with congressmen and senators. He would invite fifteen to twenty-five members of the House and Senate to confer at the White House. The purpose of these breakfasts wasn't readily apparent to Ike Hoover, the White House butler, or even to a biographer who noted the butler's disapproval. However, it appears that Coolidge was studying the legislators. The breakfasts were "to discuss matters of public business" and help build "a spirit of good fellowship" that would make governing a more harmonious affair. Often the president learned a great deal about which issues really mattered to which legislators merely by noting how many congressmen or senators, and which ones, showed up. The fact that some did everything they could to avoid the breakfasts – one lawmaker reportedly stayed out all night and could not be found – suggests that they felt the heat from the man once described as an "eloquent listener."[101] It's clear that Coolidge prided himself on maintaining effective relations with members of Congress. "I always found," he wrote in his autobiography, "members of both parties willing to confer with me and disposed to treat my recommendations fairly."[102]

*   *   *

Coolidge's use of the removal power, bolstered by his confidence in its constitutional propriety, allowed him to prevent Harding's political appointees from working against or complicating his agenda. The threat of removal often proved useful and gave his administration a needed cohesion, which in turn would help him at the nominating convention in 1924.[103] Although Coolidge decided to keep most of the Harding appointees, he defended the president's power to remove an official for any reason whatsoever and instructed his solicitor general to defend *Myers v. United States* (ultimately decided in 1926) in order to put these questions to rest. They succeeded. The Court held that the executive power had the sole power to remove executive-branch officials and need not gain the approval of the Senate or any other legislative body.

Removal power, Coolidge understood, was important because it fostered cohesion and competence, and allowed him to more effectively delegate. In this, he could follow what he would later call, in his autobiography, the "one rule of action more important than all others . . . never doing anything that some one else can do for you." This important rule "should be very strictly followed in order to prevent being so entirely devoted to trifling details that there will be little opportunity to give the necessary consideration to policies of larger importance."[104] In essence, Coolidge was articulating a policy of presidential prioritization.

Of course, this rule had what he called an "important corollary." "It is not sufficient to entrust details to some one else," he wrote. "They must be entrusted to some one who is competent." The president, Coolidge said, must carefully tailor the appointments he makes:

> The Presidency is primarily an executive office. It is a place at the apex of our system of government. It is a place of last resort to which all questions are brought that others have not been able to answer. The ideal way for it to function is to assign to the various positions men of sufficient ability so that they can solve all the problems that arise under their jurisdiction.

But Coolidge also made clear that the buck must stop with the president: "Final judgments are necessarily his own."

> No one can share with him the responsibility for them. No one can make his decisions for him. He stands at the center of things where no one else can stand. If others make mistakes, they can be relieved, and oftentimes a remedy can be provided. But he can not retire. His decisions are final and usually irreparable. This constitutes the appalling burden of his office. Not

only the welfare of 120,000,000 of his countrymen, but oftentimes the peaceful relations of the world are entrusted to his keeping. At the turn of his hand the guns of an enormous fleet would go into action anywhere in the world, carrying the iron might of death and destruction.

The power of appointment "confers the power to administer justice, inflict criminal penalties, declare acts of state legislatures and of the Congress void, and sit in judgment over the very life of the nation." While the Congress "makes the laws, it is the President who causes them to be executed." Such a power is "so vast in its implications" that it "has never been conferred upon any ruling sovereign."[105]

Coolidge knew that the power of appointment and removal is the only means by which the president can affect the growing bureaucracy. With that power, as "head of the government, charged with making appointments, and clothed with the executive power, the President has a certain responsibility for the conduct of all departments, commissions and independent bureaus."[106] This responsibility, Coolidge thought, had been recognized as far back as Jefferson, whose "wisdom" and whose "faith" in the people were part of "his constant insistence that they be left to manage their own affairs." Coolidge followed the Jeffersonian model, finding that Jefferson's "opposition to bureaucracy will bear careful analysis, and the country could stand a great deal more of its application."[107]

Coolidge knew that getting the bureaucracy right would mean nothing less than getting his presidency right. The President had to jealously guard his power because the Constitution and tradition made him "the sole repository of party responsibility." This role presented problems – mistakes at the presidential level would affect the public's perception of the entire party – but it also conferred an advantage. "It is one of the reasons that the Presidential office has grown in popular estimation and favor, while the Congress has declined. The country feels that the President is willing to assume responsibility, while his party in the Congress is not."[108]

Presidential responsibility proved to be what Professor Michael Uhlmann calls "the crown jewel" of the Constitution. Coolidge understood how the Founders had, to borrow a term from political scientist Harvey Mansfield Jr., "constitutionalized" the ancient office of king or prince and tamed its imperious nature, making it instead a servant to a republican constitution. Coolidge writes as much in his autobiography:

> It is natural for man to seek power. It was because of this trait of human nature that the founders of our institutions provided a system of checks and balances. They placed all their public officers under constitutional limitations. They had little fear of the courts and were inclined to regard legislative bodies as the natural champions of their liberties. They were very apprehensive that the executive might seek to exercise arbitrary powers. . . . It has therefore become increasingly imperative that the President should resist any encroachment upon his constitutional powers. One of the most important of these is the power of appointment. The Constitution provides that he shall nominate, and by and with the advice and consent of the Senate appoint. A constant pressure is exerted by the Senators to make their own nominations and the Congress is constantly proposing laws which undertake to deprive the President of the appointive power.[109]

To defend "the rights and liberties of the people," Coolidge added, "it is necessary for the President to resist all encroachments upon his lawful authority."[110] He must take ownership of the presidency. Perhaps that willingness to bend executive administrative bodies to his will was why the essentially modest Coolidge so often referred to his cabinet ministers possessively – as, for example, "*my* Secretary of Treasury." Given such grave duties, he knew, a president had to assume all of the power to which he was constitutionally entitled – and with which he was thereby entrusted.

Once he appointed them, though, Coolidge allowed his appointees considerable discretion, as the following scene illustrates:

Once his personal secretary, Ted Clark, came to the office and asked if he could show the President a file of papers which Secretary of Labor Davis wanted him to read.

"He would like to know whether you agree with his decision," said Clark.

"I am not going to read them," the President said. "You tell ol' man Davis I hired him as Secretary of Labor and if he can't do the job I'll get a new Secretary of Labor."[111]

Coolidge was an astute judge of the integrity of the cabinet secretaries he had inherited. Secret Service agent Edmund Starling once remarked to him that Secretary of the Navy Denby often stayed late at night at his post, so he must be an excellent man for the job. Coolidge was unimpressed, saying: "If a man can't finish his job in the day, he's not smart."[112] (Soon thereafter Denby came under fire for his involvement in Teapot Dome, and, after much tumult, he resigned.)

Yet despite (or because of) the discretion he allowed his appointees, Coolidge proved a skilled chief of the administrative state. To take one consequential example, he used the Harding-created Bureau of the Budget to aggressively rein in federal debt. With the reins in hand, he disciplined the budget; on his watch, the debt dropped from $22.3 billion in 1923 to $16.9 billion in 1929, which would prove to be the largest decline by percentage in the twentieth century.

Time and again, Coolidge fended off a Senate that hoped to use its powers to encroach upon him and his officers. On March 12, 1924, the Senate passed a resolution calling on the Bureau of Internal Revenue to release the tax records of those connected with Teapot Dome. Shortly thereafter, Coolidge rebuked the Senate for how it was handling the investigation into Teapot Dome. On April 11, 1924, Coolidge rejected the authority of Senator James Couzens of Michigan to pay attorney Francis J. Heney, at the senator's own expense, to take over part of the investigation. It was, the president contended, a violation of the law. Treasury Secretary Andrew Mellon, the subject of the investigation, worried about the precedent Couzens's move would set, warning Coolidge: "If the interposition of the private resources be permitted to interfere with the executive administration of the Government, the machinery of government will cease to function."[113]

Coolidge agreed and wrote a message to the Senate, making it clear that there should be no compliance with Couzens's request. He argued:

> The executive branch has nothing that it would wish to conceal from any legitimate inquiry on the part of the Senate. But it is recognized both by law and by custom that there is certain confidential information which would be detrimental to the public service to reveal. Such information as can be disclosed, I shall always unhesitatingly direct to be laid before the Senate. I recognize also that it is perfectly legitimate for the Senate to indulge in political discussion and partisan criticism.
>
> The constitutional and legal rights of the Senate ought to be maintained at all times. Also the same must be said of the executive departments. But these rights ought not to be used as subterfuge to cover unwarranted intrusion. It is the duty of the Executive to resist such intrusion and to bring to the attention of the Senate its serious consequences. That I shall do in this instance.

Note that Coolidge carefully portrayed the Senate squabbling as "partisan criticism" rather than faithful execution of its office, a damning criticism indeed from his standpoint. The Senate's decision to appoint Heney, Coolidge continued, "seems to have been dictated by some other motive than a desire to secure information for the purpose of legislation."[114]

"Under a procedure of this kind, the constitutional guaranties against unwarranted search and seizure break down," he warned, "and instead of a Government of law we have a Government of lawlessness." Coolidge had entered his "solemn protest" and instructed the Treasury department not to participate in it. But if they had to participate in it, and "the Government is to be thrown into disorder by it, the responsibility for it must rest on those who are undertaking it"[115] – that is, on the Senate. Coolidge appealed for a return to the "law of the land," meaning the separation of powers.

Though there was some grumbling (Senator Walsh of Montana hyperbolically called it "the most arrogant message sent by an Executive to a parliamentary body since the days of the Stuarts and Tudors"[116]), the Senate, with one-third of its members facing reelection that year, ultimately intervened to protect itself from an embarrassment. It did not want to suffer a loss of public esteem as it had when President Cleveland refused, in 1885, to allow his Cabinet members to testify or give documents in response to Senate demands.[117] Coolidge was well aware of Cleveland's precedent, and he had already indicated that he was not above ordering his Cabinet to refuse compliance.[118]

In throwing down the gauntlet, Coolidge knew, as Secretary of State Charles Hughes surmised, that the American people "detest crookedness and corruption" but also "are not fond of scandalmongers."[119] Coolidge and Hughes calculated correctly. As the *Public Ledger* of Philadelphia noted, the appointment of Heney was intended not to draft legislation, but to drive Mellon from the Treasury.[120] Were Heney's appointment allowed, he would have free rein to "prowl where he will add to the demoralization of a department already demoralized by a steady succession of vengeful partisan and personal attacks," the *Public Ledger* editorialized. "There has been nothing quite like this in the history of the Government."[121] Coolidge sought to make sure there was nothing quite like it ever again.

Coolidge not only defended the separation of powers, he energetically practiced it. Two scholars have since noted this approach, which differed from that of the Progressive presidents of his generation:

Coolidge considered his "office" correlative with Congress. Each had its equal duties. He would respect Congress and in return Congress was not to poach on presidential prerogatives. He sometimes found Congress trying, as when the Senate turned down his politically unwise nomination of Charles Beecher Warren as Attorney General, the first time since Andrew Johnson's administration that a nominee for the cabinet had been rejected.[122]

In some of his squabbles and occasional sparring matches with Congress, Coolidge turned to the courts to provide resolution. There, he found a welcome ally in the former president and now chief justice, William Taft. Chief Justice Taft happily obliged the president and handed him a series of victories, defending the pardon power[123] in *Ex parte Grossman* (1925)[124] and *Biddle v. Perovich* (1927), the pocket veto in the *Pocket Veto Case* (1929),[125] the separation of powers regarding appointments in *Springer v. Philippine Islands* (1928),[126] and the removal power in *Myers v. United States* (1926).[127] The Taft Court's reforms, in particular "massing," which led to more unanimous decisions, made it more likely that Coolidge's judicial successes would remain on the books for subsequent presidents to use. Nearly all of these decisions have stood.

Publius and Coolidge versus Wilson on the Separation of Powers: Government of Limits or Limitless Government?

In the first sentence of *Federalist* 51, Publius explains the separation of powers and asks: "To what expedient shall we finally resort, for maintaining in practice the necessary partition of power among the several departments, as laid down in the Constitution?" Following the republicans of the English Civil War and Montesquieu,[128] Publius held that to prevent a "tyrannical concentration" of powers and thus to maintain a republic, it is necessary to divide "the regular distribution of power into distinct departments."[129] "The accumulation of all powers, legislative, executive, and judiciary, in the same hands, whether of one, a few, or many, and whether hereditary, self-appointed, or elective, may justly be pronounced the very definition of tyranny."[130] That accumulation can be prevented by "contriving the interior structure of government" so that branches of government "by their mutual relations" will keep "each other in their proper places."[131] A government of limits must be limited in what it places in each branch's orbit.

Such a limited government's "interior structure" must be so arranged so that its parts are kept "separate and distinct" by design. A well-crafted separation would give "to those who administer each department, the necessary constitutional means, and personal motives, to resist the encroachment of others." By keeping the powers separate and distinct, "each department should have a will of its own"[132] to defend its territory against usurpation by other departments. This careful design would work, Publius expected, because human nature was such that officers would protect their own power even as they sought to aggrandize it. "Ambition must be made to counteract ambition," he famously cautioned. If the ambitious were set against one another, it would increase the people's trust in their government because each branch and its attendant officers would vie for dominance while distrusting the other. The self-interest of the officeholder would keep the "constitutional rights of the place" (of the office) intact, even if "parchment barriers" (the language of the Constitution) failed in this respect.[133] The branches of government would war with one another rather than on the people. The people could live undisturbed, while elements of the federal government fought among themselves for their limited powers.

The separation of powers for Publius, then, was a means to the ends of liberty and good government. If men were naturally predisposed to safeguard one another's rights and not jealously inclined to take advantage of one another, there would be no need for government – and yet there is such a need. *Federalist* 51 makes this abundantly clear: "If men were angels, no government would be necessary. If angels were to govern men, neither external nor internal controls on government would be necessary." Men, of course, are not angels. "In framing a government which is to be administered by men over men, the great difficulty lies in this: you must first enable the government to control the governed; and in the next place oblige it to control itself."[134]

Control was necessary because people are by nature jealous and hungry for power, as history proves – and Publius believed that history operated cyclically in Aristotelian fashion. In such a world, human nature is fixed. The people, who after all retained ultimate authority, would feel what Publius called "reverence" and "veneration" for the Constitution because it took both account and advantage of these timeless problems revealed by history.[135]

Publius and the Founding Fathers had, through studying history and human nature, arrived at the "political truth": that the government's structure had an "intrinsic value" that served the cause of liberty.[136] For the people, the Constitution would become as settled as a law of physics, like gravity, and as worthy of worship as the Ten Commandments.[137] With the separation of powers – what Publius calls "this invaluable precept in the science of politics"[138] or "science of government"[139] – the Constitution guaranteed the liberty that the Declaration of Independence had promised "to ourselves and our posterity" by acting to "guard the society against the oppression of its rulers."[140] If the Constitution failed and the legislature succeeded in drawing all power into its "vortex," either a hard or "soft" tyranny (the latter as described by Montesquieu) would necessarily result. What Publius calls the "experiment" would be doomed, its principles overturned by experience.

What Publius celebrated as the people's "reverence" for the Constitution, Woodrow Wilson condemned as "blind worship." Publius, he charged, had committed a sort of "political witchcraft" in persuading the people not to engage in "fearless criticism" of the Constitution. For Wilson, the separation of powers is the Constitution's "radical defect" because it induces too much "friction" in the operation of government. He expounded upon the problem as a young scholar in his book *Congressional Government* (1885), worrying that "the federal government lacks strength because its powers are divided, lacks promptness because its authorities are multiplied, lacks wieldiness because its processes are roundabout, lacks efficiency because its responsibility is indistinct and its action without competent direction."[141] The

Founders' experiment was flawed, in other words. Where Publius had sought to study "the science of government" – devising the Constitution as an apparatus to study the separation of powers[142] – Wilson disputed the need for the Constitution in the first place. In his view, the Founders were – to use a concept widely applied today – a product of their time. "The makers of our federal Constitution," Wilson wrote in *Constitutional Government* (1908),

> followed the scheme as they found it expounded in Montesquieu, followed it with specific enthusiasm. The admirable expositions of *The Federalist* read like thoughtful applications of Montesquieu to the political needs and circumstances of America. They are full of the theory of checks and balances. The President is balanced off against Congress, Congress against the President, and each against the courts. Our statesmen of the earlier generation quoted no one so often as Montesquieu, and they quoted him always as a scientific standard in the field of politics. Politics is turned into mechanics under [Montesquieu's] touch. The theory of gravitation is supreme.[143]

Montesquieu, whom Publius celebrates as an "oracle ... always consulted and cited,"[144] became in Wilson's eyes the architect of a "scheme."[145] That scheme's very design turned government into something of a Rube Goldberg machine, "conceived in the Newtonian spirit and upon the Newtonian principle," with seemingly no higher motive at work. The Founders, in Wilson's view, had the wrong scientific metaphor at the heart of their vision of government because "government is not a machine, but a living thing."[146] It is governed by "the theory of organic life" and is "accountable to Darwin, not to Newton."[147] "No living thing," Wilson argued, continuing the metaphor, "can have its organs offset against each other as checks, and live." He added: "There can be no successful government without leadership or without the intimate, almost instinctive, coordination of the organs of life and action."[148] Government needed to be

free from the separation of powers because it was, properly understood, a "body of men . . . with a common task and purpose" who thus
needed to cooperate because "their warfare [is] fatal."[149] For Wilson,
the "theory of checks and balance" – which the Constitution never
mentions in the context of the separation of powers – was "a sort of
unconscious copy of the Newtonian theory of the universe."[150]

In this argument, Wilson critically misunderstood the separation
of powers, as other scholars have noted. Far from limiting progress,
separation of powers enables the branches to specialize. Jessica Korn,
assistant professor of political science at the University of Massachusetts at Amherst, for instance, argues that such a separation
"produce[s] a division of labor so that members of the different
branches . . . develop specialized skills in pursuing the responsibilities
of legislating, executing and judging."[151] Moreover, it is clear that
Wilson's view of progress could also be consistent with a government
that honored the separation of powers. As political scientist James
Ceaser points out, separation of powers merely sets the means for
policymaking but does not prescribe an end for them.

> The doctrine of the separation of powers . . . does not define
> fully – nor was it ever intended to define fully – the exact char-
> acter of the policymaking process. The Constitution is not
> completely silent or neutral about the character of the policy-
> making process, but in the final analysis there is not one single
> constitutional model for the policymaking function but only
> constitutional limits for which models must be constructed.[152]

The separation of powers, then, is not nearly as "static" as Wilson
would have it. He also argued, however, that most power had indeed
been drawn into the legislative vortex about which Publius warned.
The "actual form of our present government is simply a scheme of
congressional supremacy,"[153] Wilson contended, and Congress was
"the predominant and controlling force, the centre and source of all
motive and of all regulative power."[154]

In seeing the Congress as (wrongly and unfortunately) the over-whelming source of power in the government, Wilson gave much thought as a young scholar to correcting the problem. He favored a series of constitutional amendments designed to radically weaken the separation of powers. One such amendment, borrowing from the British parliamentary system, would allow the president to choose cabinet members from Congress.[155] These officers, who could still introduce legislation, would have "ministerial responsibility" and would resign should Congress reject "any important part of their plans."[156] Wilson also favored lengthening the terms of the president and members of Congress[157] in order to increase the likelihood that one party would control the whole of government and therefore effect more change.

Before long, however, Wilson's view changed. He decided that the real power was in the presidency, which in the newly emerging world was now the heart of government, "the vital place of action in the system."[158] In this emerging world, Wilson argued, the president no longer merely "execut[ed] laws," but became "more and more a political and less and less an executive officer." The president was also the only truly national figure. With his "personal force" he had the power to make the presidency – the only national office – into "anything he had the sagacity or the force to make it."[159] Eleven years after Wilson's presidency, a newly elected Franklin Delano Roosevelt elaborated on this conception of the president's power: The great presidents were also "moral leaders," each of whom "in his own way and his own time, used the presidency as a pulpit," he told the press in 1932.

Calvin Coolidge disagreed. While Wilson argued against the Constitution's barriers, Coolidge celebrated them. "Our Constitution has raised certain barriers against too hasty change," he said. "I believe such a provision is wise."

I doubt if there has been any change that has ever really been desired by the people which they have not been able to secure. Stability of government is a very important asset. If amendment is made easy, both revolution and reaction, as well as orderly progress, also become easy.[160]

In urging stability of government as the higher value, Coolidge hewed to the Founders' understanding of the Constitution and the Republic. Whereas Wilson believed the president had powers that were "in their very nature personal and inalienable,"[161] – that is, they followed directly to him by virtue of having the office – Coolidge distinguished his personal opinions from his duties.[162] In doing so, he proved himself a keen student of the *Federalist Papers*, which he had read with rapt attention as an undergraduate (a fellow student later recalled Coolidge in the library "with his nose in *The Federalist*").[163] Coolidge knew that the Founders had deliberately made the presidency unitary – in charge of its branch – so as to make it powerful enough to motivate men "preeminent for ability and virtue" to seek the office.[164] The president would also be armed with a veto to force the legislature to deliberate with care.[165] The point of separation of powers wasn't to produce "deadlock," as later scholars argued, but good government. The difference here between the Founders and most modern political scientists is that the Founders understood good government to be primarily that which protects natural rights, not a force that manipulates society.

Herein lies much of the contrast with Coolidge: Wilson minimized the Declaration as a product of its time; Coolidge celebrated it as a document for all time. Wilson believed it was "impossible to apply the policies of the time of Thomas Jefferson to the time we live in."[166] Coolidge believed the opposite: "The trouble with us is that we talk about Jefferson but do not follow him. In his theory that the people should manage their government and not be managed by it, he was everlastingly right."[167] To Wilson, this was not so: The signers of the Declaration "were no theorists but practical statesmen," and Jefferson, too, was merely an "astute politician," not the articulator of a great political truth.[168] Coolidge, by contrast, credited Jefferson with the "immortal honor of having drafted the Declaration," written when Jefferson was "at his best."[169] Wilson misunderstood not only the Constitution but also the Declaration of Independence, which it was intended to fulfill.

Coolidge began his study of the Constitution early, at age thirteen, and he knew well from his studies at Amherst College under Professor Morse that the separation of powers had its origins in the English Civil War, when pamphleteers called for disentangling the executive from the legislative authority in hopes of diminishing the arbitrary power of the king.[170] These early republicans, who included *Paradise Lost* author John Milton in their company, sought to guarantee the stability of their envisioned republic by separating those who made the laws from those who executed them. John Locke, another such early republican who inspired the Founders, responded to the legacy of the English Civil War by fusing the Whiggish concern for the rule of law with the Tory love of executive prerogative; Locke aimed to found a new order in which the tug of the Whigs who wanted progress would compete with the inertia of the Tories who wanted tradition, and so preserve order and produce good governance.

While Wilson denigrated the Constitution, Coolidge celebrated it as "the most remarkable document ever struck off by the hand of man at a given time."[171] Coolidge was a lifelong student of the Constitution, its ratifying debates, and the American political founding. When it came to the separation of powers, he followed President Harding's lead: The executive's main task was to carry out legislation passed by Congress.[172] But Coolidge had also closely studied the role that each department had to play under the Constitution.[173] In addition to his intense interest in *The Federalist*, Coolidge at Amherst also "became much absorbed in the study of . . . the whole career of Alexander Hamilton."[174] Understanding Hamilton meant understanding *The Federalist* and thus the underpinnings of the Republic.[175] According to Woods:

It was especially in the field of American history that he went far beyond the range of classroom instruction and assigned reading. Here he showed marks of genuine personal initiative and zest. It was true in college, as well as amid the suggestions of his boyhood background, that he found in narratives of colonial days his chief intellectual recreation.[176]

As vice president, Coolidge spoke at a celebration of the anniversary of the birthday of Alexander Hamilton, endorsing *The Federalist* co-author's essays as "masterly."[177] Hamilton's "illuminating arguments . . . secured [the Constitution's] ratification."[178] His "intellectual force"[179] had "found the Constitution merely a plan on paper [but] made it into a living organism of government" due to his keen understanding of the separation of powers.[180] Coolidge praised the "great heritage which Hamilton bequeathed to his countrymen . . . in which every American has a share."[181] Hamilton was not only a "genius of the Revolution," but also "of the formation of the Federal Government," which he "transformed . . . into the enduring form of our Federal Union."[182] Coolidge considered it "probable that without Hamilton the American nation would not have come into being."[183]

Honoring *The Federalist*'s analysis of our constitutional system in an address at Arlington National Cemetery on May 30, 1925, Coolidge approvingly quoted a point in *Federalist* 45 that, he said, "cannot be too much emphasized": "The powers delegated to the Federal Government are few and defined. Those to remain in the hands of the State government are numerous and indefinite." Unfortunately, the people had come to forget the "real distribution of duties, responsibilities, and expenses." They had begun thinking that "if the states *will not*, the nation *must*." Coolidge worried about the trouble that he feared would follow from such thinking:

If we cannot govern ourselves, if we cannot observe the law, nothing remains but to have some one else govern us, to have the law enforced against us, and to step down from the honorable abiding place of freedom to the ignominious abode of servitude.

The nation "can only be preserved, the states can only be maintained, under a reign of national, local, and moral law, under the Constitution established by Washington."[184] Adherence to the law meant following the separation of powers.

Coolidge explained his view of the legislature's role in the separation of powers in a Memorial Day Address titled "The Destiny of America," delivered in 1923, less than three months before he assumed the presidency. In it, he exhumed an argument from *Federalist* 10.

The chief repository of power is in the legislature, chosen directly by the people at frequent elections. It is this body, which is particularly responsive to the public will, and yet, as in the Congress, is representative of the whole nation.

As a legislative body, Congress is "charged with the necessity for deliberation," a "privilege" that is sometimes "abused," just as any power "may be used unwisely," but that is also necessary as "the main safeguard of liberty" because only with deliberation – with "due consideration" – can the legislative branch serve that function.

Following the argument of *Federalist* 10 further, Coolidge said Congress and the "two great political parties" existed to "serve the interests of the whole nation" and that its members were "chosen with that great end in view." Patriotism meant "a love of the whole country," not of a "special interest" or "narrow prejudice," and "the welfare of all is equally to be sought." This important distinction meant that Coolidge saw most legislation as wrong or unnecessary. "Nine-tenths of a president's callers at the White House want something they ought not to have," Coolidge later advised his successor, Herbert Hoover (who seems not to have taken the hint). "If you keep dead-still, they will run down in three or four minutes. If you even cough or smile, they will start up all over again."

An organization that serves such special interests can have its place, Coolidge knew, but it needs to know its place. "Whenever it undertakes to serve that interest by disregarding the welfare of other interests," it harms both that organization's interest and the "public welfare in general."[185] There exists, rather, a "necessary community of interests [in the sense] that all necessarily experience depression or prosperity together. . . . No private enterprise [or particular interest] can succeed unless the public welfare be held supreme."

A concern for the national welfare, which was at base a concern for the natural rights of the people, animated the Founders who met to draft the Constitution and later saw to its ratification. The Constitution was an instrument to preserve what the Declaration maintained was the point of government: to protect the natural rights of the people, which had their basis in self-evident truths. "It was in the contemplation of these truths that the fathers made their dedication and adopted their Constitution," Coolidge said in his speech on the 150th anniversary of the Declaration. The Founders sought to "establish a free government" that would not "degenerate into the unrestrained authority of a mere majority or the unbridled weight of a mere influential few." With this goal firmly in mind, they "undertook to balance these interests against each other and provide the three separate independent branches, the executive, the legislative, and the judicial departments of the Government, with checks against each other."[186] In order to fully appreciate the political brilliance of Montesquieu or *The Federalist*, Americans "must go back and review the course which they followed," Coolidge urged. "We must think the thoughts which they thought."[187] The only progress, Coolidge knew, lay within the Constitution's separation of powers, not outside it.

CHAPTER SIX

THE "POSSIBILITIES OF SOUL"

We have seen the mere distinction of colour made in the most enlightened period of time, a ground of the most oppressive dominion ever exercised by man over man.[1]

The American theory of society is founded in part on this condition. It asserts the equality of men. That means equality of kind. All are endowed with the same kind of mind, for it is mind alone that makes man, the capacity to know the truth. That capacity, once it comes into being, does not change. It is the same now as at the dawn of its creation, however it was created.[2]

There should be no favorites and no outcasts; no race or religious prejudices in government. America opposes special privileges for any body and favors equal opportunity for every body. . . . As a plain matter of expediency, the white man cannot be protected and as a plain matter of right . . . justice is justice for everybody.[3]

AMERICA, in Coolidge's view, was destined for a special mission: the uplift of all mankind. "We must always remember that America is a missionary country, and I do not limit that word to its religious sense," Coolidge proclaimed when accepting the nomination for the vice presidency. This missionary sense came from America's founding, in which she was conceived as a "new power destined to preserve and extend the rights of mankind." As such, her people "are not without justification in assuming [she] has been called into existence to establish, to maintain, to defend, and to extend that principle," as he told an audience of black veterans.[4]

With the guidance of divine providence, Coolidge believed, America's republican system of government would instruct the world's people in the habits of successful republics. "In the fulness of time America was called into being under the most favoring circumstances, to work out the problem of a more perfect relationship among mankind that government and society might be brought into harmony with reason and conscience."[5] Such a government, grounded in reason, would sweep away all prejudice. America, in Coolidge's formulation, would teach the rest of the world how to live together. As the first nation to receive the word of the possibility of government founded on natural rights, he believed, her calling was to preach to the world's people the truth of her republican claims, inspired by the Declaration of Independence.

What the Founders had foretold was coming true, according to Coolidge. America's teachings were being disseminated – to blacks, whose progress since the Civil War foretold hope for civilizations as far away as Africa's; to Indians, who chose to fight for America, thereby earning citizenship for all their people; and to a Japanese boy, Manjiro Nakahama, who grew to be his nation's first unofficial ambassador to America. Racial prejudice was giving way to reason, and real progress on race was now possible. To be sure, "racial hostility, ancient tradition, and social prejudice are not to be eliminated immediately or easily," Coolidge granted. "But they will be lessened."[6] Fully "working out . . . in theory and in practice" the American "theory of human rights" would be "long, slow, toilsome, and laborious . . . accompanied oftentimes with disappointment and delays," Coolidge knew. "But in the progress which has been made there is every reason for encouragement and satisfaction."[7]

For Coolidge, part of man's coming into his own was a recognition, like that of the Founders, that a common fatherhood in God meant a common brotherhood, guaranteed through republican self-government. The Founders and Lincoln wrestled with how best to realize the republican government promised by the Declaration and Constitution. As previously noted, Coolidge studied their answers and joined them in considering the Declaration's moral and political teachings – what Lincoln called America's "political religion" – as the animating principle of the nation. In keeping with what Lincoln had said of the Civil War, Coolidge argued that World War I advanced a "new birth of freedom." He underscored the war's political importance in a speech in October 1925 titled "Toleration and Liberalism":

> Well-nigh all the races, religions, and nationalities of the world were represented in the armed forces of this nation, as they were in the body of the population. No man's patriotism was impugned or service questioned because of his racial origin, his political opinion, or his religious convictions. Immigrants and the sons of the immigrants from the central European countries fought side by side with those who descended from the countries which were our allies; with the sons of equatorial Africa; and with the Red men of our own aboriginal population; all of them equally proud of the name American.

That shared sacrifice furthered the sense of a shared identity, with each race attaining its rightful equality in America and no race left out. This new "Americanism," as Coolidge called it, was eased by what became known as the Coolidge Prosperity. British historian Paul Johnson has noted the sheer scope of that prosperity:

> At the time [the wealth] was as solid as houses built, meals eaten, automobiles driven, cash spent, and property acquired. Prosperity was more widely distributed in the America of the 1920s than had been possible in any community of this size before, and it involved the acquisition, by tens of millions of ordinary families, of the elements of the economic security that had hitherto been denied them throughout the whole of history.[8]

Several groups – blacks, Japanese Americans, immigrants, and Indians – benefited tremendously during the Coolidge Prosperity, when economic growth sometimes exceeded 9 percent a year. Everyone benefited:

> The 1921 GNP had been a depressed $69.9 billion; for 1923 it came to $85.1 billion, and would go on to $93.1 billion in 1924. This worked out to a growth rate of 9 percent from 1921 to 1924. . . . In this same span the consumer price index fell from 53.6 to 51.2, and the unemployment rate from 11.7 percent to 5 percent.[9]

Coolidge's political thought on these new constituencies – including women, who voted for the first time in 1920, mostly for the Harding-Coolidge ticket[10] – has seldom been explored in light of the politics of his day and with regard to his own well-informed understanding of the Founders and Lincoln.

When people in our own time explore the Founders' political thought, modern prejudices can hold sway and lead to facile condemnation. It is fashionable but wrong for so many scholars to concentrate on identity politics when considering the formation of American political thought.[11] Coolidge disliked such appeals to separatism and favored the formation of an inclusive American identity. In this, he believed as the Founders did that each of these interest groups would, in time, fade into a larger whole through the rough-and-tumble of politics. The World War, like the Revolution before it, would consecrate the flag and the nation, and through the sacrifice of its soldiers make possible a greater, more enduring union. Coolidge quoted John 15:13[12] on this point at a Memorial Day Address in 1923: "Greater love hath no man than this, that a man lay down his life for his friends."[13] That shared love of country and countrymen, and that shared service to them, produced a common identity because these experiences were an "electric cord" – as was the Declaration of Independence for Lincoln – that bound the country together.[14] Coolidge's statements on this shared sacrifice and common identity are eloquent: "We entered the war a people of many nationalities. We are united now; every one is first an American,"[15] and "the flame of patriotism swept over the whole land, consuming away the dross of all past differences, and fusing the entire people into one common national unity."[16] Unfortunately, the years of Coolidge's presidency were not as encouraging of that national unity.

Unlike other politicians of his era, Coolidge was well ahead of his time – or perhaps behind it, in the sense that he rejected the "scientific" racism of the day and especially eugenics in favor of the classical republican teachings he studied throughout his life. He fought against the Social Darwinism of the period, well expressed in the appeal to eugenics made by his secretary of labor, James Davis (who had been appointed by Harding). With a nod to egalitarianism and another to practical politics, Coolidge supported making either the census or naturalization records, not tests of mental acumen or physical ability, the basis of immigration quotas.[17] When it came to immigration, Coolidge followed Patrick Henry's "lamp of experience,"[18] not the false lights of Germanic or Darwinist "scientific" racism.

The Republican platform of 1920 explicitly supported eugenics,[19] but Coolidge did not, because it was impossible, he said, to measure the "possibilities of human soul." "It is not only what men know but what they are disposed to with that which they know that will determine the rise and fall of civilization."[20] The Darwinist notion of survival of the fittest was also similarly flawed, Coolidge suggested, for it was not through survival but through sacrifice that republics revealed their best men. Standing against the law of the jungle, which animated the German war machine, Coolidge said that republican men must "choose the sacrifice." Speaking to the Roxbury Historical Society in Massachusetts on Bunker Hill Day, 1918, as lieutenant governor, Coolidge said:

> The law of progress and civilization is not the law of the jungle. It is not an earthly law, it is a divine law. It does not mean the survival of the fittest, it means the sacrifice of the fittest. Any mother will give her life for her child. Men put the women

and children in the lifeboats before they themselves will leave the sinking ship. John Hampden and Nathan Hale did not survive, nor did Lincoln, but Benedict Arnold did. The example above all others takes us back to Jerusalem some nineteen hundred years ago. The men of Bunker Hill were true disciples of civilization, because they were willing to sacrifice themselves to resist the evils and redeem the liberties of the British Empire.[21]

True disciples of civilization lived as servants of a higher good, looking to the example of Christ – who preached to Jew and Gentile alike – and not to the false teachings of Social Darwinism.

It comes as little surprise, then, that much as Lincoln rejected the anti-immigration and anti-Catholic Know Nothings, Coolidge rejected the Ku Klux Klan, which grew with a renewed vigor in the first half of the 1920s but went into a lasting decline in the middle of his presidency. He supported legislation, and sometimes federal funding, to improve the condition of blacks, Indians, and recent immigrants: He asked Congress to appropriate about half a million dollars for Howard University to train black doctors each year; he called for a committee to look into Indian affairs; and he asked for money, from private and public sources, to help assimilate immigrants into American life.

Coolidge's purpose was to help these groups make themselves "100 percent American" – a problem that had vexed the Founders.[22] In that pursuit, the president argued for a common brotherhood of Americans in a citizenship that rested on ideals, not race, because in a republican form of government there could be no racial hierarchy. Coolidge expounded on this point before an audience that included the crown prince of Sweden: "As we do not recognize any inferior races, so we do not recognize any superior races." A refusal to recognize a racial hierarchy meant a greater recognition of the individual's contribution. "We all stand on an equality of rights and of opportunity, each deriving just honor from his own worth and accomplishments."[23]

Worth, accomplishment, and common brotherhood were on full display on the recent battlefields of Europe, where the American dead lay without regard to color. There, "the black man showed himself the same kind of citizen, moved by the same kind of patriotism, as the white man."[24] The soldiers of all races were making good the promise of America. The fact that Coolidge was himself far removed from the immigrant experience makes it all the more noteworthy that he held such views. As a biographical article in *Success* magazine in July 1924 put it: "No one could take Calvin Coolidge for anything but an American – an American not of the melting pot but of their forefathers. There is a peculiar appropriateness in the fact that he was born on the fourth of July."[25] Coolidge kept America's melting pot rhetorically to a low simmer. He supported the 1924 immigration act, which favored immigrants from countries similar to the U.S. and aimed to keep the overall immigration numbers low. The law was designed to slowly churn out Americans who honored the teachings of the nation's birth. By keeping the temperature low – and avoiding adding too many disparate immigrants to the mix – Coolidge kept the melting pot from boiling over, as it had during the wartime anti-German hysteria.

Despite this rhetoric and record, Coolidge's reputation has been savaged in recent years, with some going so far as to suggest that he was insufficiently opposed to the Ku Klux Klan. Chief among those making this claim is Robert Ferrell, the leading living Coolidge biographer. He charges that Coolidge's federal government did "little for civil rights and liberties," that "the rights of black Americans had seldom concerned their white brothers and sisters," and that the immigration laws passed were "assuredly a negative change" – all of which is false.[26]

Ferrell's claims notwithstanding, the Klan certainly didn't care for Coolidge after he asked Congress to review its involvement with lynchings, and after he refused to show up for their forty-thousand-strong parade in Washington on August 8, 1925.[27] He also refused to attend events at which Klan contingents would be present, lest he grant them legitimacy by his presence.[28] Coolidge condemned the Klan's modus operandi as "a hideous crime" and repeatedly called for Congress to pass laws against it. Theodore Roosevelt, in contrast, had announced during his presidency that the "greatest existing cause of lynching is the perpetration, especially by black men, of the hideous crime of rape – the most abominable in all the category of crimes – even worse than murder," and Taft, also before Congress, blamed lynching upon "delays in trials, judgments, and the executions thereof."[29] From Coolidge's standpoint, there were no excuses for lynchings. He repeatedly foiled the Klan's attempts to disrupt the Massachusetts Commonwealth, the Oklahoma state government, and the federal government.

Providing fodder for today's critics, Coolidge declined to condemn the Klan outright in 1924; he chose not to disturb the "Klanbake," as the press dubbed the Democratic Convention of 1924, where many delegates were fervently pro-Klan. That contentious convention ended the political careers of one of the Democrats' best politicians and hobbled the future of another. The factions supporting Governor Al Smith, a New York Catholic who was toxic to the pro-Klan side, and former treasury secretary William McAdoo, a pro-Klan Southerner and Woodrow Wilson's son-in-law, dueled long into the convention. Eventually both withdrew, leaving the politically unknown West Virginia congressman John W. Davis, Wilson's ambassador to Britain, the last man standing after the 103rd ballot. Nominated in his own right, Davis, something of a theatrical showman, hoped to use the issue of the Klan against the Republican Party as it had been used against his own. He wanted to split the Republicans, as Theodore Roosevelt had in the 1912 campaign. Davis's demands that the president denounce the Klan did pose political problems for Coolidge, especially when the popular humorist Will Rogers quipped that his new slogan was "Keep Kool with Koolidge" and attracted popular attention to Coolidge's position.[30] Still, Davis's anti-Klan gambit was ultimately for naught. Many liberals bolted from the Democratic nominee and threw their support to Senator Robert La Follette. In the presidential election, Coolidge won 60.2 percent of the three-party vote, "the largest popular majority yet recorded – 16,152,000 votes to 9,147,000," and every state outside the solid South.[31]

There is no evidence, according to Robert Sobel, one of his most recent biographers, to think that Coolidge "thought or said anything inconsistent with his belief in a colorblind society."[32] Given the very real racial prejudice harbored by his predecessors in the Oval Office, this in itself is remarkable. But to probe the dimensions of the American society Coolidge envisioned, we should closely examine how he handled racial issues and review both his successes and failures in defending what he called the "equality of rights."

Coolidge, Blacks, and the Klan

For the Founders, blacks had been a political problem. Jefferson wondered whether blacks could become a part of the American way of life. In Query 14 of his *Notes on the State of Virginia*, he proposed a method for their emancipation in Virginia, but he opposed integrating the freed blacks into American society, explaining:

> Deep rooted prejudices entertained by the whites; ten thousand recollections, by the blacks, of the injuries they have sustained; new provocations; the real distinctions which nature has made; and many other circumstances, will divide us into parties, and produce convulsions which will probably never end but in the extermination of the one or the other race.

Personal experience, which he recounted in a letter to Henri Gregoire, convinced Jefferson that blacks were not "on a par with ourselves" when it came to innate talents. Still, despite these remarks, Jefferson anticipated blacks making "hopeful advances" toward their "reestablishment on an equal footing with other colors of the human family."[33] In an earlier letter to Benjamin Banneker, Jefferson said, "No body wishes more than I do to see such proofs as you exhibit, that nature has given to our black brethren, talents equal to the other colors of men, and that the appearance of a want of them is owing merely to the degraded condition of their existence."[34] In failing to follow his thoughts on race to their logical conclusion, Jefferson fell short, to be sure. If blacks in the Jeffersonian formulation were "degraded" brothers, it would follow that Americans should do something to restore them to their place in the "human family," whether by promoting individual initiative, government policy, or some combination thereof. Jefferson was silent on such matters.

Other presidents, too, held complicated views on race, particularly in the early twentieth century. American intellectuals in the post–Civil War era increasingly questioned Jefferson's self-evident truth that all men are created equal. Anthropologist Daniel Brinton, for instance, speaking before the American Association for the Advancement of Science in 1895, praised eugenics, telling his audience that proper consideration of racial differences "supply the only sure foundations for legislation, not a priori notions of the rights of man." Sociologist John Commons began his book on immigration by attacking the Declaration of Independence's axiom that all men are created equal.[35] These notions gained popularity during Coolidge's early career and in his presidency, and Coolidge argued – and acted – forcefully against them throughout his public life. This was especially the case with regard to the Klan, which rose and fell during Coolidge's era. As Senate president in Massachusetts, Coolidge opposed the very embodiment of racial prejudice, the pro-Klan film *The Birth of a Nation*, initially titled *The Clansman*.[36]

President Woodrow Wilson, by contrast, was an early and by some accounts enthusiastic supporter of the movie. He showed it at the White House[37] and later watched it again with an audience – described as "doubtless the mo[st] [dis]tinguished that ever saw motion picture reels unraveled" – that included members of Congress, the Supreme Court, members of the diplomatic corps, and the Washington social elite. The audience "showered" the film with praise.[38]

On the issue of race, Wilson's record, like the poor records of all five presidents before Coolidge, is curiously absent in discussions of his presidency. At heart, Wilson remained a Southern man, although he made his career in a Northern state. He most likely agreed with the view of post–Civil War history that *Birth of a Nation* screenwriter Thomas Dixon endorsed, a view founded on the new racial "science" of the day. Indeed, Dixon was Wilson's longtime friend and had studied alongside him in Johns Hopkins's Progressive-oriented political-science graduate program[39] before he dropped out (against Wilson's wishes).[40] In making *Birth of a Nation*, Dixon even used material from Wilson's *History of the American People*.[41] Wilson's racist record on civil rights includes his support of the re-segregation of the District of Columbia by the new Democratic Congress and his approval of its laws against interracial marriage in the district. In addition, Wilson's cabinet was filled with pro-segregationists.[42] When Secretary of the Navy Josephus Daniels, in one of the administration's first cabinet meetings, proposed to remove "abuses" such as shared drinking fountains from Washington, Wilson supported him.[43] Soon, blacks, especially in departments headed by Southerners, were barred from using the same cafeterias, toilets, or fountains as whites.[44] With such renewed segregationist measures, and especially with what Wilson called a "new and radical departure" from the fifty-year tradition of an integrated civil service, blacks soon found that they were second-class citizens in the nation's capital. Applicants for jobs in the civil service were required to submit photographs, a measure designed to screen out blacks. The numbers of black civil servants declined as a result. Positions that had gone to blacks after the Civil War, such as the register of the Treasury and the minister to Haiti, went to whites during Wilson's administration.[45]

Although some prominent black spokesmen – such as W. E. B. DuBois; William Monroe Trotter; and Oswald Garrison Villard, a white civil rights activist – favored Wilson in 1912, they quickly found out that they were mistaken.[46] Following a rationale that became common in the aftermath of *Plessy v. Ferguson*, the 1896 Supreme Court decision upholding the constitutionality of segregation laws, Wilson maintained that segregation was good for blacks as well as whites because the two races thought differently.[47] He also argued that segregation served to preserve black jobs. At a meeting to protest

Wilson's increased segregation of the capital, one black leader denounced Wilson in a rebuttal worthy of Coolidge: Voting for someone who harbored such profoundly anti-Christian views had been a grave error, said William Monroe Trotter, an NAACP member and editor of the *Guardian*, a prominent black newspaper.[48] At base, Wilson did not believe in a common citizenship because he did not believe in the Declaration of Independence's self-evident truths.

* * *

Boston, with its long history of abolition, was a fitting staging ground for what would become a national campaign against *Birth of a Nation*. When the film opened there on April 10, 1915, it caused a "near-riot," as the *Morning Globe* reported.[49] On April 17, Trotter and ten others were arrested for demonstrating against the film inside the Tremont Theater by hurling eggs at the screen and setting off stink bombs.[50]

After meeting with Coolidge's friend William H. Lewis, a black Amherst graduate, Democratic governor David Walsh – Massachusetts's first Catholic governor, who faced an uphill reelection in 1916[51] – proposed to censor the film under a 1910 law that banned "lewd, obscene, incident, immortal or impure" art.[52] (Lewis, in spite of his shared history with Coolidge, backed John W. Davis over Coolidge in 1924 because Coolidge did not denounce the Klan.) Walsh promised that, if necessary, he would seek new legislation against the film. When a judge dismissed his attempted censorship under the 1910 law, Walsh asked the General Court to intervene. State Representative Lewis J. Sullivan of Boston moved to amend the 1910 law to include a ban on "any show or entertainment which tends to excite racial or religious prejudice or tends to a breach of the public peace."[53] After much debate, a bill emerged that proposed a censorship board that included the mayor, the state's chief justice, and the Boston chief of police. The lower chamber amended the bill to require unanimity in board decisions. The Senate changed the bill back to require a bare majority, at which point its opponents pounced, moving to send it back to committee. This would have effectively killed the bill, but Senate President Coolidge intervened.

Breaking Senate precedent, he voted for the bill, producing a tie that stopped the measure to recommit. Coolidge's parliamentary tactic earned him considerable press coverage:

"Censors Bill Near Bad Snag," said a headline in the *Boston Globe.* "Coolidge's Vote Stops Reconsideration by Senate." It went on to say: "The Boston triple censor bill advocated by opponents of the 'Birth of a Nation' came within an ace of striking a bad snag in the Senate yesterday. Only the action of President Coolidge in ordering his name called during a roll call prevented a reconsideration of the vote on Monday. . . . " The *Boston Post*'s headline was more dramatic. "Opponents of 'Birth of Nation' Win."[54]

Governor Walsh signed the bill on May 21. Silent Cal never explained the reason he voted for it, but its effect was clear. By passing legislation to censor *Birth of a Nation*, Massachusetts undermined the claim of the film's producers and promoters that prominent politicians supported the film. After the law was enacted, the film's popularity waned.[55] President Wilson was now embarrassed to have shown it at the White House.[56] Coolidge had quietly gone about doing the "day's work" and slowing the dissemination of the film that was spurring the Klan's rapid growth.

In doing "the day's work" against *Birth of a Nation*, Coolidge neatly illuminated yet another contrast between Wilson and himself on racial issues. Coolidge had come of age in a time when lynchings were rampant. As Felzenberg notes, "between 1885 and 1894 . . . an estimated 1,700 lynchings of Negroes had taken place in the United States."[57] Like the young Lincoln, Coolidge hated lynching not only because of what it did to individuals, but because of what it did to the rule of law. In contrast, A. Mitchell Palmer, Wilson's attorney general, entrusted with defending the people's law, had given a commencement speech at Swarthmore in which he defended the lynching of Italian Americans in New Orleans in 1891.[58] Unsurprisingly, with such an attorney general, lynchings *increased* during Wilson's time in office, from thirty-six nationwide in 1917, to sixty in 1918, to seventy-six in 1919.[59] To be sure, in later life Wilson said he had merely been helping out his screenwriter friend, Dixon, but Coolidge had no such friends. While Coolidge called lynching a crime against civilization and wanted to curtail it, Wilson never denounced it, even though the problem was worsening during his presidency. Wilson showed *The Birth of a Nation* at the White House; Coolidge, as Senate president, cast the definitive vote to help censor it. Wilson promised to make the world safe for democracy; Coolidge defended American democracy against the sorts of people that had watched and loved *The Birth of a Nation.*

Coolidge strongly rejected racial prejudice in whatever form it reared itself. In determining a man's worth, he argued, "we shall have to look beyond the outward manifestations of race and creed," because God had "not bestowed upon any race a monopoly of patriotism and character."[60] To Coolidge, race had no bearing on a man's character, and therefore racist beliefs and behavior were hostile toward the Union.

"The Nation," he argued at Howard University in 1924, "has need of all that can be contributed to it through the best efforts of all its citizens." It became especially clear that blacks were a part of that nation in World War I, when they had "repeatedly proved their devotion" to the "high ideals of *our* country."[61] The war prompted a more complete political equality, Coolidge stressed, because the "Negro did his part *precisely* as did the white man . . . [and] drew no color line when patriotism made its call upon him."[62] Further, "he gave *precisely* as his white fellow citizens gave, to the limit of resources and abilities to help the general cause."[63] For that service – for that general cause, which was the furtherance of American liberty – the black man "established his right to the gratitude and appreciation" of the nation. This Coolidge said and this he meant, both politically and personally.[64]

A story recounted by Coolidge's attorney general, John Sargent, noted the president's reluctance to punish groups on the basis of race.

"It seems to be a terrible thing for a person of intelligence, of educa-tion, of real character – as we know many colored people are – to be born with a different colored skin," he quoted Coolidge as saying. The president asked his cabinet officers to "find a way to give [blacks] an even chance" in government.[65] If blacks were given an even chance, Coolidge believed, they would have their rightful place in the American family, just as Jefferson had hoped. They had already con-tributed to America's and the world's welfare by fighting in Europe, where they "demonstrat[ed] the ability of America." It followed that blacks would, if given that chance, make Americans proud in other ways, too. Noting that the Germans had dismissed the American military as inferior due to the blacks in its ranks, Coolidge, while lieu-tenant governor, responded:

> What [the Germans] say in scorn, let us say in praise. We have fought before for the rights of all men irrespective of color. We are proud to fight now with colored men for the rights of white men. It would be fitting recognition of their worth to send our American negro, when that time comes, to inform the Prussian military despotism on what terms their defeated armies are to be granted peace.[66]

That fitting scene never came to pass, of course, but Coolidge's suggestion of it indicates that his political thought was not far from that of his political hero, Alexander Hamilton, who wrote in a March 14, 1779, letter to John Jay that slaves ought to earn "their freedom with their muskets."[67] Blacks were earning their place in America and "have justified the faith of Abraham Lincoln."[68]

After the war, President Coolidge concerned himself with blacks' progress, which he took as evidence that the teachings of America are universal in their appeal. He took their increasing success as evi-dence that God was still doing His work through America's people, black and white. As Coolidge noted at the opening of a hospital for wounded black soldiers, Lincoln and the Founders believed "that all people could and would finally rise" to the requirements necessary for the "high estate" of freedom.[69] But as Coolidge knew, there were many who wanted blacks to remain confined to ignorance. They were really disagreeing, he suggested, with Lincoln's hope that Americans might all be friends. "It is well for us, who live together as Americans, whatever our race or creed may be, constantly to remember his words: 'We are not enemies, but friends. We [must] not be enemies.'"[70] With this reminder, he was probably alluding to the postwar race riots of 1919, which upended life in Philadelphia, Omaha, Chicago, and St. Louis.

As racial enmity increased with the rise of the Klan, Coolidge highlighted "the negro" – his plight and his progress – in every one of his State of the Union addresses. In 1923, he reminded Congress that blacks' rights are "just as sacred as those of any other citizen" and encouraged Congress to "exercise all its powers of prevention and punishment against the hideous crime of lynching" and to "formulate a better policy [of racial reconciliation] for mutual understanding and confidence."[71] In 1924, he noted a "very remarkable improvement in the condition of the negro race" as they "work[ed] out their own destiny," were "accorded their full constitutional rights," and became "full partakers in all the blessings of our common American citizenship."[72] In 1925, Coolidge referred to the progress of blacks in "all the arts of civilization" in the last sixty years, a degree of progress he called "almost beyond belief." Blacks should be "protected from all violence and supported in the peaceable enjoyment of the fruits of their labors," he urged, and "those who do violence to them should be punished for their crimes." All Americans, irrespective of color, "have "the right to live their own lives under the protection of the public law." Coolidge channeled Lincoln, saying an "enlightened society" meant "the full right to liberty and equality before the law without distinction of race or creed."

Bigotry is only another name for slavery. It reduces to serfdom not only those against whom it is directed, but also those who

seek to apply it. An enlarged freedom can only be secured by
the application of the golden rule.[73]

The Golden Rule, taken from Matthew 7:12, teaches to do unto
others as you would have them do unto you. Lincoln once argued on
that basis: "As I would not be a slave, so I would not be a master."
Coolidge, in effect, updated this to: "As I would not be lynched, so I
would not lynch." For Coolidge, as for Lincoln,[74] Christianity neces-
sitated better treatment of blacks, who, in worshiping Christ, had
"come under its sway." Christianity's "special power" – namely, the
truth of its claims – was "something essential in our civilization." In
addition, its influence had "always and everywhere" led to the "illumination and advancement of the peoples"[75] who practiced it.

Blacks' appreciation for revelation and its dissemination through
their own, often religion-inspired, institutions suggested hope for all
mankind. "The destiny of the great African Continent, [is] to be
added at length – and in a future not now far beyond us – to the
realms of the highest civilization." Coolidge believed that black progress in America was already "one of the marvels of modern history"
and was all the more remarkable in contrast with the "slow and pain-
ful upward movement of humanity." Blacks were a part of the "long
human story," which is part of the "long evolution by which all mankind is gradually being led to higher levels ... approaching nearer
and nearer to the realization of its full and perfected destiny." This
evolution was being directed to something higher, so it was not Dar-
winian, but ordained as if by God himself. Coolidge believed that
"there is something essential in our civilization which gives it a special
power" to civilize blacks, just as he believed it civilized American
Indians, Asians, and other immigrants. The great and many "sacrifices" of blacks throughout history "were borne in a great cause" and
their recent sacrifices in World War I had proved their "devotion to
the high ideal of our country." America should have "refreshment of
faith and renewal of confidence that in every exigency our Negro fel-

low citizens will render the best and fullest measure of service whereof they are capable."[76] Similarly, in his earlier speech accepting the vice-presidential nomination, Coolidge had called for a "more general recognition" of the constitutional rights of the "colored race." After their service in World War I and in purchasing Liberty Bonds, blacks now held "the double title of citizenship, by birth and by conquest." Because they had done their duty, they were due to be "relieved from all imposition, to be defended from lynching, and to be freely granted equal opportunities."[77]

Americans also had a special obligation to end lynching as a "duty to ourselves under our claim that we are an enlightened people."[78] Although the number of lynchings dropped sharply during his presidency, probably in part because of the Coolidge Prosperity,[79] he insisted in late 1926: "We can not justify neglecting to make every effort to eradicate it by law."[80] Blacks had moved from the Emancipation Proclamation to presidential appointments, and in doing so had "shown that they have been worthy of all the encouragement which they have received."[81] Their "cooperation in the life of the Nation," Coolidge said in 1928, "is constantly enlarging."[82]

Although Coolidge asked Congress every year to enact laws against lynching, it did nothing. In 1922, the House of Representatives did pass a bill by 230 to 119 that punished lynching by five years in prison, fined offenders $5,000, and gave federal courts jurisdiction in cases of mob violence.[83] But it languished in a filibuster led by Senate Democrats. Still, the number of lynchings was on the decline.

From 1914 to 1923 the number of lynchings averaged fifty-seven a year. . . . [The 1922 bill] stirred a greater effort in some southern states toward a more orderly law enforcement, and in 1924 lynchings fell to sixteen. In 1925, when Klan activity was at its high, seventeen lynchings were reported. But then the number of lynchings began to drop. And in the first four months of 1928 not a single lynching was reported.[84]

Representative Leonidas C. Dyer, a Republican from Missouri who had witnessed the East St. Louis race riots in 1917 and who repeatedly brought the anti-lynching bill to the floor, pointed to the attention the measure received as an explanation for the decline in racial violence. More likely, demographic and economic pressures were behind the decline. With a torrent of blacks moving north toward toleration and economic opportunity, the South reformed some of its anti-black ways.[85] Without taking credit for it, Coolidge often mentioned the decline in lynchings. He believed that "just as emancipation from slavery was granted by the immortal Lincoln, so is economic emancipation being splendidly wrought out by the colored people for themselves." The Coolidge Prosperity, he said, would help blacks take "their full political rights," which had been "won through the inevitable logic of their position and the rightfulness of their claims."[86] Such a position was only logical if the Declaration's teachings were true and all men had the ability to use reason.

Unfortunately, this entire record is ignored by progressive historians who have focused almost ahistorically on a political distraction that they mistake for a matter of principle.[87] Historian David Greenberg has unfairly criticized Coolidge for "spending his political capital on another round of tax cuts" instead of the anti-lynching bill (even though such bills had long failed). Perhaps, given the economic expansion's benefits for blacks, Coolidge should have focused more on a large tax cut.[88] Greenberg ignores the possibility that these additional tax cuts may have helped blacks as well as whites by further improving the economy, as Coolidge noted to a Howard University audience on June 6, 1924.[89] In her recent history of the Depression, Amity Shlaes has noted the success of blacks at joining the middle class during this period:

> Black illiteracy decreased to 16.4 percent in 1930, from 45 percent in 1900. Fewer black babies died at birth – by half. Black life expectancy was rising. Most important, blacks were able to find work at about the same rates whites did. Data

from the 1930 census would show black unemployment nationally standing slightly below white unemployment.[90]

This progress naturally goes unnoticed by historians who have trouble grasping that blacks experienced substantial progress long before the 1960s civil rights movement, forty years before the federal government took an activist approach on the issue.[91] But there is no denying that the bustling of the economy and the movement of blacks from the South to the North were so significant that they even inspired a new term: "The Great Migration." The Coolidge Prosperity gave them good reason to migrate north.

There's a reason that many historians have ignored or even actively concealed this history of race relations: It doesn't fit the stereotype of "racist Republicans." Liberal historians such as Robert H. Ferrell have condemned Coolidge's "reluctance to speak out" against racism.[92] According to Ferrell, Coolidge did not do enough to stop the Ku Klux Klan, which was on the rise owing to what Charles P. Sweeney of *The Nation* called "the great bigotry merger" between Southern racists and white Midwestern Protestants more concerned with opposing Catholicism than with matters of political ideology.[93] Ferrell notes that Coolidge never openly denounced the Klan, which is true, but he fails to observe that Coolidge never openly mentioned *any* of his opponents by name.[94] If he was unwilling to grant honorable opponents that courtesy,[95] why would he dignify the racists who, in his view, were betraying America? Coolidge reaffirmed his own opposition to the Klan's aims by delivering the commencement address at all-black Howard University just four days before his party's convention, long before his Democratic opponent, John Davis, made it a political issue.

Coolidge's speech at Howard did not go unnoticed. Emmett Scott, secretary-treasurer of Howard, praised it and assured Coolidge that blacks knew of his "distinguished services in behalf of their race."[96] Scott was right: The number of blacks in federal employment reached a high of 51,882 in 1928, up from 22,540 in 1910.[97] These gains weren't a matter of affirmative action – the term wouldn't be invented for another fifty years – but of the meritocracy Coolidge supported. Ferrell, who denounces Coolidge for not making "any notable appointments of black Americans," neglects to mention this record at all.[98] Coolidge, humble as he was, would not have considered this additional black employment out of the ordinary; it was merely a result of his commitment to hire the best, irrespective of race. If there were fewer blacks to hire because they had not yet attained the level of whites in education, it did not mean their situation was permanent.

Felzenberg is fairer than Ferrell, granting that "while Coolidge made no specific mention of the Klan during his campaign, he did appear before assemblages of its potential victims." But this charitable admission is almost unique in Coolidge scholarship. Greenberg, in his book *Calvin Coolidge* (2006), also criticizes Coolidge for refusing to mention the Klan by name and contends that the "mildness of his opposition to the Klan" really "typified his lack of leadership on racial issues."[99] Coolidge's "silence was strategic," according to Greenberg, and may have won him several states, but it couldn't be "written off solely as election-year caution." Why it couldn't, Greenberg doesn't say. He goes on to question the timing of Coolidge's family vacation to Swampscott, Massachusetts, in August 1925 (they vacationed at that time every year)[100] – while the Ku Klux Klan marched down Pennsylvania Avenue, past the White House. Greenberg continues by impugning Coolidge's belief that states, not the federal government, should be encouraged to safeguard constitutional rights – a view Greenberg considers mistaken or morally lacking.[101] But, as the evidence shows, Coolidge worked to protect blacks at the federal level as well.

A few examples prove this. At the prompting of Ruth Whitehead Whaley, the first African American lawyer in New York state, he considered having the attorney general declare martial law whenever a lynching occurred, although he ultimately concluded that "so far, legislation seems [the] only remedy."[102] Whaley was not alone in proposing this step. In 1927, James Weldon Johnson, the first black general secretary of the NAACP, begged Coolidge to intervene, as "head of the armed forces of the United States," after the particularly horrendous lynching of Leonard Woods in Kentucky. There was, Johnson argued, a "break-down of orderly government upon the border of the states of Kentucky and Virginia."[103] Coolidge declined to use the federal government.

And yet despite the president's own words, he did not rely on legislation alone. He declined to take up the Indianapolis State Order of Hibernians on its suggestion that he follow President Grant's lead and "suppress with the arm of the federal government the invisible empire of the KKK – an organization of masked conspirators,"[104] but his refusal to directly intervene was based on prudence. He knew well that the new Klan had proved more national than its post–Civil War incarnation: Among its major areas of activity were Long Island, Maine, Kansas, Texas, California, and Oregon. With his own election in doubt – few vice presidents had won election in their own right – Coolidge probably considered the political map. He would have seen that the governors of Georgia, Alabama, California, and Oregon had all been elected with the help of the Klan.[105] And if the presidential election were decided in the House, as it might be, given the year's three-way race, the seventy-five members who owed their election in some sense to the Klan could effectively end Coolidge's career in Washington.[106] Coolidge knew that the Klan had considerable political power throughout the nation. It even threatened to disrupt the everyday functions of the federal and state governments, as evidenced by a near–civil war under way in Oklahoma.

Coolidge's decision to intervene in the crisis of the Oklahoma state government should be recognized as the profile in courage that it was. Democratic governor John C. Walton declared martial law after the Klan, during and after the Tulsa Race Riot of 1921, committed "unmentionable mutilations ... upon numerous citizens ... [while] scores of others have been taken from their homes at night and beaten and flogged in a most unmerciful way." The majority of the legislature's lower house, the governor knew, were Klansmen.[107] Walton warned that the Klan was encouraging "mob rule," and that two state governments, in effect, were vying for power. He declared martial law in Okmulgee and Tulsa Counties. In Tulsa, he suspended the writ of habeas corpus – a direct violation of the state's constitution. Walton, a Progressive, rushed into political fight after political fight during this crisis, culminating in the indiscriminate use of the state militia and a virtual war against the Klan. The pro-Klan legislature impeached him.[108] Advised by Republicans not to intervene in the matter on the grounds that the governor had, in all likelihood, abused his office by turning the state guard into his private army, Coolidge, in his circumscribed manner, barred the Klan from holding its session to impeach Walton in a federal building.[109] When Coolidge denied the Klan the use of that federal site, a newspaper ran a picture of him with the words, "He Intervenes."[110]

When a citizen wrote to him on August 9, 1924, to express dismay that a black man was running for Congress from a New York district, "in this, a white man's country," Coolidge rejected the premise of a "white man's country" and later included his reply in *Foundations of Republic*, his third and last collection of speeches. While he acknowledged the "manifest impropriety of the President intruding himself in a local contest for nomination" even to such a modest extent, Coolidge explained to readers that he was "amazed to receive such a letter" and therefore felt compelled to respond. In fulfilling their duties to their country, blacks were "just as truly citizens as are any others," he wrote. Denying them their "full political rights . . . could not possibly be permitted." As a Republican president in the tradition of Lincoln and Theodore Roosevelt, Coolidge also believed he had "a responsibility for living up to the traditions and maintaining the principles" of his party. Moreover, he had a constitutional duty to rebuff anti-black efforts:

> Our Constitution guarantees equal rights to all citizens, without discrimination on account of race or color. I have taken my oath to support that Constitution. It is the source of your

rights and my rights. I propose to regard it, and administer it, as the source of the rights of all the people, whatever their belief or race.

Blacks approved of Coolidge's rejection of the letter writer's racist sentiments. The *Chicago Defender*, a leading black newspaper, ran with the front-page headline, "Cal Coolidge Tells Kluxer When to Stop."[111] In an era of Jim Crow, Coolidge knew, as Lincoln did, that republican civilization stands between anarchy and Caesarism, and that the Republic's leaders must therefore tread carefully. They must respect the individual citizen. "The Federal Government ought to be, and is, solicitous for the welfare of every one of its inhabitants," he said in his speech accepting the Republican nomination for president on August 14, 1924, and "there should be no favorites or outcast: no race or religious prejudices in Government."[112]

Nevertheless, Coolidge's opponent in 1924, John W. Davis, unexpectedly denounced the Klan at a rally, which probably surprised the Coolidge campaign. Reporter William Lost wired a story from Plymouth Notch alleging that the president's advisers were caught unawares:

Davis's challenge dropped into the quiet village here with something akin to a bombshell last night. Secretary C. Bascom Slemp [Coolidge's chief of staff] together with newsmen motored from Woodstock to Calvin Coolidge's home and caught the President just as he was retiring. . . . Because the Klan issue wrecked the Democratic convention in New York, Republican leaders had not thought Davis would revive it and they, in turn, were not anxious to raise the issue within their own ranks.[113]

Not sure what to do, the campaign waited. For this supposed failure, Coolidge was attacked by a pro-Democratic newspaper, the *Brooklyn Eagle*:

With candidate Davis and candidate La Follette out flatly and squarely against hooded night rides of the anti-negro and anti-Jewish and anti-Catholic Ku Klux Klan, candidate Calvin Coolidge, Puritan of the Puritans, coming from the stock from which the old Know-Nothings were chiefly recruited, seems to imagine that without denouncing the Klan he can avoid loss of votes by saying nice things about the classes that are the victims of the Klan's hostility.[114]

The gauntlet had been tossed down, as the *New York Times*'s headline showed: "Davis Denounces Ku Klux Klan by Name; Challenges Coolidge to Do Likewise and Take That Issue Out of the Campaign."[115] Of course, it's not so much that Davis had a deep-seated dislike of the Klan; rather, in giving this speech before an audience of Catholics, he was deliberately attempting to inject the Klan issue into a fractious Republican Party. Although the candidate promised not to make any distinctions on the basis of race, his party certainly did. There was not a single black delegate, or even alternate, to the Democratic convention in Madison Square Garden.[116]

In all likelihood, Davis's campaign strategy was merely political rhetoric. For all his denunciation of the Klan, he nonetheless supported segregation later, arguing without fee for the state of South Carolina in favor of *Plessy v. Ferguson*'s separate-but-equal doctrine at the Supreme Court, in *Briggs v. Elliott* (1952), a companion case to, and forerunner of, *Brown v. Board of Education*.[117] Moreover, his Klan denunciations were less than met the eye, for Davis "qualified his personal condemnation [of the Klan] by saying they were sometimes almost justified, and by calling one particular group of Klansmen 'brave men.'"[118] Davis was clearly baiting Coolidge to open his mouth and split the Republican Party between La Follette supporters and Coolidge supporters, just as the Democratic Party had been split between its McAdoo and Smith factions over the issue of the Klan. Only a split between the Midwestern Progressives and the rest of the GOP would ensure a Davis victory, but he couldn't be seen to provoke this openly. But what Davis did not say openly, others said for him. Democratic senator Burton Wheeler announced flatly that "Davis is apparently after the Irish vote" and preposterously tried to brand Coolidge as the Klan's favorite candidate.[119] But events harmed Davis when the Klan refused to endorse either him or Coolidge. H. W. Evans, Imperial Wizard of the Klan, denounced La Follette as the "arch enemy of the nation," but added, "both Coolidge and Davis are nationals and Americans . . . and for this reason the Klan will take no part in the political struggle as far it is concerned."[120] Coolidge, refusing to be baited, bided his time and waited for the appropriate moment to comment.

During this campaign, he was still reeling from the sudden death of his fourteen-year-old son. Coolidge had always been a reluctant campaigner but became even more reticent upon the death of his son.[121] The task fell to his vice-presidential choice, General Charles G. Dawes, who performed admirably and barnstormed the country, delivering more than one hundred speeches in four months and traveling more than 1,500 miles.[122] On August 23, Dawes denounced the Klan by name at an event in Augusta, Maine, a state that was something of a Klan stronghold; there were few blacks in Maine, but the Klan there targeted Catholics, particularly French-Canadian immigrants. "Government cannot last if that way, the way of the Ku Klux Klan, is the way to enforce the law in this country," he said. "Lawlessness cannot be met with lawlessness if civilization is to be maintained."[123]

Although Ferrell gives the impression that Dawes thereby offended the party's sensibilities and that he was " 'spanked' for his anti-Klan utterances"[124] by party bosses, the truth is that the running mate's speech, which firmly articulated Coolidge's position, electrified his audience. Like Coolidge's, Dawes's anti-Klan position was well known and may have been the reason Coolidge and the party bosses chose him for his vice-presidential running mate. In April of 1923, more than a year before Davis and others called for the denunciation of the Klan, Dawes formed the "Minute Men of the Constitution," an organization with the stated goal of opposing the Klan in Illinois.[125]

Its charter, written by Dawes, spoke against the "wide disrespect for the law and the cowardice of political leaders in evading issues involving good government." The country, according to Dawes, needed a new "Bill of Rights to protect the country from those who are trying to dig under the cornerstones of the Constitution."[126] Dawes took great pride in the Klan's opposition to him, which, he argued, "only emphasizes the necessity of what we are doing." He bristled at the suggestion that the Klan was really an arm of law enforcement: "Why does not the Ku Klux Klan, which professes to be for law enforcement, come out from behind their sheets? The truth of the matter is that they are taking the law into their hands in many sections of the country. Lawlessness is not helped by more lawlessness."[127] Dawes reprised many of those same arguments when he denounced the Klan again, as a vice-presidential candidate.

Contrary to what Ferrell argues, there can be no doubt that Coolidge and Dawes were like-minded when it came to rejecting the Klan.[128] The president, according to a Dawes biographer, liked Dawes's speech, calling it "good" the day after it was delivered. Party officials did disapprove of Dawes's remarks, although they reacted timidly at first. Representative Everett Sanders of Indiana warned Dawes not to denounce the Klan because if he did, the Republicans could expect to lose Indiana and Maine, the two states with the most Klan members. Dawes made it clear that he would denounce the Klan anyway, notwithstanding what he called the Maine Republican Party's "extreme apprehension." Indeed, the state Republican organization had attempted to place a gag order on the mere mention of the Klan's name by Republican candidates – as Dawes found out when a Klan official who was also a high-ranking Republican sat near him on the platform.[129]

It soon appeared that Dawes's condemnation of the Klan was causing more trouble than it solved. Representative Fiorello La Guardia, a Progressive Republican from New York, charged that Dawes had "praised the Klan with faint damn" in saying the Klansmen had been wrong to use violence but right to dispense with Governor Walton in Oklahoma for his abuse of power.[130] Socialist Party presidential candidate Norman Thomas denounced as a "left-handed defense of the Klan" Dawes's suggestion that Socialists were involved in the Oklahoma mess.[131] The *New York Times* editorial page said the "trumpet of General Dawes gave a somewhat uncertain sound when he issued his blast against the Klan."[132] Dawes's denunciation was turning into political poison. There was speculation that he was summoned to the Coolidge home in Plymouth Notch for that reason, although Dawes denied it.[133]

Still, Coolidge's opponents had some success in portraying the GOP as weak on civil rights; as a result some black leaders threatened to bolt from the party. Kelly Miller, a black public intellectual, decried Dawes's statement that the Klan had been right to impeach Walton. His harsh words raised the prospect that blacks' traditional support for the Republicans might end:

> Mr. Dawes strikes the Klan a blow with the right hand, and keeps it from falling with the left. He condemns in one breath and condones in another. He speaks one word of regret and one of apology, after the manner of those who extenuate the practice of lynching and lawlessness.[134]

Secretary James Weldon Johnson, secretary of the NAACP, warned that blacks were indeed preparing to break "their historical allegiance" to the Republican Party, if Republicans failed to condemn the Klan unambiguously.[135]

Perhaps the reason Coolidge did not see a need to attack the Klan is that he had never supported it. His secretary and press secretary, C. Bascom Slemp, in replying to a letter from a Jewish voter in New York, made it clearer still: "The President has repeatedly stated that he is not a member of the order and is not in sympathy with its aims and purposes."[136] A frustrated Slemp answered yet another inquiry by insisting that Coolidge's dislike of the Klan had "long been known to those who are in touch with him."[137]

* * *

During his presidency, Coolidge knew that many state governments, in not punishing lynchings, were neglecting their duties to their citizens. But with little support from Southern Democrats or Midwestern populists, he felt his hands were tied.[138] Walking a delicate balance, he appealed to the people's sense of right and wrong. He argued in 1926:

> *The doctrine of State rights is not a privilege to continue in wrong-doing but a privilege to be free from interference in well-doing.* This Nation is bent on progress. . . . It has decided to extend the blessing of an enlightened humanity. Unless the States meet these requirements, the National Government reluctantly will be crowded into the position of enlarging its own authority at their expense. I want to see the policy adopted by the States of discharging their public functions so faithfully that instead of an extension on the part of the Federal Government there can be a contraction.[139]

Civil rights activists appreciated Coolidge's position. Writer Louis I. Jaffé, for instance, would quote this speech favorably in 1935 in his one-man crusade against lynching. Senator Carter Glass of Virginia, Jaffé charged in "Rights Fail When Duties Falter," had misused Coolidge's William and Mary speech in defending the filibuster and, by implication, lynching. On the contrary, Jaffé pointed out, Coolidge's argument "was that the Federal Government would invade the sovereignty of the States if they persevered in a policy of indifference to the action required by the 'great body of public opinion of the nation.' " Far from arguing in favor of states doing whatever they wished, Coolidge had said the federal government would intervene if states failed to deliver in "meting out justice between man and man." It was "the failure of the States vigorously to do their duty" that obligated the federal government to act.[140] Jaffé saw that lynching was a "curse on Southern life." He concluded, in language Coolidge himself could have written:

"The best way to beat it is not to rely on a State rights standard in Washington . . . but to get at the evil of lynching itself. There will be no anti-lynching bills if there are no lynchings."[141] He wanted the lynchings stopped immediately but doubted the wisdom of using legislation to stop them. When Dwight D. Eisenhower – the next Republican president to take a serious stand for civil rights – integrated Arkansas schools by declaring martial law in Little Rock, Arkansas, on September 25, 1957, after a judge's verdict, he was following in Coolidge's footsteps. David A. Nichols, author of *A Matter of Justice: Eisenhower and the Beginning of the Civil Rights Revolution* (2007), has suggested that the general turned president was one of the unsung heroes of the civil rights movement – if he was, it was because he carried Coolidge's tune.

* * *

Although Coolidge did not denounce the Klan by name in 1924, he appealed to a sense of "toleration" in 1925. He even rejected the Klan's motto, "America First," because he rejected the reasoning behind the concept.

> The generally expressed desire of "America First" can not be criticized. It is a perfectly correct aspiration for our people to cherish. But the problem we have to solve is how to make America first. It cannot be done by the cultivation of national bigotry, arrogance, or selfishness. Hatreds, jealousies, and suspicions will not be productive of any benefits in this direction. Here again we must apply the rule of toleration. . . .
>
> By toleration I do not mean indifference to evil. I mean respect for different kinds of good. Whether one traces his Americanism back three centuries to the *Mayflower*, or three years to the steerage, is not half so important as whether his Americanism is real and genuine. No matter by what various crafts we came here, we are all now in the same boat.[142]

If that last bit sounds familiar, it is because these words are said to have been uttered by another civil rights leader – Martin Luther King Jr.

Indians

Our goal is the free Indian. The orphan-asylum idea must be killed in the mind of Indian and white man. The Indians should know that he is upon the road to enjoy or suffer full capacity. He is to have his opportunity as a "forward-looking man." [143]

The Indian, though a man without a country, the Indian who has suffered a thousand wrongs considered the white man's burden and from mountains, plains and divides, the Indian threw himself into the struggle to help throttle the unthinkable tyranny of the Hun. The Indian helped to free Belgium, helped to free all the small nations, helped to give victory to the Stars and Stripes. The Indian went to France to help avenge the ravages of autocracy. Now, shall we not redeem ourselves by redeeming all the tribes? [144]

They tell us you are the thirtieth President of this great country, but to us you are our first President. [145]

Message from a Sioux chieftain to President Coolidge, 1927

As with blacks, the Founders wondered how Indians could be made a part of American national life. Jefferson's thought on the question bears scrutiny because he was not as pessimistic about harmony between Indians and whites as he was about the black–white relationship. Writing to Benjamin Hawkins, who served as general superintendent of Indian affairs to the Creeks and all tribes south of the Ohio River, Jefferson expressed his hope that there might be peace between the two groups, won through the practice of science and reason. In his first inaugural, he had criticized those Indian leaders who "inculcate sanctimonious reverence for the customs of their ancestors." And in Query 11 of *Notes on the State of Virginia*, he laments:

"Great societies cannot exist without government. The Savages therefore break them into small ones." Jefferson wished, rather, that these leaders would "induce [Indians] to exercise their reason," which was what promised them peace and a better life. This peace through better living would come when the Indians learned better forms of agriculture and household manufacture and made more productive use of the land. Once they learned agriculture and became better farmers, Jefferson predicted, "a coincidence of interests will be produced between those [educated Indians] who have land to spare, and want other necessaries, and those [white settlers] who have such necessaries to spare, and want lands."[146] This commerce would produce one people through intermarriage and shared common interest. "The ultimate point and rest for [Indians] is to let our settlements and theirs meet and blend together, to intermix, and become one people," Jefferson wrote. Union of this type would keep both parties safe and keep each from being "exposed to the many casualties which may endanger them while a separate people."[147]

Therefore Jefferson looked with joy upon the decision by an unnamed settlement of Indians to become American citizens. He encouraged Hawkins to keep trying to assimilate Indians, but he also knew that prudence demanded patience and caution, lest the novelty of the project "shock" the Indians. Gradual assimilation was far better, Jefferson reasoned, and there was some indication that this was occurring. The Cherokees in Georgia, Jefferson wrote to a neighbor, were "contemplating the establishment of regular laws" and beginning to create a "republican" form of government.[148] Such developments suggested that the Indian communities would give up their native ways and become "great societies." But Jefferson's hopes may have been in vain. A later president, John Quincy Adams, wrote in a State of the Union address, that Americans had been "far more successful in the acquisition of [Indian] lands than in imparting to them the principles, or inspiring them with the spirit of civilization."[149]

Jefferson's thoughts on Indians, did not, unfortunately, set the pattern for federal policy. Rather than intermixing as Jefferson had hoped, Indians were forcibly marched by President Jackson on a "trail of tears" to reservations, where they quickly became segregated wards of the federal government and languished in poverty. The Indian wars throughout the middle and late nineteenth century further reduced their numbers. In the post–Civil War period, Indians were seen as a plague upon the rest of America. As one secretary of the interior remarked in a report in 1865, their total destruction "has been openly advocated by gentlemen of high position, intelligence, and personal character."[150]

But twenty-two years later, policy turned back in Jefferson's assimilationist direction when Congress passed the Dawes Act in 1887. Congressman Henry Dawes of Massachusetts hoped to divide the land on reservations and thereby give the Indians private parcels. Dawes was said to claim that to be civilized meant to "wear civilized clothes . . . cultivate the ground, live in houses, ride in Studebaker wagons, send children to school, drink whiskey and own property." This was a return to the Jeffersonian expectation that Indians should give up their ancient cultures for "the habits of civilized life." Although the Dawes Act was designed to help the Indians become self-sufficient property owners, about ninety thousand Indians were in fact dispossessed. Over the law's forty-seven-year lifetime, tribes lost ninety million acres of treaty land, roughly two-thirds of the 1887 land base. Unfortunately, the acreage allocated to most Indians was not enough for economic vitality. Worse yet, the division of land between heirs upon the allottee's death led to the land's being sold off to white buyers at fire-sale prices.

And yet the Dawes Act was not a complete failure.[151] It trained a generation of young Indians – educated in boarding schools operated by the much-maligned Bureau of Indian Affairs – who became effective spokesmen for their peoples. Unlike many modern-day Indian leaders, they supported assimilation into mainstream American life.[152] The creation of the Bureau of Indian Affairs (BIA) and its twenty-five boarding schools in fifteen states sowed the seeds of the greatest civil rights success of the Coolidge years: the Indian Citizenship Act of 1924.[153]

The campaign for citizenship moved quickly. In February 1923, federal Indian Commissioner (and top official for Indian affairs) Charles Burke advised, despite "caustic criticism" from self-appointed Indian supporters, that all Indians give up their ceremonial dancing practices, which spooked Christian America. [154] In so arguing, Burke set off a row in the press with the Indian community that lasted for months.[155] Supporters of the dances pointed out that these were part of Indian culture – and therefore guaranteed protection by the Constitution. Opponents questioned the effects of native dancing and other customs.

Among those opponents was Edith Manville Dabb, director of the Young Women's Christian Association's program with Indian girls. Drawing on her experiences with the Sioux and other tribes, Dabb pointed out that young women were often forced back to reservations to be mothers, rather than educated, and that the "dance giveaways," in which the Indians destroyed their own property through neglect or gave it away altogether, tended to keep them in poverty. She argued that Americans were no more bound to respect these practices than the British were bound to respect the customs in India of *sati* (the self-immolation of a widow upon her husband's death) or child marriage. Like Jefferson, Dabb wondered what should be done about the "primitive peoples" of America.

> What shall it make of its charges since it is evident they cannot live untouched by the civilization which surrounds them? Shall it throw as many barriers around them as possible to keep them artificially isolated both from the advantages and disadvantages of modern life which threatens to engulf them? Or shall it prepare them for citizenship and the part in the march of progress which cannot eventually be denied to their descendants?
>
> Our supreme blunder, through the past 300 years, has been our generosity in giving the Indian the worst of our civilization and our failure to offset that gift with the best of our

culture, through which he might by now have slowly advanced to the point where he had outgrown the brutalities common to all primitive peoples.[156]

Joseph W. Latimer, friend of the Indian-rights activist Carlos Montezuma,[157] agreed. The Indian, he held, must be seen as a "free-born human" – and not, as current law would have him, as a "ward" or "incompetent." Every Indian had a right to claim his "human and divine right" to his "own life," but many "well-intentioned" people had lost sight of the Indian as a man possessing natural rights.[158]

The controversy came to a head when the Coolidge-appointed Committee of One Hundred met on December 12 and 13, 1923, to discuss Indians and agree on conclusions.[159] Its conclusions, released in January 1924, included recommendations that the government increase funding for health care, education,and scholarships.[160] It urged higher salaries for members of the Indian Service, in the interest of more quickly shutting down the BIA, which had made Indians into wards of the state. The committee, however, also spoke euphemistically of "protected citizens" (perpetuating, in slightly different language, the old concepts of "wards and restricted citizens"). It did so "to protect [Indians] from the rapacity of certain elements that prey upon those unable to protect themselves." This language was seized upon by the Indian advocate Latimer as proof of the committee's gaping deficiencies. Latimer wanted Indians to stop being wards.

Latimer also seized upon the committee's call for a "Court of Claims" to arbitrate disputes between Indians and the federal government. He argued that such a court would be "absolutely of no benefit to the Indian as an individual" and also contended that the recommendation was a ruse to keep the BIA relevant.[161] It is not clear whether Coolidge agreed, although he vetoed a total of fifty bills, ten of which concerned the Indians and the Courts of Claims. Since he made no statement when he vetoed these bills, it remains an open question whether he agreed with Latimer, wanted to save money, or both.

In any event, on June 2, Coolidge signed the Indian Citizenship Act of 1924 into law.[162] The magnitude of the bill's passage was remarked upon by the *New York Times*, which noted that there had been a "long road to legal absorption of the Red Man."[163] As "the 'yellow peril' recedes," *New York Times* editorial writer Ernest Harvier opined, the "opportunity of the redskin appears."[164] By Harvier's count, some 125,000 Indians out of a population of 300,000 became eligible for citizenship. The citizenship law had no effect on their property, tribal or personal, and even, he noted approvingly, "let in . . . the illiterate."[165]

The passage of the 1924 act seemed to bear out Jefferson's hope that Indians would jettison their old cultures. The *New York Times* noted that as early as 1926 many more "red men" had taken up "civilized ways" and that "only 20 of . . . 371 tribes hold to the tepee."[166] In cultivating himself in this manner, the Indian was proving himself worthy of citizenship, just as he had shown himself worthy of citizenship on the battlefield, where, as Coolidge noted, the men "of our own aboriginal population" had shown themselves "equally proud of the name American."[167] When it came to the Indians – at least fourteen thousand of whom fought for the Allied effort in World War I Coolidge had full confidence that they could assimilate.[168] This may have been because his family had Indian blood,[169] from his grandmother, Sally Thompson Coolidge.[170] In any event, Coolidge believed the Indians had proved they were not savages. "Work is not a curse," but rather "the prerogative of intelligence, the only means to manhood, and the measure of civilization," Coolidge said on February 4, 1916, before an audience of Amherst alumni. "Savages do not work."[171] Indians, who had worked in the modern sense and had become soldiers and farmers, had shown that they were fit for civilization. In the final analysis, Coolidge would have agreed with Indian Commissioner Burke's assessment that, "instead of fighting each other, they fight under one flag, having been brothers-in-arms and brothers-in-death against a common foe." Burke predicted that there would soon be an end to the wardship Indians suffered under federal control.[172]

The Indian Citizenship Act of 1924 was only a step on the road to assimilation, Coolidge acknowledged, but he hoped that the Indians would indeed become full citizens in reality as well as in law. "The condition of the American Indian has much improved in recent years," he said in 1927, but despite the grant of citizenship in 1924, "there remains much to be done."[173] Coolidge wanted to "advance [to] the time when the Indians may become self-sustaining" and wanted, "as rapidly as possible," to grant the responsibility for Indian policy to the states. The crucial test was whether or not Indians would cling to the truth of civilization, which they could do only by shedding their past. "Give a savage tribe firearms and a distillery," he feared, "and their members will exterminate each other."[174] Such were the dangers of the products of modern science if one did not have the ideals or knowledge to use them correctly. But ideals could be taught, Coolidge insisted, especially with an emphasis on Indian education.[175]

Having done his part to actualize Jefferson's ideal of harmony between the two communities, Coolidge was awarded membership in several Indian tribes in the years after the citizenship law passed. On October 22, 1924, he joined the Smoki tribe. When asked by a reporter about his decision to affiliate with another one, he replied: "Just because I belong to one tribe is no reason why I shouldn't belong to another."[176] Despite his distaste for calling attention to himself, he donned Indian garb on one occasion, a fitting symbol, perhaps, of his hope that the Indian and white communities might become one people. On August 17, 1927, Coolidge was inducted into the Sioux tribe and named "Leading Eagle."[177] He addressed the seven thousand assembled Sioux leaders about the history of Indian–white relations and shared his hope that they might, thanks to the law's provisions, unite. The new law "symbolized the consummation of what for many years has been the purpose of the Federal Government – to merge the Indians into the general citizenry and the body politic of the nation."[178] Favorably noting an 1871 law as the "first step toward individualizing them" and "making them citizens," Coolidge said the 1924 act would move in this spirit and create a "new relationship" between the Indians and the government, which would now "deal with Indians as individual men and women," rather than as tribesmen. He quoted the following section from that bill: "That hereafter no Indian nation or tribe within the territory of the United States shall be acknowledged or recognized as an independent nation, tribe or bureau with whom the United States may contract by treaty."[179]

Once whites and Indians warred, but now "peace and understanding . . . reign everywhere." Now that the hatchet had been buried between the two peoples, Coolidge continued, "the Indian problem" became "one simply of effective social service, practical philanthropy, and education." It could, in other words, be solved. There were still some complexities to be worked out, however, with the "recently primitive" peoples. "While thousands of them have succeeded in adjusting themselves to the new order of things, a great portion, mostly the older ones, still cling to the old ways." The "manifold complexities" inherit in dealing with all these different tribes made dealing with Indians difficult, according to Coolidge.

On the one hand, we find a considerable potion are so little advanced that they can speak but few English words, while on the other hand, we find tens of thousands who speak, read and write the English language, and a large percentage of this class have had a grammar school education and many are graduates of high schools, colleges, and universities.

A "practical solution" to dealing with all of these laws "cannot be effected by appeals to sentimentality, by loose talk, by ill-considered legislation, by hysterical campaigns, or by the insistence of those in charge of the administration of Indian affairs that their policies and methods are always the right ones." The missionaries had a role to play in "making them all self-supporting citizens."[180]

In spite of these problems, the Indians could become good citizens because, as Coolidge noted, so many of them had volunteered to fight and, if necessary, die for their country, making the "supreme sacrifice." He ended his speech to the Sioux by reflecting upon a scene he had witnessed at the burial of the Unknown Soldier: "A group of old

Indian warriors . . . arranged themselves around the tomb, while one, acting for the whole Indian people, laid upon the bier his war bonnet." This was "not an idle gesture," Coolidge noted. "It symbolized the outstanding fact that the red men and their neighbors had been brought together as one people and that never again would there be hostility between the two races. As one of those old warriors said: Who knows but that this Unknown Soldier was an Indian boy?" The Indians were fit for citizenship because they were fit for sacrifice.[181]

Japanese Americans

The racism of Coolidge's time was on full display in May 1913 when the newly inaugurated President Wilson refused to discuss allowing Japanese Americans to naturalize. In his campaign the previous year, Wilson had cultivated anti-Japanese and anti-Chinese prejudice, while Theodore Roosevelt emphasized fairness. Roosevelt actually won the states where that prejudice was most prevalent, California and Washington, but Wilson won the election. In short order, Wilson appointed Anthony Caminetti, the California state senator who had been the moving force behind the anti-Japanese Webb-Haney Alien Land Law of 1913, as commissioner-general of immigration. In the campaign Wilson had deliberately avoided taking a stand on the racist laws in California that limited the rights of Japanese immigrants. He argued that states had every right to pass their own laws: "Nobody can for a moment challenge the constitutional right of California to pass such land laws as she pleases." Japanese ambassador Viscount Sutemi Chinda protested the California law in 1914, but Wilson said he was constitutionally unable to do much about it.[182] This unwillingness to support Japanese Americans led to foreign-policy quarrels, just as Roosevelt had worried it might. The Japanese consul general Kametaro Ijima also protested the California law, especially the provisions banning aliens from owning property, but Wilson ignored him. Instead, Wilson implausibly blamed the Treaty of Portsmouth, which ended the Russo–Japanese war in 1905, for the growing discord between the two nations.[183] It was good politics, if poor constitutional thought or policy.[184] Wilson narrowly won California in his 1916 reelection race, defeating Charles Hughes in the state by a mere 3,800 votes out of nearly a million cast.[185] In 1920, Harding endorsed anti-Japanese restrictions and thus made sure the normally Republican state didn't tip to the Democrats again. Harding won not only California, but also every county in the Pacific-coast states.[186] Restriction was popular. Californians approved a 1920 law tightening Japanese land restrictions by a two-to-one margin, but opponents of such laws actually saw reason for hope in this, having feared that the initiative might pass by ten to one.[187] The Tokyo-based American-Japanese Relations Committee went to work trying to increase "friendship and goodwill" between "the two neighboring nations of the Pacific."[188]

On the international stage, too, Wilson rebuffed the Japanese. In February 1919, the Japanese delegation to the Paris Peace Conference proposed an amendment calling for racial equality and equality among the nations:

> The equality of nations being a basic principle of the League of Nations, the High Contracting Parties agree to accord as soon as possible to all alien nationals of states, members of the League, equal and just treatment in every respect making no distinction, either in law or in fact, on account of their race or nationality.[189]

This proposal passed by a vote of 17 to 11. But Wilson, as chairman of the conference, overturned it on the grounds that due to the existence of strong opposition, a unanimous vote was required. Japanese public opinion was very much in favor of the amendment, and the Japanese press attacked Wilson, referring to his "dangerous justice," while cursing the "female demon within him."[190] With Japanese pride so affronted, the nation's representatives pressed its territorial grievances with a keen intensity. After giving Japan most of the former German colonies in the Pacific, the Lansing-Ishii Agreement all but

ceded China to Japan. In doing so, it set the stage for the Asian war
– eventually the Asian theater of World War II – that began with the
Japanese invasion of Manchuria in 1931.

Coolidge, by contrast, admired the Japanese throughout his political career. He and his administration did all they could to prevent
some of the more unreasonable attacks against the Japanese, though
to no avail. At a speech in 1918 to the Roxbury Historical Society on
Bunker Hill Day (June 17), Coolidge cited the Japanese "reforms of
our own times" as an instance when the long-standing "conflict
between privilege and freedom" was being peacefully settled. Japan
took another step toward modernity in 1918 when Hara Takashi
became the first commoner to serve as prime minister. Coolidge's
invocation in this speech of the Japanese experiment in democracy –
he later ranked it alongside the American Revolution – is further evidence of his genuine belief that all mankind was capable of being
ruled by "reason" rather than "custom." As he said of the successful
reforms of the eighteenth century:

> Class and caste and place, all the distinctions based on appear-
> ance and accident were giving way before reality. Men turned
> from distinctions which were temporal to those which were
> eternal. The sovereignty of kings and the nobility of peers
> was swallowed up in the sovereignty and nobility of all men. . . .
> The rule of the people had begun. . . . It was an example of
> the great law of human progress and civilization.[191]

And yet, for the Japanese, progress was difficult and seemed to
have definite limits. The reformist Takashi was assassinated in 1921,
and the country descended into a combination of renewed despotism
and what one scholar called "government by assassination."[192] ("The
thirties began early in Japan," another noted.[193]) A government of
consent gave way to a government of compulsion and violence.

Coolidge could not have known the fate that would befall Takashi
in 1921, but in 1918, he looked on as Japan became what was then

called an "imperial democracy," instituting a system that was akin to Britain's parliament. Coolidge hailed this transformation and welcomed a representative of the Japanese people – "a people who have never failed to respond to an act of kindness"[194] – to Massachusetts. There, on Independence Day, the then–lieutenant governor addressed a ceremony to honor the relationship between Manjiro Nakahama and the town of Fairhaven. Nakahama was a fourteen-year-old boy who had been shipwrecked on a fishing expedition in 1841. He was found by Captain William Whitfield, an American whaler, and educated at Fairhaven's Oxford School. Nakahama wanted above all else to return to Japan, even though at the time that would mean death, the penalty for leaving the island nation. After working on board a whaling ship, he joined with two other compatriots and chartered a ship to return to Japan. He was made a *hatamoto*, or samurai, and served as a translator when Admiral Perry opened Japan to Western trade. At the ceremony in 1918, Nakahama's son Toichiro gave a sword to Fairhaven in thanks for educating his father.[195]

In speaking of the young Nakahama, Coolidge praised the Japanese people by extension. Nakahama "knew the duty of filial piety lay upon him according to the teachings of his race," and he was "determined to pursue the course which he had been taught was right." Coolidge suggested that the samurai sword was in a sense transformed into something new – a relic of republican "duty," something that unites all those associated with it. The sword, "once the emblem of place and caste and arbitrary rank," would "hereafter be a token not only of the friendship that exists between two nations but a token of liberty, of freedom, and of the recognition by the governments of both these nations of the rights of the people." It would remain in Fairhaven as a reminder of a "mutual pledge by the mutual giver and the receiver that the motive which inspired the representatives of each race to do right is to be a motive which is to govern the people of the earth."[196]

Sadly, it appeared that the Supreme Court and the Senate wanted to do wrong by the Japanese. The case of Takao Owaza, who took

his appeal to become an American citizen all the way up to the
Supreme Court in 1922, is a particularly poignant example. Owaza
had seemingly done everything worthy of praise by the standards of
the time: He spoke English at home, worked for an American company, studied at the University of California, and attended Christian
churches.[197] But when he began applying for citizenship in 1914, suc-
cessive courts denied his candidacy on the grounds that naturalization was available only to people of white or African descent. The
Supreme Court conceded that Ozawa was "well qualified by character and education," also noting the "culture and enlightenment of
the Japanese people," but still found against him, on the grounds that
the "science of ethnology" made clear that the Japanese were not
Caucasians. Still, the Court made clear that it was simply following
congressional intent and that its decision should not be taken as "a
suggestion of individual unworthiness or racial inferiority."

California senator Hiram Johnson, a leading Progressive in his
day and a former candidate for the presidency, argued that the ongoing legislative efforts that restricted all immigration on an equal
basis were wrongheaded because they failed to understand the distinct danger of the Japanese and their settlement. California's other
senator, James D. Phelan, agreed and pointed to what he called the
"incontrovertible fact that the Japanese continue ever Japanese, and
that their allegiance is always to Tokyo."[198] Phelan also said, even
more bluntly: "A Jap is a Jap," adding that unless something was done
soon, the Japanese were fully "capable of taking the place of the
White man."[199] The perceived intelligence and ethnocentrism of the
Japanese would prove their undoing when, in 1924, Congress passed
an anti-Japanese measure. The House Committee, for instance,
inserted a provision to bar "aliens ineligible to citizenship" – the Japanese, post-*Ozawa*, among them – from entering America as immigrants.[200] Congress even hired its own eugenics expert. It appeared
Coolidge would be forced by public opinion and Congress to sign the
Immigration Act of 1924, and although he acted behind the scenes
to defeat its anti-Japanese provision, he failed.[201]

*   *   *

The previous year, Japan's already precarious government had collapsed in the aftermath of a tremendous earthquake, with its attendant anarchy. In the first act of his presidency, Coolidge dispatched the Navy's Asiatic fleet[202] after an earthquake and typhoon hit Tokyo and Yokohama on September 1, 1923, killing more than 143,000 people and injuring more than 100,000.[203] The earthquake led to an inferno, as open fire grills toppled over and set the ground ablaze. The government broke down and anarchy ensued as the Japanese turned against Korean laborers, accusing them of poisoning water wells. In the panic, anyone who looked Korean was massacred.[204] Coolidge, as titular head of the American Red Cross, appealed to the American people to address the catastrophe:

> While its extent has not as yet been officially reported, enough is known to justify the statement that the cities of Tokyo and Yokohama, and surrounding towns and villages, have been largely if not completely destroyed by earthquake, fire and flood, with a resultant appalling loss of life and destitution and distress, requiring measures of urgent relief. Such assistance as is within the means of the Executive Department of the government will be rendered; but realizing the great suffering which now needs relief and will need relief in the days to come, I am prompted to appeal to the American people, whose sympathies have always been so comprehensive, to contribute in aiding the unfortunate and in giving relief to the people of Japan.[205]

Coolidge asked for $10 million in donations, and by December the American people gave $12 million, an unprecedented amount.[206]

But while the American people helped the Japanese, their congressional representatives worked to undo years of diplomatic progress. Secretary of State Hughes insisted that the Japanese-exclusion clause of the 1924 Immigration Act violated the terms of the "Gentleman's Agreement" of 1907 and would lead to a diplomatic row between Japan and America, the two powers set to dominate the Pacific. The informal arrangement, negotiated at the behest of President Roosevelt in response to the 1906 earthquake in San Francisco that led to the segregation of Japanese school children, provided that Japan would reduce emigration to America if Japanese children already in the U.S. were integrated in the schools. The Japanese government agreed to the deal out of fear that it would otherwise be subjected to a humiliating law akin to the Chinese Exclusion Act.[207] The 1924 Immigration Act threatened to undo the informal agreement, as Coolidge lamented on May 26, when he told Congress:

> I regret the impossibility of severing from it the exclusion provision, which, in light of existing law, affects especially the Japanese. I gladly recognize that the enactment of this provision does not imply any change in our sentiment of admiration and cordial friendship for the Japanese people, a sentiment which has had and will continue to have abundant manifestation. The bill rather expresses the determination of the Congress to exercise its prerogatives in defining by legislation the control of immigration instead of leaving it to international arrangements.[208]

While Coolidge was clear that he supported *restrictions* on the number of Japanese immigrants, he opposed actual exclusion. He worried that Congress had embarrassed his government in its relations with Japan. He found "this method of securing [exclusion] . . . unnecessary and deplorable." "If the exclusion principle stood alone, I should disapprove it without hesitation, if sought in this way, at this time."[209] Coolidge consistently stressed that the decision to exclude all Japanese was particularly bad at "this time" and that he did not want to "wound the sensibilities of a friendly nation."[210] We don't know whether Coolidge thought it a wise policy at *any* time. Coolidge signed the immigration law because he supported its other provisions. It proved to be, as one historian has put it, "another step on the road to war,"[211] but Coolidge could not have known that.

Immigrants

For immigrants, the picture was complicated. The party of Lincoln had jettisoned the principles of the Declaration by calling, in its 1920 presidential platform, for restricting immigration on the basis of eugenics. "The selective tests that are at present applied," it urged, "should be improved by requiring a higher physical standard, a more complete exclusion of mental defectives and of criminals, and a more effective inspection applied as near the source of immigration as possible, as well as at the point of entry."[212] Harding's secretary of labor, James J. Davis, was the son of Welsh immigrants, but he appeared to favor discrimination. Although Harding called him "one of the most humane and sympathetic men in all the land,"[213] he was also a eugenicist, believing that this new "science" proved human inequality.[214]

Eugenics proved that the Declaration of Independence's teachings were false, Davis held. To preserve the Republic, he said, Americans must distinguish between "bad stock and good stock, weak blood and strong blood, sound heredity and sickly human stuff." He favored "selective immigration" because he worried that hard-working immigrants – "beavers" – were being exploited by "rats" who were "feeble-minded, imbeciles, insane, psychologically inferior, reds, anarchists, and communists." Davis went further, drawing from his family's history as Welsh iron workers. The immigrants now arriving in America were, in his metaphor, pig iron ill suited to the hot fire of the melting pot. If all these ill-suited immigrants were allowed to continue coming to the U.S., well-suited immigrants from Northern and Western Europe would be deterred. "Labor that valued itself, labor that required a certain standard of living," would stay "at home rather than come to America to compete with slum-boarding-house conditions created by our impatient demand for quantity production at any cost."[215]

Throughout his time in government, Coolidge kept Secretary Davis, despite Davis's eugenicist views. But he did not endorse his drastic proposals for immigration restriction. As mentioned earlier, Coolidge favored, instead, making the census or naturalization records the basis for quotas (meaning they would be doled out to different countries based on the origins of Americans as of the 1920 census). This would have had much the same effect as Davis's proposals in that it would preserve America's current ethnic percentages, but it also conformed to Coolidge's thoughts on citizenship because it respected the particular immigrants who had already settled in America. Unlike Davis, Coolidge professed to take no position on the fitness of the immigrants who would have been restricted by his preferred policy. This was perhaps wishful thinking – or politics. As a life-long Republican with Whiggish sympathies and as a protectionist, Coolidge looked upon immigration restriction in much the same way as he saw the restriction of goods. "Restricted immigration is not an offensive but purely a defensive action," he told the 1924 Republican Convention. "It is not adopted in criticism of others in the slightest degree, but solely for the purpose of protecting ourselves."[216] If immigration were not restricted, the opportunity of the American people, "no matter what their origin . . . to continue in the enjoyment of their present unprecedented advantages . . . would certainly be destroyed by the tremendous influx of foreign peoples."[217] Lest he be accused of discrimination, Coolidge noted: "The first sufferers would be the most recent immigrants, unaccustomed to our life and language and industrial methods. We want to keep wages and living conditions good for everyone who is now here or who may come here."[218] As he later wrote in his post-presidential column, his criticism of excessive immigration wasn't racial, but prudential:

Every race and creed that has come here in numbers has shown examples of unsurpassed loyalty and devotion to our country. But only by coming slowly, avoiding city policies and spreading over the land do they arrive in the real United States. . . .

The economic reasons for restricting immigration are not always the most important. We have certain standards of life that we believe are best for us. We do not ask other nations to discard theirs, but we do wish to preserve ours. Standards, government, and culture under free institutions are not so much a matter of constitutions and laws as of public opinion, ways of thought and methods of life of the people. We reflect on no one in wanting immigrants who will be assimilated into our ways of thinking and living. Believing we can best serve the world in that way, we restrict immigration.[219]

He also understood that such a position could play well with the labor groups that opposed him after the Boston strike of 1919. He thought, like Samuel Gompers, president of the American Federation of Labor, "that the standards of America should not be lowered by the influx of immigrants not easily assimilable."[220] "We cast no aspersions on any race or creed," Coolidge argued, "but we must remember that every object of our institutions of society and government will fail unless America be kept American."[221] Doing that meant keeping wages high.

We ought to have no prejudice against an alien because he is an alien. The standard which we apply to our inhabitants is that of manhood, not place of birth. *Restrictive immigration is to a large degree for economic purposes.* It is applied in order that we may not have a larger annual increment of good people within our borders than we can weave into our economic fabric in such a way as to supply their needs without undue injury to ourselves.[222]

After making his economic argument, Coolidge endorsed the melting-pot metaphor as traditionally understood. American history, he said, had "demonstrated conclusively that there is a spiritual quality shared by all races and conditions of men which is their universal heritage and common nature."[223] A common heritage and common nature could mean a common politics, but only if immigrants could be readily absorbed. With lower levels of immigration, that seemed easier to achieve. Immigrants, particularly those who arrived later, "nevertheless need the opportunity to learn to read and write the English language, that they may come into more direct contact with the [American] ideals and standards of our life, political and social."[224] The task for politicians was to make sure that "education" was the "handmaid of citizenship." That meant teaching new immigrants the standards and habits of self-government. This was not an easy task, and it required time and a willingness by immigrants to shed their old ways of life. He urged immigrants to assimilate (move *toward* a sense of American identity) rather than, as John Derbyshire would later call it, "absimilate" (move *away from* American identity and keep separate). Coolidge also seemed to share the concerns of those who feared the alien radicals among America's new citizens, urging: "Those who do not want to be partakers of the American spirit ought not to settle in America."[225]

For those immigrants who did wish to join American life and to share its presuppositions, Coolidge was welcoming, but he cautioned: "New arrivals should be limited to our capacity to absorb them into the ranks of good citizenship." All Americans could agree that the wise thing to do was to assimilate immigrants slowly.

> We are all agreed, whether we be Americans of the first or of the seventh generation on this soil, that it is not desirable to receive more immigrants than can reasonably be assured of bettering their condition by coming here. For the sake both of those who would come and more especially of those already here, it has been thought wise to avoid the danger of increasing our numbers too fast.[226]

If immigrants complied with the demands placed upon them, though, they were owed a special obligation and welcome because they "came to us with stouts hearts and high hopes of bettering their state." Immigrants "have contributed much to making our country what it is." Like blacks and American Indians, they had "magnificently proved their loyalty by contributing their full part when the war made demand for sacrifices by all Americans."[227]

Coolidge had seen this participation in public life, and the hope it could stir in the breast of "stout hearts," as a young politician in Northampton when he witnessed the rise of the Irish. Though much is made of Coolidge's Puritan, Yankee background, Massachusetts was one of the most ethnically diverse states in the country, let alone New England, and Coolidge had ample experience with Irish immigrants. Unlike other immigrant groups, the Irish quickly took to political life, in part because they understood English (and, in those days of political machines, graft, though Coolidge was immune from its criminal charms). Coolidge worked with a friend, Jim Luckey, to get out the "Coolidge Irish Democrats," who always supported him – and no other Republican – on the ballot. During his campaign in the Northampton mayoral race, Coolidge wrote to his father that at least four hundred Democrats voted for him and gave him the lead, to the chagrin of the local Irish leaders. Coolidge wrote, "They knew that I had done things for them, bless their honest Irish hearts."[228]

Just what had Coolidge done? As a Northampton city councilman in 1898 and 1899, he issued a resolution to honor a deceased Irish-American Democrat.[229] The Irish typically voted Democratic, but Coolidge effectively forged a group of new "Coolidge Democrats." The *Daily Hampshire Gazette* noted his support for Irish Americans:

He said he never made any distinction between American citizens of different nationality. He had always found the Irish people good Americans and good citizens. He had appointed about 75 of them to responsible positions because he found them good Americans and well qualified for public service.[230]

Similarly, as governor, Coolidge shrewdly appointed a wide variety of people to a wide variety of positions. In 1919, he appointed fifty-five Catholics, seven Jews, two Swedes, three Italians, eight French-men, and one Pole. In 1920, he named forty-two Catholics, eight Jews, three Swedes, three Italians, two Frenchmen, one Pole, and one Portuguese.[231] His cabinet was diverse, but there is no indication that it suffered from a modern-day disadvantage of affirmative-action efforts: incompetence. On the contrary, each man seemed well placed for the job, according to the press reports at the time. Despite his appointments, nobody accused Coolidge of corruption, and none of his selections came back to harm his reputation later on. Indeed, in picking officers as president, Coolidge recognized that it was important to bring men of talent into his government, from wherever they might originate. He believed that a meritocratic system was far more attrac-tive than the anarchy or Communism that radicals of the day were offering, and he warned immigrants not to be duped by agitators who claimed America was a hostile place to which they owed no allegiance.

While Coolidge celebrated the contributions of the Irish, Wilson denigrated them. In urging the right of self-determination at the Versailles peace conference, Wilson explicitly excluded Ireland. Wil-son told Irish-American Democratic delegates at the conference that the creation of a free Irish republic was "a domestic affair for Great Britain and Ireland to settle themselves, and not a matter for outside interference."[232] President Wilson resented the Irish efforts to derail the Versailles negotiations, telling his personal aide, Dr. Cary Gray-son, that "the Irish as a race are very hard to deal with owing to their inconsiderateness, their unreasonable demands and their jealousies."[233] He questioned Irish Americans' patriotism (especially given their reluctance to fight a war for Britain) and linked them with the "pro-German forces that showed their hyphens," meaning the "hyphen which looked to us like a snake, the hyphen between 'German' and 'American,'" during the war.[234] Wilson was even willing to encourage anti-Catholic bigotry among Protestants. "I have one weapon which I can use against them – one terrible weapon, which I shall not use unless I am driven to it," he told reporter Ray Stannard Baker. "I have only to warn our people of the attempt of the Roman Catholic hierarchy to dominate our public opinion, and there is no doubt what America will do."[235] He found nothing wrong with ginning up anti-Catholic bias.

While Wilson admonished the Irish that they must behave themselves, Coolidge continued to seek the support of Irish immigrants, bragging to his family about how many Irish Americans had voted for him, speaking before Catholic organizations, and defending the Catholic Church against its enemies in the revolutionary Mexican government.[236] He did not believe that being Catholic was incompatible with American life. Catholics only needed education to embrace what was good about American institutions. Immigrants "are disposed and inclined to think our institutions partake of the same nature as these they have left behind," he said, adding, "They must be shown they are wrong."[237] It was the task of civil society, government, and everyday Americans to teach the immigrants the new ways.

While other politicians such as Senator Lodge wanted draconian laws passed against immigrants, Coolidge favored laws that would help them assimilate. The now-maligned Immigration Act of 1924 could, in this view, be seen as a means of helping immigrants who were already here. "There are among us many recent arrivals who are entitled to some consideration and assistance," he said. Immigration was mostly a federal responsibility, Coolidge believed, but states should show "an interest in their welfare, a desire to protect them from imposition, a respect for their own national spirit, and an effort to have them use that spirit in appreciating our own citizenship and supporting our own institutions." Coolidge was keenly aware that not all immigrants assimilated. He therefore urged that civil society "assist in teaching all up to middle age to speak, read, and write our language, and come in that way to an understanding of our institutions."[238]

Although not anti-immigrant, Coolidge believed with Montesquieu that some peoples were more fit for despotism and others more fit for democracy. He thought that all peoples could become democratic over time and that all men could and should be self-governing, as suggested by the Declaration of Independence. But he also accepted the teachings of his Amherst professors – teachings predominant in his generation – that the actual practice of democracy was a product of Anglo-Saxon tradition. He did not believe that the nation dedicated to the universality of natural rights could be what is now called a "universal nation." Coolidge supported immigration restrictions on the grounds that the U.S. should absorb only those immigrants who could one day become good citizens. In Coolidge's view, historical experience had shown that American society would work best if the ethnic percentages of the day were preserved. He also believed that immigration should temporarily halt during a depression or even a recession. Even in the Roaring Twenties, it seemed to him that "our present economic and social conditions warrant a limitation of those to be admitted."[239]

Coolidge's thought on immigration closely mirrored that of the Founders. Jefferson, for instance, had worried about the difficulties of welcoming immigrants from "absolute monarchies" since their "maxims" directly opposed the American principles "derived from natural right and natural reason." And unfortunately, it was

> from such, [that] we are to expect the greatest number of emigrants. [They] will bring with them the principles of the governments they leave, imbibed in their early youth; or, if able to throw them off, it will be in exchange for an unbounded licentiousness, passing, as is usual, from one extreme to another. It would be a miracle were they to stop precisely at the point of temperate liberty. These principles, with their language, they will transmit to their children. In proportion to their numbers, they will share with us the legislation. They will infuse into it their spirit, warp and bias its direction, and render it a heterogeneous, incoherent, distracted mass.[240]

Coolidge would have also found a sympathetic ear with George Washington, who wrote to Vice President John Adams in 1794:

The policy or advantage of [immigration] taking place in a body (I mean the settling of them in a body) may be much questioned; for, by so doing, they retain the language, habits, and principles (good or bad) which they bring with them. Whereas by an intermixture with our people, they, or their descendants, get assimilated to our customs, measures, and laws: in a word, soon become *one people.*[241]

And Coolidge, ever the Hamiltonian, would also have found some support from Hamilton, who argued that the "safety of a republic depends essentially on the energy of a common national sentiment; on a uniformity of principles and habits, on the exemption of the citizens from foreign bias and prejudice; and on the love of country, which will almost invariably be found to be closely connected with birth, education, and family." In one of the few times Hamilton and Jefferson agreed, Hamilton found that Jefferson's aforementioned query in *Notes on the State of Virginia* was "undoubtedly correct." As Hamilton put it:

Foreigners will generally be apt to bring with them attachments to the persons they have left behind; to the country of their nativity, and to its particular customs and manners. They will also entertain opinions on government congenial with those under which they have lived; or if they should be led hither from a preference to ours, how extremely unlikely is it that they will bring with them that *temperate love of liberty,* so essential to real republicanism?

In the recommendation to admit indiscriminately foreign emigrants of every description to the privileges of American citizens, on their first entrance into our country, there is an attempt to break down every pale which has been erected for the preservation of a national spirit and a national character; and to let in the most powerful means of perverting and corrupting both the one and the other.[242]

Given the racial rioting in America's cities and the spirit of distrust among different ethnic groups, it is understandable that Coolidge turned to the Founders for wisdom. The criticism of current historians such as Ferrell that the 1924 Immigration Act was "assuredly a negative change"[243] ignores the concerns of both the Founders and Coolidge. It's striking that Coolidge joined the Founders in rejecting at least one fundamental aspect of liberal immigration policy, the idealization of the "huddled masses yearning to breathe free," as the famed Emma Lazarus poem depicts them. For Coolidge, some immigrants yearn to breathe free, but many do not, or at least many have a variety of motives, and this is not random but correlated with nationality. Coolidge might also have discerned a key difference, which is easy to neglect, between wanting freedom for oneself and supporting free institutions for society as a whole.

Women

I go for all sharing the privileges of the government who assist in bearing its burdens. Consequently I go for admitting all whites to the right of suffrage who pay taxes or bear arms (by no means excluding females).[244]

Women have a natural and indisputable place in the affairs of state. We do not want solely a man's or a woman's world – we want a human world and we are rapidly achieving it. This does not mean that men and women are to become alike. Rather it requires each of us to make his or her peculiar contribution. Fortunately no two of us are alike. Our civilization will be sturdy and satisfying, rich and dependable just in proportion as we deepen rather than decrease the difference between men and women.[245]

We welcome women into full participation in the affairs of government and the activities of the Republican Party. We earnestly hope that Republican legislatures in states which have not yet acted on the Suffrage Amendment will ratify the amendment, to the end that all of the women of the nation of voting age may participate in the election of 1920 which is so important to the welfare of our country.[246]

What men owe to the love and help of good women can never be told."[247]

Why not?   COOLIDGE, reportedly to women's rights
                    supporters asking for more action.

Coolidge's thought when it came to women was progressive and far-sighted despite its traditional elements. The combination may be unfamiliar in our day, when the distinctions between men and women have become blurred. The ideological demand today, in the age of *Sex and the City*, is that women be unmoored from what Coolidge considered their obligations as mothers and hence deracinated from what he would have seen as their most important function – the raising of republican citizens.

Recent scholarship has suggested that the women's suffrage movement wasn't as revolutionary as modern feminists have often claimed. It was evolutionary in that it drew upon the precepts of the founding era and was spurred by the realities of life on the frontier, where women played a nearly equal role.[248] The Seneca Falls women's rights convention in 1848, led by Elizabeth Cady Stanton, appealed to the political truths of the Declaration of Independence, with its own Declaration of Sentiments, which consciously borrowed from the older document. Frederick Douglass, who was in attendance, called the 1848 declaration a "grand basis for attaining the civil, social political, and religious rights of women."[249]

Although women's rights were a long time in coming, they gradually expanded. Politicians such as Coolidge, who had long supported women's suffrage, were in some cases rewarded at the polls. He became president of the Massachusetts Senate in 1913 after the suffragettes, working to influence male voters, defeated the former president, Levi H. Greenwood, for his opposition to giving women the vote.[250]

The issue was a live one well up until Coolidge left for Washington in 1920, Massachusetts having failed to give women the right to vote in 1915. The stop-and-start nature of the political issue mirrored the changing attitudes. One the one hand, women were to be protected; on the other, they were now substantially equal citizens. It was generally believed that women, in keeping with their special family obligations, should not partake in the stresses and dangers of industrial life. They were to make the home and raise the children while the men subjected themselves to capitalism's challenges and excesses. Women and children were precious, in the view of Coolidge and others, and a progressive society rightly understood, they believed, would recognize their real worth and protect them from the assaults and deprivations they risked in a new economic era. This explains Coolidge's support of legislation that restricted the number of working hours for women and abolished child labor.[251] As a young Massachusetts politician, he fought for "humanitarian legislation" known as the Mothers' Relief Bill, which reduced a fifty-four hour week for women and minors to a forty-eight hour week.

The genius of Coolidge's political approach to women was that he saw them as they wanted to be – as both devoted mothers *and* fully engaged citizens. In his acceptance speech for the presidential nomination in 1924, he said:

> I know the influence of womanhood will guard the home, which is the citadel of the nation. I know it will be a protector of childhood, I know it will be on the side of humanity. I welcome it as a great instrument of mercy and a mighty agency of peace. I want every woman to vote.[252]

It would, of course, help if women happened to vote Republican, which in large measure they did.[253] By 200 to 102, House Republicans passed the "Susan B. Anthony Amendment" giving women the right to vote. Of the eight women elected to Congress in Coolidge's eight years as vice president and president, only one was a Democrat.

Republicans in their 1920 platform had proudly noted that of the thirty-five state legislatures that passed women's suffrage, twenty-nine were Republican-controlled. That platform called for the principle of equal pay for equal work for federal employees and also endorsed vocational aid that recognized the "special needs and aptitudes of women workers."[254] Republican women reminded the National American Woman Suffrage Association of their party's historic support for women's rights, much to the dismay of the Democrats.[255] "To the Republican Party you owe the passage of the Federal suffrage amendment," a newspaper ad said, "and it will be responsible for the ratification soon to come."[256]

While his contemporary Winston Churchill had worried that women's suffrage would mean "the loss of social structure and the rise of every liberal cause under the sun,"[257] Coolidge argued that women had always been engaged in American politics and that this engagement had always been a good thing. As Spartan mothers had helped make Spartan men, American mothers made American men. Contrary to modern feminism's frequent disregard for "stay-at-home" mothers, both parties celebrated women as mothers. President Wilson called for a federal Mother's Day as a holiday. Coolidge, unwilling to issue a federal proclamation inaugurating Father's Day, suggested that states observe a Father's Day because "such an occasion would bring about a clearer relationship between fathers and their children, and also impress upon the former their obligations."[258]

Granting women suffrage – something Coolidge had supported as early as 1907 – was a recognition of their worth to a republic that, as mothers, they had long served and shaped. To be sure, the new female citizens had to be educated, but he saw "an enormous opportunity in this direction, by example and precept."[259] This was because women had long seized the opportunities and responsibilities of citizenship. The Daughters of the American Revolution, for example, were a "powerful force for good in our country ... a body of high-minded women with such a heritage of sacrifice and devotion to an ideal."[260] As Coolidge told the DAR on April 19, 1926:

In this day, with our broadened view of the importance of women in working out the destiny of mankind, there will be none to deny that as there were fathers in our Republic so there were mothers. If they did not take part in the formal deliberations, yet by their abiding faith they inspired and encouraged the men; by their sacrifice they performed their part in the struggle out of which came our country.[261]

He quoted a letter from George Washington to this effect.[262] If the women of Washington's day were "willing to support what was only a vision, a promise," Coolidge said, "surely in this day they will be willing to go to the ballot box to support what has become an actual and permanent realization of their desires."[263] Women had always played a pivotal role because they taught the next generation from the cradle. Indeed the American epitome of the great statesman had a humble upbringing. "[Lincoln's] cradle was bare," Coolidge noted in a 1922 speech honoring Lincoln's birth, "but above it was the precious canopy of the love of a gentle mother."[264] Every mother dreams of the best for her son – Coolidge, who had lost his mother so young, wrote about this for Mother's Day in 1931: "It is hard to imagine a greater ambition than to be what our mothers would wish us to be. . . . None of us can give as much as our mothers gave us."[265]

Perhaps Coolidge understood what it means to have a woman's support because nearly every woman in his life, except his wife Grace, died before her time.[266] Of these deaths, his mother's had affected him most. Coolidge lost his mother, Victoria Josephine Moore, when he was twelve, on her thirty-ninth birthday. Later he would call her death "the greatest grief that can come to a boy." He never got over this loss but felt her presence in his life long after she was gone. Before he left for Washington, he visited her grave as he had during his boyhood. As Coolidge recalled later: "Some way, that morning, she seemed very near to me." Even in death, he talked to her often and was saddened that she didn't say much back. "I wish I could really speak to her," he told his security agent Starling. "I wish that often."[267]

Coolidge carried a picture of his mother with him in a silver case throughout his life, and it was found in his breast pocket when he died. He never spoke about Victoria publicly but probably felt that in this matter, as in others, his actions spoke for him.

How Progressive Political Thought Undermined America's Defense

The only hope for peace lies in the perfection of the arts of war.[1]

THERE IS A tragic irony in the fact that Coolidge began as a "mild Progressive" and ended his presidency hobbled by one of the Progressive measures he had long supported, the Seventeenth Amendment requiring the direct election of senators by the people. Other scholars, especially Ralph Rossum of Claremont McKenna College, have studied the damage that the direct election of the Senate has done to federalism.[2] Rossum perceptively argues that this reform, a staple of Progressivism that was finally adopted in 1913, effectively ended federalism in America's constitution by forcing the states to join alongside other interests in vying for attention – thus weakening the sovereignty and independence of the states. Coolidge had supported federalism throughout his career. He worried that it was almost at an end, but he does not seem to have realized that the direct election of senators bore much of the blame.[3]

Discussion of the proposed Seventeenth Amendment ignored the effect it might have on foreign policy. That danger would became apparent a decade later, during Coolidge's presidency. Indeed, his foreign policy suffered as a result of the democratized Senate. "The foreign relations of our country ought not to be partisan, but American," Coolidge warned.[4] Alas, the Seventeenth Amendment, by subjecting senators to a vote of the people, led to exactly that, a partisan demagoguing of defense issues. Far from being inoculated against popular prejudices as the framers of the Constitution intended, the Senate succumbed to them at least twice in Coolidge's presidency: during the anti-Japanese hysteria surrounding the 1924 Immigration Act and in debates over the Kellogg-Briand Pact, the international agreement to outlaw war. In the first instance, the Senate catered to and stoked racial fear; in the second, it played to naive hopes that the world could be safe, not only for democracy, but for all nations in all times. These two delusions – unreasonable fear and unrealistic hope – were fed and spearheaded by Senators Henry Cabot Lodge and William Borah, chairmen of the Senate Foreign Relations Committee in 1920–1924 and 1924–1933 respectively.

Writing in *The Federalist*, Publius explained the importance of the Senate as a means of checking the national government with state government. The Senate was by far the most important means of preventing excessive demagoguery in national affairs because senators elected by their state legislatures, as the Constitution provided, had to make two very distinct appeals in controversial matters and when their terms were up: directly to the legislatures, and indirectly to the people who elected the legislatures. This indirect relationship with the people protected the Senate's dignity and deliberative quality. If a revolution were attempted, it was the Senate that would prevent matters from getting out of hand. It was also the Senate that kept the balance between moderation and unrefined popular sentiment.

Before such a revolution can be effected, the Senate, it is to be observed, must in the first place corrupt itself; must next corrupt the State legislatures; must then corrupt the House of Representatives; and must finally corrupt the people at large. It is evident that the Senate must be first corrupted before it can attempt an establishment of tyranny. Without corrupting the State legislatures, it cannot prosecute the attempt, because the periodical change of members would otherwise regenerate the whole body. Without exerting the means of corruption

with equal success on the House of Representatives, the opposition of that coequal branch of the government would inevitably defeat the attempt; and without corrupting the people
themselves, a succession of new representatives would speed-
ily restore all things to their pristine order. Is there any man
who can seriously persuade himself that the proposed Senate
can, by any possible means within the compass of human
address, arrive at the object of a lawless ambition, through all
these obstructions?[5]

The Seventeenth Amendment's enactment in 1913 made the Senate subject to the same sorts of prevailing winds of public opinion
against which *The Federalist* warned. For Publius, it was essential that
government "secure the public good and private rights against the
danger of . . . faction." Factions, he warned, are dangerous because
they unite and activate citizens by "some common impulse of passion . . . adverse to the rights of other citizens, or to the permanent
and aggregate interests of the community."[6] The Constitution sought
to temper the passions of factions through the separation of powers
and through the Senate. The Senate served to keep passions in check
"until reason, justice, and truth can regain their authority over the public mind,"[7] functioning as a "defense to the people against their own
temporary errors and delusions."[8] Without a "safeguard" in place
against these temptations, the American people, like the people of Ath-
ens before them, would live under a "tyranny of their own passions."
    Publius believed foreign affairs, especially, needed to be protected
from those passions. To guarantee "the offspring of a wise and hon-
ourable policy," the Constitution deliberately placed treaty-making
in the branch of the legislature least responsive to immediate public
opinion. "It is evident that [this power] can never be sufficiently
[properly] possessed by a numerous and changeable body," Publius
argued.[9] In contrast, the Senate would have "a number so small" that
each senator would be subject to meaningful "praise and blame" for
his positions and actions. Only men of character, independent of

populist forces or party bosses, Publius predicted, would receive their state legislature's approval. Like the president, who would be chosen by the Electoral College, senators would "best understand our national interests" only if they were chosen indirectly.[10] This mode of electing senators was preferable to popular election because the latter was governed by "the activity of party zeal, taking advantage of the supineness, the ignorance, the hopes, and the fears of the unwary and [self-]interested."[11] Legislatures, in contrast, would tend to select men with a "reputation for integrity" that "inspires and merits confidence." Shaped by an upper house focused more on national concerns than parochial concerns, the foreign policy would be "afford[ed] the highest security . . . in the manner most conducive to the public good."[12]

Publius did not have the last word on the relationship between the Senate and the presidency when it came to treaty-making, however. In the Pacificus–Helvidius debates a decade later, Hamilton exhumed and expanded the arguments he had begun in *The Federalist*.[13] Hamilton supported President Washington's Neutrality Proclamation over the Jeffersonian argument against it. According to the Jeffersonians, Washington had violated the Constitution and offended the true spirit of republicanism by issuing this neutrality proclamation. Jefferson believed that Hamilton was in effect making an argument for an unlimited presidency, and he begged James Madison to take up his pen in response.[14]

Writing as Pacificus, Hamilton held that the argument advanced by Madison (Helvidius) did not bear close scrutiny. Hamilton built upon his argument in *Federalist 75* to maintain, contrary to Madison, that the treaty-making power was neither wholly executive nor wholly legislative. Instead, it came under what Locke called the "federative power" – the power to conduct foreign affairs. Hamilton touched on this power in *The Federalist*, writing that "the circumstances that endanger the safety of nations are infinite, and for this reason no constitutional shackles can be wisely imposed on the power to which the care of it is committed."[15] As Pacificus, he remarked that the executive would be "the most fit agent" in the "management of foreign relations," while the Senate's role would be limited to advice and consent. With such a division of power, the Senate would restrain the president only by affirmation or denial. Treaty negotiation, in other words, was a strictly executive function, though the Senate did have the power to decide the fate of the ultimate product. After all, treaty powers are mentioned in Article II of the Constitution – the executive article – and not Article I, which governs Congress, so the Founders clearly considered making treaties a part of the president's duties. When viewed that way, the Senate's role in treaty-making is the exception, not the rule, as Madison would have it. But in changing the *means* of electing senators, the Seventeenth Amendment changed the *ends* of Senate governance as well. The Senate was less able to douse or ignore passions, more pressured to respond to them. The separation of powers irrevocably changed with the passage of the Seventeenth Amendment, and Coolidge found himself having to deal with this new difficulty.

* * *

Coolidge's election to the presidency in 1923 was the culmination of an ongoing struggle against the new, dominating role the Senate had come to play in American politics. From the standpoint of major figures in his party, Calvin Coolidge was not supposed to be vice president, let alone president. When he was announced as Harding's running mate in mid-1920, Republican senators "chafed" at his nomination.[16] They began conspiring to limit his power in the prospective Harding administration. Woods noted that a "powerful group of senators . . . secured the nomination of one of their colleagues for President, and they were certain that they could nominate another senator for the vice-presidency."[17] But they failed. Coolidge's very presence on the Harding ticket, and then in the vice presidency, represented something of a failure to draw the presidency into the legislative and senatorial "vortex," as Publius would call it. Republican senators' displeasure at the situation did much to set the tone for Harding's presidency.

As vice president, Coolidge once called the Senate "a citadel of liberty, with a record for wisdom unsurpassed,"[18] but he ultimately took a darker view. Years later, in his autobiography, he recalled: "The Senate had but one fixed rule, subject to exceptions of course . . . that the Senate would do anything it wanted to do whenever it wanted to do it. When I had learned that, I did not waste much time with the other rules, because they were so seldom applied."[19] Throughout Coolidge's years as president, that "citadel of liberty" was beginning to fall, its edifice cracked by the Seventeenth Amendment. The Senate labored under the illusion of freedom, its officers more beholden to interest groups and public opinion than they had been before. Unmoored from its constitutional foundation, the Senate had become a prisoner of public opinion's rough, untutored utterances.

The Senate Foreign Relations Committee chairmen, Lodge and then Borah, played to unruly public opinion. French writer, academic, and geographer André Siegfried, the age's Alexis de Tocqueville, correctly called Senator Borah a "demagogue."[20] Borah was sometimes praised as the "Lion of Idaho," but he followed the whims and fancies of Progressive thought wherever they led. In December 1920, his Senate resolution calling for talks with Britain passed unanimously and even garnered attention, much of it mixed, an ocean away – in Japan. He understood the international zeitgeist and acted accordingly, to the grave peril of American foreign policy. Borah believed that war could be limited, and indeed outlawed. His thoughts found a sympathetic ear in senator-turned-president Harding, who directed Secretary of State Hughes to pursue disarmament at the Washington Naval Conference in 1921, where Japan and Britain agreed to sizeable naval reductions. Borah had less influence a couple of years later on President Coolidge and persuaded the new president to support his recommendations only reluctantly. Caring little for the complications of world affairs, Borah was a less-than-ideal senator when it came to managing the nation's foreign affairs, despite his ambition to lead in this area. At times, his thinking approached on the ridiculous. Having once consulted a mystic who predicted he would die at sea, he never traveled abroad.[21]

"If the Senate has any weakness," Coolidge wrote in his autobiography several years later, "it is because the people have sent to that body men lacking the necessary ability and character to perform the proper functions."[22] Here Coolidge was wrong. The Senate had undergone a transformation: It had been a body that favored limits; it was now one that knew no limits to its sphere of activity. The magnitude of this change only becomes clear when we consider the history of Coolidge's foreign policy.

In foreign policy as in domestic policy, Coolidge favored the use of few words. In this delicate arena, the president rationed his speech with special care. As he told the press in 1925: "It isn't helpful for me to keep talking about certain foreign relations unless there is some development that warrants some statement on my part. I didn't really want to keep rehashing practically the same thing, because it irritates foreign countries oftentimes and they wonder why the White House keeps making statements that don't appear to them to be very helpful."[23]

In this Coolidge was lucky, for his first secretary of state was a man of many words, and many considered him "the greatest statesman of his age never to become President."[24] Had he won just four thousand more votes in California, Charles Evans Hughes, then-governor of New York, would have beaten Wilson in 1916. Since he did not, he retreated from public life to his lucrative law practice. President Harding then drafted him to head the State Department. Hughes accepted because it was a "call no one could well refuse in justice to what he conceived to be his duty to his country."[25] He had little doubt that the situation that confronted the Harding administration in 1921 was dire indeed. In a later review of the conduct of America's foreign affairs prepared in 1924 for the Coolidge campaign, Hughes laid bare the foreign-policy problems that had faced the nation during Harding's years:

> It would be difficult to imagine a worse tangle in our foreign relations than that with which the Republican Administration was required to deal when it came into power on March 4,

1921. Two years and nearly four months had elapsed since the Armistice, but we were still in a technical state of war. The peace negotiations had evoked a bitter and undying controversy. In the Far East our relations were embarrassed by suspicion and distrust, giving rise to serious apprehensions. In this hemisphere old sores were still festering. For years our relations with Mexico had been unsatisfactory. The situation was a most difficult one as opportunities for disputes lay on every hand while the chances of finding adequate means of accommodation were extremely meager.[26]

As Hughes began to grapple with the mess, his first act of major diplomacy was the Washington Conference in 1921, which aimed at limiting the major powers' naval armaments. Something of a showman and a gambler,[27] Hughes had locked his keynote address speech away lest it be leaked to the press. In it, he urged the Japanese and the British – successfully, as it turned out – to sign an agreement that committed to ending construction of new naval ships for at least ten years. He pledged to immediately scuttle thirty major American ships then in existence if the Japanese would scrap seventeen and the British nineteen. The proposal would also preserve the 10:10:6 (U.S.: U.K.:Japan) ratio in naval tonnage.[28] The parties accepted, and Harding, perhaps prematurely, praised the "beginning of a new and better epoch in human progress."[29]

President Coolidge probably liked the Washington Conference naval agreement because it meant that "the burden of meeting the demand of competition in naval armaments will be lifted," as Hughes had said in his address to the conference. "Enormous sums will be released to aid the progress of civilization."[30] Favoring economy in public expenditure as strongly as he did, Coolidge no doubt appreciated having one more means to reduce the governmental burden on the economy. Still, he did not believe good foreign policy (or good government in general) could be purchased at the "bargain counter." He also recognized that although the Washington Conference had limited battleships, it left the question of submarines, aircraft, and land forces deliberately unsolved.[31]

Coolidge's foreign policy was simple but elegant. For Coolidge, America should have – and normally had honored – "one cardinal principle" in her foreign policy: "We attend to our own affairs, conserve our own strength, and protect the interests of our own citizens . . . we recognize thoroughly our own obligation to help others, reserving to the decision of our judgment the time, the place, and the method."[32] He said this in his first State of the Union address, and he meant it. His administration carried out this cardinal principle throughout its foreign policy. Despite dispatching the Marines to stabilize Nicaragua and stationing American troops in China to safeguard American property, he justly celebrated the fact that the nation was at peace during his administration. Unlike Woodrow Wilson, whose slogan promised to keep us out of war, Coolidge really did keep the peace.[33] While Wilson saw the need to meddle in other nations' affairs in order to make the world safe for democracy, Coolidge believed that America needed a humbler foreign policy. "America stands ready to bear its share of the burdens of the world," he told the American Peace Society in 1922, "but it cannot live the life of other peoples, it cannot remove from them the necessity of working out their own destiny." America should be "at peace with all peoples."[34] At the same time, Coolidge recognized that postwar America had forever turned away from isolationism. "Our interests," he noted, were now "all over the earth . . . such that a conflict anywhere would be enormously to our disadvantage."[35] Coolidge favored stability in the world order because it would protect America's considerable interests overseas, but America faced new uncertainty about its role in the world. Had the country turned away from isolationism owing to public opinion? Or was the shift a result of a new balance of international power, meaning that America could no longer afford to be isolationist because the world had irrevocably changed?

Coolidge feared that the hard-won postwar global stability was threatened by the Senate – the body constitutionally tasked with forming foreign policy. America now had tremendous goodwill from the Japanese, having created a "profound impression in the grateful hearts of suffering Japan" by aiding the country after the 1923 earthquake. According to Hughes, Prime Minister Yamamoto Gonnohyōe sent a message of thanks for the "spontaneous and prompt measures, taken by the President, the Government, and the people of the United States" after the "bewildering devastation."[36] The generous American aid, according to the prime minister as quoted by Hughes, "laid the foundation of World Peace and will greatly promote human welfare."[37]

All the goodwill won from the American fleet's delivery of assistance was at risk of being undone, however, by what Hughes called "the intemperate action of Congress" in passing the Immigration Act of 1924.[38] Hughes issued sharp warnings before the anti-Japanese provisions were added to the bill and before the bill passed, and he expressed his dismay at the comments of the anti-Japanese representative Albert Johnson of Washington, chairman of the House Committee on Immigration and Naturalization:

> The Japanese are a sensitive people, and unquestionably would regard such a legislative enactment as fixing a stigma upon them. I regret to be compelled to say that I believe such a legislative action would undo the work of the Washington Conference on Limitation of Armament, which so greatly improved our relations with Japan. The manifestation of American interest and generosity in providing relief to the sufferers from the recent earthquake disaster in Japan would not avail to diminish the resentment which would not be palliated by any act of charity. It is useless to argue whether or not such a feeling would be justified; it is quite sufficient to say that it would exist. It has already been manifested in the discussions in Japan with respect to the pendency of this measure and no amount of argument can avail to remove it.[39]

In so arguing, Hughes understood as Hamilton did that "men are ambitious, vindictive, and rapacious" and that because of this, "the causes of hostility between nations are innumerable."[40] Indeed, Hughes, looking back after World War II, seemed to suggest that the Japanese started the Pacific War because their sense of pride had been offended by what they deemed a hypocritical American foreign policy – that there was to be an open door in U.S. relations with China, but a locked door for the Japanese in America, with the passage of the Immigration Act of 1924. Hughes found it understandable that Japanese pride was offended, especially in the unstable domestic situation after the devastating earthquake and the ensuing period of "government by assassination."

Hughes's sensitivity to Japanese perceptions is to his credit, especially at a time of nationwide anti-Japanese prejudice. Experience in government had made him a particularly loyal executive officer, as the president noted when he reluctantly accepted Hughes's resignation in March 1925.[41] "Foreign affairs are perennial," Hughes told Coolidge when he tendered his resignation; but the outgoing secretary, like Coolidge, seems to have noticed a marked change in how the Senate addressed the executive branch on foreign-policy issues. It may have been why he decided to step down.[42] In calling Congress "intemperate," Hughes was concerned that the Senate wasn't acting as the sagacious, deliberative body that *Federalist* 64 had envisioned. The most intemperate of all the senators, it seemed to him, was the prestigious Henry Cabot Lodge. This presented something of a paradox: In view of Lodge's social and educational background, he would seem to be a classic example of the kind of individual (as distinct from the kind of psychology) the Founders wanted in a senator, and yet Lodge was anything but ideal. He played to the prejudices of those around him and built a coalition with anti-Japanese Californians to make sure their passionate intemperance was felt by the Coolidge administration.

* * *

The Kellogg-Briand Pact

We have come out of the war with a desire and a determination to live at peace with all the world.[43]

In the spring of 1927, Columbia University professor James Shotwell called upon French foreign minister Aristide Briand to create a multilateral pact to outlaw war. Shotwell teamed up with an attorney, Salmon Levinson, and with Senator Borah to advance his vision. The senator sought to persuade Secretary of State Frank Kellogg, who rejected Borah's ideas, and the two clashed over the issue in Senate hearings that December. Coolidge, though he agreed with Kellogg that separate arbitration treaties with individual countries were preferable, could tell that public opinion was lining up alongside Borah's position, and he maneuvered accordingly, if only to slow down Borah's tail winds.[44]

Borah's involvement in drafting the Kellogg-Briand Pact indicates the problem of senatorial involvement in foreign policy that Hamilton most feared. The prominent isolationist in the Senate remained a determined advocate of the pact. It probably seemed to Borah that it would have all the advantages of League of Nations membership (which the Senate had defeated in 1919–1920) without the League's diminution of American sovereignty. Further, the Europeans had seized the initiative by reaching their own analogous pacts at Locarno,[45] which may've made the idea of a Kellogg-Briand pact more attractive.

Kellogg, Hughes's successor and still new to the job at the time, did not have anywhere near Hughes's negotiating acumen. In addition, he saw Bolshevism as a powerful force not only in Russia but also in other countries, including China and especially Mexico, and therefore he believed that American property stood under constant threat of nationalization (which indeed happened in the 1930s). Kellogg saw that there was an agreement to be struck with the major powers, while Foreign Minister Briand, already a Nobel Prize winner, saw another such prize in the making. The proposed treaty to outlaw war, he told Kellogg, would be "the greatest accomplishment of my administration or of any administration lately."[46]

Although he went along with it, Coolidge did not think the Kellogg-Briand Pact had really outlawed war. It was, as its critics contended, "worthless, but harmless."[47] The country always wanted peace, but it also recognized, Coolidge added, that "war is not the worst of evils." Appeasement was. "There can be no peace with the forces of evil," Coolidge had told the crowd at a Memorial Day service in Northampton, Massachusetts, in 1923. "Peace comes only through the establishment of the supremacy of the forces of good."[48] Coolidge disagreed with those who "were willing to sacrifice the undoubted rights of our citizens to the maintenance of peace."[49] Coolidge quoted President William McKinley favorably on the topic of when nations should resort to war:

> "Peace," [McKinley] said, "is the national desire and the goal of every American aspiration. The best sentiment of the civilized world is moving toward the settlement of differences between nations without resorting to the horrors of war. Let us ever remember that our interest is in concord, not conflict. . . . We love peace better than war, and our swords never should be drawn except in a righteous cause, and then never until every effort at peace and arbitration shall be exhausted."[50]

There is little evidence to support the notion that the wartime lieutenant governor became a pacifist as president. In 1918, Coolidge had argued that the "only hope of a short war is to prepare for a long one."[51] And in the long run, preparing for war, by tending to prevent war, would save money as well as lives. "Past wars and national defense cost a very large sum," Coolidge reflected in his newspaper column in 1930. "It pays to be at peace."[52] He did not "claim to be able to announce any formula that will guarantee the peace of the world," but he held out hope for "plans for a codification of international law."[53] In his view, such a codification would not eliminate the need for defense but was nonetheless an important step, moving it from the realm of force to the conference table. "Proposals for promoting the peace of the world will have careful consideration" during his administration, he said at his fifth State of the Union message in 1927, but he did not believe treaties would change the hearts of men. America, according to Coolidge, knows that peace comes from "honesty and fair dealing, from moderation, and a generous regard for the rights of others." In truth, the "heart of the Nation is more important than treaties."[54] And Coolidge, ever the student of *The Federalist*, knew as John Jay did that "jealousies and uneasiness may gradually slide into the minds and cabinets of other nations."[55] America, therefore, had better be ready.

The fact that Coolidge signed a multilateral pact to outlaw war at the same time that he argued for building the world's finest navy indicates the brand of diplomacy he practiced. (Ferrell calls the simultaneous appearance of the Kellogg-Briand Pact and the hawkish naval appropriation before Congress "incongruous,"[56] but Coolidge got both of them through.) He longed for a "peace so secure as that of the Pax Romana"[57] and, like the Founders before him, considered the Navy (but not the Army, wary as he was of foreign wars[58]) instrumental in the maintenance of peace.[59] He presciently viewed the airplane as important in the national defense as well, getting Congress to appropriate money for the beginnings of an air force, a controversial concept at the time.[60] The Kellogg-Briand Pact "is the most solemn declaration against war, the most positive adherence to peace, that is possible for sovereign nations to make," Coolidge wrote in his final State of the Union message, but "[i]t does not supersede our inalienable sovereign right and duty of national defense[,] or undertake to commit us before the event to any mode of action which the Congress might decide to be wise if ever the treaty should be broken."[61] In other words, the pact, while symbolically important, would not prevent a president from faithfully defending America. Coolidge wanted to enter into more treaties like the 1921 agreement for limitations on all types of warships, guided by the ratio adopted at the Washington Conference, but when he discovered that the British and the French were maneuvering around that treaty, he quickly abandoned such a hope. One of Coolidge's final acts as president, the month before he left office in 1929, was to sign the bill authorizing fifteen heavy cruisers and two aircraft carriers, the *Saratoga* and the *Lexington*. If foreign powers would imperil American safety, he would take the necessary corrective actions.

CONCLUSION

Coolidge is probably the man of smallest caliber who has ever been made president of the United States.[1]

Liberal historians have reviled and belittled Calvin Coolidge even more than Warren Harding or Herbert Hoover, chiefly because Coolidge is a more formidable figure who presents the most serious challenge to the pretensions of Progressivism.[2]

HISTORY HAS NOT been kind to Calvin Coolidge because most professors have a skewed conception of political excellence. Modern political science is out of its depth when studying someone whose principles it doesn't much appreciate and often doesn't attempt to understand. The Maranell survey (1972) ranked him thirtieth out of the thirty-four presidents surveyed for overall accomplishment, while the Sienna Research poll (1994) ranked him thirty-sixth of forty-one and the Schlesinger poll (1996) ranked him thirtieth of thirty-nine. He is seen as insignificant, if he is seen at all. Most general-history books ignore him, moving simplistically – even propagandistically – from Woodrow Wilson to Franklin Delano Roosevelt, with little attention to the instructive decade between them or to its leading statesman.

So unable are most modern historians to comprehend Coolidge that they perpetuate all sorts of distorted images of him: He was pro-business, although he lived almost as a pauper; he was a fool, although he wrote, himself, hundreds of speeches that show otherwise. He is also assigned much of the responsibility for the Great Depression, though he loathed the policies of the Hoover administration. We don't know his stand on the Smoot-Hawley tariffs, but we can infer that he opposed the 1932 tax increase, based on his post-presidential column, in which he criticized the need for higher and higher taxes. It is often pointed out that he favored tax cuts for the wealthy, but it is not pointed out that he favored tax cuts in general – or that the tax rates became more, not less, progressive under his watch.

Today, the most frequent put-down is that he was incompetent. Why he is deemed incompetent is not often explained, but it may be that he was not as activist as many historians would like. Others have created their own Coolidges to fit the story they have neatly constructed for him. Political scientist Robert E. Gilbert suggests that Coolidge suffered from clinical depression after the death of his son and that his presidency suffered as a result. When viewed this way, the attacks on Coolidge aren't political, but psychological, as Gilbert makes clear.[3] In Gilbert's view, he was too grief-stricken by the death of his son to be a great president. This neglects the fact that great leaders have often been given to melancholy. It would be at least as accurate to note that great democratic statesmen have tended to recognize that their reach is finite and that they, like all living things, are finite, despite their place in history.

The failure of previous analyses to fully understand Coolidge is due not only to his belief in limited government and constitutionalism but also to his diffidence. He does not fit the standard image of the great man that we owe to Aristotle. The man of great soul, according to Aristotle, is "he who thinks himself worthy of great things and is worthy of them."[4] Many presidents think themselves worthy of great things – and yet are not. Coolidge, it seems, had the opposite problem. He did not think himself worthy of great things – and yet was worthy of them. It simply wasn't the shy man's style to draw the nation's attention to himself. He sought, instead, to draw attention to his principles, publishing many of his speeches so that they could live after him. His answers in his frequent press conferences were always attributed to a "White House official" because, as he said often, we need more of the midnight oil and less of the lime-light from our politicians.

So Coolidge simply worked, perhaps trusting to God that time would give him his proper due. Although memory is fickle, Coolidge's greatness is nonetheless evident in his deep humanity and his consistent faithfulness to his role as a public servant. He never lost his sense of being a part of the public. He was first among equals only, and like any good republican, he wanted to return to the people. And so it was that when Coolidge left the White House, he returned to the two-family home on Massasoit Street that he had left many years before.

Coolidge was great because he was modest, moderate, and thoroughly republican in an immodest time. He kept his appetites, politically and personally, in check and allowed himself one vice – smoking cigars. Disliking ambitious solutions to problems and opposed to complicated, unconstitutional machinery, he always reduced a problem to common sense. In doing so, he discharged his constitutional duties faithfully. If he was a dull figure in comparison with some presidents, it is because the events of his day did not demand the more obvious kind of greatness – of which he was fully capable. He believed his role as president was to let Americans be great all on their own. His decision to cut taxes four times indicated his faith that they could tend to their own business and thus serve the public good if left to their own devices. Coolidge made his position clear: Better-structured, and generally lower, taxation was not only economically wise but also moral. It was as simple as that.

Ironically, Americans with modest incomes were those most helped by the Coolidge tax cuts. "I want taxes to be less, that the people may have more," he said on September 1, 1924.[5] The people did have more, while the rich got less. Coolidge's taxation policy was progressive, a fact utterly unremarked upon by the progressive historians who have savaged his reputation. By the time he left office, 98 percent of Americans paid no income taxes at all. In 1920, those who were earning $100,000 or more paid 29.9 percent of the tax revenues. In

1929, that figure rose to 62.5 percent. Fittingly, he cared not a whit for the material grandeur around him that those very tax policies created, and so he suffered none of the excesses that the flurry of economic activity unleashed. He did not suffer much in the bursting stock bubble, for instance, because his assets were safely invested. This was because, as a Democratic admirer, Governor Alfred E. Smith of New York, noted, Coolidge was "distinguished for character more than for heroic achievement." Coolidge worked instead to safeguard the core principles of the institutions he was charged to defend. As president, Coolidge's "great task was to restore the dignity and prestige of the Presidency when it had reached the lowest ebb in our history . . . in a time of extravagance and waste."[6]

Even foreigners appreciated his temperament. Describing the silent president's state of mind during the Roaring Twenties, André Siegfried judged Coolidge correctly:

> Here is a man who is popular with the public, though possibly mostly with the lower strata. He may be less admired than Roosevelt or Wilson, but he inspires much more confidence than either of his great predecessors. He is a small, uninspiring man, and his restless eyes look at you without warmth or brilliance. He is not a hail-fellow-well-met like President Harding, nor "one of those boys" like so many politicians in both America and France. He takes no recreation, plays no games, but prefers long, prosaic walks. . . . And yet his popularity suddenly sprang up when the premature death of President Harding automatically made him chief executive. Both the House and the Senate were against him then and heaped the most humiliating abuse on him. But the public opinion judged him differently. . . .
>
> In point of fact, President Coolidge is a skillful, prudent politician, thoroughly honest; and as a good Protestant he is eager to do what is right. His much-vaunted personal economy inspires confidence in a country where every one is extravagant. He listens with consideration to business men

and does not worry them. His personality has now become the guiding factor of the doctrine or policy of his party.[7]

The Democrats of his day, Siegfried continued, "underestimated the power of Coolidge as a symbol of stability" against the union-fermented turmoil of the postwar era.[8] We, too, underestimate him today at our peril because his thought, if carefully considered and followed, might lay the ground for our own era of stability.

The new age that began within a few years after Coolidge left office – the age of big government – has turned into one of monstrous debt, deepening doubt about the viability of the American experiment, and intense partisan discord. The verve that once characterized America seems to be waning. Perhaps it is time to seriously reconsider our Republic's founding beliefs and apply them to our own time as Coolidge did to his. "The chief ideal of the American people is idealism," Coolidge said in the very same speech that was distorted into the defamatory "business of America is business" maxim. "I cannot repeat too often that America is a nation of idealists." It was his statesmanship and his keen grasp of the Republic's principles, not an unthinking pro-business stance, that led him to remind his fellow citizens:

> I favor the policy of economy, not because I wish to save money, but because I wish to save people. The men and women of this country who toil are the ones who bear the cost of the Government. Every dollar that we carelessly waste means that their life will be so much the more meager. Every dollar that we prudently save means that their life will be so much the more abundant. Economy is idealism in its most practical form.[9]

This plainspoken philosophy is as relevant today as it was then.

WHAT COOLIDGE
STILL HAS TO SAY
A Great Post-Presidency Revisited and
Lessons for Obama from Silent Cal

"THERE IS NOTHING more pathetic in life than a former president," according to President John Quincy Adams. Calvin Coolidge's brief but robust post-presidential career might give Adams cause to reconsider. With his popular column "Calvin Coolidge Says," the not-so-silent president managed a philosophic government-in-exile from the comfort of his Northampton two-family home.

There, pen in hand and typewriter at the ready, Coolidge stood athwart what he called the "socialistic" impulses of the government led by his successor, the former commerce secretary Herbert Hoover. Coolidge had reluctantly campaigned for Hoover late in the 1928 campaign but privately and dryly derided him as his "Wonder Boy." "For six years that man has given me unsolicited advice – all of it bad," he complained. Franklin Delano Roosevelt was more awed. "He is certainly a wonder," Roosevelt gushed in 1919. "And I wish we could make him President [on the Democratic ticket]. There couldn't be a better one." Hoover was, as the *New-York Tribune* described him, a "Progressive Republican of the kind [Teddy] Roosevelt loved." "He dreams of social justice," the paper reported with delight.

While commerce secretary, he had served as an unofficial – and often unwanted – "undersecretary of all other departments." Now president, Hoover gave advice that became policy in full, to disastrous effect. In his November 11, 1930, column, he criticized both parties for favoring "too much government action . . . proposing to cure human illness which no government can cure." A few weeks later, on January 23, 1931, he wrote, "Our institutions are never in so much danger from those who are openly trying to destroy them as from the misguided actions of those who think they are saving society."

Hoover was just such a misguided savior, the ex-president believed. Described by the press as a "brainy idealist," Hoover promised to "triumph over poverty" (a triumph apparently long delayed). Hoover's chief failing was his belief in his own limitless ability. As a business critic wrote in 1928: "Mr. Hoover is confident that he knows more about finance than financiers, more about industry than industrialists, and more about agriculture than agriculturists. He is so sure of his judgment in these fields that he wants to impress it on others. He is very seldom willing to take advice. Since he knows more than any advisers could, why should he?"[1]

Hoover proposed to cure the human illness of unemployment with endless conferences on jobs, while his overly friendly policies toward organized labor seemed too meddlesome and too controlling to Coolidge. On May 1, 1931, in his column, the former president warned:

> With the convocation of representatives of various lines of industry have come proposals for controlling and standardizing business. Almost all these suggestions are for artificial rules of conduct to save a situation from the inevitable consequences of the force of natural laws. . . . Neither the state nor the Federal governments can supply the information and wisdom necessary to direct the business activity of the nation. . . . The experience, skill and wisdom necessary to guide business cannot be elected or appointed. It has to grow up naturally from the people. The process is long and fraught with human sacrifice, but it is the only one that can work. Edison and Ford are not government creations.

Though Coolidge conceded that "temporary help for the needy may have been justified," he also thought "large expenditures only delay business recovery." There was a role for government, but it did not include boundless spending and regulation. The coming election of 1930 was "no time for rash experiments. The best we can get will be none too good. It is a time to use the same care in our politics that we use in our finances." If the Congress early in the Great Depression had followed "a policy of rigid economy, reduced governmental costs, avoided a deficit and more debt, the country would have looked on it as a savior." Americans "reject the theory that the bread they earn should be eaten by others," as preached by both parties. They would not fall victim to the "delusion that the people can rely on the government alone to furnish salvation."

* * *

It wasn't Coolidge's intent to argue against the Hoover presidency; he considered such squabbles gauche. He wanted to be known, he told readers of his column, "as a former President who tried to mind his own business." After six long years in office – during which he had lost both his father and his son – he wanted to go home. "When I left Washington it was because I believed my work in the government service was done," he explained in his autobiography. "I decided to withdraw from [the government] entirely. . . . I have been unwilling, therefore, in these early days of my retirement to give interviews, make speeches, or write extensively about them because I wished to avoid being an officious intermeddler." He wanted only to "engage in some dignified employment."

But various possibilities eluded him. Newspapers speculated that he could be president of a petroleum or insurance company. Told by the head of the Amherst Alumni Society that his name was in the running to head his alma mater, Coolidge politely declined. Some even wondered if Coolidge might run again, either against Hoover in 1932 or perhaps in 1936. Actor Oscar Skinner's wife implored him to consider it. "It would be the end of this horrible Depression," she suggested. "It would be the beginning of mine," Coolidge replied.[2]

The philosophizing president preferred writing to politicking. *Collier's* put it best in a May 1930 article entitled "He'd Rather Write Than Be President," which accompanied a cartoon: A female Republican elephant pining for the reluctant Coolidge while out walking hand in hand with a gussied-up Herbert Hoover; Coolidge, hard at work, didn't bother looking up from his typewriter.

"He began his writing in January 1929 and finished this autobiography in less than three and a half months," explained Ray Long, his editor at *Cosmopolitan*. He wrote for the leading magazines of his day: *Ladies Home Journal, American Magazine,* and *Cosmopolitan Magazine,* which serialized his autobiography. He sought above all to educate the public. "We would save ourselves a great deal of discouragement and impatience if we had a better historical perspective," he noted.[3]

He was also well courted for other writing ventures. The United Press Association offered him $1,000 per 1,500-word article; Doran and Company guaranteed $50,000 and syndication rates; media baron Ralph Pulitzer did one better and offered $104,000 for a weekly column "on current events – varied, as you see fit, with reviews of important periods of the Presidential career and any career experiences of your unofficial life, that may interest you." But Richard H. Waldo of McClure Newspaper Syndicate eventually won him over. He was free to wander wherever his pen led, "free to comment, criticize, moralize or recollect," as Waldo said in the *New-York Herald Tribune.* "Education, religion, business, prohibition, fundamental problems of government, fishing, farming, and a hundred other subjects are in his field."

As for matters of policy, Waldo said, "Mr. Coolidge has partly banished national politics from journalism, as he will practice it." This was only partly true, however; Coolidge himself felt that a former President "should be careful not to make comments that might embarrass the existing Administration," but at the same time he should "not impose silence on himself on all questions that enter politics." As Coolidge put it, "politics is always present."

The "Calvin Coolidge Says" column proved a great popular

success and became syndicated nationwide. Over its lifetime, it would go on to reap a total income of well over $200,000 (more than $2.7 million today).

*　*　*

"Silent Cal" was never as silent as his Progressive critics contended. As president, he gave more than five hundred press conferences; over the course of his time in public office, he wrote three collections of speeches. After retirement, he would go on to publish more than three hundred newspaper columns, which began appearing in June 1930. Composed at a critical time in American history, these works yield important lessons for understanding the Depression and Coolidge's political philosophy. Readers in today's economy who are seeking an alternative to economic interventionism à la Hoover and Roosevelt would benefit from the perspective evident in these columns (if they can get a copy – lamentably, the collected columns have long been out of print).

The words in Coolidge's first column, a year into the Great Depression, were as relevant then as they are today. As Americans we "need more faith in ourselves," he wrote, and we are too quick to blame others for the government's problems. "Largely because of some decline in trade, we have set about finding fault with nearly everybody and everything. We are told the President is wrong, the Congress is wrong, the Supreme Court is wrong, and the Cabinet Departments, the Federal Reserve Board, the chain stores, the power companies, the radio and even the religious bodies, are all wrong." And yet "our industries have changed very little from a year or two ago, when people were fairly content," he added. "We have the same country, in charge of almost entirely the same people, with substantially the same laws and administration. . . . Our country, our people, our civil and religious institutions may not be perfect, but they are what we have made them." We citizens share responsibility for our creations.

Coolidge, uniquely among American conservatives, understood

the peril that the Depression posed for self-government, even before F.D.R. took office. "When people are bewildered they tend to become credulous," he warned after the Republicans went down to defeat in the midterm elections of November 1930. "We are always in danger of expecting too much of the government. When there is distress such expectations are enlarged." Enlarged expectations – and government's failure to meet them – could lead to confusion "in the public mind as to the proper functions of the national government in the relief of distress." A breakdown of citizens' trust in their own government would only too easily follow.

Though former presidents before Coolidge had written occasionally on legal or political matters, Coolidge became "a sort of daily oracle," as the *New York Times* put it at the time. "No other ex-President ever did anything quite like this." His appeal was his likeability, which *Time* found irresistible: "Mr. Coolidge's great advantage . . . is that there are millions of people who are happy to resume relations with him. They like him. They understand his language. They approve of his mind and are happy to go on with him." He was not without his critics, to whom Coolidge is said to have responded in an interview: "They criticize me for harping on the obvious. Perhaps some day I'll write one [column] on *The Importance of the Obvious.*"

Coolidge argued in his columns that big problems, such as the Great Depression, could be solved only through sober forbearance, not by frenzied economic decision-making. "In the short era that culminated in 1929, the economic world became convinced that there was a short way to riches and power through expansion, inflation and speculation," he told readers. "A season of great avarice and extravagance brought the inevitable reaction of loss and suffering."

Only a full-scale reset would do: "Just as the political situation had to be liquidated, so the financial situation had to be liquidated. We may well be thankful it is not worse. Out of our chastening we shall emerge with less speculative and more balanced production. Economic life will be more logical and better controlled. The financial world will be on a firmer foundation." Coolidge recognized the alluring mistake of the "socialistic notions of government" (nationalizing the failing banks). "Experience is a hard school, but some learn from no other." The economy had cooled, but there would be "no salvation in repudiation [of debts] or confiscation [of property]." Spending other people's money wouldn't work either, for "the appropriation of public money always is perfectly lovely until some one is asked to pay the bill." "When the Congress passes laws requiring the expenditure of money, the people have to pay it. When a deficit exists it must be met."

Increasing taxes would cause equal harm: "Those who seek to improve our economic position by spending more tax money are going in the wrong direction." Coolidge was surprised that the American people tolerated high taxes for poor government. As he wrote on February 23, 1931:

One of the most astounding spectacles is the complacency with which people permit themselves to be plundered by extravagant governmental expenditure under the pretense of taxing the rich to help the poor. The poor are not helped but hurt. Taxes have to be collected by the rich before they are paid. They are collected from all people. A higher tax means real wages are lower. The cost of living is higher. The chance to work is less. Every home is burdened. Its value is decreased. The quality of the food, clothing and shelter of the children is reduced.

He hated "the fallacy of thinking the government can be supported by taxing the rich." A national income as large as America's "can only be secured by combined effort of all the people," he argued. "The work and expenditure of all of us contribute to it. High taxes always keep the people poor, emphasize the cleavage between the classes and retard the distribution of wealth. The people at large have a great interest in economy in public expenditures." Besides, people had little to fear from the rich. "There is little cause to fear the power of wealth. Occasionally there are those who abuse it, chiefly to their

own harm. It is difficult to find a great fortune that has been preserved through three generations. . . . Our wealth becomes distributed
by inheritance and bequest."

It was far better to trust to the churning ingenuity of American
business than "any official bureau," Coolidge insisted.

> Twenty-five years ago only a few people were engaged in [the
> automobile and aircraft industries.] The number now runs
> into the millions. We can see in these new occupations the
> natural remedy for labor temporarily displaced by machinery.
> What course our great financial and scientific resources will
> take in the next era of development we do not know. But all
> past experience teaches that it will be an important advance in
> the economic welfare of the nation.

These successes, among others, were indicative of something within
the human condition. Only a fool would ignore it. It was not possible
to understand the present or predict the future without considering
"the natural and unconquerable impulse of human nature to improve,
produce and progress," he wrote. "Left to itself it will find a way."

The government, by contrast, had demonstrated the inevitable
error of nationalization in its clumsy management of the Muscle
Shoals project in Alabama. The new federal control of an old power
plant revealed the "utter hopelessness of having any considerable
business enterprise conducted by the Congress." Every faction wanted
to dominate the negotiations and have the government on its side.
"Rivalry among power, industrial, and agricultural interests has prevented any decisive action," Coolidge explained. "Nearly all concerned
apparently have wanted to get some special advantage out of the government. That will always be the case with any business with which
the government is involved or any property the government owns."

When it came to agriculture, Coolidge further elaborated the
principle at stake:

243

Government interference to maintain prices ... disorganizes the whole economic fabric. It is the wrong method because it does not work. It is better for every one in the end to let those who have made losses bear them than to try to shift them on some one else. If we could have the courage to adopt this principle, our recovery would be expedited. Price fixing, subsidies, and government support will only produce unhealthy business.

These attempts to regulate business failed because "it is not possible to repeal the law of supply and demand, of cause and effect, or of action or reaction." "Not even the United States Treasury is powerful enough to put an arbitrary price on the great world staples with any permanent success," he noted. "Human nature, in spite of legislation, is still human nature and functions accordingly." With a touch of his characteristic understatement, he recommended that "before taking jurisdiction over other economic activities, it might be well to put those already under government control in a profitable and prosperous condition."

The economy would self-correct if government made business conditions more predictable, Coolidge urged repeatedly. "Business can stand anything better than uncertainty. ... Certainty is the basis of business confidence." If government behaves responsibly, "the paralysis of fear will be removed and confidence promoted." "One of the most powerful influences in retarding business recovery is fear. While some can afford that luxury, to many others it means lack of work and real suffering."

He favored a limited government because he believed in the tragic view of mankind: Men were fallen, but hope remained. Responsibility and hard work were critical to growth and a better society. As he wrote on December 18, 1930:

This universe into which we are born, with all its weaknesses and imperfections, yet with all its strength and progress, is the only one in which we can live, and we may as well make the best of it. The people with whom we come in contact, the business organizations which we have formed and the government we have adopted are the only ones we have and we can hope for improvement only by working with them and for them with all our ability. We cannot receive the benefits of prosperity and escape bearing the burdens of adversity.

The benefits of prosperity came from toil, not out of a government's coffers. Those like himself who opposed government's meddling in the economy "do not lack humanity," Coolidge wrote, but believed such behavior would "deprive the people of character and liberty." The people knew that "individual self-reliance is disappearing and local self-government is being undermined." On June 20, 1931, Coolidge warned that a "revolution is taking place which will leave the people dependent upon the government, and place the government where it must decide questions that are far better left to the people to decide for themselves."

The problem of recovery was, at its base, more human than economic. "We get out of life exactly what we put into it," Coolidge said, adding that the economic "failure lies in human imperfection." And much of that comes "because those in authority do not have first hand knowledge of the people and conditions with which they are attempting to deal." Coolidge found it amusing that those who had failed to predict the Great Depression could suddenly prescribe solutions to alleviate it. He took a more cyclical view. In his column of June 8, 1931, he wrote: "We have periods of economic depression which no one adequately can explain or immediately relieve. . . . It is no time for harsh words of hasty action but for patience, sympathy, and sober thought. Nor is there any reason for despair. There is a way out and it will be found. The forces of good are still superior to the forces of evil."

"We live under a system of individual freedom and self-government," Coolidge reassured his readers, "where each individual is entitled to the rewards of his own foresight and industry and is charged with his own support." Any other system would be inconsistent with the American experiment. "The only way to change this system is to restrict the freedom of the individual, let some one else govern him, give the rewards of his industry to others and make him support others. That system is slavery."

* * *

Coolidge's tragic view of human nature suggested a politics of limited possibilities. He rejected the perfection of society sought by the Progressives because he rejected the idea that government could create a perfect man. "No informed student of human affairs ever expected that democracy would be a sovereign remedy for all the ills with which morals are beset," he wrote, although self-government still offered the best possibility that America's problems would be resolved:

> The principle of self-government, applied in so far as the development of a people will admit of its application, remains as the best solution of social relations. Self-government is the expression of one of the strongest and most logical aspirations of human nature. There is no other system that is consistent with freedom. In the end it will prevail because it is everlastingly right.

If there were problems with self-government, the remedy – or the blame – would be found with the people: "We make our own government. If we fail it is our own fault."

> Every one knows that the government is not perfect. . . . Yet we all want to see it improved. We all desire progress, prosperity and an even better distribution of the rewards of industry. . . . Very few now believe that these things can be secured by more extravagance, more loafing, more politics, or more government.

Coolidge's optimism about Americans led him to predict that "if we give the best that is in us to our private affairs, we shall have little need of governmental aid." Conversely, should the citizenry prove "careless, indifferent, uninformed," the Republic "will deteriorate into a very bad form of government." We get the government we deserve, in other words. "We demand entire freedom of action and then expect the government in some miraculous way to save us from the consequences of our own acts. We want the right to run our own business, fix our own wages and prices, and spend our own money, but if depression and unemployment result, we look to government for a remedy."

Looking to the government for remedies would be looking in the wrong direction. Coolidge suggested an alternative: "The real remedy lies with the people. The laws will be enforced when the people clearly and emphatically indicate that they demand enforcement. But law is not enough. We need a change of heart." Ever the student of the classics, Coolidge knew that material wealth was necessary, but insufficient, to solve the problems of life. "We still should keep in mind that wealth is not an end but a means. We need it only for the use we can make of it. The real standard of life is not one of quantity, but of quality; not of money, but of character."

Ministering to one's character required a spiritual revolution, however, not an economic one. It required a new dedication to religion's teachings and to one's fellow men. "We build our character largely by meeting our obligations to others," he noted. "We all live in the same world. We are bound to a common destiny through a common brotherhood. The path to glory does not lie in a sordid individualism, a perverted independence, or a narrow nationalism. It lies toward the Golden Rule." The example of the Golden Rule would, in tough times, help Americans take care of one another. "Democracy is Christ's government in church and state," he said, quoting the Rev. John Wise, the pre-founding theologian. It requires sacrifice and bearing one's cross. Just as Christ had made the ultimate sacrifice for his fellow men, so too should Americans sacrifice together in their time of need. "Nothing is ever felt to be of value," Coolidge said, "which is not won as a result of sacrifice," especially not in business or politics.

To be sure, hard work comes hard for some people. Coolidge conceded that "some people can conscientiously say that they never had a chance," but "most people have failed because they did not really try." Those who do work learn "the great fact . . . that when a man dedicates his soul to his work . . . in his time of need some power outside himself directs his course and gives him the strength to prevail." Such hard workers receive "revelation." We shall "make more progress [in international and domestic relations alike] if we follow the dictates of religious enlightenment which teaches that all men are brothers." Spiritual salvation, after all, is neither allocated nor budgeted by any government program.

Workers, like the government that represented them, had to keep their expenses low. They had to be "thrifty." A thrifty person is one who "does the best that is possible to provide for suitable discharge of the future duties of life," he explained. In its essence, thrift is self-control, which at its base is the foundation of self-government. Reason, industry, and judgment are required to achieve thrift. "Contentment and economic freedom are its fruits."

Would our Republic be capable of producing such fruits? It remained to be seen. Coolidge held out hope, so long as the people took seriously their responsibilities, civic and otherwise, and chose their elected representatives well. In the run-up to the 1930 midterm elections, he issued a warning: "We have plenty of unthinking people, some vicious, and others organized for selfish exploitation of the public through governmental agencies. All of these elements vote in full force. In a light vote they will be the decisive factor." He cautioned voters not to "substitut[e] the power of entertainment for the power of accomplishment." Elections "act as a tonic for the body politic." The election should not "turn on some immaterial personal characteristic that has nothing to do with the qualifications for the office."

Coolidge also cautioned against another type of officeholder who is "always out with the square and compass seeking to find out what the political effect will be of every action they take." Fortunately, the American people are "moved by sincerity and integrity of purpose" and "pretense does not appeal to them." Statesmanship does, which is why

> those who seek popularity so seldom find it, while those who follow an informed conscience so often are astonished by a wide public approval. The people know a sham even when they seem to be trying to fool themselves and they cannot help having a wholesome respect for reality. The best political effect usually comes to those who disregard it.

*   *   *

Does the Republican Party have a standard bearer who could live up to Coolidge's description? At present, such a leader has not emerged. Indeed, it seems as if the Republican Party has decided to dispense with standards altogether. Many of its current front-runners make no pretense of even having conviction. They are, as Coolidge warned, a little too quick to bring out the "square and the compass." History may record that the individuals in 2012 who ought to have run opted out instead – a sad state of affairs, when a country's finest leaders are unwilling to minister to the Republic in her hour of need.

All is not yet lost. Our representative government represents, after all, both the vices and virtues of the American people. As Coolidge rightly knew, "good citizens cannot have a bad government." Alas, the opposite is also true: Bad citizens cannot have a good government. Let us hope that Coolidge's observations of his fellow citizens remain true of today's Americans. Surely Silent Cal would have found something admirable in the Tea Party movement and its "town meeting" language and spirit – he was immensely proud of the New England town-hall tradition. "No more effective instrument for demonstrating the principle of equality and liberty and teaching the art of self-government has been devised," he said. "Such gatherings afford the finest training in the practical elements of citizenship." Coolidge would surely have shared the Tea Party's hope that we will return to a more local, and therefore more responsive, government. The people must demonstrate "that this is their country and their government."

Lessons for Obama from Silent Cal

When President Obama demands that "millionaires and billionaires" "pay their fair share," a recurring theme of his presidency, he makes an appeal to justice, albeit justice wrongly understood. America's tax code is unjust, he argues, not because everyone doesn't pay the same rate, but because "the rich" don't pay *enough* in federal taxes. Dropping his g's, stomping his feet, seducing crowds, he goes into full sermon mode. "If you love me, then you gotta help me pass this bill," he told one swooning crowd in the run-up to the 2012 election. The campaigner-in-chief explains repeatedly that we must "spread the wealth around" and insists on raising taxes to do so. It's all about "living within our means."

But if Obama is serious about living within our means, he would do well to study President Calvin Coolidge – the last Republican president to pay down the debt while simultaneously growing the economy. There has never been a better time than now to return to the Coolidge perspective. He brought Washington's fiscal house into order. He balanced budgets, cut spending, slashed taxes, and helped expand the economy to produce prosperity. In other words, exactly what we need today.

Unfortunately, Obama's philosophy of government couldn't be further from Coolidge's. In his 1925 inaugural address, Coolidge said, "The wisest and soundest method of solving our tax problem is through economy," meaning spending restraints. His concept of our Republic differed markedly from Obama's. "The collection of any taxes which are not absolutely required, which do not beyond reason-

able doubt contribute to the public welfare, is only a species of legal-
ized larceny," he argued. "Under this Republic the rewards of
industry belong to those who earn them."[4] Americans, he reminded
an audience at the Chamber of Commerce later that same year, "are
politically free people and must be an economically free people."[5]
But under President Obama, America has become less economically
free, falling in the indexes of economic freedom.

This is chiefly because of the climate of economic uncertainty his
policies create. In 2009, President Obama rightly opposed raising
taxes in the jaws of a recession. After that, confusingly, he insisted on
raising them despite the economy's continuing contraction. Obvi-
ously he hasn't learned that taxes can't solve Washington's fiscal woes,
because to tax is to destroy the dynamic sources of our prosperity.

Coolidge knew this well, counseling his fellow citizens against the
kind of class warfare underlying Obama's economic philosophy:
"We cannot finance the country, we cannot improve social conditions,
through any system of injustice, even if we attempt to inflict it upon
the rich. Those who suffer the most harm will be the poor."[6] And the
poor have suffered dearly under President Obama: The number of
Americans living in poverty increased again in 2010, rising for the
fourth year in a row. Now, one in six Americans lives below the poverty line.

Americans instinctively dislike class warfare, Coolidge argued:
"This country believes in prosperity. It is absurd to suppose that it is
envious of those who are already prosperous." Prudence and the lessons of history, Coolidge believed, tell us that "the wise and correct
course" is "not to destroy those who have already secured success but
to create conditions under which everyone will have a better chance
to be successful."[7]

Coolidge's approach really was one of seeking the proper balance.
Government and business each "ought to be sovereign in its own sphere,"
he told same the Chamber of Commerce audience. "When government comes unduly under the influence of business, the tendency is
to develop an administration which closes the door of opportunity;

becomes narrow and selfish in its outlook, and results in an oligarchy."
On the other hand, "when government enters the field of business
with its great resources, it has a tendency to extravagance and ineffi-
ciency, but, having the power to crush all competitors, likewise closes
the door of opportunity and results in monopoly."

With his belief in big government, Obama insists that he remains
focused on creating jobs. Coolidge however, knew that government
could not create jobs directly. Job creation was the province of private enterprise. "If business can be let alone and assured of reasonable freedom from governmental interference and increased taxes,
that will do more than all kinds of legislation to relieve depression,"
the retired Coolidge later wrote during the Depression in one of his
columns. "It will be the part of wisdom to give business a free hand
to supply its own remedies."

Coolidge achieved as much as he did because he believed so deeply
in "economy," meaning frugality. He ranked it third, after only "order
and liberty," as "one of the highest essentials of a free government."
In his 1925 inaugural address, he put it simply: "I favor the policy of
economy, not because I wish to save money, but because I wish to
save people." A dollar saved was a dollar the people could spend
themselves, on their own betterment.

Unlike other politicians who espoused, even back then, a phony
fiscal conservatism, Coolidge worked to make his principles into policy. And he believed wholeheartedly in budgets, confessing a "sort of
obsession" to make the numbers come out right. "I regard a good
budget as among the noblest monuments of virtue,"[8] he proclaimed
in 1924. Compare that with President Obama's first-term budgets,
each one a monument to profligacy that failed to attract a single vote
from either party in the Senate.

Obama prefers to ramp up the rhetoric, demonizing "fat cats"
and "millionaires and billionaires." In one of his two books about
himself, he described his brief time in corporate America as a period
"behind enemy lines." Coolidge, by contrast, once remarked that
business capital is "the chief material minister to the general charac-

ter of all mankind."[9] Although he famously believed that "the chief business of America is business," he saw the business and the wealth of America as only a means, not an end.

By leaving business alone, Coolidge oversaw one of the lowest unemployment rates in American history. By keeping businesses free from excessive taxes, he protected consumers from having to pay for them with higher prices. "High taxes mean high prices," Coolidge maintained. But he also added a moral dimension: "I am opposed to extremely high rates, because they produce little or no revenue, because they are bad for the country, and finally, because they are wrong."[10]

"Debt reduction is tax reduction," as he often put it. The corollary was also true. Tax reduction was debt reduction. One of his pithiest statements bears repeating: "I want taxes to be less that the people may have more."[11] By lowering taxes, Coolidge actually produced humanitarian results. Here, even progressives might find something to admire. Those making less than $5,000 a year paid 15.4 percent of total income taxes in 1920, but only 0.4 percent in 1929. Those who earned more than $100,000 paid 65.2 percent, up from 29.9 percent over that same period. Coolidge got more revenue, too. The economic expansion led to a 28 percent increase in the proportion of the budget paid by federal income taxes. By 1927, 98 percent of Americans paid no income tax at all.

These successes were possible not only because of Coolidge's grounding in commonsense economics and his belief in limited government, but because he surrounded himself with men of accomplishment, not agenda. There were major businessmen and real statesmen in his cabinet. Among them was Andrew Mellon, his (and Harding's and Hoover's) treasury secretary. A financial wizard, Mellon had such genius and force of personality that it was said "three Presidents served under him." Another of Coolidge's outstanding appointees was Vice President Charles Dawes, who had been the nation's first director of the Bureau of the Budget in the Harding administration. Dawes devised a plan to restore post–World War I Germany and stabilize its economy and went on to win the Nobel Peace Prize in 1925.

Like many conservatives today, Coolidge was popular with the man in the street but unpopular in the Ivory Tower and in Washington. Then, as now, the educated class harbored contempt for the philosophic underpinnings of our Republic and for those who most seriously defended them. When attacks on Coolidge's philosophy failed, his critics simply got personal. Socialite Alice Roosevelt Longworth, the daughter of Teddy Roosevelt, scorned Coolidge as having been "weaned on a pickle." He was the butt of jokes and vicious rumors. He "slept more than any other President, whether by day or by night. Nero fiddled, but Coolidge only snored," wrote H. L. Mencken in 1933. When told of Coolidge's death, Dorothy Parker, the popular satirist, is said to have quipped, "How could they tell?" More recently, author William L. Shirer recalled "the incredible smugness and emptiness of the Calvin Coolidge era." He was not alone in recent years in taking such cheap shots. Pulitzer Prize–winning historian Arthur Schlesinger Jr. castigated Coolidge for being too beholden to business and pictured him as a boorish philistine.

To today's left, Coolidge was a bogeyman. The *Huffington Post* quoted an unnamed Washington Democrat who sought to tie the Tea Party to Coolidge. Mike Lux, a left-wing political consultant, linked him to the Paul Ryan budget: "[Republicans] want to take us back to the era of Calvin Coolidge, when the advances of the last 80 years simply didn't exist," Lux wrote on the *Huffington Post*.[12]

On the other hand, many on the right long for a return to Coolidge's principles. Peggy Noonan, among others, saw Coolidge in Governor Mitch Daniels of Indiana. George Will calls him "the last president with a proper sense of his office's constitutional proportions." Richard Land of the Southern Baptist Convention, who served as the honorary co-chair of one of Rick Perry's events, predicted a President Perry "would be the most conservative president since Calvin Coolidge."

Predictably, what Land hopes for, Andrew Romano of *Newsweek* fears. "Perry . . . would do more to limit the power of federal government – or at least attempt to do more – than any president since

Calvin Coolidge," Romano warned after reading an interview Perry did with his magazine in August 2011. But if Perry wants to claim the Coolidge mantle, he won't be alone. Sarah Palin's book *America by Heart* brims with favorable references to the thirtieth president. And Michele Bachmann extolled Coolidge's economic policies on the House floor in 2009.

Unlike George W. Bush, Coolidge believed that sometimes the government can't do much at all to mend people's woes. In fact, often the trick is to do nothing, which is what Coolidge did by vetoing a farm subsidy bill – the McNary-Haugen bill – in 1927 and again in 1928. As noted earlier, he once quipped to his father, "It is much more important to kill bad bills than to pass good ones."[13] In his 1926 State of the Union Address, he emphasized the rights and responsibilities of the individual: "The whole theory of our institutions is based on the liberty and independence of the individual. He is dependent on himself for support and therefore entitled to the rewards of his own industry. He is not to be deprived of what he earns that others may be benefited by what they do not earn. What he saves through his private effort is not to be wasted by Government extravagance." For President Obama, in contrast, the government is a supreme and ever-more-powerful caretaker, and its coffers must continuously expand. He insists that individuals above a certain income level – to be determined by lawmakers – give more and more of what they earn to the state, because "it's the right thing to do." "I do think at a certain point you've made enough money," he lectured. "We don't want to stop [entrepreneurs] from fulfilling *their responsibility* to help grow *our economy*."

Obama also suffers by comparison to Coolidge when it comes to eloquence. The man lauded as the greatest orator of our age uses words so indiscriminately that it seems hardly a day goes by when he doesn't deliver a major speech. These are described as major because, in Obama's view, nothing he does is minor. His favorite word is "unprecedented," which he mostly uses about himself – his eloquence being often on display when he describes his own role in the sweep of history. He has gone so far as to suggest in some remarks that he fancies himself a new Lincoln, a political messiah, another "tall, gangly, self-made Springfield lawyer." Invoking Lincoln when he announced his run for the presidency, Obama called on his fellow Americans to "gather . . . to transform a nation." The question is, What transformation does he intend? For Obama, Lincoln is personal, but for Coolidge, Lincoln was political. Coolidge, too, was thought to be Lincoln's heir, because he spoke so frequently of Lincoln's political thought, often reverently. But where Obama conceives of Americans as needing perpetual aid, Coolidge – like Lincoln – appeals to their strength and moral courage. And Coolidge, unlike Obama, never gave the impression he was the chosen one. He believed that it was the people who decided who was great. Obama, on the other hand, not limiting himself to Lincoln, uses imagery from Moses's story to describe his role. Electing him would be the "moment when the rise of the oceans began to slow and our planet began to heal," he memorably said during his 2008 campaign. Coolidge knew well the danger of letting politics go to the head. Where Coolidge responded to White House callers by keeping "dead-still" and waiting for them to "run down" till they gave up on begging for favors, President Obama seems to give such importunate visitors (such as frequent White House guest Andy Stern, president of SEIU) everything they want.

Coolidge was also determined to avoid being taken in by flatterers, and he aimed to avoid the "self-delusion" and "artificial atmosphere of adulation and exaltation" that impairs the president's judgment. He saw how easy it was for the chief executive to become arrogant and careless.[14] President Obama is rightly denounced for being both, and is prone to self-delusion, perhaps fostered by the adulation he has received during his presidency, in his 2008 and 2012 campaigns, and long before.

Conservatives should work toward nothing less than what Harding and Coolidge vowed in 1920: "a return to normalcy," by which they meant a turn away from things going "to hell in a handbasket," as they had during the Wilson years. What Harding promised, Coolidge delivered. On the eve of the 2008 election, Obama promised to "fundamentally transform" America. He delivered, too, but with "hope and change" that have left us with a changed credit rating, a foretaste perhaps of bankruptcy and irreversible dependency on the government. The task now is to return to normalcy once more, before it's too late.

It won't be easy. But it's worth repeating Silent Cal's trenchant words: "It is a great advantage to a President, and a major source of safety to the country, for him to know that he is not a great man. We draw our Presidents from the people. It is a wholesome thing for them to return to the people. I came from them. I wish to be one of them again." In 1928 he announced, "I do not choose to run," eschewed a likely election victory, and retired to Northampton, Massachusetts. Come 2016, we will have another chance to help Obama resemble Coolidge and quietly return to private life.

NOTES

INTRODUCTION

1   Arthur M. Schlesinger Jr., *A Thousand Days: John F. Kennedy in the White House* (Boston: Houghton Mifflin, 2002), 717.

2   Robert A. Woods, *The Preparation of Calvin Coolidge: An Interpretation* (New York: Houghton Mifflin, 1924), 241.

3   Paul Johnson, *Modern Times: The World from the Twenties to the Nineties* (New York: Harper Perennial, 2001), 222.

4   Johnson, *Modern Times*, 223.

5   June 9, 1925, cited in Howard H. Quint and Robert H. Ferrell, eds., *The Talkative President* (Amherst: University of Massachusetts Press, 1964), 128.

6   Calvin Coolidge, "Thought, the Master of Things," at the Annual Meeting of the American Classical League, the University of Pennsylvania, July 7, 1921, *The Price of Freedom* (Amsterdam, The Netherlands: Fredonia Books, 2001), 64.

7   Coolidge, "Great Virginians," at Fredicksburg, Virginia, July 6, 1922, *Price of Freedom*, 174. Emphasis added.

8   Maymie Richardson Krythe, *All About American Holidays* (New York: Harper, 1962), 253.

9   Coolidge, "The Destiny of America," at the Memorial Day Services at Northampton, May 30, 1923, *Price of Freedom*, 333.

10   Calvin Coolidge, *Autobiography of Calvin Coolidge* (New York: Cosmopolitan Book Corporation, 1929), 159.

11   At the White House, December 12, 1924.

12   Accepting the presidential nomination, Washington, DC, August 4, 1924.

13   To be sure, this myth was well cultivated by Coolidge himself, if only to disarm critics – he chose to appear as a simpleton to the press that he astutely courted. He reportedly spent his afternoons reading Latin, while telling the press that he was napping in the Oval Office. Eventually, his "do-nothingness" would become a cause célèbre on the right. In an essay in a new book, historian Amity Shlaes pictures him as a "windsurfer," ably bobbing and weaving with the flow of events. In my view, he had much more of a steady hand.

14   Shlaes gave this title to her talk in 2010 at the Mont Pelerin Society in Australia. By "liberal," Shlaes means classical-liberal.

15   Gene Healy, author of *The Cult of the Presidency: America's Dangerous Devotion to Executive Power* (Cato Institute: Washington, DC, 2008), seems not to have read, or carefully read, the Supreme Court decisions of the Coolidge years.

16   Mike Pence, "The Presidency and the Constitution," *Imprimis* 39, no. 10 (October 2010).

17   Though not always so: It is hard to reconcile economic liberalism with his protectionist policies on trade and immigration. Coolidge, however, did not think

of immigration solely as an economic issue, but also as one affecting America's
civic health.

CHAPTER ONE

1 Edward E. Whiting, his first biographer, cited in Claude M. Fuess, *Calvin
   Coolidge: The Man from Vermont* (New York: Little, Brown, 1939), 231.
2 Thomas T. Johnston, *Have Faith in Calvin Coolidge: Or, From a Farmhouse to the White
   House* (Boston: The Christopher Publishing House, 1925), 6.
3 *Boston Herald*, September 12, 1918. The very real fear that the strike would
   spread and hasten the overthrow of the government was omnipresent. See
   Fuess, *Man from Vermont*, 224.
4 The most recent of these is Dennis Lehane's *The Given Day*, published in 2008.
5 Larry Kudlow, for instance, when discussing the strikes in February 2011 in
   Wisconsin, invoked Coolidge's response to the police unions of 1919. Kudlow,
   "Calvin Coolidge, Call Your Office, as Unions Rage Against Democracy at Wisconsin," *New York Sun*, February 18, 2011. Cal Thomas also drew parallels in
   the *Washington Times*, February 18, 2011.
6 Reagan, borrowing from Coolidge, called the strike of the air-traffic controllers
   a "desertion in the line of duty." Coolidge had referred to the police strike as a
   "desertion of duty." See James Gertenzang, "Reagan Following Coolidge,"
   Associated Press, August 4, 1981.
7 Reagan biographer Steven Hayward, in emails to the author, suggested that the
   PATCO firings spooked *Pravda* and members of the Soviet press, who took the
   incident to mean that Reagan was serious about his political philosophy.
8 Kiron K. Skinner, Annelise Anderson, and Martin Anderson, eds., *Reagan:
   A Life in Letters* (New York: Free Press, 2003), 287.
9 Cited in Steven F. Hayward, *The Age of Reagan: The Conservative Counterrevolution,
   1980–1989* (New York: Three Rivers Press, 2009), 72.
10 Reagan explored the image that Americans have of Coolidge in a radio script
   titled "Image," which appeared in August 1975. In it, he said:

>   Calvin Coolidge – the man H. L. Mencken said had been weaned on a
>   pickle. [Editor's note: Reagan gets this wrong. It was Alice Roosevelt
>   Longworth who made this remark.] *Was he* a kind of do nothing Presi-
>   dent in one of those lulls in our Nations history? If so we should have
>   such lulls today. There was better than full employment – jobs were
>   competing for workers. The cost of living went down 2.3%...
>   During silent Cals. Presidency the number of automobiles owned by
>   Americans tripled and a great new industry, radio, went $60 mil in sales
>   to $842 mil. They laughed when Coolidge said, "the business of Am. is
>   business," but we had true peace & prosperity – those things we are

promised so often *but* given so seldom. [Ronald Reagan, *Reagan, in His Own Hand*, ed. Kiron K. Skinner, Annelise Anderson, and Martin Anderson (New York: Simon & Schuster, 2001), 252–253.]

As Reagan further noted in speech given on September 21, 1976, Silent Cal appeared to be a do-nothing man, but he was in fact doing a lot. The federal budget "actually went down & so did the Nat. debt," he said. "Consumer prices fell but unemployment stayed at a figure we only dream of – 3.5% which means everyone who wanted a job had one. Federal taxes were cut 4 times. So what if he was a 'do nothing' Pres. Do you suppose doing nothing had *something* to do with reducing the budget, reducing the debt and cutting taxes 4 times?" Ronald Reagan, *Reagan's Path to Victory: The Shaping of Ronald Reagan's Vision: Selected Writings*, ed. Kiron K. Skinner (New York: Simon & Schuster, 2004), 73–74.

11 Richard Reeves, *President Reagan: The Triumph of Imagination* (New York: Simon & Schuster, 2005), 267. Reeves got wrong the title of the biography. It is *Return to these Hills: The Vermont Years of Calvin Coolidge*, by Jane Curtis, Frank Lieberman, and Will Curtis, not *From These Hills: The Vermont Years of Calvin Coolidge*.

12 Hayward, *Age of Reagan: The Conservative Counterrevolution*, 73.

13 Mark Shields, "With All Due Respect to Cal Coolidge," *Washington Post*, July 24, 1981.

14 Cited in Hayward, *Age of Reagan: The Conservative Counterrevolution*, 72.

15 Coolidge's reputation is undergoing a bit of a restoration. Most presidential surveys since 1994 have begun placing him in the third quartile, rather than the fourth, which is one reason that the time is ripe to resuscitate Coolidge's reputation.

16 The coin was fittingly minted in commemoration of the sesquicentennial of American independence in 1926. Coolidge is pictured with George Washington.

17 William Allen White, *Calvin Coolidge: The Man Who Is President* (New York: Macmillan, 1925), 9.

18 In one area, communications, America was triumphing wildly. There were a mere sixty thousand radios in consumers' hands in 1922 and more than 7.5 million in 1928. Larry Schweikart and Lynne Pierson Doti, *American Entrepreneur* (New York: Amacom, 2009), 281.

19 Donald R. McCoy, *Calvin Coolidge: The Quiet President* (Lawrence, KS: University Press of Kansas, 1988), 256.

20 Jay Lovestone, "What's What – About Coolidge?" (Chicago: Workers Party of America, 1923), 3.

21 Robert H. Ferrell, *The Presidency of Calvin Coolidge* (Lawrence, KS: University Press of Kansas, 1998), 73.

22 Woods, in *The Preparation of Calvin Coolidge*, writes, "The gods approve the depth and not the tumult of the soul" (263). Woods understood this better than most of Coolidge's biographers:

History has shown many remarkable instances – and American history its proportion – of the deliberative type of man of action; without exception such men have encountered the same type of criticism, never without bitter stings, that has been waged against Mr. Coolidge, not only as President, but as Governor of Massachusetts. The classical instance is that of Fabius, "the incarnation of all that a Roman meant by patriotism." "Wherefore it may not be gainsaid that the fruit of this man's long taking of counsel – and (by the many so deemed) untimeous delays – was the safe-holding for all men, his fellow-citizens, of the Common Weal." "For the right moment you must wait as Fabius did most patiently, when warring against Hannibal, though many censured his delays; but when the time comes, you must strike hard, as Fabius did, or your waiting will be in vain and fruitless." (Woods, 262)

23 See generally Tom Silver, *Coolidge and the Historian* (Durham, NC: Carolina Academic Press, 1983).

24 Francis Russell, *A City in Terror: Calvin Coolidge and the 1919 Boston Police Strike* (Boston: Beacon Press, 2005), 66.

25 Coolidge, "States' Rights and National Unity," at the College of William and Mary, Williamsburg, Virginia," May 15, 1926, *Foundations of the Republic* (New York: Charles Scribner's Sons, 1926), 411.

26 Coolidge, "Public Meeting on the High Cost of Living, Faneuil Hall," December 9, 1916, *Have Faith in Massachusetts* (Boston: Houghton Mifflin, 1919), 57–58.

27 Calvin Coolidge, "The Wardens of Civilization," *The Outlook*, February 2, 1921, 188.

28 Bryce could easily have been anticipating Calvin Coolidge when he wrote the following in 1888:

A European finds that this phenomenon needs in its turn to be explained, for in the free countries of Europe, brilliancy, be it eloquence in speech, or some striking achievement in war or administration, or the power through whatever means of somehow impressing the popular imagination, is what makes a leader triumphant. Why should it be otherwise in America? Because in America party loyalty and party organization have been hitherto so perfect that anyone put forward by the party will get the full party vote if his character is good and his "record," as they call it, unstained. The safe candidate may not draw in quite so many votes from the moderate men of the other side as the brilliant one would, but he will not lose nearly so many from his own ranks. Even those who admit his mediocrity will vote straight when the moment for voting comes. Besides, the ordinary American voter does not object to mediocrity. He has a lower conception of the qualities requisite to make a statesman than those who direct *public opinion* in Europe have. He likes his candidate to be sensible, vigorous, and, above all, what he calls "magnetic," and does not value, because he sees no need for, originality or profundity, a fine culture or a wide knowledge. Candidates are selected to be run for nomination by knots of persons who, however expert as party tacticians, are usually commonplace men; and the choice between those selected for nomination is made by a very large body, an assembly of nearly a thousand delegates from the local party organizations over the country, who are certainly no better than ordinary citizens. (James Bryce, *The American Commonwealth*, vol. 1, "Why Great Men Are Not Chosen Presidents," paragraph 239)

Coolidge relished his role as an ordinary citizen and saw himself – before, during, and after his presidnecy – as one of the people. A neighbor described Coolidge's admittedly uninspiring quality but told a reporter that he nonetheless had an admirable steadiness. It soon became part of a piece about Coolidge in the widely read magazine *Current Opinion*:

Calvin has been a good representative, a good senator, and a good governor. He's honest as the day, and he's got plenty of brains, a lot of experience, and all the firmness anybody needs. I'm inclined to think he'd make a good president. You see, he never makes mistakes. He has the limitations of his Vermont Yankee hereditary [sic]. He was born cautious. All great men make mistakes, probably more mistakes than anything else. Three times out of five that great men come to bat, they strike out. The other two times are home runs tho. Calvin never takes a chance and strikes out, and never hits a home run. A base hit is his limit. He'll make that every time, to do him justice. (*Current Opinion* 68:37)

29 Coolidge, "On the Nature of Politics," May 12, 1915, Algonquin Club, Boston, Massachusetts, *Have Faith in Massachusetts*, 78.
30 Coolidge, "Written for the Sunday Advertiser and American," September 1, 1918, ibid., 132.
31 Coolidge, "Associated Industries Dinner, Boston," December 15, 1916, ibid., 66–67.
32 Coolidge, "You Own Yourself," *Hearst's International* 42 (July 1922): 5. Coolidge would have been aware of the Aristotelian principle of *eleutheria*, or of being "ruling and being ruled in turn."
33 Karl Marx, "Critique of the Gotha Programme," 1875, Part I.
34 Coolidge, "You Own Yourself," 5.
35 Coolidge, "Associated Industries Dinner, Boston," December 15, 1916, *Have Faith in Massachusetts*, 72.

36 Coolidge, "Written for the Sunday Advertiser and American," September 1, 1918, ibid., 135.

37 Coolidge, *Autobiography*, 107.

38 Robert Sobel, *Coolidge: An American Enigma* (Washington, DC: Regnery, 1998), 124.

39 Jeremy Brecher, *Strike!* rev. ed. (Boston: South End Press, 1997), 126.

40 Sobel, *American Enigma*,125.

41 "Ole Hanson, Once Mayor of Seattle," *New York Times*, July 8, 1940.

42 Robert K. Murray, *Red Scare: A Study in National Hysteria, 1919–1920* (Minneapolis: University of Minnesota Press, 1955), 65–66.

43 Sobel, *American Enigma*, 125.

44 Whittaker Chambers, in *Cold Friday*, discussed his early support for Coolidge. "I was inclined to believe that Calvin Coolidge might be another Abraham Lincoln," he wrote. "Constituting myself a one-man campaign committee, I had written to practically every Republican newspaper editor in the country, urging Coolidge's nomination for President of the United States." When that failed, he distributed handbills for Coolidge as vice president. Chambers's love for Coolidge outpaced his interests in academics, and he oftentimes failed to turn in assignments. Chambers wanted so badly to see Coolidge speak at a rally in Madison Square Garden that he climbed a fire escape in order to hear him. He knew "almost by heart" Coolidge's speeches from *Have Faith in Massachusetts*. Whittaker Chambers, *Cold Friday* (New York: Random House, 1964), 98.

45 Hanson told the audience, to applause, that even though he believed that with public support, the public utilities could be operated properly, experience convinced him that a public utility would function less efficiently than "a private corporation which has an individual reward at the end of the day." "How M.O. Works in Practice," *The Gas Record* 17, no. 5 (March 10, 1920).

46 Ole Hanson, *Americanism Versus Bolshevism* (New York: Doubleday, Pace, 1920), 47.

47 Even Canada proved fertile ground for Bolshevist thought. In Canada, on June 17, 1919, strikers in Winnipeg were convicted of a violent Bolshevist plot. The world seemed to be coming undone. (Johnson, *Modern Times*, 38)

48 Ronald J. Pestritto, *Woodrow Wilson: The Essential Political Writings* (Lanham, MD: Lexington Books, 2005), 78.

49 Ernest A. McKay, *Against Wilson and War, 1914–1917* (Malabar, FL: Krieger Publishing, 1996), 132.

50 Francis A. Russell, *A City in Terror*, 190.

51 Coolidge, "Essex County Club," Lynnfield, Massachusetts, September 14, 1918, *Have Faith in Massachusetts*, 146, 151.

52 Coolidge, "The Power of the Moral Law," address at the Community-Chest Dinner, Springfield, Massachusetts, October 11, 1921, *Price of Freedom*, 73.

53 Coolidge, "The Foundations of Our Institutions," at the N.Y. State Convention of the YMCA, Albany, April 13, 1923, ibid., 291.

54 Sobel, *American Enigma*, 249.

55 Cited in Woods, *Preparation of Calvin Coolidge*, 201.

56 Woodrow Wilson, "Survey of the War Situation in a Noteworthy Speech Before the Federal of Labor," November 12, 1917, cited in *New York Times Current History: The European War*, vol. 13.

57 Max Eastman, *Love and Revolution: My Journey Through an Epoch* (New York: Random House, 1964), 103.

58 See Jennings Cropper Wise, *Woodrow Wilson, Disciple of Revolution* (Columbus, OH: Paisley Press, 1938).

59 Eastman, *Love and Revolution*, 103.

60 Johnston, *Have Faith in Calvin Coolidge*, 27.

61 Coolidge, "Flag Day Proclamation," May 26, 1919, *Have Faith in Massachusetts*, 178.

62 Cited in Sobel, *American Enigma*, 79.

63 Upon receiving a copy of Coolidge's "Have Faith in Massachusetts" speech, Taft thanked Coolidge for "sending it to me and for giving me an opportunity to read it." (Ibid., 87)

64 Ibid., 63.

65 Lodge's subject was "The Anglo-Saxon Land Law," which made clear his pro–Anglo-Saxon racial views. Henry Cabot Lodge, *Early Memories* (New York: Charles Scribner's Sons, 1913), 263. Lodge founded the Immigration Restriction League in 1894 out of concern about the hordes of "non-Teutonic" immigrants he worried were descending upon America. Coolidge didn't seem to think it was such a problem. He cultivated the support of all recent immigrants. (See Chapter 6 for more details.)

66 Woods, *Preparation of Calvin Coolidge*, 137. There was some indication that Coolidge's political thought was catching on, however. His narrow gubernatorial victory in 1918 led to praise from the *Springfield Republican*: "Political revolutions are begotten of constructive reaction, not of liberal progressiveness." The paper encouraged the Republican Party to "wisely direct those broadening impulses of service and cooperation on the part of the individual, and of increased responsibility on the part of the Government, whether State or Nation, which are born of common sacrifice and closer union during this time of war" (Woods, 138).

67 Cited in Edward Connery Lathem, ed., *Your Son, Calvin Coolidge: A Selection of Letters from Calvin Coolidge to His Father* (Vermont Historical Society, 1968), 127.

68 Theodore Roosevelt, *Selections from the Correspondence of Theodore Roosevelt and Henry Cabot Lodge, 1884–1918* (Boston: Da Capo Press, 1971), 2:540.

69 Theodore Roosevelt, *The Letters of Theodore Roosevelt: 1914–1919*, ed. Eltin Elmore Morison (Cambridge: Harvard University Press, 1954), 1,376.

70 Cited in Sobel, *American Enigma*, 86.

71 Michael E. Hennessy, *Four Decades of Massachusetts Politics: 1890–1935* (Norwood,

MA: Norwood Press, 1935), 158.

72   White, *The Man Who Is President*, 39.

73   Sobel, *American Enigma*, 117.

74   Ibid., 90.

75   Stearns backed Coolidge to the hilt and considered him presidential material, writing as early as 1915 about his ultimate ambition for Coolidge:

> Just for a minute it does not seem best to push him for anything higher than lieutenant governor of Massachusetts, but later, of course, he must be governor and still later president. Just think what a time we will have at commencement when the president of the United States . . . comes back to commencement! (Fuess, *Man from Vermont*, 137)

76   Ibid., 119.

77   Stearns's recollection was later chronicled in Edward Connery Lathem's *Meet Calvin Coolidge: The Man Behind the Myth* (Brattleboro, VT: Stephen Greene Press, 1960), 27.

78   There is, of course, some irony in the idea that a Progressive measure – the initiative process – led to a progressive result that's also in favor of small government.

79   Fuess, *Man from Vermont*, 191.

80   Arthur Wilson Page, ed., *The World's Work: A History of Our Time* 39 (1919–1920): 377.

81   Coolidge's personal tastes may also have been a factor in his attitude toward pay raises. No matter how high his political skill took him, he cared nothing for money, preferring economy and frugality. He lived by example. Even during the speculative boom of the '20s, Coolidge kept his investments safe and his expenditures low.

82   Coolidge, "The Needs of Education," before the County Teachers' Institute and School Directors' Convention, at Reynoldsvlle, Pennsylvania, December 21, 1922, *Price of Freedom*, 225.

83   *Have Faith in Massachusetts*, 195.

84   Coolidge, "Williams College," October 17, 1919, *Have Faith in Massachusetts*, 254–255.

85   Coolidge, "Concerning Teachers' Salaries," October 29, 1919, *Have Faith in Massachusetts*, 257–258.

86   Coolidge, "Harvard University Commencement," June 19, 1919, *Have Faith in Massachusetts*, 191–192.

CHAPTER TWO

1   Coolidge, "Republican State Convention," at the Tremont Temple, Boston, October 4, 1919, *Have Faith in Massachusetts*, 244.

2   *Evening Transcript*, September 12, 1919.

3   Coolidge, "Statement Relative to the Adjustment of the Telephone Strike," April 21, 1919.

4   Sobel notes that there "had been 3,353 strikes in 1918 and another 3,630 in 1919, as against the 1,204 in 1913, the last peace-time year." The strikes "resulted in part from the inflationary economy of the period," in Sobel's view. "The cost of living in late 1919 was more than 80 percent higher than it had been in 1914, with most of this rise taking place after the United States entered the war in 1919." (Sobel, *American Enigma*, 122)

5   Ibid., 124.

6   Ibid., 131.

7   Perhaps that is why Michael Dukkakis found something to like in him.

8   Garland S. Tucker III, *The High Tide of American Conservatism* (Austin, TX: Emerald Book Company, 2010), 158.

9   McCoy, *The Quiet President*, 84.

10   Coolidge's statement in January 1919, "Massachusetts: More Revenue the Problem," as published by the American Electric Railway Association, 1919, 552. Emphasis added.

11   Coolidge appealed to this sense of self-reliance in his campaign speeches for the governorship. He "urged strongly that the Republican Party must be liberal – must be broad enough to merit the support of the various elements which make up the increasingly cosmopolitan population of Massachusetts," according to one observer. "He instances the great mass of legislation of the State for fifty years past as showing that this was the essential republican attitude. He referred, however, to the difficulties that come of too much legislation, and urged that the remedy lay in looking to the executive for a more serviceable type of public action. Such administration, however, must not destroy the will of the people through despotic bureaucracy any more than through a socialistic state." (Woods, *Preparation of Calvin Coolidge*, 136)

12   Coolidge, "Brockton Chamber of Commerce Speech," April 11, 1916, *Have Faith in Massachusetts*, 16.

13   This collection eventually became *Have Faith in Massachusetts*.

14   November 2, 1918, in *Have Faith in Massachusetts*, 149–150.

15   The original phrase is from Coolidge's Amherst Alumni Dinner address in Springfield on March 15, 1918, in which he said that the principle of the Monroe Doctrine, which had kept "European despotism" out of the Western Hemisphere, could be extended to the whole world.

16   Coolidge, "Plymouth, Labor Day," September 1, 1919, *Have Faith in Massachusetts*, 201–202.

17   Since the Russian Revolution of 1917, the postwar months saw, in Tucker's words, "a torrent of strikes." Fear of Communism was promoted, perhaps rightly, by Woodrow Wilson's attorney general, A. Mitchell Palmer. "We can get

rid of them! And not until we have done so shall we have removed the menace of Bolshevism for good." (Tucker, *The High Tide of American Conservatism*, 159)

18 Coolidge, "Plymouth, Labor Day," September 1, 1919, *Have Faith in Massachusetts*, 203

19 Ibid., 205.

20 Ibid., 206.

21 Stearns wasn't alone in thinking of Coolidge as a second coming of Lincoln. Early Coolidge biographer Thomas T. Johnston made the comparison in the opening chapter of *Have Faith in Calvin Coolidge: Or, From a Farmhouse to the White House*. Johnston returns to the comparison throughout his book. For Johnston, Coolidge is "sort of a political miracle" whose state papers are "well fitted to grace the Nation." They are "Lincoln-strong for quality." "And if Coolidge should ever be elected President, no man shall have sat in the presidential chair, since the days of the immortal Emanicipator [sic] who, to a larger measure, would receive and merit, not only the confidence and admiration but more than that, the true affection of the American people." "No man since Lincoln ever by nature and training so qualified himself for the masterful and sympathetic leadership of the people of America." See Johnston, *Have Faith in Calvin Coolidge*, 13–14, 18, 24, 25.

22 This was one fewer, interestingly, than the number tried and removed as duly appointed members of the Boston Police Department.

23 Coolidge always preferred Commonwealth to "State" when referring to Massachusetts, because the term signified public harmony and constitutionalism. It is a referral to something Plato knew well: "The things of friends are in common." Politics required the love of friends

24 Michael E. Hennessy, *Calvin Coolidge: From a Green Mountain Farm to the White House* (New York: G. P. Putnam's Sons, 1924), 98.

25 Ibid., 99.

26 These strikes ultimately did not take place. Ibid.

27 Wilson called the strike a "crime against civilization" at a political event in Montana. Later, when Coolidge was reelected governor, the president congratulated him on his "victory for law and order," adding: "When that is the issue, all Americans stand together." Senator Henry Cabot Lodge warned that if the strike were successful, "we shall be in a measurable distance of Soviet government by labor unions." Would-be presidential contenders Charles Evans Hughes and Senator Warren Harding welcomed Coolidge's victory and sent notes of congratulation.

28 Sobel, *American Enigma*, 167.

29 William Thomas Hutchinson, *Lowden of Illinois: Nation and Countryside* (Chicago: University of Chicago Press, 1957), 411.

30 Cited in Sobel, *American Enigma*, 144.

31 *Have Faith in Massachusetts*, 226–227.

32 Coolidge, "The Wardens of Civilization," *The Outlook*, February 2, 1921, 187.

33 The book in question was Raymond B. Fosdick's *American Police Systems* (The Century Company: New York, 1920).

34 Coolidge, "The Wardens of Civilization," *The Outlook*, February 2, 1921, 188.

35 Ibid.

36 Ibid.

37 Ibid.

38 Barton would go on to become a congressman and a well-known critic of Franklin Roosevelt.

39 Sobel, *American Enigma*,162.

40 Coolidge would later be criticized for being an "isolationist" or at least for not sufficiently understanding the problems of Europe. Winston Churchill even criticized him for having the "viewpoint of a New England backwoodsman" when it came to naval armaments, but Coolidge seemed to have correctly seized up the Kaiser. Fraser J. Harbutt, *The Iron Curtain: Churchill, America, and the Origins of the Cold War* (Oxford: Oxford University Press, 1988), 14.

41 Coolidge, "Essex County Club," September 14, 1918, *Have Faith in Massachusetts*, 138–139.

42 Coolidge, "Tremont Temple," November 2, 1918, ibid., 155.

43 Sobel, *American Enigma*, 113.

44 Fuess, *Man from Vermont*, 234.

45 Coolidge, "Vice-Presidential Acceptance Address," Northampton, Massachusetts, July 27, 1920, in David Pietrusza, ed., *Silent Cal's Almanack* (2008).

46 Ibid.

47 "Roosevelt Night" speech, published by the Middlesex Club, 1919.

48 As best as I can tell, this invocation of the Declaration is highly unusual for government proclamations at the time in Massachusetts.

49 Coolidge, "The Inspiration of the Declaration," celebrating the 150th Anniversary of the Declaration of Independence, July 5, 1925, Philadelphia, Pennsylvania, *Foundations of the Republic*, 449.

50 Coolidge, "The Title of American," at the Convention of the American Legion, Kansas City, Missouri, October 31, 1921, *Price of Freedom*, 83.

51 Coolidge, "Progress Toward Freedom," at the dedication of a government hospital for colored veterans of the World War, Tuskegee, Alabama, Lincoln's Birthday, February 12, 1923, ibid., 270.

CHAPTER THREE

1 Coolidge, "The Inspiration of the Declaration," July 5, 1925, *Foundations of the Republic*, 451.

2 Marion L. Burton, president of the University of Michigan, at the nomination speech at the Republican convention of 1924, cited in William Allen White, *Politics: The Citizen's Business* (New York: Ayer Publishing, 1974), 198.

3   Coolidge reminds us in his speech "Religion and the Republic": "The American Constitution was not a new theory. . . . it was the practical application of an old theory which was very new."

4   Many other writers have noted a paradox about Coolidge, but none has looked at it quite this way. His contemporaries wondered how such a man, who seemed so meek, could be behind the Roaring Twenties. Edward Connery Lathem called it a "well-seasoned paradox." Alfred Pearce Dennis put it best: "Mr. Coolidge is eighteenth century, frugal, simple, hard-bitten, set down in the twentieth-century age of jazz, extravagance in speech, dress, mad desire for pleasure, for spending." (Lathem, *Meet Calvin Coolidge*, 23)

5   Alexis de Tocqueville, *Democracy in America* 1, trans. Henry Reeve (New York: G. Adlard, 1839), 316.

6   Fuess, *Man from Vermont*, 30.

7   Coolidge, *Autobiography*, 46.

8   Fuess, *Man from Vermont*, 29.

9   Sir Walter Scott, *Marmion* (Boston: Houghton Mifflin, 1894), 287.

10 Lord Erskine was a British member of parliament and a barrister whose successful defense of William Davis Shipley, dean of St. Asaph, gave rise to the Libel Act 1792, laying down the principle that it is for the jury, and not for the judge, to decide if a publication is libel. In 1789 he was counsel for John Stockdale, a bookseller who was charged with seditious libel in publishing a pamphlet in favor of Warren Hastings, whose trial was then proceeding. Erskine's speech on this occasion, probably his greatest effort, is a consummate specimen of the art of addressing a jury. Three years later, Erskine found himself defending the controversial Thomas Paine, holding that an advocate, by refusing a brief, converted himself into a judge.

11 Daniel Webster was a Whig congressman and later a senator from Massachusetts during the antebellum period. His defense of the Union against secession from the north or the south appealed to the young Coolidge. Coolidge delivered one of his finest speeches at the home of Daniel Webster.

12 Rufus Choate, who served in the Senate before and after Webster, cultivated knowledge of the classics while serving as one of Massachusetts's finest U.S. Senators. His oratory appealed to Coolidge as much as Webster's did.

13 We do not know what works of theirs Coolidge read. The most likely ones by Carlyle are *Works* (London: Chapman and Hall, 1885–1889); *History of the French Revolution* (New York: J. B. Alden, 1885); and his most famous work, *On Heroes and Hero-Worship* (London: Chapman and Hall, 1841). It seems, given his historical interests, that Coolidge would have read Fiske's *The Critical Period of American History, 1783–89* (1888), *The Beginnings of New England* (1889), or *Civil Government of the United States* (1890).

14 Coolidge was fascinated by Cicero. According to Sobel, Coolidge discovered

NOTES

Cicero in his last year of high school and became "entranced by his orations against Cataline." Coolidge, Sobel writes,

> read all he could by Cicero, and became fairly fluent in Latin as a result. In this period in which Calvin's political consciousness was being molded, Cicero – a political moderate who looked to law and reference for tradition to preserve stability and liberty – was a profound influence. (Sobel, *American Enigma*, 29)

15 Coolidge, *Autobiography*, 73.
16 Arthur Fleser claims that Coolidge did not use literary allusions in his writing, but that statement is not borne out by an examination of the writing itself. Arthur F. Fleser, *A Rhetorical Study of the Speaking of Calvin Coolidge* (Lewiston, NY: Edwin Mellen Press, 1990).
17 Coolidge, *Autobiography*, 40.
18 Coolidge, cited in R. J. Thompson, *Adequate Brevity* (Chicago: Donahue, 1924), 11.
19 Ibid.
20 Coolidge, *Autobiography*, 47.
21 As Coolidge put it, he opposed "government bureaus which seek to regulate and control the business activities of the people." (Sobel, *American Enigma*, 330)
22 H. G. Wells, *The Outline of History: Being a Plain History of Life and Mankind* (London: George Newnes Limited, 1919–1920), 827.
23 Coolidge, "What It Means to Be a Boy Scout," July 25, 1924, address delivered at the White House and transmitted by telephone to a farewell meeting in New York for a group of Boy Scouts who were to sail July 26 to attend an international gathering of the organization in Copenhagen, *Foundations of the Republic*, 68.
24 Coolidge alludes to Peter the Hermit, Martin Luther, John Cobden, John Bright, James Otis, Patrick Henry, Daniel Webster, William Lloyd Garrison, and Wendell Phillips.
25 Gerhard Peters, "State of the Union Addresses and Messages," online at The American Presidency Project.
26 Coolidge, *Autobiography*, 41.
27 Ibid.
28 Coolidge to his father, January 15, 1893, Forbes Library.
29 Fleser, *Rhetorical Study*, 23.
30 George Whitefield (1714–1770) was an Anglican Protestant minister who helped spread the Great Awakening in Britain and especially in British North America. Thomas Chalmers (1780–1847) was a Scottish mathematician and theologian. Coolidge was most likely referring to Thomas John Knox, the seventeenth-cen-

tury Scottish prelate. Jonathan Edwards (1703–1758) was an American preacher, theologian, and president of Princeton University. Henry Ward Beecher (1813–1887) was a Congregationalist clergyman and abolitionist. Charles Timothy Brooks (1813–1883) was a Transcendentalist poet and Unitarian minister.

31   Woods, *Preparation of Calvin Coolidge*, 195.

32   Johnston, *Have Faith in Calvin Coolidge*, 35–36.

33   Coolidge, "The Place of Lincoln," Springfield, Illinois, February 12, 1922, *Price of Freedom*, 131.

34   Coolidge, "What It Means to Be a Boy Scout," July 25, 1924, *Foundations of the Republic*, 67.

35   One future admiral was listening to the president. Rear Admiral Eugene R. Fluckey, a Medal of Honor winner, four-time Navy Cross winner, and daring submarine commander, grew up in the 1920s and credited Coolidge's radio speeches as having influenced him as a boy. At age ten, the future rear admiral heard Coolidge on the radio emphasizing the importance of persistence. Fluckey was probably referring to this reported Coolidge quotation, which still finds its way into anthologies:

> Nothing in the world can take the place of persistence. Talent will not; nothing is more common than unsuccessful men with talent. Genius will not; unrewarded genius is almost a proverb. Education will not; the world is full of educated derelicts. Persistence and determination alone are omnipotent. The slogan "press on" has solved and always will solve the problems of the human race.

Inspired by the president, Fluckey named his dog after Coolidge. And Fluckey's persistence and determination led him to graduate from high school at age fifteen.

36   The speech was something of a homecoming for the would-be politician. It happened to coincide with his birthday. Coolidge, as Lincoln scholar and Coolidge admirer Harry V. Jaffa has said, was the only President born on the Fourth of July, "something he never mentioned, but never forgot." (personal recollection)

37   Fleser, *Rhetorical Study*, 12. We have no copy of this speech but rely on the memories of those who were there for it.

38   See Sir Walter Scott, *The Poetical Works of Sir Walter Scott: With a Sketch of His Life*, (Philadelphia: J. Crissy, 1838), 371.

39   Coolidge, "Amherst College Commencement," June 18, 1919, *Have Faith in Massachusetts*, 183.

40   Eliza Miner Garman, *Letters, Lectures, and Addresses of Charles Edward Garman* (New York: Houghton Mifflin, 1909), 229.

41   Coolidge, "Amherst College Commencement," June 18, 1919, *Have Faith in Massachusetts*, 185.

42 Coolidge, "Thought, the Master of Things," at the Annual Meeting of the American Classical League, the University of Pennsylvania, July 7, 1921, *Price of Freedom*, 57. Coolidge seemed perfectly at home speaking before an assembly of classicists.

43 June 25, 1919, *Have Faith in Massachusetts*, 236.

44 Coolidge, "Thought, the Master of Things," July 7, 1921, *Price of Freedom*, 57.

45 Ibid.

46 Coolidge, "Harvard University Commencement," June 19, 1919, *Have Faith in Massachusetts*, 190.

47 Making this speech before his hosts – mainly Irish Catholics – Coolidge pointed out that these criticisms "do not apply to those of the race and blood so prominent in assemblage." As proof, Coolidge offered the facts that eleven of the signatures of the Declaration of Independence were of Irish birth or lineage; that "on the roll of Washington's generals were Sullivan, Knox, Wayne," and Richard Montgomery; and that "a generous portion of the rank and file of the men who fought in the Revolution and supported those who framed our institutions was not alien to those who are represented [at Holy Cross]." According to the plaque outside City Hall honoring the Irish contribution to the Declaration of Independence in Philadelphia, Coolidge missed a few signers. They are in full: Charles Carroll, John Hancock, John Hart, Thomas Lynch, Thomas McKean, Thomas Nelson, Robert Treat Paine, George Read, Edward Rutledge, James Smith, George Taylor, Matthew Thornton, William Whipple, and Charles Thompson, who served as secretary. Coolidge might also have listed others in the Army and Navy, such as Clinton, Dillon, Hand, Irvine, Lewis, Moylan, Stark, Stewart. John Barry, the father of the American Navy, and Jeremiah O'Brien, who won the first naval battle of the Revolutionary War at the Battle of Machias, also deserve mention. Truly William Pitt the Elder was right when he said: "The whole Irish Nation favors America. Ireland is with them to a man."

48 Polybius, *The Histories*, Loeb Classical Library edition (Cambridge: Harvard University Press, 1922–1927), 6:439.

49 Coolidge, *Autobiography*, 59.

50 Fleser, *Rhetorical Study*, 12.

51 Record of course transcript, Morgan Hall, Amherst College. Cited in Fleser, *Rhetorical Study*, 9.

52 Coolidge, *Autobiography*, 60, 71.

53 John Almon Waterhouse, *Calvin Coolidge Meets Charles Edward Garman* (Rutland, VT: Academy Books, 1984), 75.

54 Ibid., 3.

55 Fuess, *Man from Vermont*, 69–70.

56 Horace Green, *The Life of Calvin Coolidge* (New York: Duffield, 1924), 29.

57 Woods, *Preparation of Calvin Coolidge*, 91–92.

58 Coolidge, *Autobiography*, 61.

59 *Have Faith in Massachusetts*, 161. Emphasis added.

60 This becomes clear when we consider another Coolidge discussion about laws. "The process of civilization consists of the discovery by men of the laws of the universe, and of living in harmony with those laws." Coolidge, "The Supports of Civilization," at the Amherst College Alumni Dinner, New York City, November 27, 1920, *Price of Freedom*, 3.

61 Coolidge, "Inaugural Address as Governor," January 2, 1919, *Have Faith in Massachusetts*, 161–162.

62 Coolidge, *Autobiography*, 61–62.

63 Houston Peterson, *Great Teachers* (New York: Vintage Books, 1946), 105, cited in Waterhouse, *Coolidge Meets Garman*, 8.

64 Claude M. Fuess, *Amherst Memorial Volume* (Amherst College Press,1926), 239, cited in Waterhouse, *Coolidge Meets Garman*, 16.

65 Peterson, *Great Teachers*, 106, cited in Waterhouse, *Coolidge Meets Garman*, 9.

66 Fuess, *Amherst*, 240, cited in Waterhouse, *Coolidge Meets Garman*, 12.

67 Morrow, who would go on to become a successful banker and diplomat, wrote Garman in 1894: "I don't believe, Professor, that you can fully appreciate what a strong hold you have on Amherst today. It isn't only with the senior class with whom you come into contact. Underclassmen go to the seniors for advice continually because they know the seniors have something which they do not" (Sobel, *American Enigma*, 36). Harlan Stone was brought in after the disgrace that followed the Daugherty hearings. Stone seems to have done a good job – Coolidge elevated him to the Supreme Court. Secretary of Commerce William F. Whiting, of Whiting Paper Company fame, served after Herbert Hoover stepped down to run for president.

68 Coolidge, *Autobiography*, 63–66.

69 For these reasons, Thomas Le Duc describes Garman like this:

> [He] might be termed a Christian Hegelian. The "idea" realizing itself in history is the atonement; the "state" is the good society. Human progress is not blind, but is directed unequivocally towards the promised coming of the Kingdom. Penetrating all of Garman's writings is an optimistic assurance tantamount to millenarianism. But the concept of the state which he offers is not German, but Puritan; the individual remains the focal entity and Jesus, the ultimate authority. [Thomas Le Duc, *Piety and Intellect at Amherst College, 1865–1912*, (New York: Ayer Publishing, 1977), 114.]

70 Fuess, *Amherst*, 240, cited in Waterhouse, *Coolidge Meets Garman*, 11.

71 Le Duc, *Piety and Intellect at Amherst*, 105, 107.

72 Waterhouse, *Coolidge Meets Garman*, 11.

73 Le Duc, *Piety and Intellect at Amherst,* 106.

74 Coolidge, *Autobiography,* 99–100.

75 It is not clear whether Garman thought that this was a requirement of that age, or whether he was just suggesting it to make the students feel as if their own age was important, as, indeed, every age is. He always tried to make his courses timely. Garman, *Letters, Lectures, and Addresses,* 455, cited in Waterhouse, *Coolidge Meets Garman,* 10.

76 McCoy, *The Quiet President,* 18.

77 Waterhouse, *Coolidge Meets Garman,* 19.

78 Hewitt H. Howland, *Dwight Whitney Morrow: A Sketch in Admiration* (New York: The Century Company, 1930), 10, cited in Waterhouse, *Coolidge Meets Garman,* 21.

79 Coolidge, *Autobiography,* 66.

80 Le Duc, *Piety and Intellect at Amherst,* 116.

81 Sobel points out that nearly three-quarters of a million people went out on strike in Chicago in 1894. The government's finances were similarly in disarray. J. P. Morgan bailed out the United States in 1895, the year Coolidge graduated. (Sobel, *American Enigma,* 34)

82 Garman, *Letters, Lectures, and Addresses,* 378.

83 Ibid.

84 Ibid.

85 Garman, *Letters, Lectures and Addresses,* 373. Consider also: "Whenever we make our ultimate appeal to quality instead of quantity, all men become persons and peers with God." Ibid., 366.

86 Coolidge, "Brockton Chamber of Commerce," April 11, 1916, *Have Faith in Massachusetts,* 18.

87 Ibid.

88 Ibid.

89 Garman to William Orr, manuscript letter of April 29, 1908, and Garman's undated letter to J. H. Seelye, attributed to 1894.

90 Walter E. Edge to Coolidge, August 9, 1923, Calvin Coolidge Papers (Manuscript Division, Library of Congress).

91 Ambrose Clark to Coolidge, August 23, 1923.

92 After being appointed to run the U.S. Forest Service, Pinchot became convinced that President Taft's new appointee at the Department of Interior, Richard A. Ballinger, wanted to "stop the conservation movement," after Ballinger reversed the previous administration's policy on environmental development. Pinchot charged that Ballinger had sided with private interests over the development of water power. He arranged a meeting with President Taft and Louis Glavis, who served as chief of the Portland, Oregon, division of the General Land Office. President Taft was presented with Glavis's fifty-page report that accused Ballinger of improperly handling coal claims in Alaska. Taft, though, upon consulting with his attorney general, issued a public letter exonerating

Ballinger and firing Glavis. Glavis pivoted and turned to the press and to Pinchot to tell his story. On January 10, Pinchot sent an open letter to Senator Jonathan P. Dolliver to be read into the Congressional Record. The letter criticized Taft, praised Glavis, and called for investigations into the alleged impropriety. Furious, Taft fired Pinchot, and the House held hearings on Ballinger, who, after a five-month process, was cleared of any wrongdoing. Pinchot was a close friend of Roosevelt's, and his treatment prompted Roosevelt to challenge Taft for the presidency. See John T. Ganoe, "Some Constitutional and Political Aspects of the Ballinger-Pinchot Controversy," *The Pacific Historical Review* 3 (September 1934).

93 Mark Sullivan in the *New-York Tribune*, August 12, 1923.

94 Ibid.

95 Ferrell, *Presidency of Calvin Coolidge*, 51. Coolidge seems to have internalized Napoleon's great maxim: "Never interrupt your enemy when he is making a mistake."

96 This suggestion was clever. Coolidge knew that there was a growing split in the party that dated back to the Ballinger–Pinchot controversy between development supporters and conservationists. By encouraging other sources of energy, Coolidge was encouraging the conservation faction in the short term and the development faction in the long term.

97 "Interviews had appeared in the press in which he was represented as announcing that he was going to offer the government a solution of the coal problem," Hammond noted in his autobiography. John Hays Hammond, *The Autobiography of John Hays Hammond* (New York: Ayer Publishing, 1974), 684.

98 The report's findings were helpfully summarized by Hammond, who, like Coolidge, opposed excessive government interference in mining. He noted his views on the coal problem in his autobiography. Since the coal industry substantially affected the economy, operators and miners couldn't be allowed to "fight each other to a standstill." The federal government therefore had "a right to supervise and regulate, though fixing of prices and wages was not advised [in the report], nor was compulsory arbitration."

> We recommended that the responsibility for the smooth running of the industry should lie within the industry itself; we felt that legislative action would tend to diminish efficiency rather than increase it, and that private development, if carried on honestly and as a quasi-public utility, ought to be encouraged. (Hammond, *Autobiography*, 684)

99 Ibid., 685.

100 Sobel, *American Enigma*, 256.

101 Ferrell, *Presidency of Calvin Coolidge*, 52.

102 M. Nelson McGeary, *Gifford Pinchot, Forester-Politician* (Princeton, NJ: Princeton University Press, 1960), 309.

103 Ibid.

104 Ibid.

105 "Coal: Anthracitis," *Time Magazine*, September 3, 1923.

106 Robert H. Zieger, "Pinchot and Coolidge: The Politics of the 1923 Anthracite Crisis," *The Journal of American History* 52, no. 3 (December 1965): 573.

107 Ibid., 575.

108 McGeary, *Gifford Pinchot*, 309.

109 Ibid., 310.

110 Zieger, "Pinchot and Coolidge," 578.

111 Ferrell, *Presidency of Calvin Coolidge*, 52.

112 *New-York Tribune*, August 24, 1923; *New York Times*, August 26, 1923.

113 The fact that Coolidge came to share Garman's hostility to expediency is apparent in statements such as these:

> "The age of science and commercialism is here. . . . The wise desire is not to destroy it, but to use it and direct it rather than to be used and directed by it, that it may be, as it should be, not the master but the servant, that the physical forces may not prevail over moral forces, and that the rule of life may not be *expediency* but righteousness" (Coolidge, *Price of Freedom*, 59). The monuments to the revolutionaries who fought at Bunker Hill are "not monuments to *expediency* or success, they are monuments to righteousness" (Coolidge, *Have Faith in Massachusetts*, 119). If those two and a half years, before the American declaration of war [in WWI], shall appear . . . to have been characterized by a balancing of . . . *expediency* against justice [by refusing to fight] they will be counted as a time of ignominy for which a victorious war would furnish scant compensation" (Coolidge, *Have Faith in Massachusetts*, 107). (Emphasis added in all.)

114 Coolidge, *Autobiography*, 67

115 Ibid., 52

116 "The Hard Part of the Hard Coal Settlement," *Literary Digest* 78 (September 22, 1923): 9.

117 See Chapter 2 for more details on how Coolidge settled strikes.

118 David Greenberg, *Calvin Coolidge* (New York: Henry Holt, 2007), 93.

119 McGeary, *Gifford Pinchot*, 310.

120 Ibid., 311.

121 Just to be on the safe side, Coolidge offered him the ambassadorship to London.

122 Coolidge, State of the Union Address, December 6, 1923.

123 This did not mean that the president would do nothing. As he told Cooper, "We will have to seem to be doing something; do the best you can without much hope" (Sobel, *American Enigma*, 327). The fluctuations with the price of corn had borne this out, Coolidge argued, and so the political question was all but decided:

At every cabinet meeting for a year or so back, Secretary Henry Wallace [of Agriculture] used to be grumbling and complaining about the price of corn and was always wanting the government to do something about it. Then corn took a rise. The government didn't do it. I noticed that Wallace had shut up on the price of corn. (Ibid.)

124 Coolidge, State of the Union Address, December 6, 1923.

125 Richard B. Scandrett Jr., *Do the Day's Work – A Sketch of the President* (Published by a Coolidge Reelection Committee, n.d.), 4, cited in Waterhouse, *Coolidge Meets Garman*, ix.

126 See Chapter 5 for a discussion of his executive theory.

CHAPTER FOUR

1 Coolidge, "Daniel Webster," July 4, 1916, *Have Faith in Massachusetts*, 25. Coolidge understood how the Founders saw themselves, and he grasped the true magnitude of the risky decision to sign the Declaration:

> They knew that the duty between the citizen and the State was recipro-cal. They knew that the State called on its citizens for their property and their lives; they laid down the proposition that government was to pro-tect the citizen in his life, liberty, and pursuit of happiness. At some expense? Yes. Those prudent and thrifty men had no false notions about incurring expense. They knew the value of increasing their mate-rial resources, but they knew that prosperity was a means, not an end. At cost of life? Yes. These sons of the Puritans, of the Huguenots, of the men of Londonderry, braved exile to secure peace, but they were not afraid to die in defense of their convictions. They put no limit on what the State must do for the citizen in his hour of need. While they required all, they gave all. Let us read their conclusion in their own words, and mark its simplicity and majesty: "And for the support of this Declara-tion, with a firm reliance on the protection of Divine Providence, we mutually pledge to each other our lives, our fortunes, and our sacred honor." There is no cringing reservation here, no alternative, and no delay. Here is the voice of the plain men of Middlesex, promising York-town, promising Appomattox. ("Daniel Webster," 33–34)

2 Coolidge, "Message for the Boston Post," April 22, 1918, ibid., 108.

3 Coolidge, "Westfield," September 3, 1919, ibid., 207.

4 Coolidge, "Tremont Temple," November 3, 1917, ibid., 90.

5 Coolidge, "The Instruments of Progress," address before the American Uni-versity, Washington, DC, June 7, 1922, *Price of Freedom*, 166.

There are two great standards, and two alone, by which men measure progress – creation and redemption. . . . Wherever you may explore the high places of American history you come upon this same motive as the main cause of the action of her people. It was the thought of the early settlers where they raised up their altars and established their schools. It was the meaning of the life of Washington, of the great Declaration, or of the greater Federal Constitution. It is the explanation of Abraham Lincoln and the all-embracing freedom wrought out in his day. Finally, it sent two million men across the sea, that the cause of a Christian civilization might still remain supreme.

The power of creation and the power of redemption have come down through all the ages with mankind in ever-increasing proportions. They are the power to build and the power to endow with righteousness. They represent intelligence and sacrifice, the state and the church, the material and the spiritual. These are the forces upon which mankind can rely. They do not fail; they endure. (163–166)

6   The Germans, Coolidge would have agreed, denied Jefferson's assessment that "the mass of humanity has not been born with saddles on their backs nor a very few booted and spurred ready to ride them legitimately by the grace of God." (Jefferson, in a letter to Roger C. Weightman, June 24, 1826)

7   Coolidge, "Daniel Webster," July 4, 1916, *Have Faith in Massachusetts*, 33.

8   Ibid., 33–36

9   *Autobiography*, 67.

10   Coolidge, "Great Virginians," July 6, 1922, *Price of Freedom*, 178.

11   Coolidge, "Thought, the Master of Things," July 7, 1921, ibid., 59.

12   Coolidge, "Letter to Thomas Alva Edison, Jr.," February 11, 1927. "Your inventions, placing the forces of nature at the service of humanity, have added to our comfort and happiness and are a benefaction to all mankind for generations to come," Coolidge wrote. He reasoned from the example of Edison and other inventors that the nature of progress in science was gradual.

13   Coolidge, "The Inspiration of the Declaration," July 5, 1926, *Foundations of the Republic*.

14   Sobel, *American Enigma*, 63.

15   Fuess, *Man from Vermont*, 123.

16   Coolidge, "Riverside," August 28, 1916, *Have Faith in Massachusetts*, 40.

17   It is significant that Coolidge acknowledged the need for a constitutional amendment, an approach that progressives – who in this period used the Sixteenth, Seventeenth, and Eighteenth Amendments to enact the income tax, the direct election of senators, and women's suffrage – haven't emphasized much since, preferring to win new policies by means of court rulings, by executive order, or by passing legislation with little regard to constitutionality.

18   Coolidge, "Education: The Cornerstone of Self-Government," at the Convention of the National Education Association, July 4, 1924, *Foundations of the Republic.*

19   Coolidge, "Inaugural Address as Governor," January 2, 1919, *Have Faith in Massachusetts*, 161.

20   May 12, 1915, ibid., 75.

21   Burton Folsom Jr., "An Enabler of Prosperity," *Why Coolidge Matters* (Chatsworth, CA: National Notary Association, 2010).

22   "The Inspiration of the Declaration," July 5, 1926, *Foundations of the Republic.*

23   Coolidge, "The Supports of Civilization," November 27, 1920, *Price of Freedom.*

24   Coolidge, "Thought, the Master of Things," July 7, 1921, ibid., 58. Emphasis added.

25   Paul Johnson, "Calvin Coolidge and the Last Arcadia," cited in *Calvin Coolidge and the Coolidge Era: Essays on the History of the 1920s*, ed. John Earl Haynes (Washington, DC: Library of Congress, 1998), 9.

26   The title of Coolidge's second book of speeches comes from an address he gave in Evanston, Illinois, January 21, 1923:

> Of course it would be folly to argue that the people cannot make political mistakes. They can and do make grave mistakes. They know it; they pay the penalty. But compared with the mistakes which have been made by every kind of autocracy they are unimportant.... Oftentimes the inconvenience and loss fall on the innocent. This is all a part of the price of freedom. We have to bear one another's burdens whether we will or no. We have to make personal sacrifice for the common good. We cannot have what is good unless we pay the price. Unless the people struggle to help themselves, no one else will or can help them. It is out of such struggle that there comes the strongest evidence of their true independence and nobility, and there is struck off a rough and incomplete economic justice, and there develops a strong and rugged national character. It represents a spirit for which there could be no substitute. It justifies the claim that they are worthy to be free. (*Price of Freedom*, 241–242)

27   Coolidge, "The Supports of Civilization," November 27, 1920, ibid., 3.

28   Coolidge, "The Needs of Education," December, 21, 1922, ibid., 216.

29   Coolidge, "The Things That Are Unseen," June 19, 1923, ibid., 381.

30   Coolidge, "The Instruments of Progress," June 7, 1922, ibid., 163.

31   Coolidge, "Amherst College Commencement," June 18, 1919, *Have Faith in Massachusetts*, 183.

32   Coolidge, "Education: The Cornerstone of Self-Government," July 4, 1924, *Foundations of the Republic*, 58.

33   Coolidge, "Amherst College Commencement," June 18, 1919, *Have Faith in Massachusetts*, 186.

34 Ibid., 187.

35 Ibid., 185.

36 Coolidge, "The Inspiration of the Declaration," July 5, 1926, *Foundations of the Republic*, 449.

37 Ibid., 448.

38 Here Coolidge quotes from Revelation 22:13: "I am Alpha and Omega, the beginning and the end, the first and the last." Like history, democracy is, according to Coolidge, a revelation. See "Daniel Webster," July 4, 1916, *Have Faith in Massachusetts*, 448

39 Coolidge, "The Inspiration of the Declaration," July 5, 1926, *Foundations of the Republic*, 452.

40 Coolidge, "Daniel Webster," July 4, 1916, *Have Faith in Massachusetts*, 24.

41 Letter of November 2, 1923, reel 4, Coolidge's private papers.

42 Albert Galloway Keller, *Earth-hunger and Other Essays*, ed. William Graham Sumner (New Haven: Yale University Press, 1913), 234.

43 Coolidge, "Education: The Cornerstone of Self-Government," July 4, 1924, *Foundations of the Republic*, 51.

44 Interestingly, Coolidge, like Lincoln, was deeply religious but seldom attended church, despite his Congregationalist inclinations. He officially joined one such church after leaving the presidency. (Sobel, *American Enigma*, 33)

45 Coolidge, "Religion and the Republic," at the unveiling of the Equestrian Statue of Bishop Francis Asbury, Washington, DC, October 15, 1924, *Foundations of the Republic*, 153.

46 Coolidge, quoted in *Our Paper* 38 (February 12, 1923): 78.

47 Coolidge, "The Spiritual Unification of America," at the laying of the cornerstone of the Jewish Community Center, Washington, May 3, 1925, *Foundations of the Republic*, 211–212. Emphasis added.

48 Coolidge knew, for instance, of Washington's letter to the Jews of Newport, Rhode Island, in which the first President promised that in America – unlike other systems under which the Jews had suffered – Jews would be free from persecution. Washington wrote, "For happily the Government of the United States, which gives to bigotry no sanction, to persecution no assistance, requires only that they who live under its protection should demean themselves as good citizens, in giving it on all occasions their effectual support."

49 Coolidge, "The Destiny of America," May 30, 1923, *Price of Freedom*, 353.

50 Coolidge, "Address before the National Council of the Boy Scouts of America," Washington, DC, May 1, 1926, online at The American Presidency Project, www.ucsb.edu.

51 Coolidge, "The Progress of a People," at Howard University, June 6, 1924, *Foundations of the Republic*, 31. The speech is about the progress of black Americans.

52 Coolidge, "The Genius of America," to a delegation of foreign-born citizens at the White House," October 16, 1924, *Foundations of the Republic*, 164.

53   Woods, *Preparation of Calvin Coolidge*, 238.

54   Coolidge, "Religion and the Republic," October, 15, 1924, *Foundations of the Republic*, 153.

55   Coolidge, "The Genius of America," October, 16, 1924, ibid., 164.

56   Coolidge, "Toleration and Liberalism," at the American Legion Convention at Omaha, Nebraska," October 6, 1925, *Foundations of the Republic*, 296.

57   Woodrow Wilson, "The Author and Signers of the Declaration of Independence," in *American Progressivism: A Reader*, ed. Ronald J. Pestritto and William J. Atto (Lanham, MD: Lexington Books, 2008), 97.

58   Wilson, "The Author and Signers of the Declaration," 97, cited in *Progressivism: A Reader*. Emphasis added.

59   Although he rejected social evolution as preached by the Progressives, Coolidge, at least as a young man, had great respect for Charles Darwin:

> I see [Oliver Wendell] Holmes [Sr.] is dead, the Autocrat of the Break-fast table on whom the years sat so lightly and who had only just declared that he was 85 years young. No one but [William] Gladstone is left of those great men that were born in 1809. Darwin is gone, the great expounder of evolution, a scientist equal to Newton. Our own Lincoln finished his life's work when he struck the shackles from four millions of slaves and saw the surrender of General Lee. (Coolidge to his father, November 2, 1894, in Lathem, *Your Son, Calvin Coolidge*)

60   Coolidge, "Theodore Roosevelt," address before the Women's Roosevelt Memorial Association, New York City, January 23, 1921, *Price of Freedom*, 17.

61   Coolidge, "Westfield," September 3, 1919, *Have Faith in Massachusetts*, 208.

62   Coolidge, "The Place of Lincoln," February 12, 1922, *Price of Freedom*, 126.

63   Woods, *Preparation of Calvin Coolidge*, 272.

64   Coolidge, "The Place of Lincoln," February 12, 1922, *Price of Freedom*, 131.

65   The world, Coolidge recognized, had come to see Lincoln as a man for all peoples. Coolidge applauded future Argentine president Domingo Faustino Sarmiento for writing a biography of Lincoln. (Address before the First Pan American Congress of Journalists, Washington, DC, April 8, 1926, online at The American Presidency Project)

66   Coolidge, "Andrew Carnegie: Organizer for Service," at the Founders' Day Celebration of Carnegie Institute, Pittsburgh, Pennsylvania, April 28, 1921, *Price of Freedom*, 37.

67   Coolidge, "Daniel Webster," July 4, 1916, *Have Faith in Massachusetts*, 21.

68   Coolidge, "Great Virginians," July 6, 1922, *Price of Freedom*, 171.

69   A reference to Romans 12:16.

70   Coolidge, "The Place of Lincoln," February 12, 1922, *Price of Freedom*, 131.

71 Coolidge, "What It Means to Be a Boy Scout," July 25, 1924, *Foundations of the Republic*.

72 Gamaliel Bradford, *The Quick and the Dead* (New York: Houghton Mifflin, 1931), 257.

73 Ibid.

74 Fuess, *Man from Vermont*, 351.

75 "10 Reasons Why Coolidge and Dawes Should Have Your Support," http://www.lincoln-highway-museum.org/Coolidge/Coolidge-Index.html. The loss of Coolidge's son seems to have affected vice-presidential candidate Charles Dawes also. Dawes, who had lost a son in 1912, recalled the turmoil in the Coolidge house on July 2, 1924, five days before Calvin Jr.'s death.

> As I passed the door of [young] Calvin's room I changed to look in. He seemed to be in great distress. The president was bending over the bed. I think I have never witnessed such a look of agony and despair that was on the president's face. From that moment I felt a closeness to Coolidge I never felt before, and have never lost. (Sobel, *American Enigma*, 295–296)

76 Coolidge, Inaugural Address, March 4, 1925, *Foundations of the Republic*. Emphasis added.

77 Coolidge, "Holy Cross," June 25, 1919, *Have Faith in Massachusetts*, 234–235.

78 In his "Classics for America" speech, delivered at the Second Annual Meeting of the American Classical League at the University of Pennsylvania, Philadelphia, on Thursday, July 7, 1921, Coolidge told the audience:

> It is impossible for society to break with its past. It is the product of all which has gone before. We could not cut ourselves off from all influence which existed prior to the Declaration of Independence and expect any success by undertaking to ignore all that happened before that date. The development of society is a gradual accomplishment.

79 Coolidge, "The Price of Freedom," January 21, 1923, *Price of Freedom*, 233. The phrase "a little lower than the angels" is a reference to Psalm 8:5, which gave man "glory and honor."

80 Coolidge, "Authority and Religious Liberty," address delivered to the Holy Name Society, Washington, DC, September 21, 1924, online at The American Presidency Project.

81 Ibid.

82 Pestritto, *Wilson: Essential Political Writings*, 11.

83 Congressional advocates hadn't pressed the matter, but Coolidge still acted, telling reporters at a November 1923 press conference that even though he did not

"like the term political prisoners," he was ordering an inquiry into their status.

84 Woodrow Wilson, *Constitutional Government in the United States* (New York: Columbia University Press, 1908), 65.

85 *Have Faith in Massachusetts*, 63.

86 Coolidge, "Tremont Temple," November 1, 1919, *Have Faith in Massachusetts*, 266.

87 Coolidge, "Daniel Webster," July 4, 1916, ibid., 26.

88 Coolidge, "Authority and Religious Liberty," September 21, 1924, online at The American Presidency Project.

89 The full quotation reads, "I have never had a feeling politically that did not spring from the sentiments embodied in the Declaration of Independence. I have often pondered over the dangers which were incurred by the men who assembled here and framed and adopted that Declaration of Independence." Lincoln at Independence Hall in Philadelphia, February 22, 1861.

90 Coolidge, "The Instruments of Progress," June 7, 1922, *Price of Freedom*, 166.

91 Coolidge, address dedicating a monument of General George Gordon Meade, Washington DC, October 19, 1927, online at The American Presidency Project.

92 Coolidge, "The United Nation," at the Confederate Memorial, Arlington National Cemetery, May 25, 1924, *Foundations of the Republic*, 15.

93 Ibid.

94 Fuess, *Man from Vermont*, 155.

95 Jules Abels, *In the Time of Silent Cal* (New York: G. P. Putnam's Sons, 1969), 16.

96 Those articles appeared in the following order: *Washington Post*, October 20, 1920; *Washington Post*, August 4, 1923; *New York Times*, February 11, 1924; *Los Angeles Times*, March 24, 1924.

97 Coolidge, "Preface," in Carl Schurz, *Abraham Lincoln, an Essay* (New York: Houghton Mifflin, 1920), iii–iv.

98 Coolidge, "Lincoln Day Proclamation," January 30, 1919, *Have Faith in Massachusetts*, 167.

99 Ibid., 166–167.

100 Coolidge, "Address at the Memorial Exericises at Arlington, Virginia," May 31, 1926, online at The American Presidency Project.

CHAPTER FIVE

1 Coolidge, *Autobiography*, 241.

2 Coolidge, "Authority and Religious Liberty," September 21, 1924, *Foundations of the Republic*, 104.

3 Coolidge, *Autobiography*, 195.

4 Stéphane Laussane, editor of *Le Matin*, quoted in "Paris Would Know Coolidge's Policy," *New York Times*, August 5, 1923.

5 See Fuess, *Man from Vermont*, ch. 14.

6   Nathan Miller, *The Founding Finaglers* (Philadelphia: David McKay, 1977), 341.

7   "Republican Control of Senate in Balance," *New York Times*, August 4, 1923.

8   George H. Nash, "The 'Great Enigma' and the 'Great Engineer': The Political Relationship of Calvin Coolidge and Herbert Hoover," in Haynes, *The Coolidge Era*, 132–148.

9   *New York Times*, August 4, 1923.

10   Gilbert C. Fite, *Peter Norbeck: Prairie Statesman* (Columbia, MO: University of Missouri, 1948), 114.

11   Sullivan diary, September 19, 1923, copy in Herbert Hoover presidential library.

12   Fuess, *Man from Vermont*, 337.

13   Sidney M. Milkis and Michael Nelson, *The American Presidency: Origins and Development 1776–2002* (Washington, DC: CQ Press, 2003), 265.

14   John D. Hicks, *Republican Ascendancy, 1921–1933,* (New York: Harper & Row, 1960), 81

15   Coolidge, perhaps alluding to Wilson, later wrote: "It has become the custom in our country to expect all Chief Executives, from the President down, to conduct activities analogous to an entertainment bureau." (*Autobiography*, 118)

16   James E. Watson, *As I Knew Them: Memoirs of James Watson, Former United States Senator from Indiana* (Indianapolis, IN: Bobbs-Merrill, 1936), 239.

17   President Coolidge later advised his Secretary of War, Dwight F. Davis: "You know, Mr. Secretary, I have found in the course of a long public life that the things I did not say never hurt me." (Fuess, *Man from Vermont*, 473)

18   Alben William Barkley, *That Reminds Me* (New York: Doubleday, 1954), 124.

19   September 16, 1924. Quint and Ferrell, *The Talkative President*, 10.

20   Duff Gilfond, a Coolidge hagiographer, titled one of his chapters "The Sphinx Propounds a Riddle." See generally Duff Gilfond, *The Rise of Saint Calvin: Merry Sidelights on the Career of Mr. Coolidge* (New York: The Vanguard Press, 1932).

21   At times, John Hammond noted, Coolidge "became a most interesting conversationalist," but this was only in private. According to Hammond, Coolidge once remarked to a friend "Well, after all, you'll have to admit that what I didn't say has never cost me anything." (Hammond, *Autobiography*, 695)

22   "President Has Busy Day," *New York Times*, August 5, 1923.

23   *New York Times*, December 7, 1923.

24   Chapter 8 of Lord Bryce's *The American Commonwealth* (in the 1888 edition) is titled "Why Great Men Are Not Chosen Presidents." In crafting his carefully formed public persona of "Silent Cal," the Yankee everyman, Coolidge may have taken much of his inspiration from this chapter.

25   Woods, *Preparation of Calvin Coolidge*, 89.

26   This "adequate brevity" compliment comes from President Alexander Meiklejohn of Amherst College, who paid it to Coolidge in June 1918, when he conferred an honorary degree upon Coolidge.

27 Coolidge's decision to delay announcement of his retirement until the afternoon after the markets closed so as to not deleteriously affect them illustrates well that he knew when to speak – and when not to. (Sobel, *American Enigma*, 369)

28 On August 5, 1923, he told the *New York Times*: "Gentlemen: There isn't a thing I can say at the present time about policies of the Administration. There will not be anything until after the final interment of the late President. I am glad of the opportunity to greet and shake hands with you. The executive offices will always be open, so far as is possible, to give your readers what may be given to them. A good many of you I know personally. This is your Government. You can exercise a great and helpful influence over the Administration and I know you will give the Administration that necessary cooperation."

29 Clinton Wallace Gilbert, *You Takes Your Choice* (New York: G. P. Putnam's Sons, 1924), 27.

30 Milkis and Nelson, *American Presidency*, 265.

31 As others have noted, this relationship allowed Coolidge to become the first "Great Communicator": "The Coolidge press conference marked the beginning of serious presidential meetings with the press. . . . It remained for the careful Coolidge to put press conferences on a schedule, to solicit press backing for his administration, generously giving them news and hoping that on their side the press would respond with sympathetic stories. Usually they did so. In *The Nation* of March 16, 1927, Frank Kent noted, 'Since Mr. Coolidge entered the White House he has had more solid press support than any other President. Frequently he has through the Spokesman expressed his appreciation. It would be strange indeed if he did not feel it.' " (Quint and Ferrell, *The Talkative President*, 20)

32 Coolidge, *Autobiography*, 224.

33 Ibid., 197.

34 Sobel, *American Enigma*, 17.

35 State of the Union Address, December 6, 1923, online at The American Presidency Project.

36 Delegates to the constitutional-ratification debates in 1787 decided that there should be no limits to how many times a president could be reelected; Senator Cummins disagreed with their views. He told the *New York Times*: "Of course, President Harding would have been renominated had he lived, but I always have believed one term is enough. The great responsibility and the tremendous strain of the office are more than any man can stand. . . . We should limit the President to one term. It might be made a six-year term, but I am not so sure about that, even." "Cummins Advocates One-Term Presidency," *New York Times*, August 6, 1923.

37 President Coolidge issued a total of 1,545 pardons and clemencies during his time in office, which is a yearly average of 281, placing him in the top three for most pardons and clemencies per year. F.D.R. and Wilson each had a yearly

average of slightly more than three hundred. Coolidge's number is by far the highest for any Republican president.

38 Coolidge's fifty-plus vetoes were almost always based on constitutional or limited-government grounds.

39 In his five and a half years in office, he issued the second-highest number of executive orders per year – 224.6 – and had a career total of 1,253, with a yearly average of 224.6. (F.D.R. issued the most per year.)

40 When Coolidge became president, an interviewer asked him if he had ever wanted to be president. Coolidge responded that he wanted to be a lawyer, but "of course when I became Lieutenant-Governor, I wanted to be Governor." The interviewer wasn't persuaded, saying: "The steps in your progress as an incumbent of public office have followed so inevitably that there must have been a purpose to it." The President replied, "There was a purpose to it; but it was not mine." (Woods, *Preparation of Calvin Coolidge*, 216)

41 Coolidge won 382 electoral votes (15.7 million popular votes) to Democrat John Davis's 136 (8.4 million). With 54 percent of the vote, Coolidge crushed his two opponents.

42 Fite, *Peter Norbeck*, 114.

43 Sobel, *American Enigma*, 210–211.

44 Woods, *Preparation of Calvin Coolidge*, 196.

45 Ibid., 190.

46 Steven G. Calabresi and Christopher Yoo, *The Unitary Executive: Presidential Power from Washington to Bush* (New Haven, CT: Yale University, 2008), 261.

47 Coolidge, *Autobiography*, 172–173

48 Woods, *Preparation of Calvin Coolidge*, 225.

49 Charles E. Hughes, *The Autobiographical Notes of Charles Evans Hughes*, ed. David J. Danelski and Joseph S. Tulchin (Cambridge, MA: Harvard University Press, 1973), 200.

50 Coolidge, *Autobiography*, 163–164.

51 Ibid., 175.

52 "There is considerable speculation as to whether I am likely to change or not. I don't anticipate to change very much. I have tried in the conduct of my office to be natural and I don't want to change that attitude. There are two or three people that have served with me in the conduct of affairs of the United States that I should be pleased if they changed a little – that have to change from saying 'no' to saying 'yes.' " (November 11, 1924, cited in Quint and Ferrell, *The Talkative President*, 11)

53 March 1, 1929, ibid., 19.

54 Coolidge, *Autobiography*, 216.

55 Nathan Miller, *New World Coming: The 1920s and the Making of Modern America* (Cambridge, MA: Da Capo Press, 2004), 135.

56 Ibid., 135.

57 Sobel, *American Enigma*, 242–243.

58 Gerald D. Nash, *United States Oil Policy, 1890–1964: Business and Government in Twentieth Century America* (University of Pittsburgh Press, 1968) 74.

59 Ibid.

60 Fall's fall has been great indeed. *Time Magazine*, in a special report titled "Top 10 Worst Cabinet Members," listed him among the ten worst cabinet members in American history.

61 Fall once said that he "st[oo]d for opening up every resource." Gerald D. Nash comments on his political approach, "[Fall]'s record revealed a decided predilection for rapid resource development. In regard to timber, for example, he opposed placing of restrictions on private operators in national forests, but urged federal road construction in these federal preserves to hasten their development. He also expressed doubts about the inclusion of grazing lands in federal forest preserves when such lands might be made available to cattlemen. That he criticized the Forest Service's administration of federal properties did not endear him to Pinchot." (Nash, *Oil Policy*, 76)

62 Ibid., 77.

63 Ibid.

64 La Follette ran for president in 1924 as the Progressive Party nominee and garnered a good 17 percent of the vote.

65 Coolidge would later outfox Pinchot by giving the governor the power to settle a coal dispute that proved much too difficult to handle, as discussed in a previous chapter.

66 Nash, *Oil Policy*, 78.

67 Ibid. Nash notes that there was an attempt to win over Secretary of Agriculture Henry C. Wallace, who criticized Fall's policies in cabinet meetings, further sowing dissent.

68 The Democratic nominee, John W. Davis, hoped to make political hay out of Teapot Dome, telling an interviewer matter-of-factly, "I am inclined to think that the Democrats will pay particular attention to that issue [Teapot Dome] in the campaign." "Davis Sees in Oil Big Campaign Issue," *New York Times*, August 7, 1924.

69 At the time, people knew that government ownership of the oil reserves had led to increased draining of Teapot Dome naval oil reserves, confirming an old pattern: When government owns something, it tends to take poor care of it. October 18, 1923, *New York Times*; and October 19, 1923, *Washington Post*.

70 In today's terms, that sum is equivalent to well over $5 million.

71 Nash, *Oil Policy*, 80.

72 This is more than $25 million in today's dollars. Stratton, *Tempest Over Teapot Dome: The Story of Albert B. Fall* (Norman, OK: University of Oklahoma Press, 1998), 392–394.

73 Nash, *Oil Policy*, 80–81.

74 As commander in chief, Coolidge oversaw much of the development of the United States Air Force. To provision that Air Force, he knew, oil would be necessary. Oil was therefore a matter of national security, and Coolidge became alarmed at the waste that seemed commonplace in oil fields' development. "Present methods of capturing our oil deposits [are] wasteful to an alarming degree," he noted in a public statement. "Developing aircrafts indicate that our national defense must be supplemented, if not dominated, by aviation. It is even probable that the supremacy of nations may be determined by the possession of available petroleum and its products." Coolidge statement December 19, 1924, "At the Appointment of the Federal Oil Conservation Board." Coolidge promptly appointed his Secretaries of War, Navy, Interior, and Commerce to the board.

75 Sobel, *American Enigma*, 262.

76 Chapter 183, "Prerogatives as Related to the Executive," in *Cannon's Precedents*, vol. 6. March 21, 1921 (U.S. Government Printing Office), online at gpo.gov.

77 Congressional Record, February 13, 1924, p. 2,335.

78 "Denby Won't Resign; Defies the Senate," *New York Times*, January 30, 1924.

79 "Denby to Leave March 10; Coolidge, in Accepting, Says Honesty Has Not Been Impugned," *New York Times*, February 19, 1924.

80 McCoy, *The Quiet President*, 212.

81 Sobel, *American Enigma*, 262.

82 Ibid.

83 Ibid., 263–264.

84 McCoy, *The Quiet President*, 212–213.

85 Marian C. McKenna, *Borah* (Ann Arbor: University of Michigan Press, 1961), 202; and Claudius O. Johnson, *Borah of Idaho* (New York: Longmans, Green, 1936), 289.

86 McCoy, *The Quiet President*, 213.

87 Taft had been a "constant adviser" to the Coolidge presidency. (Hammond, *Autobiography*, 712)

88 McCoy, *The Quiet President*, 214.

89 Ibid., 216.

90 "Seeks Tax Returns Made by Oil Men," *New York Times*, February 29, 1924.

91 Coolidge, "Special Message to Senate" (April 11, 1924), cited in Calebresi and Yoo, *Unitary Executive*, 270. See also "Coolidge Refuses Income Tax Returns," *New York Times*, March 7, 1924.

92 Calabresi and Yoo, *Unitary Executive*, 268.

93 According to Sobel, Daugherty talked Harding out of dropping out of contention for the nomination in 1920. He convincingly explained why he thought Harding would win. Despite having failed to win "nomination to the posts of state attorney general, congressman, governor, and three times for senator,"

Daugherty was a "skilled political operative" (Sobel, *American Enigma*, 171). It seems only logical that such skill produced enemies.

94 "House Votes $100,000 to Coolidge to Prosecute in Oil Lease Scandal," *New York Times*, January 29, 1924.

95 McCoy, *The Quiet President*, 216.

96 Quoted in Harry M. Daugherty, *The Inside Story of the Warren G. Harding Tragedy* (New York: Books for Libraries Press, 1932), 312. Emphasis added.

97 Sobel, *America Enigma*, 267.

98 Calabresi and Yoo, *Unitary Executive*, 270.

99 Sobel, *American Enigma*, 267.

100 Coolidge, *Autobiography*, 198–199.

101 Ferrell, *Presidency of Calvin Coolidge*, 142–143.

102 Coolidge, *Autobiography*, 223.

103 Coolidge was one of very few vice presidents to get the nomination in his own right after the death of a seated president. The other famous example in that time period is Theodore Roosevelt.

104 Coolidge, *Autobiography*, 196.

105 Ibid., 196–198.

106 Ibid., 211–212.

107 Ibid., 214.

108 Ibid., 231–232.

109 Ibid., 233–234.

110 Ibid. 234.

111 Lathem, *Meet Calvin Coolidge*, 77, quoting Edmund W. Starling, a member of the Secret Service detail assigned to the White House.

112 Ibid.

113 Phillip H. Love, *Andrew W. Mellon: The Man and His Work* (Whitefish, MT: Kessinger Publishing, 2003), 91.

114 "The President's Rebuke to the Senate," *Literary Digest*, April 26, 1924, 5–6.

115 Ibid.

116 Ibid.

117 Ibid.

118 Sobel notes that "of all the presidents, an argument might be made that Coolidge resembled Cleveland more than any other." Both "considered the role of the president to be that of executing legislation passed by Congress and vetoing those measures of which he did not approve." (Sobel, *American Enigma*, 6)

119 Love, *Mellon*, 102.

120 Ibid., 97.

121 Ibid., 98.

122 Quint and Ferrell, *The Talkative President*, 87.

123 In matters of Prohibition, which he defended as law despite his view that Prohi-

bition was inadvisable, Coolidge often relied upon the pardon power. Mayor Roswell O. Johnson of Gary, Indiana, for instance, was indicted with seventy-five other persons for his part in a liquor ring. Johnson, along with fifty-four other conspirators, was found guilty. He was given the most severe punishment possible, eighteen months in federal prison and a $1,000 fine. President Coolidge pardoned him, thereby restoring his civil rights and allowing him to run again for mayor, a position he wound up winning. Johnson was not the only public official that Coolidge pardoned for Prohibition-related offenses. Municipal Judge William M. Dunn was also sentenced to serve time in a federal prison, but had his conviction overturned by official pardon. Robert A. Hill and Marcus Garvey, eds., *The Marcus Garvey and Universal Negro Improvement Association Papers* (Berkeley, CA: University of California Press, 1991), 7:65.

124 At issue was whether the President had the power to pardon Phillip Grossman for violating the Volstead Act. The Court unanimously agreed that, according to Section 2, Clause 1 of Article II, Coolidge had the power to pardon Grossman.

125 The issue at hand concerned the ten-day requirement to override a veto. Congress had passed a law concerning Native Americans, and before ten days had passed, it promptly adjourned in violation of Article II, Section 4, Clause 2 ("unless the Congress by their Adjournment prevent its Return, in which Case it shall not be a Law"). The bill did not become law after the Supreme Court ruled in a 9–0 decision.

126 In a 6-to-3 ruling, the Court agreed that when it came to the control of the government-owned corporations of the Philippines, the executive branch, not the legislature, controlled the power of appointment to the governing boards of those corporations. Justice Sutherland, writing for the Court, found that it was an executive function to "enforce [the laws] or appoint agents charged with the duty of such enforcement." The legislature "cannot engraft executive duties upon a legislative office, since that would be to usurp the power of appointment by indirection."

127 In a 6-to-3 vote, the Taft Court found that an 1876 statute requiring Senate consent for removing executive officers was unconstitutional because it interfered with executive prerogative. Taft wrote a very lengthy opinion of more than seventy pages in which he argued that the authority to remove officers was an inherent part of executive power. His argument was essentially a separation of powers argument, to the effect that if the Founders had intended to allow Congress to have the power to approve removal, it would have meant "unlimited discretion to vary fundamentally the operation of the great independent branch [the executive] and most seriously weaken it." The absence of such a power, for Taft, is evidence that "none was intended." While the Senate has "full power" to reject "newly proposed nominees," no such power exists when it comes to vetoing removal. The President, after all, is more alert to the "defects" of a cabinet officer

than the Senate, because he must serve with that officer daily. If the President "loses confidence in the intelligence, ability, judgment or loyalty" of a cabinet officer, "he must have the power to remove him without delay."

128 The Founders praised "the celebrated Montesquieu" (see *Federalist* 47). For the eighteenth-century French political philosopher, political liberty was "a tranquility of mind arising from the opinion each person has of his safety" (see Montesquieu, *Spirit of Laws*, Chapter 17, no. 9).

129 Alexander Hamilton, James Madison, John Jay [Publius], *Federalist Papers* (New York: Signet Classic, 2003), *Federalist* 48.

130 *Federalist* 47.

131 *Federalist* 51.

132 Ibid.

133 Ibid.

134 *Federalist* 51.

135 *Federalist* 49.

136 *Federalist* 47.

137 Laws allow men to "know their Duty," as John Locke explained. Without reverence for the law, "their Peace, Quiet, and Prosperity will be still at the same uncertainty, as it was in the state of Nature." It was important, then, for men to be "govern'd by *declared Laws*" – hence Publius's and the Founders' project, a written constitution. David F. Epstein, *Political Theory of the Federalist* (Chicago: University of Chicago Press, 2007), 128.

138 *Federalist* 47.

139 *Federalist* 37.

140 *Federalist* 51.

141 Pestritto, *Wilson: Writings*, 167.

142 These questions about the balance of powers, according to *Federalist* 37, "puzzle the greatest adepts in political science."

143 Pestritto, *Wilson: Writings*, 176.

144 *Federalist* 47.

145 Pestritto, *Wilson: Writings*, 176.

146 Coolidge wasn't immune from thinking of government in machine-like terms. Earlier in his career, he encouraged the state legislature to work for progress in the following language: "In its promotion of human welfare, Massachusetts happily may not need much reconstruction, but like all other living organizations forever needs construction" (Woods, *Preparation of Calvin Coolidge*, 141). Yet Coolidge also bristled at the kind of paternalism implicit in Wilson's appeal to leadership. He disagreed with the rush to regulate during the Wilson administration, arguing, for instance, that it would stifle private initiative. It was far better to intervene only when necessary, for "self-reliance and self-control will be increased" in such a world. "Society will remain a living organism sustaining hope and progress, content to extend its dominion, not by conquest, but by service" (ibid., 198).

147 Given the confusion introduced into American constitutional government with Wilson, perhaps a better metaphor can be borrowed from the theory of modern atomic physics – Heisenberg's uncertainty. We are all uncertain as to what exactly we are observing whenever we delve into the modern workings of government, given how far we seem from the Constitution.

148 Wilson, *Constitutional Government*, 56–57.

149 Pestritto, *Wilson: Writings*, 176.

150 Wilson, *Constitutional Government*, 54–56.

151 Jessica Korn, *The Power of Separation: American Constitutionalism and the Myth of the Legislative Veto* (Princeton, NJ: Princeton University Press, 1998), 12.

152 James W. Ceaser, "In Defense of Separation of Powers," cited in *Separation of Powers – Does It Still Work?* ed. Robert A. Goldwin and Art Kauffman (Washington, DC: American Enterprise Institute, 1986), 178.

153 Woodrow Wilson, *Congressional Government: A Study in American Politics* (New York: Houghton Mifflin, 1901), 6.

154 Ibid., 11.

155 Woodrow Wilson, 1882, "Government by Debate: Being a Short View of Our National Government as It Is and as It Might Be," in *The Papers of Woodrow Wilson*, ed. Arthur S. Link (reprint, Princeton, NJ: Princeton University Press, 1967), 2 (1881–1884): 202.

156 Wilson, "Cabinet Government in the United States," in *The Papers of Woodrow Wilson*, vol.1 (1856–1880), in Pestritto, *Wilson: Writings*, 131.

157 Wilson, 1882, "Government by Debate," 202.

158 It bears considering that this whole analysis was first published in 1908 after the presidency of Theodore Roosevelt, one of the most charismatic and aggressive presidents in American history.

159 Wilson, *Constitutional Government*, 68–69.

160 Coolidge, "Ordered Liberty and World Peace," address delivered at the dedication of a monument to Lafayette, September 6, 1924, *Foundations of the Republic*, 96.

161 Wilson, *Constitutional Government*, 67.

162 Coolidge told his cousin, H. Parker Willis, the editor of the *New York Journal of Commerce*, who doubted Coolidge's opinion on a matter of finance: "*I regard myself as representative of the government and not as an individual.* When technical matters come up I feel called upon to refer them to the proper department of the government which has some information about them and then, unless there is some good reason, I use this information about them as a basis for whatever I have to say; but *that does not prevent me from thinking what I please as an* individual." (Sobel, *American Enigma*, 380, emphasis added)

163 William Allen White, *A Puritan in Babylon* (New York: Capricorn Books, 1965), 37.

164 *Federalist* 68.

165 *Federalist* 10, 69, and 73.

166 Woodrow Wilson, "An Address of Thomas Jefferson," in Pestritto, *Wilson: Writings*, 93.

167 Coolidge, *Autobiography*, 214.

168 Woodrow Wilson, "The Author and Signers of the Declaration of Independence," in Pestritto, *Wilson: Writings*, 99.

169 Coolidge, "Great Virginians," July 6, 1922, *Price of Freedom*, 178; "Daniel Webster," July 4, 1916, *Have Faith in Massachusetts*, 25.

170 Morse believed in the Whig interpretation of history, in which history moved upward and onward toward progress. Hendrik Booraem, writing in *The Provincial: Calvin Coolidge and His World, 1885–1895*, recounts Morse's views:

> History, as Morse presented it, was a subject full of meaning. It was essentially political, the story of the human rise from barbarism and servitude to self-government and democracy. It has heroes: men like Simon de Montfort and Luther, Cromwell and Jefferson, rebels all against some kind of oppression, helped on by progress, that wonderful warm engine that Morse, like so many late-nineteenth-century Americans, sensed churning beneath the surface of history. Where "conditions are healthful and progress is normal," he wrote in a major paper the year Coolidge was studying under him, "the humblest citizen becomes to the full measure of his capacity a sharer" in the goods of society, including political power. To Morse, there was nothing wrong with political parties; each was "the self-realization of a group of citizens within the state." This broad, basically optimistic vision of history Morse presented with remarkable sweep and detail. . . . Morse's vision held the full attention of Calvin Coolidge. [Hendrik Booraem, *The Provincial: Calvin Coolidge and His World, 1885–1895* (Cranbury, NJ: Associated Press, 1994), 179.]

171 Coolidge, "Our Heritage from Hamilton," January 11, 1922, *Price of Freedom*, 105.

172 Sobel, *American Enigma*, 212.

173 Coolidge defended the separation of powers in this constitutional argument:

> Some people do not seem to understand fully the purpose of our constitutional restraints. They are not for protecting the majority, either in or out of the Congress. They can protect themselves with their votes. We have adopted a written constitution in order that the minority, even down to the most insignificant individual, might have their rights protected. So long as our Constitution remains in force, no majority, no matter how large, can deprive the individual of the right of life, liberty or property, or prohibit the free exercise of religion or the freedom of speech or of the press. If the authority now vested in the Supreme

Court were transferred to the Congress, any majority no matter what their motive could vote away any of these most precious rights. Majorities are notoriously irresponsible. After irreparable damage had been done the only remedy that the people would have would be the privilege of trying to defeat such a majority at the next election. Every minority body that may be weak in resources or unpopular in the public estimation, also nearly every race and religious belief, would find themselves practically without protection, if the authority of the Supreme Court should be broken down and its powers lodged with the Congress. ("Ordered Liberty and World Peace, address delivered at the dedication of a monument to Lafayette," September 6, 1924, *Foundations of the Republic*, 94–95.)

174 Woods, *Preparation of Calvin Coolidge*, 89.
175 One of his first biographers, William Allen White, points to his spiritual and political upbringing: "Coolidge's spiritual line ran straight back to the Puritan leader John Winthrop, and he believed with the writer in *The Federalist* in the beneficent despotism of the 'rich, wise, and good.' He was a conservative Republican, only as liberal as the challenging times required him to be" (White, *A Puritan in Babylon*, 170). This dismissiveness of Coolidge's conservatism is something of a hallmark of his biographers.
176 Woods, *Preparation of Calvin Coolidge*, 89.
177 Coolidge, "Our Heritage from Hamilton," January 11, 1922, *Price of Freedom*, 105.
178 Coolidge, "William McKinley," at the Convention of Spanish War Veterans, Harvard University, April 17, 1923, ibid., 300.
179 Coolidge, "The Purpose of America," at Johns Hopkins University, February 22, 1922, ibid., 141.
180 Coolidge, "The Destiny of America," May 30, 1923, ibid., 340.
181 Coolidge, "Our Heritage from Hamilton," ibid., 108.
182 Ibid., 103.
183 Ibid., 106.
184 Coolidge, "The Reign of Law," Memorial Day Address at Arlington National Cemetery, May 30, 1925, *Foundations of the Republic*, 233.
185 Coolidge was not exactly forthright here. Special-interest organization are by definition selfish – they do, after all, hold their interests as special and therefore worthy of consideration – and yet he wants them to consider the public good. Coolidge may not have thought this fully through, or perhaps he was trying to have it both ways.
186 McCoy, *The Quiet President*, 295.
187 Coolidge, "The Insipiration of the Declaration of Independence," July 5, 1926, *Foundations of the Republic*, 453–454.

CHAPTER SIX

1   James Madison, "Speech at Constitutional Convention," June 6, 1787, in *Records of the Federal Convention of 1787*, ed. Max Farrand (New Haven: Yale University Press, 1937), 1:135.

2   Coolidge, "The Power of the Moral Law," October 11, 1921, *Price of Freedom*, 72.

3   Calvin Coolidge, *The Mind of the President, as Revealed by Himself in His Own Words*, ed. C. Bascom Slemp (Garden City, NY: Doubleday, Page, 1926), 247.

4   Coolidge, "Progress Toward Freedom," February 12,1923, *Price of Freedom*, 274.

5   Coolidge, "The Purpose of America," February 22, 1922, ibid., 136.

6   Coolidge, "The Progress of a People," June 6, 1924, *Foundations of the Republic*, 34.

7   Coolidge, "Progress Toward Freedom," February 12, 1923, *Price of Freedom*, 279.

8   Johnson, "The Last Arcadia," in Haynes, *The Coolidge Era*, 8.

9   Sobel, *American Enigma*, 278

10 There is some indication that women tipped the election in 1920 to the Republican Party in Tennessee. Tennessee was the last state to ratify the Nineteenth Amendment. It also very narrowly voted for the Harding-Coolidge ticket in 1920, becoming one of the few post–Civil War southern states to vote for the Republican presidential ticket until after World War II. Sobel notes that the Republican Party carried the state, for the first time since 1868, by less than two thousand votes. Coolidge may well have tipped the balance, having visited Tennessee on the campaign trail. (Sobel, *American Enigma*, 207)

11 When I recently visited Independence Hall in Philadelphia, the tour guide excoriated America for not being "inclusive" or sufficiently democratic. "When they said all men were created equal, they didn't mean women, or gays, or even poor white people," she said.

12 The Gospel of John was a particular favorite of Coolidge's, and he took the oath of office on March 4, 1925, with the Bible opened to the first chapter of John. He had learned to read that chapter to his grandfather when he was a small boy. (Quint and Ferrell, *The Talkative President*, 42)

13 Coolidge, "The Destiny of America," May 30, 1923, *Price of Freedom*, 352.

14 Abraham Lincoln, "Electric Cord Speech," Chicago, Illinois, June 10, 1858, in *The Collected Works of Abraham Lincoln*, ed. Roy P. Basler (New Brunswick, NJ: Rutgers University Press, 1953), 11:499–500.

15 Coolidge, "Essex County Club," September 14, 1918, *Have Faith in Massachusetts*, 143–144.

16 Coolidge, "The Title of American," October 31, 1921, *Price of Freedom*, 85–86.

17 Hans P. Vought, *The Bully Pulpit and the Melting Pot: American Presidents and the Immigrant, 1897–1933* (Macon, GA: Mercer University Press, 2004), 187.

18 In his commencement speech before Holy Cross in 1919, Coolidge quoted Patrick

Henry's speech before the Continental Congress favorably: "I have but one lamp by which my feet are guided and that is the lamp of experience." Coolidge also noted, echoing Henry: "The present is ever influenced mightily by the past."

19 Vought notes the platform's pro-eugenics language: "The selective tests that are at present applied should be improved by requiring a higher physical standard, a more complete exclusion of mental defectives and of criminals, and a more effective inspection applied as near the source of the immigration as possible, as well as at the port of entry." (Vought, *Bully Pulpit*, 162)

20 Speech in December 1922 in Reynoldsville, Pennsylvania, cited in Vought, *Bully Pulpit*, 188.

21 Coolidge, "Roxbury Historical Society," June 17, 1918, *Have Faith in Massachusetts*, 118–119.

22 I will turn to what the Founders thought later in this chapter but mention here, in passing, Washington's thought on immigration policy. He supported making America an "asylum to the *virtuous* and persecuted part of mankind, to whatever nation they may belong," but only if those who came were in such numbers as could be readily "assimilated to our customs, measures, and laws: in a word, soon become *one people*." Edward J. Erler, Thomas G. West, John A. Marini, *The Founders on Citizenship and Immigration: Principles and Challenges in America* (Lanham, MD: Rowman & Littlefield, 2007), 85; Thomas G. West, *Vindicating the Founders: Race, Sex, Class, and Justice in the Origins of America* (Lanham, MD: Rowman & Littlefield, 2001), 151.

23 Coolidge, "Address at the Dedication of the Statue of John Ericsson," Washington, DC, May 29, 1926, online at The American Presidency Project.

24 Coolidge, "The Progress of a People," June 6, 1924, *Foundations of the Republic*.

25 *Success*, July 1924, p. 12, enclosed in Walter Hoff Seely to Calvin Coolidge, 12 June 1925, Calvin Coolidge Papers, President's Personal File (PPF) 166 (reel 7), Forbes Library, Northampton, Massachusetts.

26 Ferrell, *Presidency of Calvin Coolidge*, 95, 107, 112.

27 "Will Ask Congress to Review the Klan," *New York Times*, June 25, 1925.

28 Coolidge, according to one of the secret agents, had a low opinion of the Klan. Agent Starling recalled a conversation about which play Coolidge wanted to see:

> What's at the National?, Coolidge asked. . . .
> I don't think the National would interest you, I said. I took Mr. Sargent (the Atty General) there last night. It's just an ordinary leg show.
> I'd better not take my wife there, he said, and you'd better not let the folks in Vermont know John Sargent is going to leg shows. . . . What about the Belasco?
> It is rented this week to the Ku Klux Klan.
> Well, we won't go there. That's worse than a leg show.

See Alvin S. Felzenberg, 1988, "Calvin Coolidge and Race: His Record in Dealing with the Racial Tensions of the 1920s," lecture delivered at the JFK Library, in *New England Journal of History* 55, no. 1 (Fall 1998): 83–96.

29   Theodore Roosevelt, State of the Union Address, December 3, 1906; William Howard Taft, State of the Union Address, December 7, 1909; Calvin Coolidge, State of the Union Address, December 6, 1923.

30   Will Rogers, *Will Rogers' Weekly Articles*, ed. James Smallwood and Steven K. Gragert (Stillwater, OK: Oklahoma State University Press, 1980), 326.

31   Johnson, "The Last Arcadia," in Haynes, *The Coolidge Era*, 2.

32   Sobel, *American Enigma*, 320.

33   Thomas Jefferson, letter to Henri Gregoire, February 25, 1809.

34   Thomas Jefferson, letter to Benjamin Banneker, August 30, 1791.

35   West, *Vindicating the Founders*, 171.

36   The Klan unsurprisingly owed its growth partly to the film's popularity and the national sensation it caused. To modern eyes, *Birth of a Nation* – one of the industry's earliest and most technically advanced major efforts – looks dated, cartoonishly racist, and more than a bit hokey. But these perceptions are deceiving, for the film's influence would be hard to overstate. A recent history of the movie describes it as the nation's first "blockbuster." That was just one of its many "firsts." As Melvyn Stokes notes in *D.W. Griffith's* The Birth of a Nation: *A History of "The Most Controversial Motion Picture of All Time"* (Oxford: Oxford University Press, 2007):

> This film would bring about a revolution in American moviegoing. *The Birth of a Nation* was the first American film to be twelve reels long and to last around three hours. It was the first to cost $100,000 to produce. It was the first to be shown mainly in regular theaters at the same admission prices of up to $2 that were charged for live performances. It was the first to have a specially compiled musical score to accompany the film's exhibition. It was the first movie to be shown at the White House, the first to be projected for judges of the Supreme Court and members of Congress, the first to be viewed by countless of millions of ordinary Americans, some of whom had made long journeys to see it, the first to run in so many places for months at a time, the first to attract viewers who returned to see it, sometimes again and again, and the first to have its existence treated as a story in its own right in local newspapers. . . . The men who advertised and publicized it created ways of promoting movies that would soon become standard across the American movie industry. In many ways, in fact, *Birth of a Nation* was the first "blockbuster": it was the most profitable film of its time (and perhaps, adjusted for inflation, of all time), it helped open up new markets (including

South America) for American films, and it may eventually have been seen by worldwide audiences of up to 200,000,000. (3)

37 According to legend, President Woodrow Wilson exclaimed his admiration of the film: "It is like writing history with lightning. And my only regret is that it is all so terribly true." This was probably one of many myths that cropped up around the film. Stokes reported what the only survivor of that White House screening remembered, in 1977, some fifty-two years later: She recalled that the president "seemed lost in thought during the showing" and that he "walked out of the room without saying a word when the movie was over." (Ibid., 111)

38 Ibid., 112.

39 At Johns Hopkins, Dixon – and presumably Wilson – learned much of his belief in the superiority of the Anglo-Saxon peoples from historian Herbert Baxter Adams. Adams had trained in Germany and believed in a "germ" theory of American self-government. Adams, according to Stokes, held that the "roots of American democracy could be traced back to the primitive arrangements of medieval German tribes" (ibid., 32). Wilson did not believe in natural rights, as noted in Chapter 1.

40 Ibid., 33.

41 Ibid., 21.

42 Felzenberg notes that the number of black presidential appointees "dropped sharply – from 33 to 9" during the Wilson years. Blacks-only divisions were created "beginning with the Departments of Treasury, Post Office, Navy, and later the Interior, all headed by Southerners." (Felzenberg, "Calvin Coolidge and Race")

43 J. W. Schulte Nordholt, *Woodrow Wilson* (Berkeley: University of California Press, 1991), 99.

44 Michael J. Klarman, *From Jim Crow to Civil Rights: The Supreme Court and the Struggle for Racial Equality* (Oxford: Oxford University Press, 2004), 68.

45 Klarman, *Jim Crow to Civil Rights*, 68. The contrast with Coolidge is clear. His chief of staff, C. Baston Slemp, pointed out in his memoirs that Coolidge appointed a "semi-diplomatic commission, composed exclusively of Negroes, to visit the Virgin Islands" in what Slemp called "the first diplomatic recognition of this kind of the Negro . . . in the history of the United States." (Slemp, *Mind of the President*, 245)

46 This was perhaps because many blacks in those days increasingly supported socialism, which Wilson also supported in that he advocated the government-run ownership of industries. See Chapter 1. Blacks might have realized that Wilson would not be a ready ally if they had noted his background. Until 1910, after all, he had been president of Princeton, one of the very few Northern colleges that completely barred blacks. (Klarman, *Jim Crow to Civil Rights*, 68)

47 This was a position that soon found a voice in the Coolidge administration, too, in the person of Secretary of Labor James Davis, who supported eugenics. In language that seems as if it could have been written yesterday, Davis argued that while he opposed hiring on the basis of race, he believed that "in cases where department heads have been confronted with special problems growing out of interracial relationships, a solution could be expedited by the employment of Negro experts of broad vision, understanding, and training." Davis also had on his staff a "Negro commissioner of conciliation" to advise him on "interracial issues and industrial problems that had arisen through (racial) mis-understandings." (Felzenberg, "Calvin Coolidge and Race")

48 Trotter, who represented the NAACP, was eventually banned from the White House by Wilson for that argument. (Nordholt, *Woodrow Wilson*, 100)

49 "'Birth of a Nation' Causes Near-Riot," *Morning Globe* [Boston], April 18, 1915.

50 Stokes, *D. W. Griffith's* The Birth of a Nation, 146.

51 Governor Walsh lost his reelection to Samuel McCall. In 1917, Coolidge served as McCall's lieutenant governor.

52 Lewis, the son of former slaves, served as Taft's assistant U.S. attorney general and was elected to the Massachusetts General Court four years before Coolidge was. Alvin S. Felzenberg, *The Leaders We Deserved (And a Few We Didn't): Rethinking the Presidential Rating Game* (New York: Basic Books, 2008), 307.

53 Stokes, *D. W. Griffith's* The Birth of a Nation, 146.

54 Felzenberg, "Calvin Coolidge and Race."

55 Stokes, *D. W. Griffith's* The Birth of a Nation, 148–149.

56 Ibid., 149.

57 Felzenberg, "Calvin Coolidge and Race."

58 Vought, *The Bully Pulpit*, 149.

59 Klarman, *From Jim Crow to Civil Rights*, 122.

60 Coolidge, "Toleration and Liberalism," October 6, 1925, *Foundations of the Republic*, 285.

61 Coolidge, "Progress of a People," June 6, 1924, ibid., 31–36. Emphasis added.

62 Ibid. Emphasis added.

63 Ibid. Emphasis added.

64 One anecdote might be illustrative. Secret Service Agent Edmund Starling referred off-handedly to Arthur Brooks, the White House butler, as "a fine, colored gentleman." Coolidge quickly corrected him, saying: "Brooks is not a colored gentleman. He is a gentleman." (Felzenberg, "Calvin Coolidge and Race")

65 Sobel, *American Enigma*, 320.

66 Coolidge, "Somerville Republican City Committee Speech," August 7, 1918, *Have Faith in Massachusetts*, 129.

67 http://www.vindicatingthefounders.com/library/hamilton-to-jay.html

68 Coolidge, "Progress Toward Freedom," February 12, 1923, *Price of Freedom*, 277.

69 Ibid., 275.

70 Ibid.

71 Coolidge, State of the Union Address, December 6, 1923.

72 Coolidge, State of the Union Address, December 3, 1924.

73 Coolidge, State of the Union Address, December 7, 1925.

74 Lincoln likened unequal treatment to original sin: "the same old serpent that says you work and I eat, you will work and I will enjoy the fruits of it." This was the opposite of the Golden Rule, and unless it was expunged, it would drag down the whole Republic. Abraham Lincoln, *Abraham Lincoln: Complete Works, Comprising His Speeches, Letters, State Papers, and Miscellaneous Writings*, ed. John G. Nicolay and John Hay (New York: Century, 1894), 2:259.

75 Coolidge, "The Progress of a People," June 6, 1924, *Foundations of the Republic*, 31.

76 Ibid., 31–36.

77 Coolidge, "Vice-Presidential Acceptance Address," July 27, 1920.

78 Coolidge, State of the Union Adress, December 7, 1926.

79 Historian Robert Ferrell notes, for instance, that between 1925 and 1929, the chief years of the Coolidge Prosperity, the lynching rate fell. Also see generally Felzenberg, "Calvin Coolidge and Race."

80 Coolidge, State of the Union Address, December 7, 1926.

81 Coolidge, State of the Union Address, December 6, 1927.

82 Coolidge, State of the Union Address, December 4, 1928.

83 The Republican House passed the bill "with Negroes cheering in the galleries and Southerners cursing on the floor." William B. Hixson Jr., "Moorfield Storey and the Defense of the Anti-Lynching Bill," *New England Quarterly* 42, no. 1 (1969): 74.

84 "Prosperity and the Coolidge Years," Macrohistory and World Report, http://www.fsmitha.com/h2/ch15-9.htm.

85 Ferrell notes that between "300,000 to 400,000 blacks went north to replace the labor of white immigrants who moved up the economic scale or entered the army." (Ferrell, *Presidency of Calvin Coolidge*, 107)

86 "Coolidge Pledges Right to Negroes," *New York Times*, August 22, 1924.

87 Here I refer to John W. Davis's baiting of Coolidge on the issue of denouncing the Ku Klux Klan.

88 Greenberg, *Calvin Coolidge*, 87.

89 Coolidge was speaking here about blacks' economic and intellectual progress in the more than fifty years since emancipation. His detailed knowledge of their success is evident in the following quotation and argues against the charges of contemporary and later critics that Coolidge was indifferent toward blacks:

> Looking back only a few years, we appreciate how rapid has been the progress of the colored people on this continent. Emancipation brought them the opportunity of which they have availed themselves. It has been calculated that in the first year following the acceptance of their

status as a free people, there were approximately 4,000,000 members of the race in this country, and that among these only 12,000 were the owners of their homes; only 20,000 among them conducted their own farms, and the aggregate wealth of these 4,000,000 people hardly exceeded $20,000,000. In a little over a half century since, the number of business enterprises operated by colored people had grown to near 50,000, while the wealth of the Negro community has grown to more than $1,100,000,000. And these figures convey a most inadequate suggestion of the material progress. The 2,000 business enterprises which were in the hands of colored people immediately following emancipation were almost without exception small and rudimentary. Among the 50,000 business operations now in the hands of colored people may be found every type of present day affairs. There are more than 70 banks conducted by thoroughly competent colored business men. More than 80 per cent of all American Negroes are now able to read and write. When they achieved their freedom not 10 per cent were literate. There are nearly 2,000,000 Negro pupils in the public schools; well nigh 40,000 Negro teachers are listed, more than 3,000 following their profession in normal schools and colleges. The list of educational institutions devoting themselves to the race includes 50 colleges, 13 colleges for women, 26 theological schools, a standard school of law, and 2 high-grade institutions of medicine. Through the work of these institutions the Negro race is equipping men and women from its own ranks to provide its leadership in business, the professions, in all relations of life. (*Foundations of the Republic*, 33–34)

90 Amity Shlaes, *The Forgotten Man: A New History of the Great Depression* (New York: Harper Perennial, 2008), 43.

91 Liberal historians have been reluctant to grant what economist Thomas Sowell has demonstrated:

Black education rose substantially, both absolutely and relative to white education, in the decades *preceding* the civil rights legislation of the 1960s and the affirmative action policies that began in the 1970s. What economic changes accompanied this rise in black education? As of 1940, 87 percent of black families had incomes below the official poverty line. By 1960, this was down to 47 percent of black families. This dramatic 40-percentage-point decline came at a time when there was no major federal civil rights legislation. But this was a time not only of rising black education, but also a time of massive exodus of blacks out of the South – more than 3 million people – escaping both the Jim Crow laws and the substandard Southern black schools. In short, this was a time when vast numbers of blacks lifted themselves out of poverty – "by their own bootstraps," as the phrase goes. [Thomas Sowell, *Affirmative Action Around the World: An Empirical Study* (New Haven: Yale University Press, 2004), 119.]

92 Ferrell, *Presidency of Calvin Coolidge*, 113.
93 Charles P. Sweeney, "The Great Bigotry Merger," *The Nation*, July 5, 1923.
94 Sobel, *American Enigma*, 51.
95 And Coolidge did think some of his opponents were honorable. "My most serious regret at the election is that you cannot share the entire pleasure of the result with me," he wrote to an early opponent. He continued: "I value your friendship and good opinion more than any office and I trust I have so conducted the campaign that our past close intimacy and good fellowship may be more secure than ever." (Sobel, *American Enigma*, 73)
96 Felzenberg, "Calvin Coolidge and Race."
97 "Prosperity and the Coolidge Years," Macrohistory and World Report.
98 Ferrell, *Presidency of Calvin Coolidge*, 110.
99 Greenberg, *Calvin Coolidge*, 86.
100 Years later *Newsweek* criticized President Ronald Reagan's repeated homage to Coolidge by pointing to the fact that Coolidge took "two-month vacations" (Hayward, *Age of Reagan: The Conservative Counterrevolvution*, 73). Coolidge, it seems, is damned if he does and damned if he doesn't.
101 Greenberg also seizes upon Coolidge's State of the Union Address in 1923, in which the new president suggested that lynchings were "to a large extent local problems which must be worked out by the mutual forbearance and human kindness of each community." In quoting this, he leaves out the next part. "Such a method," Coolidge added, "gives much more promise of a real remedy than outside interference."
102 Felzenberg, "Calvin Coolidge and Race."
103 Alexander Leidholdt, *Editor for Justice: The Life of Louis I. Jaffé* (Baton Rouge: Louisiana State Press, 2002), 222.
104 Felzenberg, "Calvin Coolidge and Race."
105 Sobel, *American Enigma*, 281.
106 Ferrell, *Presidency of Calvin Coolidge*, 111.
107 Felzenberg, "Calvin Coolidge and Race."
108 Dewey W. Grantham, *The Life and Death of the Solid South: A Political History* (Lexington, KY: University Press of Kentucky, 1988), 81.
109 Felzenberg, "Calvin Coolidge and Race."
110 Ibid.
111 "Cal Coolidge Tells Kluxer When to Stop," *Chicago Defender*, August 16, 1924, cited in Jonathan Bean, *Race and Liberty in America: The Essential Reader* (Lexington: University Press of Kentucky, 2009), 153.

112 "Calvin Coolidge Will Act on Klan Challenge," *New York Times*, August 14, 1924.

113 See Felzenberg, "Calvin Coolidge and Race."

114 Cited in Sobel, *American Enigma*, 319.

115 *New York Times*, August 23, 1924.

116 Ferrell, *Presidency of Calvin Coolidge*, 110.

117 Raymond Wolters, *The Burden of Brown: Thirty Years of School Desegregation* (Knoxville: University of Tennessee Press, 1992), 137.

118 "Davis Wins Praise for Attacking Klan," *New York Times*, August 24, 1924.

119 "Wheeler Jabs at Coolidge," *New York Times*, August 23, 1924.

120 "Klan to Fight La Follette: But Is 'Neutral' as Between Coolidge and Davis, Evans Asserts," *New York Times*, August 23, 1926.

121 In those days, it was considered unpresidential to campaign for reelection. "Front porch campaigns" were the standard for Republican candidates, like James Garfield in 1880, Benjamin Harrison in 1888, William McKinley in 1896, and Warren G. Harding in 1920. Coolidge, a lifelong Republican, probably saw no reason to break with the tradition.

122 Sobel, *American Enigma*, 302.

123 Bascom Nolly Timmons, *Portrait of an American: Charles G. Dawes* (New York: Henry Holt, 1953), 235.

124 Ferrell, *Presidency of Calvin Coolidge*, 111.

125 Timmons, *Portrait of an American*, 211.

126 Ibid., 212.

127 Ibid., 214.

128 Coolidge's advice to Dawes when giving speeches indicates that they were of one mind: "The more simple you can keep it, the better they will like it." He also advised: "Keep as much as you can to an expression of general principles, rather than attempting to go into particular details of legislation." (Sobel, *American Enigma*, 303)

129 Timmons, *Portrait of an American*, 234–235.

130 "Maine," *New York Times*, August 25, 1924.

131 "Sees Klan Defense in Dawes's Attack," *New York Times*, August 24, 1924.

132 "Break the Klan Now," *New York Times*, August 26, 1924.

133 "Dawes's Plans Changed Suddenly," *New York Times*, August 25, 1924; "Coolidge Discusses Campaign Policies with General Dawes," *New York Times*, August 26, 1924.

134 Kelly Miller, "The Negro and the Klan," *New York Times*, September 7, 1924.

135 "Negroes Threaten to Bolt on Klan," *New York Times*, September 17, 1924.

136 "Coolidge Opposes Aims of Klan, Says Slemp, in Reply to Questionnaire from New York," *New York Times*, September 3, 1924.

137 "Slemp Reiterates Coolidge Klan Stand," *New York Times*, October 12, 1924.

138 Coolidge appealed to the spirit of Lincoln in favoring charity to all and malice toward none. By expressing his "thoughtful sympathy with Southern sentiment,

through the results of his study of Southern colonial history and particularly
through his reverence for the character of General Robert E. Lee," Coolidge
earned the admiration of the South. "In the campaign, and later, he showed
the white South that he could express to the Negroes his conviction that they
were justifying Lincoln's faith, without giving a rebuff to the new but characteristic impulse among the best Southern leaders toward fully and fairer understanding between the races" (Woods, *Preparation of Calvin Coolidge*, 185). In other
words, Coolidge was trying to bring people together, in a Lincolnian fashion.

139 Coolidge, "States' Rights and National Unity," May 15, 1926, *Foundations of the Republic*, 411. Emphasis added.

140 Leidholdt, *Editor for Justice*, 346.

141 Ibid., 347.

142 Coolidge, "Toleration and Liberalism," October 6, 1925, *Foundations of the Republic*, 298–300.

143 Annual Report of Secretary of the Interior Franklin K. Lane, 1915, cited in Francis Paul Prucah, *The Great Father: The United Sates Government and the American Indian* (Lincoln, NE: First Bison Books, 1995), 880.

144 Dr. Joseph K. Dixon, 1924, cited in "1924 Indian Citizenship Act" at nps.gov.

145 Message from a Sioux chieftain to President Coolidge, 1927, on the induction of Coolidge into the Sioux tribe at Fort Yates, North Dakota.

146 Thomas Jefferson, letter to Colonel Benjamin Hawkins, Washington, February 18, 1803.

147 Ibid.

148 Thomas Jefferson, letter to Francis W. Gilmer, Monticello, June 7, 1816.

149 John Quincy Adams, State of the Union Address, December 2, 1828.

150 Annual report of the Department of the Interior, 1865, submitted by Secretary James Harlan.

151 The Coolidge administration later assessed the Dawes Act for itself. In 1926, Secretary of the Interior Hubert Work commissioned a study of federal admin-istration of Indian policy and of the Indians' condition. Completed in 1936, *The Problem of Indian Administration* – commonly known as the Meriam Report after the study's director, Lewis Meriam – documented fraud and misappro-priation by government agents. In particular, the report found that the Dawes Act had been used to illegally deprive Native Americans of their land rights.

152 The most prominent of these organizations was the Indian Rights Association.

153 Indian leaders had generally sought citizenship, as provided for in the 1924 law, but had also wished to abolish the BIA because of its heavy-handed policies.

154 Arthur C. Parker, "Defining our Indian Policy," *New York Times*, January 20, 1924.

155 "The Indians' Lament," *New York Times*, August 19, 1923.

156 Edith Manville Dabb, "Evils of Tribal Dances," *New York Times*, December 2, 1923.

157 Carlos Montezuma (~?1867–1923) was an Indian-rights leader and physician

who urged citizenship and the abolition of the BIA. He promoted these causes in his monthly newsletter *Wassaja*. He drafted the Indian-citizenship bill that became law after his death. Montezuma was also among the founders of the Society of American Indians, an organization that emphasized two main political goals: citizenship for all Indians and dismantling the BIA.

158 Joseph W. Latimer, "Rights of the Indian," *New York Times*, December 22, 1923.

159 The Committee of One Hundred was a group of experts appointed by Secretary of the Interior Hubert Work.

160 The committee's language revealed its belief that the public schools could produce a common citizenry: "The public school system of our country should be fully open to the Indian as an effective means of preparing him for good citizenship." "Interior Department appropriation bill, hearing before subcommittee of House Committee on Appropriations," 1925, Washington, G.P.O., 1924.

161 Joseph W. Latimer, "Indian's Day in Court," *New York Times*, January 28, 1924.

162 The Indians were far from a homogeneous group. As the *New York Times* noted, "of the various Indian tribes . . . there are 371 speaking 58 different languages" "Red Men Take Up Civilized Ways," *New York Times*, April 18, 1926. It was difficult to assimilate so many diverse groups with a uniform policy.

163 "Absorbing the Indian," *New York Times*, March 7, 1926.

164 Ernest Harvier, "Indians to Vote Next Election Day," *New York Times*, September 7, 1924.

165 As the *Times* noted, that was a large number: "In 1920, of the Indian population 10 years of age and over, 20.8 per cent could not speak English and 34.9 per cent were classed as illiterate." "Absorbing the Indian," *New York Times*, March 7, 1926.

166 "Red Men Take Up Civilized Ways," *New York Times*, April 18, 1926.

167 Coolidge, "Toleration and Liberalism," address before the American Legion Convention, Omaha, Nebraska, October 6, 1925, *Foundations of the Republic*, 298.

168 It was hoped that the Indians' sacrifice on foreign fields in World War I might help them. Joseph K. Dixon, secretary of the American Indian Association, appealed to President Woodrow Wilson and the nation before Congress's subcommittee on military affairs with the following proposal, entitled "The Emancipation of the North American Indian":

1. Declare all Indians who have served in any capacity in the United States military forces, to be, from even date, full citizens of the United States.
2. Declare all Indians of age to the date of April 6, 1917, the day war was declared, to have full citizenship.
3. Declare all Indian children born after April 6, 1917, to have full citizenship upon reaching their majority.
4. Declare the abolition of the reservation system. . . .

Sweep clean the national house of democracy and put the crown on the goddess of victory by issuing a proclamation of emancipation for the North American Indian, who has shed his blood for a country and a flag that he could not call his own.

... when America is focused in the eye of all the world ... such a proclamation as has been suggested would not only work out justice and fair play to a long-oppressed race of people, but the fiat would stand out as the most striking consummation of our wonderful achievement at arms in bringing freedom to all peoples.

United States Congressional House Committee on Military Affairs, "Reorganization of the Army: report of a sub-committee of the Committee on Military Affairs Relating to the Reorganization of the Army" (Washington, DC: Government Printing Office, 1919), 2,149.

169 Fuess, *Man from Vermont*, 13.

170 Booraem, *The Provincial*, 197.

171 Coolidge, "Amherst College Alumni Association," February 4, 1916, *Have Faith in Massachusetts*, 13 .

172 John McNeely, "American Indian Strides Forward," *New York Times*, September 12, 1926.

173 Coolidge, State of the Union Address, December 6, 1927.

174 Coolidge, "Amherst College Commencement," June 18, 1919, *Have Faith in Massachusetts*, 183.

175 John McNeely, "American Indian Strides Forward," *New York Times*, September 12, 1926.

176 Quint and Ferrell, *The Talkative President*, 14–15.

177 His name was not, contrary to one press report at the time, "Still Water," although that would have been fitting for him.

178 "Coolidge Addresses 10,000 Sioux Indians as Supreme Chief," *New York Times*, August 18, 1927.

179 "Tribesmen Hear Their Big Chief," *Lawrence Journal-World*, August 17, 1927.

180 Ibid.

181 Ibid.

182 Vought, *The Bully Pulpit*, 111.

183 Ibid.

184 McDougall writes that the laws to restrict Japanese settlement in California failed. The population of Japanese adults grew from 32,785 in 1910 to 47,566 in 1920. Japanese landholdings "quadrupled since 1913." Walter A. McDougall, *Let the Sea Make a Noise: A History of the North Pacific from Magellan to MacArthur* (New York: Harper Perennial, 2004), 536.

185 Hughes's career would be affected by the Japanese issue again, when it nearly brought about his resignation as secretary of state.

186 When Harding embraced Asian restriction as a means of currying favor with Californians, he was reversing himself. In 1908, he had condemned California for defying the federal government and risking a war with Japan over exclusion, but in 1920, after meeting with Governor Stephens to discuss "Oriental exclusion," Harding concluded that "there is abundant evidence of the dangers which lurk in racial differences." (Vought, *Bully Pulpit*, 164)

187 Izumi Hirobe, *Japanese Pride, American Prejudice: Modifying the Exclusion Clause of the 1924 Immigration Act* (Palo Alto, CA: Stanford University Press, 2001), 6.

188 McDougall, *History of the North Pacific*, 537.

189 Ray Stannard Baker, *Woodrow Wilson and World Settlement* (Garden City, NY: Doubleday, Page, 1923), 234.

190 Ibid., 239.

191 Coolidge, "Roxbury Historical Society," June 17, 1918, *Have Faith in Massachusetts*, 116–117.

192 See generally Hugh Byas, *Government by Assassination* (New York: Routledge, 2011, first published in 1943).

193 McDougall, *History of the North Pacific*, 535.

194 Coolidge, "Fairhaven," July 4, 1918, *Have Faith in Massachusetts*, 122.

195 *The Presentation of a Samurai Sword* (Fairhaven, MA: Millicent Library, 1918), http://www.archive.org/stream/presentationofsa02mill#page/22/mode/2up.

196 Coolidge, "Fairhaven," July 4, 1918, *Have Faith in Massachusetts*, 125.

197 Hirobe, *Japanese Pride, American Prejudice*, 7.

198 McDougall, *History of the North Pacific*, 537.

199 Ibid., 536.

200 Vought, *Bully Pulpit*, 189.

201 At a press conference on May 24, the president acknowledged his and Secretary of State Hughes's failure in this respect. (Quint and Ferrell, *The Talkative President*, 92)

202 Reading the wire-service news, Coolidge turned to the acting secretary of state and said, "You might tell [the fleet] to go right away to Yokohama." (McDougall, *History of the North Pacific*, 535)

203 William F. Nimmo, *Stars and Stripes Across the Pacific: The United States, Japan, and Asia/Pacific Region 1895–1945* (Westport, CT: Greenwood, 2001), 112.

204 Ibid. 113

205 Coolidge's statement to the American people is cited in Joshua Hammer, *Yokohama Burning: The Deadly 1923 Earthquake and Fire That Helped Forge the Path to World War II* (New York: Simon & Schuster, 2006), 224.

206 Ibid., 227.

207 Greenberg, *Calvin Coolidge*, 83.

208 Cited in Vought, *Bully Pulpit*, 191.

209 McCoy, *The Quiet President*, 232.

210 Quint and Ferrell, *The Talkative President*, 91.

211 Sobel, *American Enigma*, 269.

212 Vought, *Bully Pulpit*, 162.

213 Ibid., 170.

214 Davis fondly and routinely quoted eugenicist Harry H. Laughlin, a previous House Immigration Committee consultant. After listening to Laughlin's testimony on the mental acuity of immigrants, Davis proposed "strict but just tests of physical and mental health." He asked A. E. Hamilton, who worked at the Carnegie Institution's Station for Experimental Evolution with Laughlin and Charles B. Davenport, to prepare thirty-seven pamphlets titled, "Selective Immigration or None." (Vought, *Bully Pulpit*, 173–174)

215 Ibid., 174–176.

216 Coolidge, "Accepting the Republican Presidential Nomination," August 14, 1924, in Slemp, *Mind of the President*, 216–217.

217 Coolidge, "The High Place of Labor," September 24, 1924, *Foundations of the Republic*, 83.

218 Coolidge, "The Genius of America," October 16, 1924, ibid., 162.

219 "Calvin Coolidge Says," December 13, 1930.

220 Samuel Gompers, *Seventy Years of Life and Labor: An Autobiography*, 2 vols. (New York: E. P. Dutton, 1925), 1:557.

221 Coolidge, "Accepting the Republican Presidential Nomination," August 14, 1924.

222 Coolidge, State of the Union Address, December 8, 1925. Emphasis added.

223 Coolidge, "Contribution of the Norsemen to America," before the Norwegian centennial celebration, at the Minnesota State Fair Grounds, June 8, 1925, *Foundations of the Republic*, 250.

224 Coolidge, "Education: The Cornerstone of Self-Government," July 4, 1924, ibid., 60.

225 Thompson, *Adequate Brevity*, 50.

226 Coolidge, "The Genius of America," October 16, 1924, *Foundations of the Republic*, 162.

227 Ibid., 162–163.

228 Fuess, *Man from Vermont*, 105.

229 Vought, *Bully Pulpit*, 184.

230 *Daily Hampshire Gazette*, November 8, 1911.

231 Vought, *Bully Pulpit*, 185.

232 Ibid., 142.

233 Cary T. Grayson, diary entry, March 5, 1919, in Wilson, *Papers* 55:443.

234 Vought, *Bully Pulpit*, 147.

235 Ray S. Baker, diary entry, May 31 1919, in Vought, *Bully Pulpit*, 145–146.

236 On this last point, Coolidge made clear that his defense of religious liberty in Mexico was not a matter of supporting Catholicism as such; it was more

generally that he supported justice for American property owners there. (Quint and Ferrell, *The Talkative President*, 239)

237 Cited in Vought, *Bully Pulpit*, 184.

238 Ibid.

239 Coolidge, State of the Union Address, December 6, 1923.

240 Thomas Jefferson, *Notes on the State of Virginia*, 84–85.

241 George Washington, letter to John Adams, November 15, 1794.

242 Hamilton, "The Examination," nos. 7–9 (1802), Harold C. Syrett, ed., *Papers of Alexander Hamilton* (New York: Columbia University Press, 1961), 25:491–501.

243 Ferrell, *Presidency of Calvin Coolidge*, 112.

244 Abraham Lincoln, "In Favor of Equal Suffrage and Public Improvements," *Early Speeches, 1832–1856: Including Legislative and Congressional Resolutions, Political Circulars, Notes, Etc.*, ed. Marion Mills Miller (New York: Current Literature, 1907), 3:8.

245 Marion L. Burton, "Nominating Speech for Calvin Coolidge," *The Man Coolidge* (Chicago: RNC, 1924).

246 "Republican Party Platform of 1920," online at The American Presidency Project.

247 Coolidge, *Autobiography*, 44.

248 Akhil Amar points out that the first states to give women the right to vote were frontier states (which also tended to be Republican states). Women were an "especially rare and precious resource in the West." "Under the laws of supply and demand," Amar writes, "when women were exceptionally scarce, men had to work that much harder to attract and keep them." Perhaps suffrage resulted from a recognition not so much of how women were treated (or mistreated) in general, but from an appreciation of their value in the frontier environment. Akhil Amar, *America's Constitution: A Biography* (New York: Random House, 2006), 419.

249 Frederick Douglass, *North Star*, July 28, 1848, as quoted in *Frederick Douglass on Women's Rights*, ed. Philip S. Foner (New York: Da Capo Press, 1992, originally published in 1976), 49–51.

250 Fuess, *Man from Vermont*, 117.

251 Coolidge, although he was a committed federalist who believed most legislation should be up to the states, favored a constitutional amendment to abolish child labor entirely. But he was also loyal to the Constitution in opposing federal legislation on the issue. When the Supreme Court invalidated federal child-labor laws, Coolidge defended the rationale behind the decision. The decision "does not mean that the court or nation wants child labor," he explained, but "simply means that the Congress has gone outside of the limitations prescribed for it by the people in their Constitution and attempted to legislate on a subject which the several States and the people themselves have chosen to keep under their own control."

> Should the people desire to have the Congress pass laws relating to that over which they have not granted to it any jurisdiction, the way is open and plain to proceed in the same method that was taken in relation to income taxes, direct election of senators, equal suffrage, or prohibition – by amendment to the Constitution.

Giving the Congress the power to pass laws that could not be reviewed by the courts would lead to disaster, for "such a provision would make the Congress finally supreme [and i]n the last resort its powers practically would be unlimited." ("The Limitations of the Law," address before the Ameican Bar Association, San Francisco, August 10, 1922, *Price of Freedom*, 202)

The constitutional amendment failed, but child labor increasingly became a relic of a bygone era as skilled labor replaced unskilled in the Roaring Twenties. It was not until the Great Depression that laws ending child labor passed without clamor. This was as much economic as it was political. With national unemployment over 25 percent and adults willingly doing jobs previously done by children, the political will existed to outlaw child labor.

252 Cited in Melanie S. Gustafson, *Women and the Republican Party: 1854–1924* (Champagne-Urbana, IL: University of Illinois Press, 2001), 191.

254 Ibid., 5.

254 While conservatives may recoil at this precursor of the ill-fated Equal Rights Amendment, it is worth considering that its rules would have applied only to *federal* workers, not private workers as modern-day feminists want. See generally "Republican Party Platform of 1920," June 8, 1920, online at The American Presidency Project.

255 "Suffragists Split by Party Politics," *New York Times*, February 13, 1920.

256 Ibid.

257 Winston Churchill long opposed the suffrage movement. He found himself "hen-pecked" by suffragettes for this. Winston Churchill, *Churchill Speaks: Winston S. Churchill in Peace and War: Collected Speeches, 1897–1963*, ed. Robert Rhodes James (New York: Chelsea House, 1980), 83.

258 Ralph LaRossa, *The Modernization of Fatherhood: A Social and Political History* (Chicago, IL: University of Chicago Press, 1997), 173.

259 Coolidge, "The Things That Are Unseen," June 19, 1923, *Price of Freedom*, 383.

260 Coolidge, "The New Responsibilities of Women," April 19, 1926, *Foundations of the Republic*, 379.

261 Ibid., 378.

262 "I do not suppose that George Washington could be counted as one who would have favored placing upon the women of his time the duty and responsibility of taking part in elections. Nevertheless he had seen such a deep realization of the importance of their influence upon public affairs at the time when we were adopting our Federal Constitution, that he wrote to one of them as follows:

A spirit of accommodation was happily infused into the leading charac-
ters of the continent and the minds of men were gradually prepared, by
disappointment, for the reception of a good government. Nor could I
rob the fairer sex of their share in the glory of a revolution so honorable
to human nature, for, indeed, I think you ladies are in the number of
the best patriots American can boast. ("The Duties of Citizenship,"
November 3, 1924, address by radio from the White House, *Foundations
of the Republic*, 177–178)

263 Ibid., 178.

264 Coolidge, "The Place of Lincoln," February 12, 1922, *Price of Freedom*, 120.

265 Cynthia D. Bittinger, "A Champion of Women's Rights," in *Why Coolidge Matters*, 51.

266 His mother, grandmother, stepmother, and sister all died fairly young. His sister,
Abbie, died when she was sixteen. In a letter, Coolidge tried to reassure his
father about her loss: "I . . . hope you are better now. We must think of Abbie as
we would of a happy day counting it a pleasure to have had it and not a sorrow
because it could not last forever." When his father was too old to travel,
Coolidge wrote him from Washington in 1925: "It is getting to be Christmas
time again. I always think of mother and Abbie and grandmother and now of
Calvin. Perhaps you will see them all before I do, but in a little while we shall all
be together for Christmas." (Lathem, *Your Son, Calvin Coolidge*, 216)

267 Greenberg, *Calvin Coolidge*, 17.

CHAPTER SEVEN

1   Coolidge, "Amherst College Alumni Association," February 4, 1916, *Have
Faith in Massachusetts*, 13.

2   See generally Ralph Rossum, *Federalism, the Supreme Court, and the Seventeenth
Amendment: The Irony of Constitutional Democracy* (Lanham, MD: Lexington Books,
2001). See also Todd Zywicki, "Repeal the Seventeenth Amendment," *National
Review*, November 15, 2010.

3   For a perceptive rumination on the problems of federal and state government,
see generally Coolidge's "The Reign of Law," his address at Arlington National
Cemetery, May 30, 1925, in *Foundations of the Republic*.

4   Coolidge, "Vice-Presidential Acceptance Address," July 27, 1920.

5   *Federalist* 63.

6   *Federalist* 10.

7   *Federalist* 63.

8   Ibid.

9   Ibid.

10   *Federalist* 64.

11   Ibid.

12 Ibid.

13 Hamilton, writing to G. F. Hopkins, who had finished an edition of *The Federalist* in 1802, recommended that Hopkins add his letters written as Pacificus to the collection. According to Hamilton, "some of his friends had pronounced [it] . . . his best performance."

14 "Nobody answers him, & his doctrine will therefore be taken for confessed. For God's sake, my dear Sir, take up your pen, select the most striking heresies, and cut him to pieces in the face of the public. There is nobody else who can & will enter into the lists with him." Jefferson to Madison, July 7, 1793, *The Papers of James Madison*, ed. Thomas A. Mason, Robert A. Rutland, and Jeanne K. Sisson, (Charlottesville: University Press of Virginia, 1985) 15:43; and below, 54.

15 To be sure, Hamilton worried still about a state of perpetual emergency: "Every breach of the fundamental laws, though dictated by necessity, impairs that sacred reverence which ought to be maintained in the breast of rulers towards the constitution of a country, and forms a precedent for other breaches where the same plea of necessity does not exist at all, or is less urgent and palpable." (*Federalist* 25)

16 Woods, *Preparation of Calvin Coolidge*, 188.

17 Ibid.

18 Ibid., 189.

19 Coolidge, *Autobiography*, 162.

20 André Siegfried, *America Comes of Age: A French Analysis* (Whitefish, MT: Kessinger, 2005), 247.

21 Sobel, *American Enigma*, 352.

22 Coolidge, *Autobiography*, 163.

23 April 10, 1925, in Quint and Ferrell, *The Talkative President*, 25–26.

24 McDougall, *History of the North Pacific*, 524.

25 Ibid., 525.

26 Hughes, *Autobiographical Notes*, 209.

27 Although his father was a Baptist minister, Hughes delighted in smoking cigarettes and playing poker and baseball. At Brown University, he earned money by one of the most questionable means: writing essays for fellow students. (McDougall, *History of the North Pacific*, 524)

28 Ibid., 528.

29 "Harding Sees Dawn of a Better Epoch as He Lauds Conference," *New York Times*, February 7, 1922.

30 Hughes, "Washington Naval Agreement on Capital Ships," 1921.

31 Coolidge, "Speech before Associated Press," April 28, 1924.

32 Coolidge, State of the Union Address, December 6, 1923.

33 Still, some thinkers question Coolidge's custodianship of national defense. In an email exchange with me, conservative historian Larry Schweikart, author of the recent *A Patriot's History of the United States*, essentially blamed Coolidge for

balancing the budget at the expense of American military preparedness – a common refrain in light of the Japanese surprise attack on Pearl Harbor. Others continue to criticize him for the Kellogg-Briand Act of 1928, which purported to outlaw war, and the Dawes Plan, which (some allege) failed to predict or prevent the rise of the Nazis, who violated every one of the plan's tenets.

34 Coolidge, "The Purpose of America," February 22, 1922, *Price of Freedom*, 148.

35 Coolidge, "Address at the Observation of the Tenth Anniversary of the Armistice under the Auspices of the American Legion," November 11, 1928, online at The American Presidency Project.

36 Hughes, *Autobiographical Notes*, 249.

37 Ibid.

38 Ibid.

39 Ibid.

40 *Federalist* 6.

41 Hughes, *Autobiographical Notes*, 280.

42 His daughter, Elizabeth Hughes Gossett, said he was "very much exercised" over the Japanese-exclusion bill and considered it "one of his great disappointments." (Ibid., 252)

43 Coolidge, "Progress Toward Freedom," February 12, 1923, *Price of Freedom*, 279.

44 Sobel, *American Enigma*, 356.

45 In 1925, Germany and France pledged to respect the post–World War I Rhineland frontier, while Germany, Belgium, and the U.K. pledged never to go to war against one another, save for self-defense.

46 Sobel, *American Enigma*, 356.

47 Greenberg, *Calvin Coolidge*, 123.

48 Coolidge, "The Destiny of America," May 30, 1923, *Price of Freedom*, 352.

49 Coolidge, "The Title of American," October 31, 1921, ibid., 87.

50 Coolidge, "William McKinley," April 17, 1923, ibid., 305.

51 Coolidge, "Somerville Republican City Committee," August 7, 1918, *Have Faith in Massachusetts*, 129.

52 "Calvin Coolidge Says," December 4, 1930.

53 Coolidge, "Speech before Associated Press," April 28, 1924.

54 Coolidge, State of the Union Address, December 6, 1927.

55 *Federalist* 4. In his post-presidential syndicated column, Coolidge made reference to Jay's opinion on Washington's decision to make a treaty with England in 1794: "Almost every important agreement ratified with a foreign power has been accompanied in this country by bitter criticism of our own government, and wholesale assaults upon the other contracting country. Yet in the light of history, it would be hard to find such an agreement that has not been fairly justified by the results. After the bad temper of the period has been dissipated by time and reason, the mutual advantages have been apparent. Our diplomacy

has not been inferior. Our statesmen have been able to be just to ourselves and fair to others." ("Calvin Coolidge Says," September 11, 1930)

56 Quint and Ferrell, *The Talkative President*, 173.

57 Coolidge, "Thought, the Master of Things," July 7, 1921, *Price of Freedom*, 65.

58 In his 1925 State of the Union Address, Coolidge hoped for steps toward a "reduction of armies rather than navies." Indeed, he considered such a goal "of the first importance to the world at the present time."

59 In a speech before the graduating class of the U.S. Naval Academy at Annapolis on June 3, 1925, Coolidge spoke movingly about the Navy. "I feel warranted in asserting it to be true that your success lies in giving a very large support to the civilian life of the Nation and to the promotion of the public peace." (*Foundations of the Republic*, 238)

60 In this thinking, Coolidge followed the controversial General Billy Mitchell, who perceptively argued that bombers could already sink battleships; Mitchell organized a series of bombing runs on stationary, unmanned ships to prove it. Like Coolidge, Mitchell was skeptical that World War I would be the last war. "If a nation ambitious for universal conquest gets off to a flying start in a war of the future, it may be able to control the whole world more easily than a nation has controlled a continent in the past," he said. "The advent of air power has made every country and the world smaller. We do not measure distances by the unit of miles, but by the unit of hours. . . . Should a nation, therefore, attain complete control of the air, it could more nearly master the earth than has ever been the case in the past." William Mitchell, *Winged Defense: The Development and Possibilities of Modern Air Power – Economic and Military* (1925; reprint, New York: Dover, 1988), 25–26.

61 Coolidge, State of the Union Address, December 4, 1928.

CONCLUSION

1 *The New York Call*, a Socialist newspaper, 1927.

2 Steven Hayward, *The Politically Incorrect Guide to the Presidents* (Washington, DC: Regnery, 2012), 77.

3 Gilbert reads everything through that prism and notes the mentions of his depression in the writings of Coolidge biographers, whose names he rattles off:

> Rose describes Coolidge as expressing "his commitment to the principle of a do-nothing Presidency by publicizing that he slept eleven of every twenty-four hours that he was in the White House" (1988, p. 22) while Neustadt states simply that Coolidge had no "drive" (1990, p. 204). Warren writes that "Coolidge voluntarily abdicated the leadership which the Constitution intended that the chief executive should exercise. . . . " (1964, p. 146). Bailey states that Coolidge "lacked both imagination

and idealism" and was a below average President (1966, p. 317). Murray cites Coolidge as a "figure-head" President (1973, p. 143) and Plesur refers to Coolidge's presidential performance as "lackadaisical" (1974, p. 188).

See Robert E. Gilbert, *Calvin Coolidge, Death, and Clinical Depression* (Westport, CT: Praeger, 2003).

4   Aristotle, *Lectures in the Lyceum, or Aristotle's Ethics for English Readers*, ed. St. George Stock (London: Longmans, Green, 1897), 257.

5   Coolidge, "The High Place of Labor," September 1, 1924, *Foundations of a Republic*, 84.

6   Cited in Robert Sobel, "Coolidge and American Business," 1988, at calvincoolidge.org.

7   Siegfried, *America Comes of Age*, 282.

8   Ibid., 302.

9   Coolidge, Inaugural Address, March 4, 1925.

AFTERWORD

1   Thomas H. Gammack, "A Wall Street View of Hoover," *The Outlook*, June 27, 1928.

2   James Dodson, "The Funniest President of Them All," *Yankee Magazine*, September 1987.

3   "Calvin Coolidge Says," October 13, 1930.

4   Coolidge, Inaugural Address, March 4, 1925.

5   Coolidge, "Address Before the Chamber of Commerce of the State of New York," New York City, November 19, 1925, at The American Presidency Project.

6   Coolidge, Inaugural Address, March 4, 1925, *Foundations of the Republic*.

7   Ibid.

8   Coolidge, "Telephone Remarks to the Federation of Jewish Philanthropic Societies of New York City, Assembled at the Hotel Pennsylvania," October 26, 1924, online at The American Presidency Project.

9   Thompson, *Adequate Brevity*, 18.

10 Coolidge, Inaugural Address, March 4, 1925.

11 Coolidge, "The High Place of Labor," September 1, 1924, *Foundations of the Republic*, 84.

12 Mike Lux, "The Cal Coolidge/Paul Ryan Budget," *Huffington Post*, April 6, 2011.

13 Cited in Sobel, *American Enigma*, 75.

14 Coolidge, *Autobiography*, 241.

SELECTED BIBLIOGRAPHY

Abels, Jules. *In the Time of Silent Cal.* New York: G. P. Putnam's Sons, 1969.

Amar, Akhil. *America's Constitution: A Biography.* New York: Random House, 2006.

Aristotle, *Lectures in the Lyceum, or Aristotle's Ethics for English Readers.* Edited by St. George Stock. London: Longmans, Green, 1897.

Baker, Ray Stannard. *Woodrow Wilson and World Settlement.* Garden City, NY: Doubleday, Page, 1923.

Barkley, Alben William. *That Reminds Me.* New York: Doubleday, Page, 1954.

Bean, Jonathan. *Race and Liberty in America: The Essential Reader.* Lexington: University Press of Kentucky, 2009.

Booraem, Hendrik. *The Provincial: Calvin Coolidge and His World, 1885–1895.* Cranbury, NJ: Associated Press, 1994.

Bradford, Gamaliel. *The Quick and the Dead.* New York: Houghton Mifflin, 1931.

Brecher, Jeremy. *Strike!* Rev. ed. Boston: South End Press, 1997.

Bryce, James. *The American Commonwealth.* 2 vols. New York: Macmillan, 1888.

Burton, Marion L. Burton, *The Man Coolidge.* Chicago: Republican National Committe, 1924.

Byas, Hugh. *Government by Assassination.* New York: Alfred A. Knopf, 1942. Reprint, Routledge, 2010. Page references are to 2010 reprint.

Calabresi, Steven G., and Christopher Yoo. *The Unitary Executive: Presidential Power from Washington to Bush.* New Haven, CT: Yale University, 2008.

Chambers, Whittaker. *Cold Friday.* New York: Random House, 1964.

Churchill, Sir Winston. *Churchill Speaks: Winston S. Churchill in Peace and War: Collected Speeches, 1897–1963.* Edited by Robert Rhodes James. New York: Chelsea House, 1980.

Coolidge, Calvin. *Autobiography of Calvin Coolidge.* New York: Cosmopolitan Book, 1929.

———. *Foundations of the Republic.* New York: Charles Scribner's Sons, 1926.

———. *Have Faith in Massachusetts.* Boston: Houghton Mifflin, 1919.

———. *The Mind of the President, as Revealed by Himself in His Own Words.* Edited by C. Bascom Slemp. Garden City, NY: Doubleday, Page, 1926.

———. *The Price of Freedom.* 1924. Reprint, Amsterdam, The Netherlands: Fredonia Books, 2001.

Daugherty, Harry M. *The Inside Story of the Warren G. Harding Tragedy.* New York: Books for Libraries Press, 1932.

Eastman, Max. *Love and Revolution: My Journey Through an Epoch.* New York: Random House, 1964.

Epstein, David F. *Political Theory of the Federalist.* Chicago: University of Chicago Press, 2007.

Erler, Edward J., Thomas G. West, and John A. Marini. *The Founders on Citizenship and Immigration: Principles and Challenges in America.* Lanham, MD: Rowman & Littlefield, 2007.

Farrand, Max, ed. *Records of the Federal Convention of 1787.* New Haven: Yale University Press, 1937.

Felzenberg, Alvin S. "Calvin Coolidge and Race: His Record in Dealing with the Racial Tensions of the 1920s." *New England Journal of History* 55, no. 1 (Fall 1998): 83–96.

———. *The Leaders We Deserved (And a Few We Didn't): Rethinking the Presidential Rating Game.* New York: Basic Books, 2008.

Ferrell, Robert H. *The Presidency of Calvin Coolidge.* Lawrence, KS: University Press of Kansas, 1998.

Fite, Gilbert C. *Peter Norbeck: Prairie Statesman.* Columbia, MO: University of Missouri, 1948.

Fleser, Arthur F. *A Rhetorical Study of the Speaking of Calvin Coolidge.* Lewiston, NY: Edwin Mellen Press, 1990.

Foner, Philip S., ed. *Frederick Douglass on Women's Rights.* 1976. Reprint, New York: Da Capo Press, 1992.

Fuess, Claude M. *Calvin Coolidge: The Man from Vermont.* New York: Little, Brown, 1939.

Garman, Eliza Miner. *Letters, Lectures, and Addresses of Charles Edward Garman.* New York: Houghton Mifflin, 1909.

Gilbert, Clinton Wallace. *You Takes Your Choice.* New York: G. P. Putnam's Sons, 1924.

Gilbert, Robert E. *Calvin Coolidge, Death, and Clinical Depression.* Westport, CT: Praeger, 2003.

Gilfond, Duff. *The Rise of Saint Calvin: Merry Sidelights on the Career of Mr. Coolidge.* New York: The Vanguard Press, 1932.

Goldwin, Robert A., and Art Kauffman, eds. *Separation of Powers—Does It Still Work?"* Washington, DC: American Enterprise Institute, 1986.

Gompers, Samuel. *Seventy Years of Life and Labor: An Autobiography.* 2 vols. New York: E. P. Dutton, 1925.

Grantham, Dewey W. *The Life and Death of the Solid South: A Political History.* Lexington, KY: University Press of Kentucky, 1988.

Green, Horace. *The Life of Calvin Coolidge.* New York: Duffield, 1924.

Greenberg, David. *Calvin Coolidge.* New York: Henry Holt, 2007.

Gustafson, Melanie S. *Women and the Republican Party: 1854–1924.* Champagne-Urbana, IL: University of Illinois Press, 2001.

Hamilton, Alexander. *Papers of Alexander Hamilton.* Edited by Harold C. Syrett. New York: Columbia University Press, 1961.

———, James Madison, and John Jay [Publius]. *The Federalist Papers.* 1788. Reprint, New York: Signet Classic, 2003.

Hammer, Joshua. *Yokohama Burning: The Deadly 1923 Earthquake and Fire That Helped Forge the Path to World War II.* New York: Simon & Schuster, 2006.

Hammond, John Hays. *The Autobiography of John Hays Hammond.* New York: Farrar and Rhinehart, 1935. Reprint, New York: Ayer Publishing, 1974. Page references are to 1974 reprint.

Hanson, Ole. *Americanism Versus Bolshevism.* New York: Doubleday, Pace, 1920.

Harbutt, Fraser J. *The Iron Curtain: Churchill, America, and the Origins of the Cold War*. Oxford: Oxford University Press, 1988.

Haynes, John Earl, ed. *Calvin Coolidge and the Coolidge Era: Essays on the History of the 1920s*. Washington, DC: Library of Congress, 1998.

Hayward, Steven F. *The Age of Reagan: The Conservative Counterrevolution, 1980–1989*. New York: Three Rivers Press, 2009.

Healy, Gene. *The Cult of the Presidency: America's Dangerous Devotion to Executive Power*. Cato Institute: Washington, DC, 2008.

Hennessy, Michael E. *Calvin Coolidge: From a Green Mountain Farm to the White House*. New York: G. P. Putnam's Sons, 1924.

———. *Four Decades of Massachusetts Politics: 1890–1935*. Norwood, MA: The Norwood Press, 1935.

Hicks, John D. *Republican Ascendancy, 1921–1933*. New York: Harper & Row, 1960.

Hill, Robert A., and Marcus Garvey, eds. *The Marcus Garvey and Universal Negro Improvement Association Papers*. Berkeley: University of California Press, 1991.

Hirobe, Izumi. *Japanese Pride, American Prejudice: Modifying the Exclusion Clause of the 1924 Immigration Act*. Palo Alto: Stanford University Press, 2001.

Hughes, Charles E. *The Autobiographical Notes of Charles Evans Hughes*. Edited by David J. Danelski and Joseph S. Tulchin. Cambridge, MA: Harvard University Press, 1973.

Hutchinson, William Thomas. *Lowden of Illinois: Nation and Countryside*. Chicago: University of Chicago Press, 1957.

Jefferson, Thomas. *Notes on the State of Virginia*. First published in France, 1785. Reprint, New York: Penguin Classics, 1998.

Johnson, Claudius O. *Borah of Idaho*. New York: Longmans, Green: 1936.

Johnson, Paul. *Modern Times: The World from the Twenties to the Nineties*. New York: Harper Perennial, 2001.

Johnston, Thomas T. *Have Faith in Calvin Coolidge: Or, From a Farmhouse to the White House*. Boston: The Christopher Publishing House, 1925.

Keller, Albert Galloway. *Earth-hunger and Other Essays*. Edited by William Graham Sumner. New Haven: Yale University Press, 1913.

Klarman, Michael J. *From Jim Crow to Civil Rights: The Supreme Court and the Struggle for Racial Equality*. Oxford: Oxford University Press, 2004.

Korn, Jessica. *The Power of Separation: American Constitutionalism and the Myth of the Legislative Veto*. Princeton, NJ: Princeton University Press, 1998.

Krythe, Maymie Richardson. *All About American Holidays*. New York: Harper, 1962.

LaRossa, Ralph. *The Modernization of Fatherhood: A Social and Political History*. Chicago: University of Chicago Press, 1997.

Lathem, Edward Connery. *Meet Calvin Coolidge: The Man Behind the Myth*. Brattleboro, VT: Stephen Greene Press, 1960.

———, ed. *Your Son, Calvin Coolidge: A Selection of Letters from Calvin Coolidge to His Father*. Vermont Historical Society, 1968.

BIBLIOGRAPHY

Le Duc, Thomas. *Piety and Intellect at Amherst College, 1865–1912.* New York: Columbia University Press, 1946. Reprint, New York: Ayer Publishing, 1977. Page references are to 1977 reprint.

Leidholdt, Alexander. *Editor for Justice: the Life of Louis I. Jaffé.* Baton Rouge: Louisiana State Press, 2002.

Lincoln, Abraham. *The Collected Works of Abraham Lincoln.* Edited by Roy P. Basler. New Brunswick, NJ: Rutgers University Press, 1953.

———. *Complete Works, Comprising His Speeches, Letters, State Papers, and Miscellaneous Writings.* Edited by John Hay. New York: Century, 1894.

———. *Early Speeches, 1832–1856: Including Legislative and Congressional Resolutions, Political Circulars, Notes, Etc.* Edited by Marion Mills Miller. New York: Current Literature, 1907.

Lodge, Henry Cabot. *Early Memories.* New York: Charles Scribner's Sons, 1913.

Love, Phillip H. *Andrew W. Mellon: The Man and His Work.* Whitefish, MT: Kessinger, 2003.

Madison, James. *The Papers of James Madison.* Edited by Thomas A. Mason, Robert A. Rutland, and Jeanne K. Sisson. Charlottesville: University Press of Virginia, 1985.

McCoy, Donald R. *Calvin Coolidge: The Quiet President.* Lawrence, KS: University Press of Kansas, 1988.

McDougall. Walter A. *Let the Sea Make a Noise: A History of the North Pacific from Magellan to MacArthur.* New York: Harper Perennial, 2004.

McGeary, M. Nelson. *Gifford Pinchot, Forester-Politician.* Princeton, NJ: Princeton University Press, 1960.

McKay, Ernest A. *Against Wilson and War, 1914–1917.* Malabar, FL: Krieger, 1996.

McKenna, Marian C. *Borah.* Ann Arbor: University of Michigan Press, 1961.

Milkis, Sidney M., and Michael Nelson. *The American Presidency: Origins and Development 1776–2002.* Washington, DC: CQ Press, 2003.

Miller, Nathan. *The Founding Finaglers.* Philadelphia: David McKay, 1977.

———. *New World Coming: The 1920s and the Making of Modern America.* Cambridge, MA: Da Capo Press, 2004.

Mitchell, William. *Winged Defense: The Development and Possibilities of Modern Air Power— Economic and Military.* 1925. Reprint, New York: Dover, 1988.

Montesquieu, Charles de. *The Spirit of the Laws.* 1750. Edited by Ann. M. Cohler, Basia C. Miller, and Harold S. Stone. Cambridge: Cambridge University Press, 1989.

Murray, Robert K. *Red Scare: A Study in National Hysteria, 1919–1920.* Minneapolis: University of Minnesota Press, 1955.

Nash, Gerald D. *United States Oil Policy, 1890–1964: Business and Government in Twentieth Century America.* University of Pittsburgh Press, 1968.

Nimmo, William F. *Stars and Stripes Across the Pacific: The United States, Japan, and Asia/ Pacific Region 1895–1945.* Westport, CT: Greenwood, 2001.

Nordholt, J. W. Schulte. *Woodrow Wilson*. Berkeley: University of California Press, 1991.

Pestritto, Ronald J. *Woodrow Wilson: The Essential Political Writings*. Lanham, MD: Lexington Books, 2005.

———, and William J. Atto, eds. *American Progressivism: A Reader*. Lanham, MD: Lexington Books, 2008.

Polybius. *The Histories*. Loeb Classical Library edition. Cambridge: Harvard University Press, 1922–1927.

The Presentation of a Samurai Sword. Fairhaven, MA: Millicent Library, 1918. http://www.archive.org/stream/presentationofsa02mill#page/22/mode/2up.

Quint, Howard H., and Robert H. Ferrell, eds. *The Talkative President*. Amherst: University of Massachusetts Press, 1964.

Reagan, Ronald. *Reagan: A Life in Letters*. Edited by Kiron K. Skinner, Annelise Anderson, and Martin Anderson. New York: Free Press, 2003.

———. *Reagan, in His Own Hand*. Edited by Kiron K. Skinner, Annelise Anderson, and Martin Anderson. New York: Simon & Schuster, 2001.

———. *Reagan's Path to Victory: The Shaping of Ronald Reagan's Vision: Selected Writings*. Edited by Kiron K. Skinner. New York: Simon & Schuster, 2004.

Reeves, Richard. *President Reagan: The Triumph of Imagination*. New York: Simon & Schuster, 2005.

Rogers, Will. *Will Rogers' Weekly Articles*. Edited by James Smallwood and Steven K. Gragert. Stillwater, OK: Oklahoma State University Press, 1980.

Roosevelt, Theodore. *The Letters of Theodore Roosevelt: 1914–1919*. Edited by Eltin Elmore Morison. Cambridge, MA: Harvard University Press, 1954.

———. *Selections from the Correspondence of Theodore Roosevelt and Henry Cabot Lodge, 1884–1918*. 1925. Reprint, Boston: Da Capo Press, 1971.

Rossum, Ralph. *Federalism, the Supreme Court, and the Seventeenth Amendment: The Irony of Constitutional Democracy*. Lanham, MD: Lexington Books, 2001.

Russell, Francis A. *A City in Terror: Calvin Coolidge and the 1919 Boston Police Strike*. Boston: Beacon Press, 2005.

Schlesinger, Arthur M., Jr. *A Thousand Days: John F. Kennedy in the White House*. Boston: Houghton Mifflin, 2002.

Schurz, Carl. *Abraham Lincoln, an Essay*. New York: Houghton Mifflin, 1920.

Schweikart, Larry, and Lynne Pierson Doti. *American Entrepreneur*. New York: Amacom, 2009.

Scott, Sir Walter. *Marmion*. Boston: Houghton, Mifflin, 1894.

———. *The Poetical Works of Sir Walter Scott: With a Sketch of His Life*. Philadelphia: J. Crissy, 1838.

Shlaes, Amity. *The Forgotten Man: A New History of the Great Depression*. New York: Harper Perennial, 2008.

Siegfried, André. *America Comes of Age: A French Analysis*. Whitefish, MT: Kessinger, 2005.

Silver, Tom. *Coolidge and the Historian*. Durham, NC: Carolina Academic Press, 1983.

Sobel, Robert. *Coolidge: An American Enigma*. Washington, DC: Regnery, 1998.

Sowell, Thomas. *Affirmative Action Around the World: An Empirical Study*. New Haven: Yale University Press, 2004.

Stokes, Melvyn Stokes. *D. W. Griffith's* The Birth of a Nation: *A History of "The Most Controversial Motion Picture of All Time."* Oxford: Oxford University Press, 2007.

Stratton, David. *Tempest Over Teapot Dome: The Story of Albert B. Fall*. Norman, OK: University of Oklahoma Press, 1998.

Thompson, R. J. *Adequate Brevity*. Chicago: Donahue, 1924.

Timmons, Bascom Nolly. *Portrait of an American: Charles G. Dawes*. New York: Henry Holt, 1953.

Tocqueville, Alexis de. *Democracy in America* 1. Translated by Henry Reeve. New York: G. Adlard, 1839.

Tucker, Garland S., III. *The High Tide of American Conservatism*. Austin, TX: Emerald Book Company, 2010.

Vought, Hans P. *The Bully Pulpit and the Melting Pot: American Presidents and the Immigrant, 1897–1933*. Macon, GA: Mercer University Press, 2004.

Waterhouse, John Almon. *Calvin Coolidge Meets Charles Edward Garman*. Rutland, VT: Academy Books, 1984.

Watson, James E. *As I Knew Them: Memoirs of James Watson, Former United States Senator from Indiana*. Indianapolis, IN: Bobbs-Merrill, 1936.

West, Thomas G. *Vindicating the Founders: Race, Sex, Class, and Justice in the Origins of America*. Lanham, MD: Rowman & Littlefield, 2001.

White, William Allen. *Calvin Coolidge: The Man Who Is President*. New York: Macmillan, 1925.

———. *Politics: The Citizen's Business*. New York: Macmillan, 1924. Reprint, New York: Ayer, 1974. Page references are to 1974 reprint.

———. *A Puritan in Babylon*. 1938. Reprint, New York: Capricorn Books, 1965.

Why Coolidge Matters. Chatsworth, CA: National Notary Association, 2010.

Wilson, Woodrow. *Congressional Government: A Study in American Politics*. New York: Houghton Mifflin, 1901.

———. *Constitutional Government in the United States*. New York: Columbia University Press, 1908.

———. *The Papers of Woodrow Wilson*. Edited by Arthur S. Link. 69 vols. 1966–1994. Vol. 2, *1881–1884*, reprint, Princeton, NJ: Princeton University Press, 1967.

Wise, Jennings Cropper. *Woodrow Wilson, Disciple of Revolution*. Columbus, OH: Paisley Press, 1938.

Wolters, Raymond. *The Burden of Brown: Thirty Years of School Desegregation*. Knoxville: University of Tennessee Press, 1992.

Woods, Robert A. *The Preparation of Calvin Coolidge: An Interpretation*. New York: Houghton Mifflin, 1924.

INDEX